D0891771

Playing THE Game

Sport and the Physical Emancipation
of English Women, 1870–1914

Kathleen E. McCrone

The University Press of Kentucky

Published in the United States of America
by The University Press of Kentucky
Scholarly publisher for the Commonwealth,
serving Bellarmine College, Berea College, Centre
College of Kentucky, Eastern Kentucky University,
The Filson Club, Georgetown College, Kentucky
Historical Society, Kentucky State University,
Morehead State University, Murray State University,
Northern Kentucky University, Transylvania University,
University of Kentucky, University of Louisville,
and Western Kentucky University.

Editorial and Sales Offices: Lexington, Kentucky 40506-0024

Library of Congress Cataloging-in-Publication Data

McCrone, Kathleen E., 1941–
    Playing the game: sport and the physical emancipation of English
women, 1870–1914/Kathleen E. McCrone.
        p. cm.
    Bibliography: p.
    Includes index.
    ISBN 0-8131-1641-4
    1. Sports for women — England — History — 19th century. I. Title.
GV709.18.G7M33   1988
796'.01'940941 — dc 19   87-32038
                                                                        CIP

Printed and bound in Great Britain

Contents

To my brother
Alistair William McCrone
and to our parents
Hugh MacMillan McCrone and Kathleen Forth McCrone

Illustrations

Preface

The idea of writing a book on Victorian women and sport occurred to me in 1979. By that date, I had studied various aspects of the history of women in nineteenth-century England for over a decade, and while preparing a review of Ann Phillips's *Newnham Anthology*, I was struck by the frequency and pleasure with which Old Girls from Newnham College, Cambridge, recalled their sporting activities. I was struck too by the important conjunction between these activities and the broader process of emancipation in which Newnhamites were involved, and by the irony that while definitions of woman emanated largely from the physical there were no studies centred on Victorian women's experience with physical activity.

The resulting study can be situated within the history of women, women's education, women's rights, sport, leisure and recreation. Its aim is not to establish or submit to review what is known or thought to be known about the Victorian world-view and woman's place within it, but rather to investigate reactions against this view and the emergence of a counter-view through sport and exercise. An attempt is made to rescue the English sportswoman from the obscuring mists of the past, to discuss her as a transitional figure between opposing views of womanhood and to place her within the context of the general movement for the emancipation of women as an important effect and cause — without necessarily assuming what women's status in sport and in society should have been. Included is a good deal of descriptive material and themes that may at times seem repetitious, for the basic data remain largely unavailable elsewhere and patterns repeated themselves. Analyses are contained mainly within chapter conclusions and the conclusion to the book.

Deliberately eschewing the complicated definitions of sport offered by philosophers and sociologists, I use the term 'sport' broadly and simply to include organised, competitive physical games with spatial and temporal limitations — like hockey and lawn tennis — and non-competitive, unorganised recreational pursuits, mostly undertaken out of doors and involving a degree of physical skill — like cycling. Dancing, an important form of physical activity for females, enjoyed an enduring reputation as a fashionable art integral to the ideal of ladyhood, but it falls outside my definition's perimeters and has thus been excluded.

I also chose to exclude working-class women and to concentrate on those of the rising middle ranks. The Victorian feminine ideal was a middle-class construct that limited middle-class women from business and professional backgrounds. As was the case with many aspects of the advancement of women during the late-nineteenth century, change permeated downward. It was the physical frustrations, needs and aspirations of middle-class women that were asserted first, because it was they whose sporting consciousness was raised by educational and recreational experiences and they who had the free time and financial resources that participation in sport required. With only a few exceptions, between 1870 and 1914 sport among working-class women was virtually non-existent since the requisite leisure, schooling and money were lacking.

Still another deliberate exclusion, apart from incidental references, involves the non-English areas of the British Isles, because the revolution in women's sport was centred in England and treating the whole United Kingdom would have involved too much information for a single volume. The use of St Leonards School, St Andrews, Scotland, as a case study in Chapter 3, is not inconsistent, for it was essentially an 'English' school in that it was patterned on English models and staffed largely by English-educated women.

My study makes no claim to being definitive. Rather, it hopes to provide a catalyst to the huge task of research which obviously remains to be done. Future explorers of the subject will find themselves on a fascinating journey, and will undoubtedly discover — as have most searchers for the women hitherto hidden from history — that the dearth of readily available information is only superficial and that an abundance of resources can be found if one digs deeply enough. They will discover too a story of ups and downs, of parallel advances and reversals, rather than one of uninterrupted progress.

Acknowledgements

I extend sincere thanks to the Social Sciences and Humanities Research Council of Canada for two major research grants; to the University of Windsor for leaves which allowed me to spend two years in England; and to administrators, librarians, archivists, physical educators and faculty members at the Cheltenham Ladies' College, the North London Collegiate School, Roedean School, Brighton, St Leonard's School, St Andrews, Wycombe Abbey School, High Wycombe, the Girls' Public Day School Trust, London, Girton and Newnham Colleges, Cambridge, Lady Margaret Hall, St Anne's, St Hilda's and Somerville Colleges, Oxford, the City of Birmingham and Thames Polytechnics, the Chelsea School of Human Movement of the Brighton Polytechnic, the Bedford College of Higher Education, the All England Women's Hockey Association, the All England Women's Lacrosse Association, the Women's Cricket Association, the Kenneth Ritchie Wimbledon Library, the British Library, the Bodleian Library and the Cambridge University Library, for their generous assistance. I am also grateful to Clare Hall, Newnham College and Wesley House, Cambridge, William Goodenough House, London, and my British relations and friends for providing hospitality and accommodation; to the sources indicated in the list of illustrations for reproduction permission, and to the *Journal of British Studies* and the *British Journal of Sports History* for permission to reprint material in Chapters 2 and 3 that has appeared previously.

Particular thanks go to Ann Phillips, the librarian at Newnham College, for her abundant help with the project from its inception; to Gillian Sutherland, also of Newnham College, for her insights and assistance in making useful contacts; to Netta Rheinberg, author and retired cricketer, for sharing information from her private collection; to Jennifer Hargreaves, June Kennard and Shirley Reekie for lending copies of their excellent theses; to Robin Myers, archivist at the North London Collegiate School, for valuable aid that evolved into warm friendship; to Neville Thompson, Professor of History at the University of Western Ontario, for reading the manuscript and providing much-needed affirmation; and to Pauline Olafson, my graduate assistant, for her help with proof-reading.

Acknowledgements

Finally, I wish to acknowledge a profound debt to four friends: Peter Wilkinson, whose help and support in the crucial early stages were critical to the project's successful launch; James Flanagan, whose insights and unfailing interest convinced me of the wisdom of applying inter-disciplinary perspectives to the subject matter and contributed significantly to the writing of the first draft; Ann Johnston, whose encouragement and skilful editing proved invaluable to the manuscript's completion; and Colin Atkinson, whose editorial assistance facilitated essential pruning in the final stages.

1

Introduction

> Girls are sometimes pretty and wear nice clothes, and can sit on
> coaches to watch us play cricket . . . but girls cannot run, jump or
> climb trees.[1]

Although in recent years Victorian specialists have eagerly
cultivated the fields of sport and women's history, they have
produced surprisingly little relating the two areas. Historians of
women have neglected the physical dimension of the struggle for
emancipation, while historians of sport have reflected sport's
traditional male orientation by virtually ignoring the distaff side,
even though the history of women's participation in sport reflects
different themes and patterns and raises different questions from
that of men. As W.J. Baker notes, 'The history of British women
in sports . . . stands high on the agenda of work to be done.'[2]

Sport is a complex phenomenon which acts as an important
agent of both social change and social control and modifies and
defines female roles in society at large. Sport creates and reflects
tensions surrounding definitions of sex and gender roles, and
perhaps more clearly than any other institution reveals how status,
functions and power are assigned on the basis of biological
differences. Because of the particular place of the body in definitions of woman, and because of the attack of women's sport on
physical norms — the factors that controlled and subordinated
women the most — barriers to women's participation in sport
were among the last to fall. Normally a conservative institution,
sport is laden with rituals, symbols and preconceptions that
disseminate, affirm and reinforce idealised and dominant values.
As an essentially male preserve related to other forms of patriarchal control, sport embodies and recreates the principles and

1

practices of gender inequality and male dominance and privilege in other realms of life.

At the same time, however, sport has considerable potential for social disruption, since it can operate as an important channel for underprivileged groups to challenge existing social arrangements and express hostility to and deviance from established norms. Its masculinity makes it an obvious sphere for women to attempt to penetrate — or at the very least to challenge by creating parallel worlds of their own — in their efforts to counter external definitions of female physical and emotional frailty.

In the case of English women in the late-nineteenth century, sport was perplexingly ambiguous because it stood on the threshold between male and female and between the past and future. It was a repressive and constraining mechanism that deliberately idealised maleness and kept women separate from and inferior to men. But it was also a transforming and liberating one, that offered women unprecedented opportunities to free themselves from some of the more entrenched and pervasive tenets of the Victorian ideology of femininity. Sport is therefore an excellent monitor of how far women have travelled along the road to equality and the distance yet to go, and it is crucial to an understanding of society at large and the patterns of social relations in which sport and women were embedded.

Sport and physical recreation have been significant and pervasive forms of social action in the life of England since the Middle Ages. Until recently, however, women's place in this long and distinguished sporting tradition was peripheral and primarily passive, since sport involved essentially masculine activities requiring physical and psychological attitudes and behaviour considered unnatural to respectable females. It is now known that women were never completely excluded from sport, and that more participated and in more sports than was previously suspected, but the fact remains that women in English sport were a social anomaly for centuries.

During the medieval period separation of roles according to gender was often indistinct among ordinary people. Fresh air and exercise were all in a day's work for both sexes; and during fairs and holy day festivities women as well as men participated in ball games, foot races and contests of strength. Some women also made a living as itinerant dancers and tumblers, entertaining at court, castles and local celebrations. At the other end of the social spectrum a minority of noble ladies hunted and hawked with considerable skill, either in parties of their own or within protected situations. Until the late-fourteenth century, when Anne of Bohemia, the wife of Richard II, popularised the side-saddle, women often rode astride, like the Wife of Bath, 'who sat her ambler easily'. Literary and artistic sources also depict ladies playing with balls; and the first treatise on sport in the English language is attributed to a woman, Dame Juliana Berners, prioress of Sopwell Abbey in Hertfordshire. *The Book of St Albans* (c. 1486) deals knowledgeably with hunting and hawking, and was so popular that it was reprinted more than any other work of its time except the Bible. The medieval lady's usual recreations, however, involved needlework and sedentary games of chance. The main sports of the age — archery, fencing and jousting — were related to military training and hence identified with men alone. The lady's primary sporting role was as spectator who awarded prizes and provided inspiration and applause at tournaments, a passive pose her descendants emulated for centuries.

The medieval pattern of female exercise continued in the early modern period, with common folk playing crude games and the upper classes dancing, hunting and hawking. Henry VIII is said to have complained of the expense of keeping Anne Boleyn in archery equipment;[3] and the prowess in the hunting field of Mary Queen of Scots and Queen Elizabeth I is well known. The latter, at the age of 66, was reported to be still 'exceedingly disposed to hunting, for every second day she is on horseback, and continues the sport long'.[4] Tudor ladies also played real tennis and battledore and shuttlecock; but there was little physical play and exercise in their education.

Juan Luis Vives, tutor to the Princess Mary and author of *The Instruction of a Christian Woman* (1524), the leading theoretical manual in Europe on female education, had nothing to say about exercise or games; and while Erasmus expressed concern about the bodily health of little girls, he believed they would derive sufficient exercise from the active performance of household tasks. Similarly, Thomas Elyot, a Tudor bureaucrat who was inspired by Renaissance views on the conjunction of mind and body to write *The Governor* (1531), the first treatise in English on the value of exercise to the health, character and social success of gentlemen, completely ignored the education of women apart from condescending advice on how to be good wives.

In the seventeenth century Jacobean theories on the patriarchal and hierarchal structure of society combined with changes in productive mechanisms and the growth of commercial capitalism to diminish the status of women. Except during the Puritan revolution, women were subjected to increasing restraints which reinforced the image of a 'weaker sex' and reduced opportunities for exercise. Dancing, which was designed to produce graceful movement rather than physical fitness, was the only exercise integral to a young lady's training. John Locke was one of the few educational reformers to recognise that children of both sexes were physical animals, and that girls as well as boys needed moderate, open-air exercise for reasons of strength and good health. Even embryonic feminists like Bathsua Makin and Mary Astell expressed little interest in physical education. It is thus not surprising to find seeds of the debilitating Victorian concept of femininity in *The Ladies' Dictionary's* advice in 1694 to 'beware of taking straddling steps or running ahead for those are indecent for a lady'.[5]

Unusual incidents of an exhibitionist nature involving women of the lower classes, such as horse and foot races, and football, boxing and stoolball matches, continued to be recorded. The odd rural Andromache still hunted and rode, occasionally even in breeches, ignoring negative comments about her talk of horses and hounds and audacious leaping over gates. Queen Anne herself was an avid hunter when young, and her love of horse racing led to the laying out of the Ascot course and the acceptance of respectable women as spectators. But such activities were considered exceptional and did nothing to compromise the view that sport was essentially a man's business.

The situation changed little during the Georgian period, although from the middle of the eighteenth century warnings about the need for girls to have exercise and criticisms of its limitation in the name of gentility appeared in print with increasing frequency. For example, Thomas Gisborne, prebendary of Durham, argued in 1747 that, while girls did not require the hardy amusements of boys, they needed more vigorous bodily exercise in order to become healthy, strong and alert. John Gregory, in his famous advice to daughters in the 1770s, compromised his adherence to the tenets of female inferiority sufficiently to recommend outdoor exercise and horse-back riding energetic enough to produce rosy cheeks and good health. Twenty years later Erasmus Darwin, although convinced that women's sexual function limited their intellectual capacity and required the cultivation of mildness and reticence, argued that social convention, not nature, made schoolgirls sedentary and that ball games, shuttlecock, dumb-bell exercises and vigorous walking and dancing would improve their health. During the 1790s, too, the bluestockings Catherine Macaulay Graham and Hannah More agreed that female weakness was the result of false notions of beauty and educational regimes that corrupted the powers of the body and mind, and they recommended exercise as an antidote.[6]

Only Mary Wollstonecraft, however, got to the heart of the matter. In her seminal work on the rights of women (1792) she identified the liberation of women's bodies as among those that most needed vindicating. Wollstonecraft acknowledged the superior bodily strength of men, but urged females to take up masculine types of exercise to demonstrate 'how far the natural superiority of man extends'. Bodily dependence produced mental dependence and weak mothers weak children, she warned.[7]

A number of works of fictional literature in the eighteenth century also approved of female exercise. George Farquhar's Silvia (1706) could 'gallop all the morning after the hunting-horn, and all the evening after a fiddle. In short [she could] do everything with [her] father but drink, and shoot flying'.[8] Thomas Holcroft's Anna St Ives (1792) demanded female physical training and called the supposition that men were better able to climb walls than women 'weakness and folly'.[9] William Wordsworth assured '. . . a Young Lady, who had been reproached for taking long walks in the country' (1802) that continuation of the habit would make her 'healthy as a shepherd boy', in marked contrast to her critics;[10] and in *Pride and Prejudice* (1813) and *Northanger Abbey* (1818) Jane Austen condoned Elizabeth Bennett's walking three miles to Netherfield in wet weather and arriving 'with weary ankles, dirty stockings, and a face glowing with warmth and exercise' and Catherine Morland's liking for cricket and 'all boys' plays', and she strongly condemned the censure both heroines received.[11]

All the arguments about girls' pressing need of open-air pursuits were assiduously ignored by educational practitioners, however. The growing number of private boarding and day schools for girls from affluent families deliberately neglected genuine physical and mental training in favour of stylish accomplishments. Mistresses supported only demure walking and decorous dancing which supposedly contributed to the becoming postures and social skills required of a polished lady.

The traditional view that English women rarely engaged in sport and physical recreation before the mid-nineteenth century has been challenged recently by Shirley Reekie, who argues that before and during the early stages of the Industrial Revolution women participated in a wide range of activities, the nature and extent of which were largely determined by place of residence and social class.[12] Reekie's evidence indicates that despite strenuous labour and restricted time for play the common people's rural sports were a vibrant force in which women participated freely — if with less frequency and variety then men — and that women's activities included cricket, stoolball, trapball, football, golf, foot races, pugilism, rowing, sword-fighting, swimming and dancing.

Among the upper classes, Reekie claims, social convention, confining fashions and more clearly defined gender roles restricted women's opportunities for vigorous recreation, while at the same time leisure, affluence and privileges of rank allowed some to ride, hunt, shoot, fish, swim, climb, walk, sail, dance and play battledore and cricket. That sporting ladies were not unknown is confirmed by their appearance in art and literature — John Collet's famous painting of 'Miss Wicket and Miss Trigger' (c. 1770), for example, and the *Sporting Magazine's* inclusion, without adverse comment, of occasional articles on ladies who excelled in the field, such as the Marchioness of Salisbury, who enjoyed a national reputation as a daring rider and was master of the Hertfordshire foxhounds from 1775 to 1819.[13]

Reekie nevertheless concludes that only a minority of women in any class were actively involved in sport between 1700 and 1850, and that in the early-nineteenth century among people of all classes and both sexes, sport in general experienced a decline precipitated by a complex combination of forces related to urbanisation, industrialisation and the moral attitudes of the rising middle classes.[14] Among respectable women the decline of sport was related to attempts by the middle ranks to compensate for their lack of inherited status and establish their respectability by behaving in a manner appropriate to the social position to which they aspired. One result was the evolution of the Victorian ideal of femininity which embodied the conviction that the genteel lady was destined by God and nature to be man's helpmate, nurture his children and protect the sanctity of his home. Passive, gentle, emotional and delicate, she had neither the strength nor inclination to undertake strenuous exercise and competitive games.

Some women of the landed classes continued to hunt and ride, while other women performed light callisthenic exercises and competed in archery and, from mid-century, croquet contests that combined little physical effort with welcome opportunities for respectable social encounters. On the whole, however, the world of the early- and mid-Victorian lady was an indoor and sedentary one. The arbiters of acceptable behaviour considered it undignified for the daughters of gentlemen to develop muscles or exhibit athletic prowess; and they regarded the elements of competition and qualities of character intrinsic to many sports as inimical to the female role.

These attributes were ultimately based upon notions of physiology, which held that woman's reproductive capacity and sexual organisation, specifically the ovaries and uterus, controlled her entire nature and existence from puberty to menopause, that these organs were the seat of disease and the centre of sympathies, and shaped everything from social roles and characteristics to common ailments and personal, intellectual and physical abilities and disabilities. To woman's peculiar physiology doctors attributed the ideal feminine characteristics — intuition, timidity and dependence — and the female proneness to illness and breakdown. On the basis of no scientific evidence whatsoever, they related biology to behaviour and opined that women who behaved in an 'inappropriate' and 'unfeminine' manner, that is, who displayed symptoms of aggression, ambition and competitiveness, were incompletely developed and prone to disease, and that they had probably become so by living unphysiological lives in ignorance of or indifference to the 'fact' that they could become sterile or transmit acquired characteristics to their children, who in turn in all likelihood would be nervous, undersized, dyspeptic and degenerate.

The change from girlhood into womanhood was considered the greatest crisis in a female's life; and during puberty, particularly during menstrual periods when susceptibilities were most acute, doctors said, great care had to be taken to make sure that fertility was not permanently jeopardised by unladylike behaviour and a squandering of vital energies. They knew nothing of the chemical basis of sex differentiation, and generally believed that how a girl behaved, dressed, worked and played at puberty controlled the development of her primary and secondary sex characteristics, and that the physical events of puberty triggered the psychological manifestations of femininity. Normal puberty was connected with normal behaviour, which was identified with mental, physical and behavioural characteristics defined as feminine, while women with masculine interests, ambitions, thoughts and actions were identified as defectively sexually developed. Women were thus caught in a double bind. They were told that sickness was the result of being female and at the same time that they got sick when they behaved in an unfeminine manner.[15] Furthermore, as dependents on others they were deprived of the right to decide for themselves about the role of physical activity in their life-style.

During childhood girls, unlike boys, were constantly reminded of their sex's purpose and nature and of the need to curb their natural exuberance. They were taught that facial colour and muscular strength were signs of having to work for a living; that physical effort, like running, jumping and climbing, might damage their reproductive organs and make them unattractive to men; and that the capacity to walk a couple of miles at a brisk pace without fatigue was undeniable proof of want of refinement. Having been socialised thus, it is hardly surprising that women not delicate by nature eschewed vitality by cultivating indolence and dressing in fashions which inhibited movement, or that their antipathy to exercise was difficult to overcome. There was, however, another side to the story.

As the standards of fashion and decorous behaviour made physical activity increasingly unpopular and inaccessible, a host of works poured from the pens of concerned male, female and anonymous authors, advocating moderate and supervised exercise to improve health and remedy an apparent epidemic of postural defects. Their relative obscurity invites a brief and selective summary.

In a series of *Reflections on the Present Condition of the Female Sex* (2nd edition 1817), Priscilla Wakefield, a prolific writer on natural history and travel, urged parents to worry less about daughters soiling their clothes and offending against good manners and more about their receiving physical education that would improve maternal capacities. Lant Carpenter, Unitarian minister and father of Mary Carpenter, the noted social reformer, lamented, in *Principles of Education* (1820), the exaggeration of the physical distinctions between the sexes and the damage exercise was thought to inflict on girls' manners, and instead recommended active pastimes, like running, swinging, jumping and rope-skipping, to better prepare them to bear and train the next generation. An anonymously authored *Manual of Elegant Recreations, Exercises, and Pursuits* (1829) designated dancing, archery and riding as suitable amusements for young ladies. An article in the *Penny Magazine* (1833) criticised the false standards of dress and decorum in boarding schools that restricted the free exercise health required; and a handbook on physical education for young ladies (1838) by a French medical professor associated a sound mind with a sound body in both sexes, although it simultaneously described girls as much more illness-prone than boys and advocated restricting their exercise to slow walking and gentle gymnastics.[16]

By far the most important of the early Victorian defences of female physical training was Donald Walker's *Physical Exercises for Ladies* (1836), a work intended as an authoritative guide to regular activity 'suited to the female constitution and character', despite its author's lack of scientific training. Walker branded what passed for the teaching of exercise as 'frivolous and lacking in system', and argued strongly that women needed exercise to improve their health. But his basic premise, that 'the constitution of women bears only moderate exercise', typified the whole Victorian concept of womanhood.[17]

Because all women's parts, tissues and fibres were finer and more delicate than men's, because their grace, beauty and gentleness had to be preserved and because overly fatiguing activities tended to produce rheumatism, muscle inflammation, nervous exhaustion and premature ageing, and worst of all, endangered their 'peculiar function of multiplying the species', Walker insisted that exercise must be restrained and non-violent. He especially recommended activities beneficial to balance, deportment and the correction of deformities, and requiring little strength or 'inconvenience', such as light callisthenics, the use of dumb-bells and Indian clubs, smooth dancing and walking at a pace that did not necessitate steps exceeding the length of the foot. Owing to the 'excessive shocks' running and leaping communicated, and the 'one-sidedness' produced by archery, these Walker discouraged, while horse-back riding in particular he considered anathema because it coarsened the voice and complexion, twisted the body, bestowed a masculine air and 'produced an unnatural consolidation of the bones of the lower part of the body, ensuring a frightful impediment of future function, which need not be dwelt on'.[18]

However influential, Walker's work was far from the last word, and during the 1840s and 1850s the litany continued. In a general treatment of physical education (1845) Captain James Chiosso, the supervisor of fencing and gymnastic exercises at University College School, associated mental with physical health in both sexes. Damning fashions and schools for preventing adequate exercise, he proposed for women a rational and moderate system of physical education supervised by trained personnel, the result of which, he predicted with more perspicacity than usual and more than he himself realised, would be graceful carriages, good health, mental acuity, the ability to cope with physical danger, a life-long love of exercise and a confident consciousness of physical ability.[19]

Even conservative arbiters of female behaviour, such as Sarah Stickney Ellis and Matilda Pullan, entered the debate. No one believed in the mental and physical inferiority of women more strongly than Ellis, whose manuals of advice to the daughters, wives and mothers of England are particularly revealing of the Victorian ideal. Although forbidding girls to run lest they 'heat themselves' and so weaken their chests, she regretted the 'morbid listlessness' of too many, and recommended up to three hours of open-air exercise a day on foot or horse-back.[20] Similarly, in maternal counsel to daughters (1855), Mrs Pullan advised that 'a certain amount of exercise must be taken daily to maintain the health', either through walking or arm callisthenics or 'by the simpler method of doing some portion of the household work', there being 'no better exercise in the world than rubbing a table or sideboard, or sweeping a room'.[21]

Of a different ilk was Herbert Spencer, the future Social Darwinist who thought himself a great liberal. In a series of *Essays on Education* (1859), Spencer attacked as misconceived the ideal of womanhood that was responsible for the neglect of physical exercise in girls' schools, and asked why, if sporting behaviour among boys did not prevent their growing into gentlemen, physical play among girls should prevent their becoming ladies. Spencer's interest in female exercise arose not from an advocacy of women's rights, however, but from a desire to assure the production of healthy mothers who would protect England against racial degeneration.[22]

Individually and collectively these works and others like them provide insights into the ideal Victorian woman and the attitudes and practices that guaranteed her exclusion from realms of power and status. It could be argued that they were progressive in so far as they criticised the lack of exercise that typified female education and life-styles and the fashions that constricted vital organs and impeded motion; moreover, their assertion that properly conceived exercise posed no threat to gentility may have helped establish a climate of opinion which eventually accepted a degree of sport and physical education for respectable females. But while they manifested an obvious concern for the health of women and a genuine desire that women take more exercise, they lacked any semblance of a feminist perspective. Almost all considered females naturally inferior to and weaker than males. They cautioned constantly against overstrain and were obsessed with worry about the effects of exercise on maternity and propriety. Their recommendations were thus exceedingly cautious. Few indicated any sympathy for the idea that women had a right to develop their bodies as fully as possible, and none saw sport as a means of their doing so, since sport was inevitably equated with masculinity and threats to true womanliness.

Not until the middle of the nineteenth century did even the most moderate advice about the advantages of exercise begin to be taken. Then, however, the same powerful socio-economic forces that had produced the feminine ideal in the first place created other forces destined to undermine it. Two of critical importance to the physical emancipation of women were the revolution in sport and the movement for women's rights.

The sporting revolution was the most spectacular aspect of a larger revolution in leisure and recreation that had profound implications for social control and transformed forever the nature of English daily life. To understand it one must recall that sport in the pre-industrial period was either for the landed classes or labourers, and comprised activities that were largely spontaneous, unorganised and local. Industrialisation shattered traditional, agrarian patterns. Mechanisation, the reorganisation of periods of labour, improvements in transportation and communication, population growth, urbanisation and the emergence of new classes with time and money at their disposal, all contributed to the creation of a vastly different society with different attitudes and needs, and different patterns of leisure and recreation. Its primary architects were members of the rising middle classes, to whom fell the pleasures and problems of using the free time which accompanied their growing affluence in a manner that was both enjoyable and morally legitimate. Given their work and self-improvement ethics, activities that could be justified as edifying and utilitarian, as well as recreational, had a particular appeal.

Sport seemed to fill the bill perfectly. It offered satisfaction of a sedentary urban group's need for physical exercise that could be taken within confined spaces; it also recommended itself as a duty because of the apparently beneficial effects on health, work and character. Furthermore, it accorded with the prevailing competitive spirit, and offered a powerful new agent of moral and social discipline.[23]

Around mid-century the public schools, where bourgeois boys were turned into gentlemen, provided the locus for the cultivation of a new, peculiarly middle-class ideology of sport derived from traditional games and the Englishman's natural love of outdoor exercise. A unique cult of athleticism and organised team games that encouraged manliness developed and rapidly exploded into and around the world, a phenomenon Helen Meller describes as 'one of the greatest forces considered to be on the side of the angels' during the whole Victorian period, and proof of the Victorians' creativity in responding to the complicated process of cultural reconstruction by both developing new concepts of leisure time and new ways of filling it.[24]

The Victorians 'taught the world to play' by redefining the old and by introducing new sports. Whereas at the beginning of their period only cricket and golf were organised and played under generally accepted rules, rowing was still 'boating', football and hockey were tests of strength rather than skill and lawn tennis had yet to be invented, by the 1890s a comprehensive range of sports had developed.[25] Under the impetus of the trend towards bureaucratisation and rationalisation in society at large, various sports became subject to governing bodies; rules were standardised and a complex competitive structure implemented; greater numbers participated; and new techniques and improved equipment increased skills. Sport became the most popular recreational activity among middle- and upper-class males, and certain of its manifestations, like football, became big business catering to a mass audience in a mass society.

In leisure and recreation, as in society at large, class and gender were important variables that reflected potent power relationships. The arbiters of the new sporting culture were middle-class males who were determined to control the direction of social change and shape the evolution of the social order to their own advantage. This meant, during the early stages of the leisure revolution, attempting to suppress the traditional sporting pastimes of the working classes for fear of the potentially evil uses to which spare time might be put. When this proved not completely possible, and when workers began to enjoy more spare time and spare cash, the emphasis shifted from control by suppression to control by providing rational recreations such as sports, which would teach order and discipline and so minimise the danger of social disruption.[26] If properly handled, sport was perceived as a means of reinforcing rather than blurring distinctions of class and territory. The middle classes — including women — usually had no desire to play with their social inferiors, and erected a variety of barriers to protect the cohesion of the bourgeois world and the integrity of its recreational activities.

Fear of social disruption of a different sort lay behind attempts to control the sporting activities of women. Besides reinforcing class identity and social standing, the patterns of Victorian leisure and recreation partially strengthened gender distinctions and reflected the different roles and privileges historically ascribed to the sexes. As the chapters that follow demonstrate, women of leisure and financial means certainly shared in the Victorian sporting revolution, but as a release from the unnatural confinement of their drawing rooms and from boredom brought on by too much free time, rather than from too much work. Once the delights of sport were discovered, the lure proved irresistible despite the threat to traditional values; and it combined with a relaxation of social constraints and redefinition of the ideal of womanhood to provide women with increased sporting opportunities. But women were allowed to 'play the game' only within limited behavioural boundaries which confirmed the separate spheres of the sexes and the superiority of men.

As Jennifer Hargreaves perceptively notes, 'perhaps more than any other leisure activity, sport was associated with "male" characteristics, and hence sexism received heightened expression in this context'.[27] The new world of sport was one of sexual apartheid. Men's and women's sports, with a few exceptions, remained strictly segregated, and women's sport was severely circumscribed by the patriarchal nature of social relations and by women's willingness, as in so many other areas, to allow men's perception of what was suitable to influence the choice and nature of their activities. To protect sport's 'sacred' masculinity from pollution by inferior beings and to protect the male monopoly of power that sport represented, men used the excuse of women's best interests to perpetuate the view that unless women were careful sport would masculinise their appearance and behaviour, damage their vital organs and distract them from their crucial domestic duties. An anomalous situation was created in which women — the element in the middle class with the most free time at its disposal — had the fewest choices of how to fill it. Their sporting activities may have expanded significantly, but they remained curtailed by an uncomfortable element of compulsion, based on a concern for the protection of status and respectability, that limited options and trapped them in a confined gender role. Only sports activities and behaviour that were 'feminine' and legitimated the male-dominated social structure were considered acceptable, and even these were to be set aside if they conflicted with established social norms. To paraphrase Sheila Fletcher, the experience of Victorian women relative to men was thus circumscribed not only by poor education, disenfranchisement and inferior property rights, but by tightly-laced corsets, not having their legs free and not riding astride, in other words by not having free access to vigorous games and exercise.[28] This was a situation the Victorian women's movement sought to rectify.

Born in mid-century when the forces of change were beginning to make the incompatibility of the Victorian feminine ideal with reason and reality increasingly obvious, the women's movement raised questions about women's disabilities and constricted place in society and sought a partial redefinition of gender roles and the admission of women into spheres previously dominated by men. One of them was sport. Unlike the fight for legal and political rights, there was no organised campaign to promote women's sport, and its development was somewhat removed from the centres of feminist controversy. As has been the case recently, however, the entry of women into sporting activities was a significant part of the general movement for female emancipation, for its translation of demands for equity 'into demands for privileges and practices attendant to the male competitive model'[29] conflicted with existing views of femininity and hence challenged and helped to undermine constraints that prevented women from developing all their powers and exercising control over their own lives and bodies.

The early feminists viewed education as particularly critical to women's efforts to live under their own control, and tied self-development to the exercise of reason. As long as women remained ignorant they could not notice their inferior situation in sufficient numbers to turn the isolated complaints of individuals into an effective movement, nor could they completely refute the argument that women were ill-equipped for broader legal, vocational and political horizons. That their pleas for educational reform were not confined solely to mental requirements was due to a growing concern about the health of future mothers and to the convictions that the widely held idea concerning the inseparability of healthy minds and healthy bodies applied to women as well as men and that lack of exercise was largely to blame for women's poor health.

In 1850 Harriet Martineau, the distinguished political economist, repudiated the notion that a 'little gentle amble with a hoop' did anything for a girl's physical and moral development, and asserted that girls should be allowed to do unladylike things such as climb trees, walk briskly, run, leap, row and swim.[30] Shortly thereafter Bessie Rayner Parkes, one of the earliest and most distinguished campaigners for women's rights, observed with regret that 'most people endeavoured to check the physical power of their daughters as much as that of their minds.[31] Damning educational regimes that stunted girls both mentally and physically, she argued:

> Women should try to become as tall, as strong, as capable of enduring mental and bodily exertion as it is possible for them to be; and till they have attained this maximum point, they have not fulfilled the intention of God . . . The usual and purely arbitrary notion of only certain games and certain bodily motions being decorous for the female sex is a miserable restriction on the 'individuality' of the individual. It is a cruel thing to maim the fair forms and cripple the light limbs of one generation of women after another in deference to a false ideal and a corrupted eye.[32]

In 1858 Parkes and several other pioneer feminists founded the *English Woman's Journal*, the first literary voice of the embryonic women's movement. From its inception the *Journal* and its successor, the *Englishwoman's Review*, included articles expressing concern about the suffering visited upon girls by the training they received in school. Blaming physical inactivity for excessive sensibility and poor health, contributors urged educators to ignore convention and parental whims in order to provide playgrounds and adopt such activities as swimming, scientific gymnastics, uninhibited dancing and vigorous games, which would improve students' health and physical development. Teachers were told they must constantly impress upon parents and pupils that mental and bodily vigour were inter-dependent; that if girls were allowed to develop their physical faculties as fully as boys they would become more rather than less feminine; and that whatever their futures, girls required all the physical strength and soundness of constitution of which they were capable.[33]

About the same time, Frances Power Cobbe, another leading feminist, perspicaciously linked exercise and games to women's entry into meaningful work. Noting the 'singular difference between the fresh and genuine enjoyment of men's sports by men, and the flaccid and dawdling indifferentism' of ladies' recreational employments, she lamented:

> Not one lady in five hundred past girlhood cares for any game or sport in the world as men care for these things. Most women care, indeed, for social pleasure, with all their bearings on the affections, on ambition, and on vanity; but a game of any sort, for the game's own sake, or a sport in which she should have no companion, are little or nothing to an ordinary woman . . . Except in cases of women with a strong dash of the masculine element in their disposition, there is hardly such a thing to be seen as a grown-up lady, thoroughly eager about any pleasure of the kind we are speaking of, for its own sake . . . The reason [is that] . . . ladies do not work, and therefore cannot play. It is not because they are more serious and earnest than men that they do not care for amusement, but because they are too commonly shut out from all serious and earnest aims, and therefore they have no appetite for it . . . How is all this to be remedied? . . . We should give ladies work to do, in the first place, if it were only that, in the second, they might enjoy play. Real work, of course . . . work that has some object and purpose . . .[34]

If women were allowed training and to enter the professions, she predicted, their dreary lives would be transformed, and they would learn to relax through participation in activities involving muscular exercise, activities like riding, swimming, archery and croquet. Cobbe considered women physically inferior to men, and could not envisage their playing such 'masculine' games as cricket. But her equation of physical freedom with other aspects of liberation was absolutely fundamental to women's emancipation.

The report of the Taunton Commission (1868), the first royal commission to consider female education, concurred, and was harshly critical of the physical as well as mental aspects of girls' schooling. On the basis of evidence that clearly revealed the relation between beliefs and practices regarding physical activity in female education and women's future roles in adult society, it described 'the important subject of bodily exercise' as 'imperfectly attended to', and the 'want of systematic and well-directed physical education' as one of the main impediments to good health and academic success.[35] The commissioners noted an absence of competitive behaviour in students' leisure and educational pursuits; a regrettable tendency to consider vigorous exercise undignified; and a general lack of playgrounds and provision for outdoor exercise and games. Among 100 private girls' schools in London, for example, they found 32 that provided nothing but a form of gentle callisthenics, while 60 offered only 'walking-abroad, croquet and dancing',[36] the latter activities apparently performing an important socialising function in the lives of women when they were the maximum physical exertion permitted by a society dominated by males.[37]

The views of educational reformers, feminists and royal commissioners collectively fell on fertile ground, for during the mid-nineteenth century reforms of all kinds were the order of the day. The Industrial Revolution was finally acknowledged as having created a pressing need for an educated population, and positive practical steps began to be taken towards providing training that would make women learned rather than merely accomplished. These included the foundation of several schools which deliberately tried to educate female minds and to educate bodies as well by providing students with more exercise; and even at less progressive schools drill lessons, supervised by NCOs from local army regiments, and slightly more energetic callisthenics were gradually instituted.

Progress, however, was painfully slow, for if education was a crucial arena for the working out of advances in the status of women, it also involved accommodations to prevailing stereotypes and rules of propriety. Conservative mistresses who improved opportunities for exercise remained more interested in graceful deportment than genuine physical fitness. Fathers often baulked at paying extra fees for gymnastic lessons; and too many teachers as well as parents continued to believe 'a girl was doing all that could be expected of her if she learned to keep her head up, her stomach in and her back straight'.[38]

Even reformers inevitably recognised that the more rigorous academic programmes they sought to introduce violated many established norms concerning the proper socialisation of young ladies and would provoke strong criticism. If they were to succeed in the long run, they would have to proceed cautiously to allay the fears of parents already nervous about the deleterious effects such an academic education might have on their daughters and who would have found intolerable the added fear of introducing vigorous exercise. Thus, although they made sure students took more exercise than was customary in the past, even the most advanced girls' school continued to insist on impeccably ladylike behaviour. The transition from gentle callisthenics and crocodile walks to real physical education and competitive games was gradual and did not occur to any extent before at least the 1880s. Indeed, games really entered girls' schools only with the first generation of Oxbridge-educated mistresses who had learned to appreciate them at university.

Notes

1. 'Eton Boy', quoted in *Physical Culture*, vol. 1 (November 1895), p. 334.

2. William J. Baker, 'The State of British Sport History', *Journal of Sport History*, vol. 10, no. 1 (1983), p. 64.

3. Marjorie S. Loggia, 'On the Playing Fields of History', published in the American feminist periodical *MS.*, vol. 2, no. 1 (1973), p. 63.

4. Rowland White to Robert Sidney, 12 September 1600 in Roger Longrigg, *The History of Fox Hunting* (London, 1975), p. 39.

5. *The Ladies' Dictionary* (1694), quoted in Loggia, 'On the Playing Fields', *MS.*, vol. 2, no. 1, p. 63.

6. Thomas Gisborne, *An Enquiry into the Duties of the Female Sex* (London, 1747), pp. 90–1; John Gregory, *A Father's Legacy to his Daughters* (London, 1774; reprint edn, New York, 1974), pp. 47–51; Erasmus Darwin, *A Plan for the Conduct of Female Education in Boarding Schools* (London, 1797), pp. 10, 68–70; Catherine Macaulay Graham, *Letters on Education* (London, 1790), pp. 24–5, 203–9; Hannah More, *Strictures on the Modern System of Female Education* (2 vols, London, 1799; reprint edn, New York, 1974).

7. Mary Wollstonecraft, *A Vindication of the Rights of Woman*, Miriam Kramnick (ed.) (Harmondsworth, 1975), pp. 182–3. See also pp. 81–3, 123–30, 286–7, 291–9.

8. George Farquhar, 'The Recruiting Sergeant' in William Archer (ed.), *George Farquhar* (London, 1949), p. 262.

9. Thomas Holcroft, *Anna St Ives* (7 vols, London, 1792), vol. 5, p. 234.

10. William Wordsworth, *The Poetical Works of William Wordsworth* (6 vols, London, 1857), vol. 2, p. 193.

11. Jane Austen, *Pride and Prejudice*, 3rd edn, R.W. Chapman (ed.) (Oxford, 1932), p. 36; Jane Austen, *Northanger Abbey and Persuasion*, 3rd edn, R.W. Chapman (ed.) (Oxford, 1933), p. 13.

12. Shirley H.S. Reekie, 'The History of Sport and Recreation for Women in Britain, 1700-1850', unpublished PhD thesis, Ohio State University, 1982, pp. 33-152.

13. *Sporting Magazine*, vol. 4 (June 1794), pp. 154-5, vol. 22 (June 1803), pp. 133-7.

14. Reekie, 'History of Sport', pp. 166-70.

15. Joan Burstyn, *Victorian Education and the Ideal of Womanhood* (London, 1980), pp. 84-98; Deborah Gorham, *The Victorian Girl and the Feminine Ideal* (Bloomington, Ind., 1982), pp. 86-90.

16. Priscilla Wakefield, *Reflections on the Present Condition of the Female Sex*, 2nd edn (London, 1817), pp. 19-26; Lant Carpenter, *Principles of Education, Intellectual, Moral and Physical* (London, 1820), pp. 329-87, 404-21; *The Young Lady's Book* (London, 1829); 'On the Ill Effects of Insufficient Exercise, Constrained Positions, and Tight Stays on the Health of Young Women', *Penny Magazine*, vol. 2 (28 February 1822), pp. 77-80; A.M. Bureaud-Riofrey, *Physical Education: Specially Adapted to Young Ladies* (London, 1838), p. 330.

17. Donald Walker, *Exercises for Ladies*, 2nd edn (London, 1837), pp. xvii–xviii, 72. This work is a striking contrast to Walker's *British Manly Exercises* (London, 1834), in which he identified as 'manly' rowing, sailing, riding, driving, walking, running, leaping, vaulting, balancing, skating, climbing, swimming, wrestling, boxing, tennis, bowling, curling, golf and cricket.

18. Walker, *Exercises for Ladies*, pp. 44-5. See also pp. 18, 71-5, 128, 131.

19. James Chiosso, *Remarks on Physical Education* (London, 1845), pp. 3-38.

20. Sarah Stickney Ellis, *The Women of England* (London, 1839), p. 17; Sarah Stickney Ellis, *The Mothers of England* (London, 1843), p. 324; Sarah Stickney Ellis, *The Daughters of England* (London, 1845), pp. 11-12, 228.

21. Matilda M. Pullan, *Maternal Counsels to a Daughter* (London, 1855), p. 104.

22. Herbert Spencer, *Essays on Education and Kindred Subjects* (London, 1910), pp. 136-7, 150-1; Herbert Spencer, *The Principles of Biology*, (2 vols, London, 1898), vol. 2, pp. 512-13. See also Chapter 7.

23. Peter Bailey, '"A Mingled Mass of Perfectly Legitimate Pleasures": The Victorian Middle Class and the Problem of Leisure', *Victorian Studies*, vol. 21, no. 1 (1977), pp. 8-13.

24. Hellen Meller, *Leisure and the Changing City 1870-1914* (London, 1976), pp. 17, 146, 225. See also J.A. Mangan, *Athleticism in the Victorian and Edwardian Public School* (Cambridge, 1981).

25. Peter C. McIntosh, *Physical Education in England Since 1800* (London, 1968), pp. 15-16. See also Charles Tennyson, 'They Taught the World to Play', *Victorian Studies*, vol. 2, no. 3 (1959), pp. 211-12.

26. Peter Bailey, *Leisure and Class in Victorian England* (London, 1978)

p. 1; Hugh Cunningham, *Leisure in the Industrial Revolution c. 1780–c. 1880* (London, 1980), p. 15; Meller, *Leisure and the Changing City*, p. 6.

27. Jennifer A Hargreaves, 'Playing Like Gentlemen While Behaving Like Ladies: The Social Significance of Physical Activity for Females in Late Nineteenth and Early Twentieth Century Britain', unpublished MA thesis, University of London Institute of Education, 1979, p. 56.

28. Sheila Fletcher, *Women First* (London, 1984), p. 9.

29. Jan Felshin, 'The Triple Option . . . For Women in Sport' in M. Marie Hart (ed.), *Sport in the Socio-Cultural Process*, 2nd edn (Dubuque, Ia., 1972), pp. 434–5.

30. Harriet Martineau, 'How to Make Home Unhealthy', *Harper's Monthly*, vol. 1 (October 1850), pp. 602, 617–18.

31. Bessie Rayner Parkes, *Remarks on the Education of Girls* (London, 1854), p. 8.

32. Ibid., pp. 11–12.

33. *English Woman's Journal*, vol. 1, no. 3 (1858), pp. 145–57; vol. 1, no. 6 (1858), pp. 189–90; vol. 1, no. 6 (1858), pp. 413–16; vol. 3, no. 16 (1859), pp. 217–29; vol. 3, no. 17 (1859), pp. 316–24; vol. 6, no. 36 (1861), pp. 262–5; *Englishwoman's Review*, no. 24 (July 1872), pp. 178–83.

34. *Every Saturday*, vol. 9 (12 February 1870), p. 101.

35. Great Britain, Royal Commission on School Education, *Report* (1868), vol. 1, p. 522. See also vol. 6, pp. 389, 588 and vol. 9, p. 299.

36. Ibid., vol. 7, pp. 556–7.

37. J.W.T. Hughes, 'Socialization of the Body Within British Educational Institutions — An Historical View', unpublished MSc thesis, University of London Institute of Education, 1975, p. 52.

38. Barry Turner, *Equality for Some* (London, 1974), p. 27.

2

The 'Lady Blue': Sport and Exercise at Oxbridge Women's Colleges

Girton College Hockey Song
(Tune 'Wot Cher')

To our ground there came a hostile force,
They were bent on beating us of course,
And the College cheered till it was hoarse
While fiercer still and fiercer grew the fray;
See our players in their scarlet shirts,
Tassel'd hockey caps and short blue skirts,
Little reck they of their wounds and hurts,
These are the order of the day.

Chorus: 'Play Up!' all the College cried
'Pass out to the wing, girls!'
'That's the sort of thing, girls'.
'Run! I thought I should have died'
'Knocked it through the Newnham Goal!'[1]

Victorian women's entry into sport was directly related to the campaign for female higher education which began in the 1860s and was one of the most crucial aspects of the women's rights movement, even though many of its leaders were not especially notable as advocates of the general emancipation of women. The successful establishment of women's colleges at Oxford and Cambridge Universities resulted from the collective efforts of men and women who shared an interest in broadening women's opportunities and promoting educational institutions which emphasised academic achievement. The significance of these colleges cannot be exaggerated, for their example was imitated at other universities; and, since education was the principal means for the pursuit of women's social mobility, they were a spectacular demonstration of tangible progress towards the day when sound education would be generally accessible to women and a new ideal of female excellence would be accepted.

The founders of the women's colleges were primarily concerned with establishing and developing the intellectual capacities of women in order to prepare them better for both domestic and professional roles. They believed, in addition, that women had a right to develop their bodies; and through games and exercise they sought to make students as fit as possible in order to prove that women could endure, without damage, the strain of higher learning. The latter was of critical importance, for the most potent and durable arguments against higher education were that maturing females possessed only a finite amount of energy; that energy expended in one area diminished the amount available in others; that the brain and reproductive system could not develop simultaneously; and that the hard labour required by university training would produce permanent damage, to the detriment of future generations.

It was no accident that the most eloquent, value-laden and apocalyptic 'scientific' critiques of higher education for women coincided with the establishment of the first women's colleges and a crusade to demonstrate the environmental rather than natural basis of women's intellectual inferiority. In the 1870s an attack was launched against the university-educated woman by two eminent physicians who were convinced that a tide of feminist reform threatened traditional roles and relationships and presaged gynaecological and racial disaster. Dr Edward Clarke of Harvard University and Dr Henry Maudsley of University College, London, issued polemics, in 1873 and 1874, in which they insisted there was sex in the mind as well as in the body. The physiological distinctions between the sexes, especially those connected with women's reproductive organs, they argued, dictated significant differences in behaviour, functions, abilities and education, and ordained the incompatibility of good health and rigorous mental activity. University life, they concluded, was 'out of harmony with the rhythmical periodicity of the female organisation', so college-educated women were bound to experience health problems ranging from anaemia, weakness, nervosity, melancholy, epilepsy and even insanity, and worst of all, the stunted growth of their sex organs. Clarke and Maudsley thus branded the higher education of women as calamitous to the future of the human race and a crime before God and humanity.[2]

Paradoxically, medical opinion was at first relatively

unconcerned about the potentially high energy demands of exercise, perhaps because there was little exercise to worry about. In fact, doctors not only failed to invoke the constitutional over-strain theory in the case of exercise, but actually supported moderate types and amounts as a counter-weight to serious study, and so were partly responsible for the introduction of sport and physical education at educational institutions for women.

Couched as it was in scientific terms, the medical case gave apparent legitimacy to opponents of the higher education of women and threatened to deal a fatal blow to women's ambitions in every direction except the domestic. The pioneer educators Frances Mary Buss and Emily Davies thus persuaded Elizabeth Garrett Anderson, the second woman to practise medicine in England, to issue a similarly scientific rebuttal.

Garrett Anderson conceded that, since rapid growth during adolescence taxed girls' 'nutritive powers', excessive mental effort should be avoided; but she insisted at the same time that normal girls were quite able to sustain ordinary amounts of brain work, and that health problems were much more likely to result from poor diet, improper clothing and too little mental and physical exercise. Denying Maudsley's charge that feminists sought to change women into men, she argued further that the promoters of higher education simply sought to enable women to develop their potential fully and that that potential would only be demonstrated if they were given the same educational opportunities as males. In response to Maudsley's charge that reformers neglected physical education, Garrett Anderson responded that in fact 'the same people who recently have attempted to improve the mental training of girls have continually been protesting in favour of physical development . . . [and have been] the first to introduce gymnastics, active games, daily baths and other hygienic reforms sorely needed in girls' schools'.[3]

Reforming educators generally agreed that there was an important conjunction between students' physical and mental health and a need to avoid over-strain. But whereas critics of women's higher education assumed that intellectual effort would deplete physical reserves, supporters suggested that gender differences assumed to be natural were more closely related to conformity to cultural norms than to absolute biological determinants. Since one of the most potent arguments against females receiving a sound education was that they were too weak, new institutions deliberately set out to prove they were not and at the same time to make them stronger. This was the root of most of the early physical activities within them and it dictated their form.[4]

It was certainly the case at the women's university colleges, and explains why they became centres of athletic pioneering as well as intellectual advancement. Their visionary founders usually resisted compromising principles by watering down academic programmes, and instead emphasised physical fitness as an important corollary of academic success. From the start they encouraged students to take exercise and engage in sport; and the response was enthusiastic. By the 1870s when the first women's colleges were established, sport was becoming an increasingly regular feature of university life, and not unnaturally the young women who pursued a course of study similar to men's sought to emulate, however imprecisely, other aspects of the male under-graduate experience.

Cricket and country pursuits comprised the main physical recreations of Oxbridge undergraduates in the early-nineteenth century, but from the 1850s, in the wake of the introduction of organised games in public schools, university sport grew more systematised. As early as 1868, although games were far from universal among university men, although their importance varied markedly from college to college, and although the element of compulsion and exaggerated self-consciousness characteristic of school sport was much less obvious, Mark Pattison, the venerable rector of Lincoln College, Oxford, deplored publicly the growth of athleticism and athletocracies, and of their corollary, anti-intellectualism, within the universities. But his words fell largely on deaf ears.

By the late-nineteenth century the universities and public schools were connected by what J.A. Mangan calls a 'circle of causality' wherein 'the successful games player at public school flourished in the same capacity at university and then returned to school as lauded assistant master to set another generation of devotees along the same route'.[5] By the end of the century, too, the university boat race and cricket match were mass spectator sports that attracted national attention through extensive press coverage. The typical memory of university life was of idle years of cricket, football and rowing, during which academic work weighed lightly; besides, the receipt of a blue in a major sport was as much a guarantee of future success as a first in the honours examinations. As at public schools, sport acquired dispropor-tionate significance as a powerful mechanism of social control, enhancing physical and moral qualities essential to national and imperial governance, and creating a life-long sense of community and institutional attachment.[6]

Although its nature was very different, sport also eventually played an important socialising role at the women's colleges as well. For years, however, discretion was the watchword. The rules forbidding the marriage of fellows were abolished only in 1882, and until then there were few women in university life. Many university men, undergraduates and dons alike, strongly disapproved of the presence of female students on the public grounds that higher education was incompatible with true womanhood and on the more important private ones that it threatened clerical and male control of the universities. Furthermore, they had a 'strong sense that admission of women to the privileges of higher learning would be derogatory to the dignity of the learned craft'[7] — not to mention of sport. The nature of the prejudice university women faced was revealed with dramatic clarity in a sermon preached in 1884 by John Burgon, the Dean of Chichester, in response to Oxford University's decision to admit women to most of the same examinations as men. Burgon called higher education 'plainly subversive' to women's best interests, and predicted 'to their great injury', that it would lead them to become independent and competitive and to 'imitate the manners, the demeanour, the phraseology of the undergraduate rivals . . . [worst of all they would even] adopt men's games where it is possible'.[8]

However revolutionary their aims and ambitions for women, the first heads of the women's colleges internalised many of the values of their culture, and became locked into a defensive mode of respectability by the hostility of men and repeated allegations that overwork would produce infertility and mental breakdown.[9] Fully aware that all eyes were upon their students, and that any inconvenience or offence would provoke censure and jeopardise chances of acceptance, they insisted upon discreet, inconspicuous behaviour. Every detail of conduct was closely monitored for years, and exercise, while encouraged, was circumscribed.

Cambridge

The story of women's collegiate sport began modestly in 1869 when Emily Davies's plans to make university education accessible to women resulted in the opening of Hitchin College in

Hertfordshire to five young ladies, who immediately undertook the work prescribed to candidates for Cambridge honours degrees under the watchful eyes of several lecturers who generously volunteered their services. Early in her campaign for educational reform Davies noted the 'importance of physical health to the life of the nation', and lamented that 'women are not healthy . . . it is a rare thing to meet with a lady of any age who does not suffer from headaches, languor, hysteria, or some ailment showing a want of stamina'.[10] At Hitchin her concern for physical as well as mental development was expressed in encouragement to students to take long country walks, properly chaperoned of course, and to play croquet, fives and a crude form of cricket in the seclusion of the college garden, which they apparently did 'with great laughter and fun, but small skill'.[11] Since none of the students could swim, Davies urged them to patronise the local open-air bath on the one day a week it was open to ladies, and even provided an aquatic role model by taking to the water herself. When they began to play a very mild form of football, however, she quickly forbade it on the grounds that outside knowledge of such overtly masculine activity would be taken as incontrovertible proof of the unsexing consequences of higher education.[12]

By 1873, when Hitchin College moved to Girton on the outskirts of Cambridge, women had hardly begun to participate in sport. But from the first, despite a lack of facilities, the authorities of the new college considered the students' health of such importance that free time for physical recreation was provided each afternoon. During the next decade the growing number of Girtonians obtained 'exercise and pleasure' from such activities as walking, rackets, fives, croquet, badminton, gymnastics and lawn tennis.

Plans for the first college buildings included a gymnasium; and, although the death of the donor delayed its construction, students in the early 1870s 'seem to have been greatly taken with gymnastics . . . and . . . tried to learn from each other vaulting, handswing, rope ladder and fencing'.[13] The question of appropriate gymnastics attire caused friction among Miss Davies's students and members of college, until the liberal view prevailed that students should be allowed to choose their own costume as long as it was worn only for gymnastics and included nothing 'unfitting and objectionable'. In 1877 a building designated 'the gymnasium', but not fitted out as such, containing a rackets court at one end and fives court at the other, was finally opened. Its multi-purpose use caused problems, and a letter to the *Girton Review* in 1882 complained about the storage of old lumber and broken furniture and the cramped conditions ensuing when rackets were played while gymnastic exercise was being taken. Three months later the *Review* announced the removal of the lumber and the acquisition of new apparatus through the generosity of members of a recently formed gymnastics club, whose disinclination to practice regularly resulted four years later in the club's disbandment.

The first game to capture the interest of Girton women was the newly invented lawn tennis. Despite a lack of proper courts, in 1873 student initiative lead to the playing of matches on the 'scanty and rough' lawn outside the dining hall. In this connection an informal club gradually arose, followed by a second and formal one in 1878, and the amalgamation of the two in 1883. Gravel courts were also built, and came under the management of a separate club instituted in 1882. Inter-college competition began in 1878 when Girton accepted an informal challenge to a doubles match by the recently founded Newnham College, and won a victory that marked the commencement of a domination that lasted to 1914. From 1882 the inter-collegiate was an annual fixture of considerable importance in the lives of both colleges, and from 1883 a silver challenge cup, presented anonymously by Charlotte Scott, Girton's first wrangler, was the reward for the doubles champions. Singles competition was added in 1883, and although there was no challenge cup until 1891, those who participated received silver racquet badges, the quest for which greatly 'increased the level of play and keenness'.[14]

Women's inter-university sports competition was inaugurated in 1883 when two representatives of Girton and Newnham engaged two from Lady Margaret and Somerville Halls, Oxford, in a doubles match on a private court in Essex safely away from the public eye. Cambridge, with four times as many students to choose from, was victorious, as was usually to be the case for many years. Simultaneously, the oldest challenge trophies in women's inter-university sport were introduced when two men on the Girton committee presented gold medal and silver owl prizes for the first and second champions of the winning side. By 1894, when an Old Girtonian presented a silver challenge cup, the inter-university tennis match had long since become a regular institution. Because they were held on courts belonging to private clubs and individuals, inter-university matches could be watched by past and present students and their friends without the risk of a scandal arising from players making themselves publicly conspicuous. The Archbishop of Canterbury was the host of the 1890 match at Lambeth Palace in memory of his late daughter, a student at Lady Margaret Hall, while that in 1894 was played before about 200 'enthusiastic spectators' at the All-England Club, Wimbledon.

Throughout the pre-First World War period lawn tennis remained a major sport at Girton. Over the years the number of courts, players and contests increased steadily. By the early 1890s, for example, the college had eight courts, four lawn and four gravel. The tennis club, born in 1886 from an amalgamation of the separate grass and gravel court clubs, boasted 63 members out of a college enrolment of approximately 114. A self-governing body with elected officers who took their activities very seriously, it developed elaborate rules for different types of competitions, arranged dates, locations and order of play, provided badges and cups and specified attire.

From the early 1890s, Girton also played outside matches against the women's colleges of London University, which, with university women around the country, were emulating the Oxbridge athletic model. Spectators travelled with the team to lend moral support; the college team increased in size; a second team was organised, as were diverse contests within Girton involving individuals, years, tripos, and old Girtonians, 82 of whom had formed the Girton College Lawn Tennis Club Honorary Members Association in 1882, thereby giving substance to exercise-advocates' hope that an interest in sport developed at college would be carried on afterwards.

Lawn tennis was a sport that even the staunchest male athletic exclusionist had difficulty in condemning, since for years it was played in impeccably feminine style and costume, which meant there was little running, stretching or vigorous movement. Girton's tennis records are free of controversy, apart from occasional indications that early players sometimes experienced a struggle between their urge to 'play the game' and retain, unsullied, their femininity. It was such a struggle that moved the college magazine, in 1883, to condemn

> . . .the tendency shewn by some players to consider attitudes and what they are pleased to think 'good style' as of the first importance [which] . . . if allowed to spread will have the most disastrous results on play in general. Quiet style is above all things important, but low hard strokes well

to the back of the court and into the corners, and good
judgement in waiting for and placing the balls will do more
to make a good game and to win a match than any amount
of attitudes and so-called 'pretty play'.[15]

Students apparently eventually concurred, for by the end of the
century, as skill became more important than appearance, the
Girton Review had forsaken expressions like 'quiet style' and 'pretty
play' for 'hard returns', and 'spirited volleys', 'sharp backhands'
and 'deadly overhand serves'.

Meanwhile, enrolment and confidence in Girton increased.
Whereas in the early days the majority of students had been
educated at home, by the 1880s half the freshers had attended a
public school, which meant they were better prepared for university work and competitive examinations and more used to taking
exercise. Tripos examination results demonstrated women's intellectual capacities and ability to stand the strain of higher learning
to such an extent that in 1880 college authorities sought official
recognition from the university. The senate responded the following year by formally opening honours and previous examinations
to women, placing their names on the public lists of examination
results and granting them certificates attesting to the places they
would have obtained had they been 'duly qualified' — in other
words, had they been men.

Hand-in-hand with women's rising academic ambitions came
the formation of all sorts of clubs and societies, after the fashion
of men's colleges, and more varied and vigorous exercise.

Apparent risks to body and propriety delayed the introduction
of hockey until late in 1890, when the lawn tennis club passed a
motion that a hockey club be formed. Prospective players had
little difficulty persuading authorities to provide a ground on the
site of an asphalt tennis court and the tennis club to donate £20
towards its preparation. Despite fears that 'the revelation that
"those Girton girls had actually taken to hockey"', would create
a 'national shudder',[16] the game rapidly developed into the main
sporting attraction. Between 1891 and 1895 a miscellany of
matches between years, and against Old Girtonians, Newnham
and Oxford, were arranged. The Newnham contest, which dated
from the Easter term of 1892 and was played for a cup presented
by an Old Newnhamite the next year, immediately became the
major event of the athletic year at both colleges, the one which
aroused the greatest excitement and emotion among players and

spectators alike. Also exciting, if somewhat less so, was the inter-university match between Oxford and Cambridge, an annual event from 1894, and from 1898 played for a trophy presented by two sisters who had attended Newnham and Somerville. As with tennis, participants in the inter-collegiate and inter-university competitions received distinctive silver badges.

Following the narrow victory by Cambridge in the first match, at the Wimbledon Hockey Club, Mr Punch manifested the generally contemptuous male attitude towards women's sport when he laughed uproariously at the whole 'hilarious' spectacle, and in a parody of 'The Battle of the Baltic' sarcastically warned that the Cambridge ladies' triumph rendered insignificant any victories in other sports by teams of Oxford men.[17] If he was still laughing 20 years later, however, it was less heartily, for by that time hockey had become established as the premier women's team game in the country. The annual inter-university women's match attracted several hundred Old Girls, parents, friends, and college and school staff and students to a ground in Richmond, and by 1913 even coverage in *The Times*.[18]

In 1895 Girton, along with several other colleges, became a charter member of the All England Women's Hockey Association (AEWHA), and students formed a second college XI and Old Girtonians, a Ladies' Hockey Club Honorary Members Association. Five years later membership on the college team was regularised when Girton (and Newnham) agreed that only residential students were eligible, and so excluded those who had gone down.

The primacy of hockey was demonstrated by the *Girton Review's* devotion of far more space to it than to any other sport or activity, the enlargement of the hockey ground several times and the constant expansion of the list of home and away fixtures involving schools, university and physical training colleges and women's clubs. Matches of all sorts were watched and played with great enthusiasm; a militant 'Beat Newnham' hockey song was sung to the tune of 'Knocked 'em in the Old Kent Road'; and playing on the college first XI came to be considered one of the greatest honours a Girtonian could attain. There was one prominent Girtonian, however, who was distinctly unenthusiastic about the game. Constance Jones, who became Mistress in 1903, is reported to have cautioned her charges, 'if you *must* play hockey, do try to hit the ball gently!'[19]

As attitudes to women became more liberal, as students' pre-university sports experience increased and as enrolment grew, sporting activities at Girton became increasingly diverse, vigorous and frequent. From the early days, students went for long walks in the Fens. A rackets club, formed in the mid-1870s when a court was fitted out in the new gymnasium, survived for about ten years until the attractions of outdoor sport proved irresistible. Between 1891 and 1902 the college had a golf club and its own nine-hole course; and although Newnham declined an invitation to participate in an inter-college match, there was a good deal of interest within Girton, particularly in the mid-1890s, in competing for a challenge brooch donated by an Old Student in 1893. Until 1900, when past students were prohibited from playing hockey, the brooch was the only trophy limited to students resident in college. Enthusiasm for golf waned around the turn of the century, and the club disbanded in 1902 when a new building was constructed on part of the course.

In the realm of aquatic sports, the swimming bath that opened in 1900, thanks to the largesse of Old Students and friends of the college, immediately went into 'constant use'. Students formed a swimming club the next year, which arranged races and water-polo matches between students in different subjects and years. From 1907 inter-college and inter-university meets were held, the latter involving first Oxford and then London Universities. Because of Girton's distance from the river the boating club that students started for recreational purposes in 1906 did not become popular and received no mention in the *Review* after 1907. Although 'not a strenuous thing at all' and involving 'no races or anything competitive', boating appeared potentially dangerous, and for safety's sake the club required members to pass proficiency tests in swimming and rowing.[20]

As regards team sports, students played a primitive form of cricket from the Hitchin days, and continued to do so at Girton. Hertha Ayrton, a scientist who assiduously avoided sport while up in the late 1870s, wrote to Barbara Bodichon of her fellow students' cricket playing, 'You have no idea how funny they look; they run shockingly with their heads a mile in front of them . . . I suppose they will improve in time but at present they send me into fits of laughter.'[21] Girton's records indicate that cricket was not taken particularly seriously, but a club was established in 1893 and matches were played 'on a grassy space sheltered from the public eye'[22] — the hockey ground and then the golf course. Informal matches against Newnham were held during the long vacation for some years prior to the first formal contest in 1897, for which a challenge cup was donated by an Old Newnhamite. There were no inter-university matches prior to 1914 since very little cricket was played at Oxford; but contests between years, students and lecturers were organised within Girton, and in 1907 a professional coach, with the 'highest testimonials' to his character, was engaged.

The game of lacrosse was introduced to Girton by students from St Leonards School, St Andrews. A club was formed in 1899 as a result of initiatives taken by the new games club, but it laboured 'under difficulties as hockey is so much played . . . that there is little time for those who wish to practise lacrosse'.[23] These difficulties evidently killed it, for in 1913 the *Review* reported on the formation of a new lacrosse club and on the commencement of intra-college matches. Later the same year it made much of a Girton side's defeat of Newnham for a trophy donated by Girton, and in 1914 of Girtonians' membership on a combined Cambridge team that defeated Oxford for a trophy given by Lady Margaret Hall, before a small crowd at that bastion of male sport — Lord's.

Finally, no history of sport at Girton would be complete without mention of the activity which, although not strictly speaking a sport at all, made the greatest contribution to the physical liberation of women. This was bicycling. Like women everywhere during the 1890s, few Girtonians could resist its lure. Promises to parents to do nothing so 'fast' as ride a cycle were quickly forgotten, and students soon found themselves being 'measured for a cycling skirt, with little elastic stirrups sewn into the hem to keep it down to the ankle'.[24] A cycling club, organised in 1894, became instantly popular, and each term so many new cycles were brought up that there was a storage problem until, in 1910, the college built a new bicycle shed with space for 160 machines.

Prior to the advent of the bicycle Girton's distance from central Cambridge kept students safely secluded and forced them to travel about in horse-drawn cabs irreverently called 'Girton hearses'. Fearing the effects of the new mobility on university opinion and students' morals, college authorities at first subjected cycling to strict regulations. Riders had to pass a proficiency test before they could go into town, and they were not allowed to ride on Sundays until 1900, nor around Cambridge until 1903, by which time female cyclists had ceased to be stared at as an extraordinary novelty. The following year students gained permission to ride to lectures after dark, unaccompanied by a don, as long as at least three went together, and by 1906 all restrictions had disappeared.[25]

Sport and physical recreation were so prevalent at Girton by the turn of the century that some observers thought there was an 'all-pervading athletic spirit' in the college which prevented students from 'becoming blue-stockings and bookworms'.[26] Unlike men's colleges such as Jesus, however, Girton never developed an athletocracy or worshipped at the altar of a cult of athleticism. A few students might have become obsessed with games, and some might occasionally have skipped lectures in order to practise or play an important match. But 'playing the game' never completely lost its therapeutic purpose, and to students and staff alike it was always distinctly secondary to academic achievement.

Simultaneous with Emily Davies's establishment of Girton College, Anne Jemima Clough (the sister of poet Arthur Hugh Clough) and a group of prominent men and women did similar work elsewhere in Cambridge. In the mid-1860s Clough helped Davies to form the London Society of Schoolmistresses and, in addition, associations in major Midland cities to assist teachers and to obtain advanced instruction for women through lectures by university dons. The union of the latter in 1867 into the North of England Council for Promoting the Higher Education of Women marked the beginning of the influential university extension movement.

The sizeable audiences the council's lectures attracted indicated the desire of a substantial number of women to cultivate their minds and, along with girls' recent admission to the Cambridge Local Examinations, encouraged the council to inform Cambridge University of 'the great want which is felt by women of the upper and middle classes, particularly by those engaged in teaching, of higher examinations suitable to their own needs'.[27] Since there was no suggestion of competition with men or infringement of their domain, the university quickly agreed.

The first women's examination in May 1869 was followed almost immediately by the establishment of a series of lectures for women in most subjects of examination by a university committee led by Professor Henry Sidgwick, whose keenness to recognise the needs of women was part of a larger plan to modify the whole university system. The unexpectedly large attendance created a problem of accommodation, and in 1871 Anne Jemima Clough was invited to take charge of a house of residence for five students in Regent Street. Thus was born Newnham College.

Unlike the Girton pioneers, who insisted on the pursuit of academic programmes identical to those of men in order to establish the intellectual equality of the sexes, Newnham's founders lacked a sense of mission or involvement in a stirring campaign for women's rights. They accepted diluted courses and tests; and although by 1890 most Newnhamites prepared for honours examinations, for several years they were allowed to pursue a variety of courses at a variety of levels and speeds, which meant a relatively high turnover and short length of stay.

Nevertheless, the foundation of Newnham created a new forum for women's higher education, where from the first those in charge were concerned about maintaining and improving the students' health. Since the original house in Regent Street had no garden, opportunities for exercise were limited. Mary Paley, one of the original five and later wife of Alfred Marshall, the Professor of Political Economy, recalled, 'We went twice a week to the town gymnasium, but otherwise walks were our only form of exercise. We watched the undergraduates playing games on Parker's Piece, and envied them.'[28] Merton Hall, the larger premises near St John's College obtained in 1872, had a spacious private garden where, according to Clough, 'the students tried croquet and cricket . . . but they happily could not do cricket'.[29] But Newnham Hall, the first permanent building, which opened in 1875, sat amidst two acres of grounds.

Sport at Newnham evolved along lines similar to those at Girton, except that in due course Newnham offered even greater variety. From the start the afternoon hours between lunch and tea were set aside for fresh air and exercise, and lawn tennis quickly became the most popular pastime. An ash court was laid out and a tennis club organised in 1876. When new halls opened in 1880 and 1888, students formed clubs, arranged intra- and inter-hall matches, and keenly fought for the requisite cups presented in 1882 for the hall singles championship by a member of parliament whose daughter had been at Newnham, and for doubles by Arthur James Balfour whose sister Eleanor married Henry Sidgwick and in 1892 became Newnham's second principal.

Over the years as enrolment expanded the number of tennis players increased and facilities improved. The annual inter-college match created much excitement, and membership on the college and university teams became coveted as a great honour. Tennis at Newnham occasioned one of the first breaks in the social segregation of Cambridge men and women, when in 1899 the college tennis club

> . . . represented to the authorities how much improved our
> play would be if we had the advantage of playing with men,
> and the suggestion was favourably received. The Tennis Six
> who played in inter-college matches, were allowed to invite
> men on certain days, brothers, cousins or old family friends
> and were of course carefully chaperoned. The Tennis Six
> interpreted the term 'cousin' rather liberally.[30]

Mixed sets, predictably, became very popular.

The Newnhamites' other physical recreations in the 1870s and 1880s included walking, gymnastics and fives. Gymnastics was considered useful for the maintenance of health and the production of a good carriage, so early on students paid ten shillings a year to use a private gymnasium in town. Following the opening of the college's own facility in 1879, gymnastics enjoyed temporary popularity, but interest declined in the face of growing opportunities for outdoor sport. Fives, although never widely played, developed a devoted following. During the mid-1880s and early-1890s, donations by past and present students enabled the building of a court, a club was started, and a cup for hall competition and colours for club members were awarded.

As at Girton, the big sporting breakthrough came in 1890 with the formation of a hockey club, but whereas at Girton the tennis club provided the initiative, at Newnham it came directly from the principal. Despite 'ridicule and disapprobation from select circles',[31] Miss Clough actively encouraged hockey on the grounds that such experiences of college life were almost as valuable to students as book learning, and that participation in games and other college societies taught them to be business-like and co-operative. Hockey quickly became Newnham's premier sport, and by 1894 it threw such 'a spell over its votaries' that they would 'not hear of anything being compared to it'.[32]

During the 1890s, a hockey ground was provided, hall and college clubs were formed, and cups were donated for hall and freshers' competitions by friends and Old Students. Matches between past and present students were arranged following the formation of an Old Newnham Students Hockey Club. It immediately joined the Old Girtonians in hiring a ground near London for matches every second Saturday, but, like other such clubs, soon had to allow friends of members to play since, as a result of family obligations and scepticism about the sport for adult women, too few turned out regularly to make up full sides. The college hockey team adopted as colours a white blouse and scarlet cap and tie, and navy-blue serge skirts, which proved a 'voluminous impediment' to play since modesty dictated that they be no more than eight inches off the ground. At Christmas in 1894 Newnham sent the first women's hockey team on tour, a group of past and present students who accepted an invitation to play in Ireland; shortly thereafter the college became one of the charter members of the AEWHA.[33]

By the early-twentieth century internal and external matches abounded, and there were three college XIs. The attention of the whole college became riveted by the annual contest against Girton, detailed reports of which appeared in the college magazine, and inevitably included highly charged expressions like 'men of Newnham', 'noble defenders', 'intense enthusiasm', 'keen excitement', 'great pride' and 'glorious victories'. When Girton was vanquished the college XI dined together in hall while the rest of the students assembled to cheer; and at the close of a successful season, a dance — for women only, of course — was held to celebrate.

In the 1890s the style of hockey at Newnham was described as 'at once exciting and pretty to watch', proof that the game could be a 'graceful amusement'.[34] But on occasion grace apparently gave way to excitement and competitive instincts. Although Newnham lacked a college song, the halls certainly had theirs, and during keen contests the 'men of Clough' or the 'men of Sidgwick' were urged to 'fight' and be 'tough' by a cacophony of voices raised to a most unladylike pitch. Propriety was also forgotten after the Freshers' Cup championship when students cheered, shouted, sang and rang fire-bells and gongs, and by the students who occasioned the following query in the *Thersites*:

> Is it usual during a hockey match for one side to shout complaints against the other which may be heard all over the field, or having thrown down the Captain of that side to accuse her of holding your leg by the crook of her stick, while lying on the ground?[35]

Had such behaviour been known to the outside world it would have confirmed predictions about the sport's defeminising character, but what it demonstrated internally was the healthy, liberating effects of sport on young ladies who were normally models of gentility.

In addition to tennis and hockey, Newnhamites eventually participated in a remarkable variety of other sports and physical recreations. They went for long walks through the Fen country, by the river or to Girton, although without special permission restricted to a ten-mile radius of the college. When the river froze they ice-skated, some of the more adventurous as far as Ely; and a few wealthy girls rode horses. By 1891, properly chaperoned of course, a number boated up and down the Cam 'to some little inn where they have tea before returning'.[36] A rowing society was organised shortly thereafter, and by 1910 it was conducting trials for two divisions, to the apparent risk of the Clare Bridge. To forestall criticism Mrs Sidgwick noted that the few Newnhamites who rowed did so in an unstrenuous manner, and that the rules of the boat club were designed primarily to ensure the safety of students who boated for pleasure rather than to promote skilled rowing and sculling.[37] Between 1896 and 1914 Newnhamites also formed croquet, cricket, swimming, fencing and lacrosse clubs. They even started a ju-jitsu class, which enjoyed temporary popularity, following a demonstration by a Japanese gentleman around 1906; and at the end of the period some introduced netball for the sake of those who had played no other game at school.

During the 1890s Newnhamites — lecturers and students alike — also contracted cycling fever. In 1894:

> The Council . . . decided that students may ride the bicycle with certain restrictions. The art must not be acquired at College; only inveterate proficiency is countenanced, and this is tested in a searching examination in corner-turning, etc., before candidates received a diploma.[38]

Dons conducted the tests, after having instructed students on the finer points of turning and mounting and dismounting gracefully; and a list of approved riders was posted. The fact that Eleanor Sidgwick rode, and rode well, helped to destroy any residual feelings that cycling was an unwomanly activity. Riding to lectures was not officially permitted until 1910, however, although by that date the rule against it was honoured more in the breach than the observance.

Newnham's diversity and abundance of sport were the result of a combination of student initiative and deliberate encouragement by college authorities who, though concerned about the possibility of excess and overstrain, considered most sports an important contribution to physical, moral and scholastic development. In the words of Miss Clough:

> It is undeniable that they [games] frequently occupy a place in girls' thoughts which might be filled by something more fruitful, but one also has to take the probabilities into account and consider what would be likely to be in the heads that games fill, and I incline to think there might easily be less wholesome matters. Games, I do believe, drive out much silliness; they occupy the vacant space, and they also produce an antiseptic atmosphere. An active game I hold more likely to produce a healthy atmosphere, a healthy outlook on things, the complete forgetfulness of self, and the quickening of the blood which accompany it.[39]

Perhaps because there was no indication that athletic and academic achievement were incompatible, the only caution in the Newnham records against excessive devotion to sport was the 'word of warning' issued in 1912 by the college magazine to all, 'particularly the younger members, [to] beware of too much hockey'.[40] Philippa Fawcett, whose historic placing above the senior wrangler in the first part of the mathematical tripos in 1890 was a great triumph for the cause of women's higher education, played on the first college hockey team. Florence Stawell, the college tennis champion in 1892, was the first woman in the first division of the first class of the classical tripos the same year; and the *Thersites'* regular column on 'Those in Authority' frequently featured students who excelled in both study and sport.

Oxford

The development of women's sport at Oxford followed a pattern similar to that of Cambridge, although at Oxford there was less variety in activities and more emphasis on boating. There were also eventually combined university clubs in tennis (1899), hockey (1901) and lacrosse (1912), that were selected from the best players from all the women's colleges and from which the university teams were chosen, and that brought women from across the university together in a way unusual at the time.

The history of women at Oxford began in 1873 with the formation of a committee of women to develop a scheme for women's lectures and examinations. Two years later its lobbying, and that of a number of Oxford men, resulted in the university adding to its statute governing the examination of non-members a provision for the examination of women above the age of 18 and the creation of preparatory lectures. Both lectures and examinations were very successful, and in 1878 an Association for the Promotion of the Higher Education of Women in Oxford (AEW) was founded to arrange lectures, engage lecturers and furnish residential accommodation. To the latter end Lady Margaret and Somerville Halls opened without fanfare in 1879.

Although in 1884 the Oxford convocation admitted women to the final honours examinations in mathematics, natural science and modern history, unlike Cambridge it did not confine the honours schools to resident students; so Oxford women were not matriculated, which meant they could take as long as they liked to sit examinations, and until 1910 their societies had no official standing.

Also unlike Cambridge, Lady Margaret and Somerville were strictly halls of residence at first. But from the early days, whereas Girton and Newnham women heard lectures on site, their students went to special lectures arranged by the AEW or professional or college lectures to which the AEW had secured their admission if they came suitably chaperoned. By 1901 most of the lectures Oxford women attended were in men's colleges, which perhaps explains why they identified more closely with the university than did their Cambridge sisters who would have said 'When I was at Newnham' to the Somervillian's, 'When I was at Oxford'.[41] But at Oxford as much as at Cambridge, the first generations of female students were there on sufferance and lived lives far removed from those of the undergraduates to whom they were strange curiosities. Apart from laboratory work, male and female students had little communication until after the First World War; and to women the university with its undergraduate activities seemed entirely marvellous and remote.[42]

As did their Cambridge counterparts, the pioneers of women's education at Oxford had to allay strong prejudices against women yet maintain high ideals about the nature of female education. Aware that their students were on probation and that any false step might destroy chances of acceptance, they too insisted on discreet, inconspicuous behaviour, while students for their part felt a responsibility to live up to the privileges of study, and so dutifully observed irksome rules framed in deference to opinion in men's colleges that did not even acknowledge their existence.

Lady Margaret Hall, which had strong ties with the Church of England, began life in a house in Norham Gardens with a complement of nine students. Its principal from 1879 to 1909 was Elizabeth Wordsworth, a mild-mannered and conservative woman who did not share Emily Davies's view on women's rights or their need to follow the same academic programmes as men. Wordsworth urged students to cultivate womanliness and put marriage high on the list of desirable careers, which perhaps explains why Lady Margaret Hall became known as a kind of finishing school for ladies. At the same time she seriously promoted the cultivation of intellects, and for health reasons, and because of her girlhood experience at a Brighton boarding school where the only exercise provided was dancing and crocodile walks, she encouraged the playing of outdoor games.[43] Practising what she preached, Wordsworth herself took a walk each morning; and in her annual reports she commented regularly on the attention given to physical development, on general and individual health and on the hall's sporting activities.

Although the Norham Gardens house lacked facilities for games, Wordsworth's and the Lady Margaret Hall Council's concern for physical as well as mental growth meant that two hours were set aside each afternoon for recreation and exercise. The latter consisted initially of croquet, taking country walks in pairs or groups, skipping in corridors on wet days and playing tennis on a couple of makeshift courts. The first permanent building, which opened in 1882, included a small gymnasium, thanks to the generosity of donors,[44] and on its spacious grounds proper grass and asphalt tennis courts were promptly constructed. For years thereafter tennis was the chief outdoor amusement. A club was formed, trophies were donated, matches against Somerville were played 'amidst much cheering and excitement' and the results of contests at all levels were regarded as important news.

Between 1881 and 1884 the hall council raised money for and conducted protracted discussions regarding a rackets court. When no suitable site proved obtainable, in 1885 the council approved the diversion of funds to the purchase of a boat and boathouse on the River Cherwell, which flowed past the hall garden. Thereafter boating loomed large in the students' lives. Since few could swim, those wishing to boat were required to obtain written permission of parents and principal — permission Wordsworth was pleased to give for she regarded early morning swims as conducive to health — and to produce a certificate of proficiency or pass a swimming test of 50 feet. As the number of boats increased through student subscriptions and private and conciliar donations, the qualifying test became more stringent. But despite the 'grim and nerve-wracking rituals' the test involved, the joy of taking a boat out proved irresistible.[45]

By the turn of the century, when a boat club was belatedly formed under the presidency of Miss Wordsworth, most students could swim and many could be found any day but Sunday happily boating on the Cherwell. They were not allowed on the River Isis, however, for they might have interfered with what were considered the much more important boating activities of undergraduates; and there was no question of inter-college competition. Boating at Lady Margaret Hall was for fun, not serious exercise, and the complicated club rules and qualifying regulations had more to do with increasing safety than skill.[46]

Paradoxically, the hall council no sooner approved boating than it banned hockey. In the spring of 1885 Miss Wordsworth conceded that 'perhaps there was too great a preponderance on the out-of-door athletic side of life throughout the term'.[47] But she was exceedingly annoyed that the council, 'feeling the strength of certain objections to the game of hockey, think it desirable that it should be discontinued for the present'.[48] The minutes of the council meeting are bland in the extreme and give no indication of the nature of the 'certain objections', or the controversy that must have ensued during the discussion of the prohibition. There are, however, several possible explanations: a concern that too much games-playing was responsible for the hall's examination results the previous year being inferior to Somerville's; disapproval of Lady Margaret students behaving like undergraduates and in the full flush of a victory over Somerville building a bonfire in the hall garden; and, at what was a very early date for young ladies to be playing hockey, the conviction that it was improper. Whatever the reasons, Miss Wordsworth was unconvinced, and her next report acidly blamed the poor health at the hall on the diminution of outdoor games.

The ban lasted until 1893 when the council, responding to the winds of change, finally gave students 'leave to play hockey in a field to be hired for the purpose; the parents' permission to be obtained in each case'.[49] The students immediately formed a hockey club and in short order arranged a variety of inside and outside matches, to the evident satisfaction of the principal who reported in 1894 that 'the good deal of hockey' that was played 'told favourably on [students'] health and spirits'.[50]

The next 20 years saw the number of college XIs increase to three; coaching at first by male dons and then by an expert especially hired for the purpose; graduating students' donation of a cup for inter-house competition; the abandonment of the Somerville ground for home matches when the hall obtained facilities of its own; and the formation of an Old Lady Margaret Hall Hockey Club which, despite much enthusiasm, had difficulty getting sufficient players together. They also saw the *Fritillary*, the magazine of the Oxford women's halls, comment on occasion about the poor attendance at hall hockey practices and about the inexcusability of the first team's losing its collective head during matches. Learning how to 'play the game' evidently took time.

In addition to tennis and hockey, hall students eventually participated in a variety of other physical activities, including athletic sports, skating, swimming, lacrosse and, of course, cycling.[51] Permission to cycle aroused a degree of excitement second only to that over hockey. A cycling club was formed in 1895 by 37 of the hall's 53 students, despite the dangers of scrapes and sprained ankles, and the inevitable restrictions on where and when students could ride. Sunday riding was prohibited at first, unless it facilitated attendance at church, as was riding over the Magdalen and Folly bridges; but Lady Margaret women were never prevented from cycling into Oxford. When, at the age of 60, Miss Wordsworth herself took up tricycling, out of a conviction that it would decisively benefit her health, restraints became less stringent than elsewhere. And at Lady Margaret, as at all the women's halls, the bicycle had an immediate impact on the relaxation of chaperonage rules.

One sport students were not allowed was cricket. The subject first came up in 1886 when Somerville refused to allow Lady Margaret Hall to use its grounds for the purpose, and it arose again in 1901 when students petitioned the hall council 'that they might be allowed to play cricket with the High School Games Club or any other Ladies' Clubs in Oxford'.[52] The council's negative response was supported by Miss Wordsworth, who regarded the game as entirely too masculine, and in this it was not alone. None of the Oxford women's halls fielded cricket teams prior to 1914, although St Hilda's and the Home Students' Society permitted individual women to play with local clubs.

For a number of years the academic demands at Lady Margaret Hall were not great, but the interest in sports was. They loomed large in students' lives and conversations, and if play was amateurish by later standards, it was vigorous and enthusiastic. Winifred Knox Peck, who was up from 1901 to 1903, recalled:

> Hockey in spring wind or rain or misty autumn sunshine on our admirable ground, our great matches with Cambridge and Somerville, and long, long conversations about them over tea-tables by blazing fires, were the centre of our early terms. When summer came we filled punts and canoes with gay cushions and pushed off from our boathouse in the Cherwell, feeling that Lady Margaret was our world. We did not even attend the inter-college debates or societies of the women's colleges.[53]

But sport was never allowed to dominate life. Elizabeth Words-worth, for all her promotion of the athletic spirit as an aid to good health, shared her generation's concern about excess and overstrain, and was always careful to guard against athleticism becoming a cult.

> Are we not carrying the reaction in favour of physical culture a little too far [she asked in 1894]? It is no secret among medical men that many of our young women have already fallen victim to the overstrain which an eager nature, acted upon by that *esprit de corps* which is so strong in school and college girls, has often led them to undergo in playing, when a sensible mother would have insisted on their declining to do so. If our young men sometimes sacrifice their health to an overenthusiasm for games that is no reason why our young women should do likewise.[54]

Although Lady Margaret and Somerville Halls shared a common birthdate, the two were not identical twins. While Lady Margaret had strong Church of England connections, Somerville was non-denominational, less strict and more academic. 'Born of enlightened ideas and in particular a progressive conception of women which clothed itself discreetly in the hereditary feminine garb of modest manners and watchful tact',[55] Somerville stood for complete intellectual and religious liberty as well as scholarship and culture. A strong spirit of individualism permeated its atmosphere, and in due course it earned a reputation for cultivating in women a sense of professionalism and the need to fight women's battles.

Somerville Hall opened in October 1879 to twelve students. Its first principal, Madeleine Shaw Lefevre, was the sister of George John Shaw Lefevre, the member of parliament for Bradford and post-master general in Gladstone's second ministry. Her tact, moderation and unqualified womanliness were a great help in disarming the hostile criticism that was directed against women's higher education and in laying secure foundations for the hall.

Shaw Lefevre shared Elizabeth Wordsworth's views on the necessity of impeccably ladylike behaviour and on the health-producing combination of study and physical recreation. She thus urged Somervillians to take exercise during their free afternoon hours, albeit in inoffensive ways. Playing space was not a problem since the hall was surrounded by three acres of ground, and in no time 'the girlies' began playing pat-ball tennis on the lawn 'in flounced skirts and with lop-sided racquets'.[56] When they were invited to tennis parties elsewhere, they were 'conveyed in a closed cab since it was not considered decorous . . . to be seen walking through the streets of Oxford with a racquet'.[57]

The development of tennis followed the usual pattern involving the students' formation of a club, laying down of proper courts, intra- and extra-college contests and appropriate rewards. It was a distinguished Old Somervillian, Lilian Faithfull (1883–6), who in 1890 first recommended that special badges be awarded to all those who competed for Oxford and Cambridge in the women's inter-university tennis match, so they could say, like the undergraduates, that they had received their blue. All four colleges concerned implemented the suggestion the very next year, and thus the 'lady blue' was born.[58]

As at Lady Margaret, hockey at Somerville had a chequered career. Students started a club in 1885, and the game immediately became popular. Lilian Faithfull, the first hockey captain, recalled the excitement of the inaugural match against Lady Margaret Hall and the disgust at Somerville's defeat after the captain was laid low by a blow in the eye from an errant stick.[59] In 1887, however, for unexplained but calculable reasons, hockey was unceremoniously forbidden.

Following its revival in 1893, hockey rapidly became the sporting queen. The requisite club was organised, and it helped form the AEWHA two years later. Donations permitted the acquisition of a sports field that could accommodate a full-size ground; more and more outside matches were played; additional XIs were formed; a rule designed to improve mobility and quality of play required skirts to be cut a daring seven inches off the ground; colours were awarded on the basis of merit to members of the first XI; and a woman coach, an ex-All England player, was engaged. Senior students impressed on promising freshers the role they might play in winning or losing the all-important inter-collegiate hockey cup; and when, in 1912, the Oxford women defeated Cambridge to win the inter-university championship for the first time in 15 years, Somerville hosted the great celebration.

Hockey's only serious rival was boating, which was allowed on the upper Cherwell from 1884 for recreational purposes, at times when undergraduates were unlikely to be encountered. The river proved widely appealing, and before long, despite increasingly exacting swimming tests that initially prevented some of the best athletes from joining, the boat club boasted a large membership and ownership of several craft that were in 'constant use'.[60]

The slowness of attitudinal changes and the longstanding pressure on women to defer to masculine interests, however, is strikingly revealed in the following contemporary observation:

> Athleticism is as strong a point at Somerville as at any of the women's colleges of the present advanced day. But here again great care is taken that the college should not clash with the men's colleges. A Somerville boat would be very much disliked on the river, so, though the college owns five boats, two canoes and a punt, these are kept on the Cherwell . . . On the lower river these boats never appear; they sometimes go on the upper river for picnics, but that is all.[61]

The Somervillians' other sporting options eventually included horse-back riding, fencing, gymnastics and cycling. A 'covered gymnasium for the use of students' was provided in 1891 'at her own cost' and 'with great liberality' by a Miss Forster, an old friend of Miss Shaw Lefevre.[62] Initially a sergeant from a nearby boys' school came over to give lessons in fencing and gymnastics that proved popular in the winter though rather less so in good weather when students preferred being outdoors.

As for bicycling, cyclists first appeared at Somerville in 1893, and the garden was soon rendered 'dangerous' by the feats of riders with varying levels of skill. Riding to lectures or alone was considered unseemly and was thus forbidden; on rides short or long at least one companion was required.

All things considered, sport, however popular, was never over-done at Somerville. The college's reputation for scholarship was well deserved; and the view of successive principals, that athletics in moderation were beneficial to health and character, but that overstrain was a danger, prevented excess.

The sporting history of the other women's halls at Oxford was largely unexceptional.

At St Hugh's (1886), founded by Elizabeth Wordsworth for those unable to afford the fees at Lady Margaret, low enrolment impeded the development of sport. Students did, however, organise tennis, walking, boating and hockey clubs, although in the latter instance, while the majority belonged, play remained erratic because of fluctuations in enthusiasm and a certain reluct-ance to attend practice.[63]

At St Hilda's (1893), established by Dorothea Beale, primarily for graduates of the Cheltenham Ladies' College who intended to become teachers, small numbers also limited sporting activity. But from the start, for health reasons, students were expected to spend time outdoors between lunch and tea walking, cycling and playing croquet and tennis.[64] Since the River Cherwell flowed past the hall garden, they soon formed a boat club, the male coach of whose four must have been amused to see his charges encircling their skirts with elastic bands to prevent entanglement in sliding seats. Its eight, the first at a women's college, was used only on a secluded part of the river so as to avoid the undesirable attention such a masculine activity would have attracted. St Hilda's even had a canoe club from 1901, to which instruction was given for a time by a Canadian Rhodes Scholar.[65]

As for other sporting realms, students joined the inter-college tennis competitions in 1898; they ice-skated when the Cherwell froze; some took instruction at a local fencing club; a few tried lacrosse; and in 1900 an energetic player organised a hockey club. 'Regrettably', however, so 'large a number of St Hilda's students declined to play hockey',[66] that a regular team could not be fielded until 1911.

What was unique about St Hilda's sport was the rifle club, the existence of which, at a hall whose students were not particularly athletically inclined, provides an excellent example of the emulation of male models. Formed in October 1909 by 28 of the hall's 44 members, it competed for a fine silver goblet donated by one Alice Edwards, whose largesse stemmed from the unusual conviction that 'if any of our students go to the colonies they might find this art useful'.[67] For the next five years, until the demands of war produced an ammunition shortage and the commandeering of the local rifle range, an average of 20 devotees held weekly practices. Several apparently became first-class shots; it is not recorded whether their skill was ever of any use in the colonies.

After the opening of the various halls of residence for women at Oxford, there remained some who preferred living in private homes. To these the term Home Students was first applied in 1890–1; and in 1898 the council of the AEW officially designated them the Society of Oxford Home Students.

Among the Home Students, small numbers, a variety of ages and nationalities, scattered quarters and the lack of their own grounds retarded the growth of sport. Nevertheless, they established boat, tennis and hockey clubs in the 1890s, and were warmly encouraged to do so by Bertha Johnson, their principal, who strongly supported activities like sport that brought students together as a recognised body and developed among them a corporate identity. The boat club enjoyed consistent popularity, despite exacting swimming tests and strict rules that prevented students from boating alone or unchaperoned with young men. But attendance at tennis and hockey practices was insufficiently large or regular to maintain standing teams for more than a few years at a time.[68]

The situation to 1914

Although their students generally came from the well-to-do middling middle class of business, manufacturing, politics and learning, the Oxbridge women's colleges were far from being all of a piece. There were obvious and subtle differences between them involving size, endowments, fees, living arrangements, attitudes and social standing, which affected to some extent both academic and athletic orientation.[69] The evidence is overwhelming, however, that large and small, strongly academically oriented and less so, 'up- and down-market', by 1914 the majority of college students were physically active, and even of those who were not, most were involved as spectators. Enthusiasm for games may not

have been quite universal, and on occasion may have been more
a matter of pressure to keep up with the athletic Joneses than
genuine inclination, but there is no doubt that sport played a
major social and socialising role in female collegiate life. On going
up, freshers were vigorously lobbied to join sports clubs, a
complicated series of which, at the university, college, hall and
Old Students level in a range of major and minor activities, made
regulations about eligibility, behaviour and dress, levied subscription fees, purchased equipment, hired coaches, awarded an extensive array of cups and colours, and arranged practices and
matches that involved competition from the university level down
through colleges, halls, years and subjects of study. Photographs
and club and team membership lists reveal a remarkable number
of familial athletic dynasties and all-rounders, such as the four
Martin-Leake sisters who played tennis for Girton between 1882
and 1899; Gertrude Bell, the Middle Eastern explorer and
archaeologist, who while at Lady Margaret Hall in the late 1880s
swam, rowed, fenced, walked and played tennis; and Violet
Cooper of Girton, who cycled and played hockey, cricket, tennis
and golf between 1906 and 1909. Athletes of distinction were
major personages, and the annual tennis and hockey matches
between major colleges riveted everyone's attention and generated
excitement comparable to that inspired by the publication of the
honours examination lists, for upon their results college honour
was thought to depend. The larger colleges developed extensive
sporting facilities in which they took great pride; and 'lady blues'
on occasion experienced the thrill of playing for their university
before crowds numbering several hundred at sporting meccas like
Wimbledon and Lord's.

The quality of performance, always a relative thing, is difficult
to assess. In the early days tennis was nothing more than pat-ball,
and hockey and cricket were more akin to play than genuine sport.
Equipment was makeshift, teams were incomplete and rules were
either unknown or ignored. College magazine commentaries
varied from complimentary to critical, and the expertise of
writers, and the standards on which they based their judgements,
cannot be determined adequately. Nevertheless, over the years
quality must have improved markedly, as genuine skill, seriousness of purpose and greater vigour became the rule rather than the
exception. Quality must have risen too as enrolment increased,
students with prior games experience came up, games themselves
evolved, practices became more regular, rules were fixed,

equipment and facilities were improved, limbs were partially liberated, health and physical fitness improved, coaching was obtained, and definitions of feminine behaviour were reformed.

Sport probably never gave more joy than it did to the first generations of college players, to at least some of whom it meant freedom and an exhilarating awareness of physicality and the potential significance of body control. Filtered and enhanced by the passage of time, memories of long hours on playing fields, tennis courts and the river, and of the paroxysms of excitement and nervousness that preceded major matches, were among those most cherished. Years later Old Students recalled the feeling of bliss that accompanied running at full tilt in relatively comfortable sports costumes, or, as one put it, 'the rightful joy in suppleness of body and in speed of foot'.[70] They recalled too the stiffening of their characters, the welcome relaxation during matches of the formality that normally governed relations between senior and junior students and between students and dons, the pride in being chosen for a first team, the thrill of travelling to away matches, the precious friendships formed, the sense of responsibility that accompanied election to a captaincy or sports club executive, and the tremendous feeling of achievement evoked by improvement of skills, receipt of colours and the gaining of victory. At times, with Olive Dunlop, one can almost 'smell the damp grass of the old [Girton] hockey ground' where 'the ghosts even of our old age will be fluttering . . . playing once again the game of ball and the game of life'.[71]

Unlike the situation in some of the men's colleges, however, while sport at the women's colleges developed a vigorous life of its own, and while some students were undoubtedly games-mad, athleticism never became a cult, for its dangers were appreciated by principals and mistresses and forestalled early on. Neither was athletic success worshipped above academic, nor was it an apparent deterrent. The Oxbridge pioneers never forgot that their primary purpose was to demonstrate and develop the capacity of the female mind, or that integral to the ideology they developed to justify their efforts was the encouragement of exercise and sport as a means of improving and maintaining the health of students to make them better able to tolerate the stresses and strains of higher learning.

In comparison with the prolonged and heated debate on the subject of degrees for women, the emergence of the collegiate sportswoman created remarkably little controversy. There was never any question of the competition between the sexes in the classroom — that men found so menacing and women so essential to intellectual respectability — being extended to the playing field, despite the conservative prediction in the 1890s that if women were allowed to become full members of the universities, 'the boat race, which is far more popular . . . than the progress of Women, would be replaced by a vapid contest at lawn tennis between the Women of Cambridge and the Men of Oxford'.[72] In addition, except for cricket at Girton and Newnham, overtly masculine games were eschewed; and although the female manner of games-playing gradually became more vigorous and skilled, it always occurred in appropriately modest attire and carefully avoided flagrant violations of behavioural rules. Women's sports thus remained so far removed from the male variety as to minimise stress in participants and offer little threat to womanliness or masculine exclusivity. Descriptions of players as graceful and ladylike as well as healthy and athletic presented a reassuring compromise between images of the old and New Woman. In addition, for years women's play was conducted within the sheltered confines of college or private grounds and was thus virtually invisible to the public; and it was always given a degree of legitimacy by its acknowledged value as a curative or preventive of the physical and mental defects supposedly caused by higher education.

Lest an overly optimistic picture be painted, however, it must be recalled that the debate on the physical, psychological and social effects of university education on women continued for years, since, despite overwhelming evidence to the contrary, the view that it prejudiced a woman's health and femininity was not entirely eradicated. In the midst of the debate, the fact that sport did not entirely escape controversy is clear from the bans on hockey and cricket at Lady Margaret and Somerville Halls in the mid-1880s and the strict rules everywhere surrounding the use of bicycles. It is also evident at the individual level, in letters between Violet Cooper of Girton and her fiancé, Cecil Brown, in which she promised not to 'overdo' hockey, tried to minimise his 'shock' over the news that she intended to qualify for boating and wear a 'short' skirt for golf and walking tours, and indicated that she would not play hockey for a women's club after going down if he disapproved.[73]

Even more to the point is that women were still not really part of the universities by 1914. Male and female students lived very separate lives, and many Oxbridge men simply ignored women throughout the pre-First World War period, except when their presence offered inconvenience or became a national issue, such as when the contentious questions of degrees or votes were raised. Certainly, despite the fact that on occasion men coached women's teams and provided funds for the purchase of facilities, equipment and trophies, and men's colleges chivalrously loaned tennis courts and hockey grounds for women's matches, and despite occasional coverage of major women's events in *The Times*, women's sport was usually either assiduously ignored or summarily dismissed, for the simple reason that like women themselves it had 'little place in the general life of the universities'.[74]

Although it regarded Cambridge as extremely sympathetic to the claims of women, the *Cambridge Review* opposed the demands for degrees, and its extensive columns on 'College Sports' and 'College Correspondence' included men's activities only. The opinion of the Cambridge matron reported by the *Review* in 1913, that a satisfactory Girtonian 'was a nice girl, with rosy cheeks and nice manners and nicely dressed . . . [who] you would never have thought knew anything'[75] about either the classics or cricket, was a reflection of the views of many members of the university. In 1896 'gentlemanly' Cambridge undergraduates, in an act more powerfully symbolic than they probably realised, hung an effigy of a bloomer-clad lady cyclist across from the Senate House to celebrate the senate's rejection once again of degrees for women, in one gesture condemning females of the intellectually and physically liberated variety. The *Review's* first report on the women's inter-university hockey match, in 1913, and its congratulations to the Cambridge victors, represented only a slight change of opinion.[76]

The *Oxford Magazine* revealed the same story of lengthy and unfriendly coverage of the degree issue, extensive treatment of men's athletic activities and none whatsoever of women's, with the result that when the undergraduate paper, the *Isis*, offered the women's colleges a 'Woman's Page' in 1913, they proudly refused on the grounds that their own paper, the *Fritillary*, would continue to serve them far better than an obscure corner in a men's publication.[77]

College women may have imitated male undergraduates in the nature and organisation of some of their games and in adopting the rituals and symbols that made sport a powerful mechanism for the development of traditions and allegiances. But the heart of the matter was that, while men's sport was considered natural, desirable, serious and important, women's continued to be regarded as somewhat unnatural, amusing and frivolous. Moreover, despite notable advances in the status of women by 1914, the wider world of club, army, education, business, Church, civil service and empire, that sport in general and the earning of a blue in particular opened to university men, remained firmly closed to women, athlete and non-athlete alike. About the only professional use to which a woman could put a college sports career was in acquiring a teaching post at a school where games were emphasised.

Ultimately, however, the significance of women's sport lay not in what university men or even public opinion thought of it, but in what it meant to the women themselves. This, in a word, was freedom. To attend a woman's college between 1870 and 1914 was to become a member of a small, privileged society of serious-minded, generally hard-working young women, a number of whom felt part of a stirring campaign. It meant participation in an exhilarating experiment which, despite the restrictions of college life, brought freedom to mix with women of similar background, and freedom to be alone on occasion and to look after one's own needs rather than those of others. It also brought a plethora of unique new experiences and the opportunity to think, achieve and take genuine physical exercise, and to some, an awareness of the potential and reality of mental and physical power.[78]

Active feminism played little part in the entrance of university women into the world of sport. Most collegiate sportswomen participated for fun not in defence of the physical rights of their sex. Furthermore, while pioneering principals and mistresses may have shared a vision of intellectual and physical liberation, they were rarely militant feminists, and usually held liberal views on only selected aspects of the woman question. Their encouragement of sport certainly helped to make it a respectable activity for young ladies. But, like their counterparts in the public schools, they actually perpetuated the identification of vigorous physical activity with masculinity by continuing to perceive games-playing females as acting in a masculine manner, by insisting on moderate, feminine behaviour, and by rejecting certain sports, ways of playing and costumes as unacceptable. The female collegian was thus compelled to accept limitations on the playing field which had been rejected in the classroom. Her sporting image and activities compromised with and accommodated to middle-class mores without radically challenging them, although they 'revitalized them in ways which allowed some adaptation to the broader social changes occurring at the time'.[79]

Despite accommodations with socially-approved female roles and behaviour, however, it was extremely important to the emancipation of women that university educators took up mental and physical aspects simultaneously. The Oxbridge women's colleges were a special domain, a circumscribed social world in which training and development occurred outside traditional spheres. Their enrolment may have been small, and the majority of middle-class women may have remained at home in a kind of psychological and physical bondage. But they could not be other than significant instigators of social change and pioneers in the drive towards greater female autonomy, for their establishment was an aggressive act, a deliberate attack on the Victorian attitude that held the incapacity of women to be perpetual. When college women successfully emulated male academic and athletic models, these became less exclusively masculine. In the process, both society's and women's own expectations about their intellectual and physical abilities began to be transformed. Whether they realised it or not, the early games players headed a drive towards greater female autonomy and provided extremely valuable role models. Every sphere of university life women penetrated, whether it was the lecture hall, the honours examinations or the sports field, told in favour of opening up new spheres and conceding to women rights to personal and public liberty.[80]

The 'lady blue' was thus a major actor in a larger social drama, as important in her own way as the lady wrangler. Her very existence made a significant contribution to eradicating the view that physical weakness was natural and admirable in women, and it epitomised the fundamental feminist principles of self-determination and emancipation. Furthermore, she had a profound influence on the development of women's sport beyond the Cam and Isis, for it was she who first introduced games into girls' public schools.

Notes

1. Girton College, College Songs, 1894.
2. Edward H. Clarke, *Sex in Education* (Boston, 1873); Henry

Maudsley, 'Sex in Mind and in Education', *Fortnightly Review*, vol. 15 (January–June 1874), pp. 466–83.

3. Elizabeth Garrett Anderson, 'Sex in Mind and Education: A Reply', *Fortnightly Review*, vol. 15 (January–June 1874), p. 587.

4. Jonathan Gathorne-Hardy, *The Public School Phenomenon, 597–1977* (London, 1977), pp. 271–2.

5. Mangan, *Athleticism*, pp. 126–7.

6. S.H. Jeyes, 'Our Gentlemanly Failures', *Fortnightly Review*, vol. 61 (1 March 1897), p. 387; J.R. de S. Honey, *Tom Brown's Universe* (New York, 1977), pp. 110–13; Mangan, *Athleticism*, p. 124; J.A. Mangan, '"Oars and the Man": Pleasure and Purpose in Victorian and Edwardian Cambridge', *British Journal of Sports History*, vol. 1, no. 3 (1984), pp. 245–56.

7. Thorstein Veblen, '*The Theory of the Leisure Class*' in L.D. Abbott (ed.), *Masterworks of Economics* (Garden City, NY., 1946), p. 750.

8. John William Burgon, *To Educate Young Women like Young Men, and with Young Men — a Thing Inexpedient and Immodest* (Oxford, 1884), p. 23.

9. Martha Vicinus, '"One Life to Stand Beside Me": Emotional Conflicts in First Generation College Women in England', *Feminist Studies*, vol. 8, no. 3 (1982), p. 605–7.

10. Emily Davies, *On Secondary Instruction as Relating to Girls* (London, 1864), pp. 8–9.

11. Louisa Lumsden, *Yellow Leaves* (London, 1933), p. 51.

12. Muriel C. Bradbrook, *'That Infidel Place'* (London, 1969), p. 43; Catherine B. Firth, *Constance Louisa Maynard* (London, 1949), pp. 113–14; E.E. Constance Jones, *Girton College* (London, 1913), p. 24; Barbara Stephen, *Emily Davies and Girton College* (London, 1927), pp. 224–5; Barbara Stephen, *Girton College 1869–1921* (Cambridge, 1933), p. 3.

Infᵒ⁻ ᵃtion on exercise and sport at Hitchin and Girton Colleges was deriᵛ ᵈ primarily from Kathleen Waldron, 'Won on the Playing Fields: The Story of Some School and College Challenge Trophies', *Girl's Realm* vol. 4 (November 1902–October 1903), pp. 678–81; 'Are Athletics Over-Done in Girls' Colleges and Schools? A Symposium', *Woman at Home*, vol. 6 (April 1912), pp. 247–52; and the following archival material: V.E.L. Brown, *The Silver Cord* (Sherborne, Dorset, c. 1954); College Songs; *Girton College Clubs, Etc.* (London, 1898); *Girton College Register, 1869–1946* (Cambridge, 1948); *Girton Review* (1882–1914); *Life at Girton* (1882); Photograph Album (1887–1905); Tennis Club Minutes (1883–1924, 1886–1905).

13. Constance Louisa Maynard, quoted in Firth, *Maynard*, p. 114.

14. *Girton College Clubs*, p. 10; *Girton Review* (July 1883), p. 10.

15. *Girton Review* (July 1883), pp. 10–11.

16. Kathleen Waldron, 'Hockey for Ladies', *Lady's Realm*, vol. 3 (February 1898), p. 399.

17. *Punch* (24 March 1894), p. 141.

18. *The Times*, 11 March 1913.

19. Bradbrook, *'Infidel Place'*, p. 103.

20. Brown, *Silver Cord*, p. 37.

21. Evelyn Sharp, *Hertha Ayrton 1854–1923* (London, 1926), pp. 71–2.

22. Sara A. Burstall, *English High Schools for Girls* (London, 1907), p. 64.

23. *Wycombe Abbey School Gazette*, vol. 2 (March 1902), p. 25. In 1896 a games club was created when the tennis, hockey, golf and cricket clubs, while retaining their separate existences, agreed to amalgamate their finances for the sake of efficiency. Students usually headed individual sports clubs, but mistresses occasionally served as president, and frequently played.

24. Bradbrook, *'Infidel Place'*, pp. 106–7.

25. B. Megson and J. Lindsay, *Girton College* (Cambridge, 1960), pp. 40–1.

26. *Windsor Magazine*, vol. 6. (June–November 1897), p. 351.

27. Alice Zimmern, *The Renaissance of Girls' Education in England* (London, 1898), p. 50.

28. Mary Paley Marshall, *What I Remember* (Cambridge, 1947), p. 15. Millicent Garrett Fawcett, the leader of the non-militant campaign for women's suffrage for 50 years, was the students' gymnastics chaperone and apparently the best climber on the long rope.

29. B.A. Clough, *A Memoir of Anne Jemima Clough* (London, 1897), p. 201.

Information on exercise and sport at Newnham College was derived primarily from an interview with Mrs A.B. White (Newnham 1911–15), Cambridge, 16 November 1984, and from the following archival material: letters; Newnham College Club, Cambridge Letter and Newnham College Letter (1881–1914); *Newnham College Register 1871– 1971*, vol. 1 (Cambridge, 1971); Newnham Roll (1875–1902); North Hall Diary (1875–1914); photographs; *Thersites* (1901–14); unpublished reminiscences.

30. Ann Phillips (ed.), *A Newnham Anthology* (Cambridge, 1979), p. 46.

31. Clough, *Memoir*, p. 243.

32. *Strand Magazine*, vol. 8 (July–December 1894), p. 513.

33. Of the approximately 159 students at college, 100 belonged to the hockey club during the Michaelmas term in 1894.

34. *Strand Magazine* (July–December 1894), p. 513.

35. *Thersites*, no. 12 (4 November 1910).

36. *Century Magazine*, vol. 42 (1891), p. 289.

37. 'Are Athletics Over-Done?', p. 247. The first rowing eight at Newnham was established in 1919.

38. Newnham College Club, Cambridge Letter (1894), pp. 11–12.

39. Anne Jemima Clough, quoted in Burstall, *English High Schools*, p. 99.

40. *Thersites*, no. 28 (6 December 1912).

41. *Brown Book* (December 1928), p. 96.

42. Ruth F. Butler and M.H. Prichard (eds), *The Society of Oxford Home Students* (Oxford, c. 1930), p. 114; interview with Ruth F. Butler (Oxford Home Students 1902–5), Oxford, 14 November 1981. Men and women were seated separately at lectures.

43. Georgina Battiscombe, *Reluctant Pioneer* (London, 1978), p. 90.

Information on exercise and sport at Lady Margaret Hall was derived primarily from Gemma Bailey (ed.), *Lady Margaret Hall* (Oxford, 1923), and from the following archival material: Annual Reports (1879–1914);

Boat Club Minutes (1899–1914); Council Minute Books (1878–1914); *Fritillary* (1894–1914); *Lady Margaret Hall Register, 1879–1966* (Oxford, 1970); Lady Principals' Reports (1879–1914); Log Book (1878–1915); Old Students' Association, *Brown Book* (1891–1915); photographs; Sports and Students' Committee Minute Books (1908–12).

44. In 1893 the gymnasium was sacrificed to the enlargement of the chapel.

45. Leonard Miller (ed.), 'Unpublished Diary of Irene M. Martin (Lady Margaret Hall 1912–15) c. 1894–1970', in the hall archives.

46. While the London University women's colleges encouraged competitive rowing prior to 1914, it was not allowed at Oxford until the 1920s. A women's boat race between Oxford and Cambridge was inaugurated in 1965.

47. Lady Margaret Hall, Lady Principal's Report (May Term 1885).

48. Lady Margaret Hall, Council Minutes (22 October 1885).

49. Ibid. (16 February 1893). See also Lady Margaret Hall, Log Book (16 February 1893), p. 32.

50. Lady Margaret Hall, Lady Principal's Report (Lent Term 1894).

51. In 1907 a student-run sports committee was formed to co-ordinate the activities of the various clubs and approve their rules and regulations.

52. Lady Margaret Hall, Log Book (7 March 1901), p. 56.

53. Winifred Knox Peck, *A Little Learning* (London, 1952), pp. 157–8.

54. Elizabeth Wordsworth, *First Principles in Women's Education* (Oxford, 1894), p. 12.

55. Muriel S. Byrne and Catherine H. Mansfield, *Somerville College, 1879–1921* (Oxford, 1922), p. 12. See also Helena C. Deneke, *Grace Hadow* (Oxford, 1946), p. 28.

56. Byrne and Mansfield, *Somerville College*, p. 78; *Lady's Pictorial* (6 March 1920), p. 301.

Information on sport and exercise at Somerville College was derived primarily from the following archival material: Annual Reports (1879–1914); *Fritillary* (1894–1914); Log Book (1879–1907); Somerville Students' Association Reports (1888–1914).

57. Byrne and Mansfield, *Somerville College*, p. 78.

58. Somerville Students' Association, Report (September 1890), p. 8, (September 1891), pp. 9–10.

59. Lilian M. Faithfull, *In the House of My Pilgrimage* (London, 1924), p. 62.

60. In 1898 approximately 40 of Somerville's 76 students belonged to the boat club, and in 1901, 58 of 82. Most of the boats were gifts to the club from friends of the hall or Old Students. By 1909 they included five sculls, two punts and three canoes. In 1898 the boat, tennis, hockey and gymnastics clubs formed an amalgamated games club, to which they turned over their funds.

61. *Ladies' Field* (31 December 1898), pp. 106–8.

62. Somerville College, Annual Report (November 1890), p. 7.

63. *Fritillary*, no. 6 (December 1895), p. 106.

64. Christine M.E. Burrows, 'History of St Hilda's College', Chapter 7 (c. 1952), in St Hilda's College archives.

65. St Hilda's Hall, House Rules (1898), in St Hilda's College archives.

66. *Fritillary*, no. 36 (December 1905), p. 598.

67. Burrows, 'History of St Hilda's', chapter 7. See also *Fritillary*, no. 48 (December 1909), p. 837, no. 51 (December 1910), pp. 900–1; Chronicle of Old Students' Association (1910), pp. 19–20, in St Hilda's College archives. The Lady Margaret Hall *Brown Book* (p. 30) noted the formation of a rifle club in 1910, but mentioned it no further. Most of the men's colleges had rifle corps whose purpose was to train future soldiers.

68. *Fritillary*, no. 12 (December 1897), p. 208; Oxford Home Students Committee, Annual Report (1903–4), p. 10 and Minutes (Hilary Term 1904), in St Anne's College archives.

69. Gillian Sutherland, 'The Social Location of the Movement for Women's Higher Education in England, 1840–1880', unpublished paper (1980), pp. 1–17.

It is difficult to relate sport and the socio-economic background of college students. But match results indicate that the colleges with more well-to-do students were likely to be successful in individual sports like tennis, and those with the somewhat less so, in team games like hockey. Although the records make no mention of it, one can speculate that membership fees charged by sports clubs, which varied from one to three shillings a term, and the necessity for students to pay for their own sports clothes, travel expenses and equipment and contribute to the upkeep of grounds, may well have affected those on limited budgets.

Approximate comparative college enrolment figures based on college registers and annual reports were as follows:

	1887	1897	1913
Girton	91	105	163
Newnham	112	167	173
Lady Margaret Hall	96	52	72
Somerville	31	76	110
St Hugh's	9	25	52
St Hilda's		16	47
Home Students		32	101

70. Olive J. Dunlop, *Leaves from a Cambridge Note-Book* (Cambridge, 1907), p. 76.

71. Ibid., pp. 76–9

72. Charles Whibley, 'The Encroachment of Women', *Nineteenth Century*, vol. 41 (April 1897), p. 534.

73. Brown, *Silver Cord*, pp. 41–5.

74. Howard Savage, *Games and Sports in British Schools* (New York, 1926), p. 77.

75. *Cambridge Review*, vol. 35 (2 November 1913), p. 122. See also vol. 34 (24 April 1913), p. 385.

76. Ibid., vol. 34 (17 April 1913), p. 364, extra number, vol. 34 (19 April 1913), p. 34.

77. Vera Brittain, *The Women at Oxford* (London, 1960), pp. 132–4.

78. Hilda Jackson (Somerville c. 1902), letter, 19 September 1970, in Somerville College archives; Peck, *A Little Learning*, pp. 155–6; Vicinus, '"One Life"', p. 606.

79. Hargreaves, 'Playing Like Gentlemen', pp. 200–1.

80. As indicated briefly in the text, inspired by the Oxbridge example, late-Victorian women also sought the privileges and pleasures of higher education beyond the Cam and Isis, and in certain cases with rather more success. By the turn of the century, of the 16 universities in the United Kingdom only Oxford and Cambridge denied women degrees and full membership. London University started admitting women on equal terms with men in 1878, and four years later graduated 15. By 1914 it had several women's colleges, in all of which sport had developed to varying degrees; the co-educational University College had women's sport as well; and the University Athletic Union even had a women's branch. At Birmingham, Manchester, Liverpool and Durham Universities women also established their sporting rights, although not without a struggle.

For further information see Bedford College, Council Minutes (1867–1914), Students' Association Committee Minute Book (1894–1911), Physical Education Sub-Committee (1903–4); *Bedford College Magazine* (1886–1914); *King's College Magazine* (1896–1914); Royal Holloway College, Boat Club Minute Book (1905–14), College Letter (1890–1900, 1908–14), College Meeting Minute Books (1890–1914), Hockey Club Record Books (1890–1904), Students' Meeting Minute Books (1895–1914), Swimming Records and Minutes (1899–1914), Tennis Club Minute Books (1889–1914); *University College Gazette* and *Union Magazine* (1886–1904); University College Women's Union Society, Athletic Union, Lawn Tennis, Hockey, Swim and Gymnastic Clubs Records; University of London Athletic Union Annual Reports (1909–13); Westfield College, *Hermes* (1892–1910), Diaries of Constance Maynard (1871–1913); Eleanora M. Carus-Wilson (ed.), *Westfield College, University of London, 1882–1932* (London, 1932); Negley B. Harte, *The Admission of Women to University College London: A Centenary Lecture* (London, 1979); F.J.C. Hearnshaw, *The Centenary History of King's College London, 1829–1928* (London, 1929); Marilyn Hird (ed.), *Doves and Dons: A History of St Mary's College Durham* (Durham, 1982); Janet Sondheimer, *Castle Adamant in Hampstead: A History of Westfield College, 1882–1982* (London, 1983); Margaret Tuke, *A History of Bedford College for Women, 1849–1937* (London, 1939); Mabel Tylecote, *The Education of Women at Manchester University, 1883–1933* (Manchester, 1941).

3

Sport, Exercise and the
Public Schools Phenomenon

To Good St Andrews Ancient Town
(Air: The Vicar of Bray)

When Queen Street first gave house and home
Its rooms became scholastic,
Our sums were worked in drawing rooms
In coach-house our gymnastics.
The back-green cramped the batsman's 'four',
Yet cricket came in fashion
And hurdles races, goals galore,
And games became a passion.[1]

Complementing the creation of university colleges for women, closely tied to their development and part of the same network of elite institutions was an even more powerful agent in the Victorian educational revolution, girls' public day and boarding schools. Their introduction of sport was an important extension of women's entry into the academic and physical context of the university world, for it was 'reformers of girls' education . . . who have had the advantage and privilege of residence at a University who must insist on the necessity of physical development, thus shewing that a University justifies its name by the universality of its education'.[2] The introduction of sport was also related to the emulation of male models, specifically the old boys' public schools and the new ones founded in mid-century to cater for the sons of socially ambitious professional and merchant families which came to exert an immense influence on Victorian education and society.

Before the 1850s games-playing was an irregular feature of male public school life. But by the end of the century, as schools grew in number and rivalry, athleticism and manliness — the

59

fusion of moral rectitude and physical robustness — had become essential hallmarks, and supported a huge, voracious and self-perpetuating games machinery centred on rowing, cricket and football.[3] Supporters praised the qualities of endurance, self-reliance, discipline, courage, loyalty and decisiveness they supposedly instilled in the future leaders of country and empire, qualities implicit in Sir Henry Newbolt's moralistic exhortation to Victorian gentlemen to 'Play Up! Play Up! and Play the Game!' and so put the world to rights.[4] Critics, on the other hand, were appalled by what J.A. Mangan describes as the games system's 'simplistically decoded Darwinian interpretation of existence which harmonised with the intensely competitive values of the time'[5] and involved an unrelenting struggle in which only the fittest survived. They thus branded the exaltation of the games ethic as distorted and hypocritical, as an insidious form of social control whose ultimate ends were status and power, and whose emphasis on character to the disparagement of brains produced arrogant, selfish and belligerent men, lacking in maturity, imagination and aesthetic sensibility.

Manliness, of course, was contrasted with feminine weakness and passivity; so passage through the proving ground of the public schools made games-playing progressively more masculine. To the muscular Christian gentleman a woman's only role in sport was to watch and applaud. Yet the significance for the education of women of games at boys' public schools was considerable, since it was their curricula, organisation and life-style that many reformers of female education sought to emulate, and it was at similar institutions for girls of the same class that female sports made some of their first appearances.

The first public schools for girls, the North London Collegiate School and the Cheltenham Ladies' College, were founded in the 1850s, but the girls' public school phenomenon began in earnest only after the passage of the Endowed Schools Act in 1869. During the next three decades about 200 new schools were established which differed markedly from the private ladies' academies of the past in ownership, funding, fees, patterns of authority, size, students' ages, residency requirements, social composition, religious affiliation, behavioural norms, curricula and activities. They also differed among themselves; but their similarities were striking and important. Most intended to prepare the daughters of business and professional families for more active and socially useful roles in the public and domestic spheres. Many instituted entrance and attendance requirements and developed curricula which rejected polite accomplishments in favour of academic subjects and ties with university colleges that enhanced their authority and reputation. Many were overseen by largely male boards of governors, but were almost completely controlled by commanding headmistresses who shared similar aspirations and legendary reputations.

These women were often progressive conservatives whose strategies manifested contradictions and ambivalences. The fulfilment of their aims necessitated an accommodation to the demands of femininity and social class along with a revision of the feminine ideal to include the possibility of intellectual development and careers other than marriage. In other words, they embraced a 'double conformity' or 'divided aim' that involved the simultaneous acceptance of two things which appeared mutually exclusive — male academic standards and the constraints of ladylike behaviour. Most remained committed to Victorian values concerning family and womanliness and to the view that men and women had different missions. But at the same time they held that if females were not to be relegated to a position of second best in perpetuity, and if they were to have productive and useful lives within and without the domestic sphere, they must have opportunities for intellectual and personal development similar to those of males. Although adaptation not slavish imitation was their watchword, and they made deliberate efforts to avoid the errors of the male experience, they perceived masculine values as the norm and essentially 'female' subjects as inferior. Their highest priority was thus the provision of sound intellectual training through the introduction of curricula, examinations and rewards modelled on those in boys' schools.[6]

Connected to this were the important issues of health and fitness, for most reformers of female education also subscribed to the male belief in the intimate connection between intellectual and physical health, and voiced the distinctly unconventional view that sporting activities incorporating both competition and play should be an intrinsic part of the educational life of girls as well as boys. Their expectations of the benefits of participation in games were both high and varied. Games-playing, they insisted, would improve girls' health and child-bearing potential, counteract mental overstrain, stimulate study and aid discipline. Above all it would impart valuable moral qualities, like honour, loyalty, determination, resourcefulness and courage, that had previously been ascribed exclusively to males.[7]

Among the new schools, those that took boarders emulated male models particularly closely. The house system, with all its emphasis on conformity and its scope for ideological indoctrination, was usually introduced. Games were vigorously promoted by university-educated mistresses who had learned to appreciate their value and pleasurableness while at college, and were eager to enlighten students and continue to play themselves. Modern research shows that teachers are powerful role models in transmitting gender-appropriate behaviour to students;[8] and in more and more schools that were headed and staffed by progressive women who were concerned about mental and physical development, drill and callisthenics gradually gave way to scientific physical training and competitive games. As early as 1877 the Association of Head Mistresses recorded its conviction that to prevent overwork

> . . . it is desirable to give especial attention to the physical education of girls, and to attach to schools, a gymnasium in which regular daily exercise can be taken, and if possible to secure the use of a swimming bath, also to encourage active games such as ladies' cricket, fives, etc.[9]

Educational rights had first to be won, however, before games and physical training could be recognised as suitable for girls, so progress on the physical was slower than on the academic front. Only years of experience showed that girls required further freedom for healthy physical development alongside the possession of a wider field in which to exercise their mental abilities. By no means all schools for middle-class girls accepted the efficacy of rigorous physical training. Beyond the end of the century reformers continued to lament the neglect of exercise in private academies, like Queenwood in Eastbourne, that retained the ambience of a home, prepared students exclusively for domestic careers and restricted their exercise to decorous walks in pairs. But in the best public schools, both day and boarding, physical and academic work were treated together. A balanced and complete theory and practice of physical education were developed, which included attention to the physical development and therapeutic needs of individual students, scientifically designed systems of exercise, regular medical inspection by qualified practitioners, organised games and the employment of professionally trained teachers of physical training and sports. Gymnastics, drill and games were welded into a comprehensive system of physical education, which put girls' schools well ahead of their male counterparts where the cult of athleticism continued to brook no rival.

Day schools

One of the first notable events in the practical reform of female secondary education was the establishment in 1850 of the North London Collegiate School for Ladies. Its founder, Frances Mary Buss, was convinced that girls were as able as boys, and determined to prepare them for any position in life. Her particular aim was to provide middle-class girls of limited means with an education which would minimise social gradations and develop morals, character and intellect.

Buss took the dangerously advanced step of introducing science and mathematics; and because she considered health a primary concern, she provided students with lessons on its laws and required them to take physical exercise. Early prospectuses and timetables noted that a large garden was available for gentle callisthenics under the tutelage of Captain James Chiosso. In 1864 Buss informed the Schools Inquiry Commission that, since schoolgirls normally got too little exercise, she required students over the age of twelve to attend callisthenics classes four times a week and encouraged those younger to exercise out of doors, and in addition that the formal part of the school day ended at about 1.00 p.m. in order to leave the afternoon hours free for playing.[10] Shortly thereafter, she introduced the musical gymnastic system of Dio Lewis to counteract 'any ill effect of the great amount of mental work caused by preparation for the Cambridge Local Examinations', because it was 'easy, graceful and not too fatiguing' and cultivated rhythm of movement, while 'wonderfully' improving figures and benefiting health.[11]

In the early 1870s, as Buss's thinking developed, she acknowledged 'the need of a covered place for exercise' and her hope 'that in the future, not very remote, we may have funds to build a gymnasium'.[12] Meanwhile, she succeeded in gaining limited access for students to the St Pancras Baths, engaged a swimming instructor, arranged for the student who made the most progress to receive a prize, and encouraged mistresses to give up free time to supervise. As a result, despite some girls' fear that lengthy stays in the water would be fatiguing and injurious, the number of bathers increased steadily. Buss was less successful in arranging for a skating rink because of prohibitive costs, but her continuous agitation for a gymnasium resulted in one being provided in the new school building that opened in 1879 and was enlarged five years later. The first gymnasium in a girls' school, it was a dark, beam-ceilinged room containing ropes, parallel bars, wall-ladders, a giant-stride, a vaulting horse and barbells.

In the tradition of progressive conservatism, Buss commended gymnastics for enhancing health and improving educational efficiency while 'admirably . . . cultivating . . . grace and elegance of movement';[13] and she ensured that every student took systematic exercise by giving gymnastics a more regular place in the morning's work. The whole school, in different divisions, was required to participate in short daily drills and an additional half-hour of exercise twice a week; and optional gymnastics lessons were offered during the afternoon. An eclectic method with a German bias was used since it included dancing and was thus considered by Buss to be more feminine than the better known Swedish system.

Since Buss believed that many students were physically abnormal, she concluded that the whole management of exercise should be in the hands of properly trained women. As a result, shortly after the gymnasium opened she engaged a female teacher with experience in German gymnastics and a part-time female doctor, an innovative step that was widely imitated elsewhere. All students in gymnastics classes were required to undergo inspection by the medical superintendent who prescribed remedial exercise under the supervision of the physical education mistress and recorded improvements. The records of the second medical inspector, Dr Frances Hoggan, if taken literally, would compel the conclusion that most of the girls at the school were indeed physically unsound. Hoggan described only six of 335 girls as strong and vigorous. The rest, she reported, had problems ranging from curvature of the spine, to weakness, delicacy, anaemia, languor, ruptures, acne, knock-knees, lung congestion, flat chests and heart mischief. Her usual remedies involved dumb-bell and breathing exercises, but she advised at least one poor student with a weak back 'to hang from a pole for three minutes night and morning'.[14] Hoggan excused girls from gymnastics classes during menstruation only if they complained of dysmenorrhea, despite prevailing medical wisdom's recommendation of complete rest.

The development of games at the school was seriously handicapped for years by the lack of an adequate playing field. Nevertheless, a sports programme of sorts quietly evolved. In 1885, the students established a games club to organise badminton, fives and ninepins contests in the gymnasium during the early afternoon dinner break, with the result that, 'instead of girls sitting listlessly about and talking', all was excitement. Four years later the different forms created separate games clubs, for the purpose of playing rounders and fives and holding competitions in the playground, the 'animation' and 'disorder' of which necessitated stricter procedures for selecting captains.[15] A few students began competing for prizes in swimming races in the 1880s; and in 1890 swimmers participated in the school's first outside sports competition, races at the Kensington Public Baths against the Notting Hill High School. The North Londoners' victory created 'much excitement' and a heightened interest in swimming, which resulted in 1895 in the formation of a swimming club whose officers were kept busy providing badges for students who fulfilled certain qualifications and arranging lessons, life-saving classes, aquatic sports days, form team meets, school championships and inter-school competitions.

Squash rackets was introduced in the winter of 1889 by players who used tennis racquets and balls against a wall of the gymnasium; and at the end of the term '32 teachers and girls entered a tournament [conducted] before a large and enthusiastic audience including Miss Buss and the Cambridge Examiners'.[16] The next year a long rivalry with Notting Hill in tennis began, but it was a number of years before the champions on each side accepted overhand services as anything other than inelegant, and ten years before a club — for fifth and sixth form girls only — was created under the presidency of the headmistress. Interest in tennis grew substantially only when membership in the club was opened to all students, and a series of internal and external matches and colours for championship players were inaugurated.

Students also organised annual athletic sports days from July 1890 involving competitions in the gymnasium in running, throwing, jumping and obstacle contests for prizes 'useful and ornamental'. When their popularity created an accommodations problem they were moved out of doors to a ground in Epping. By the early-twentieth century, sports days attracted the whole school, along with several hundred Old Students and visitors,[17] and the range of activities expanded to include cricket-ball throwing, and slow bicycle, potato and egg and spoon races for such prizes as challenge cups, inkpots and picture frames. As elsewhere, sports days involved fun rather than serious sport, but they were an integral part of a serious ritual process of affiliation with an identifiable community.

Despite a continuing problem with inadequate facilities, sport grew considerably at the North London Collegiate School during the 1890s. A gymnastics club promoted outside competitions as well as extra callisthenics and gymnastic classes. Fives and rounders, the great games internally, were encouraged by flourishing clubs. Their popularity, however, succumbed to that of netball, a game considered particularly good at developing self-control and unselfishness. Netball was begun in 1899 by students who used waste-paper baskets perched atop jumping poles as goals, and it quickly became competitive at the form and inter-school levels, acquiring a variety of legitimating paraphernalia — team badges and ties, a challenge cup for internal competition and a club presided over by the headmistress.[18]

The appearance of the great team game of hockey was delayed by the lack of a playing field and Buss's fear that only rough girls would participate. When Buss died in 1895, however, she was succeeded by Mrs Sophie Bryant, who was more enthusiastic about sport than her predecessor and an ardent sportswoman herself.[19] The following year hockey was finally introduced by teachers who had learned the sport at Girton, and who agreed that, to avoid giving offence, girls must obtain parental permission to play; and in short order teachers and senior students started a club which hired grounds for practices on Saturday mornings and Thursday afternoons from a private school in Hendon and from the Maria Grey Training College for Teachers. The club was reorganised in 1900 under the presidency of the headmistress, and new arrangements were made to play on grounds in Golders Green and Highgate. In the years thereafter, the club joined the Southern Ladies' Hockey Association and the AEWHA; form matches and clubs for Old Pupils and girls under 14 were organised; second and third school XIs were formed; an Old Pupil was appointed as hockey coach; a hockey song was composed; dark blue and yellow were adopted as the club colours; and a system of colours was developed to reward good play.

Finally, in 1909, sports in general and hockey in particular received a much needed boost. That year, after an almost decade-long fund-raising campaign, the North London Collegiate School acquired a half-share — with its sister institution, the Camden School for Girls — in a 2.5 acre ground to be used for tennis, netball and hockey, the governors having finally recognised that the lack of sports facilities was detrimental to the school's otherwise progressive image.

All things considered, exercise in the broadest sense was fundamental to the purposes of the school. Frances Buss and Sophie Bryant believed that in order to develop the whole woman and demonstrate the abilities of the female sex, both mind and body had to be challenged and cultivated. This led to the gradual implementation of a comprehensive programme of physical education directed towards the needs of individuals, which included optional sports and games plus compulsory gymnastics under the supervision of a medical doctor and trained physical educators, and which led to a significant reformation in students' dress.[20] Sport, however, never became as significant at the North London Collegiate School as at boarding schools or at those of the Girls' Public Day School Company which were its chief sporting rivals.

While Miss Buss and Mrs Bryant supported athletic as well as academic competition, their primary concern was always the intellectual. Bryant rejected Buss's lingering fear that 'rough' games such as hockey would cause overstrain, but she shared her mentor's concern that an excessive interest in games was detrimental to health and schoolwork and that if games-playing were made compulsory the critical characteristics of play and fun would be eliminated. As a result, in 1895 sports practices were forbidden the day before a gymnastics display, and in 1900 a rule was adopted that no form was to spend more than a half-hour on games and a half-hour on drill in the same day. Similar concerns, as well as the feeling that more students should have an opportunity to play for the school, moved the games club a few years later to prohibit students from playing field games more than twice a week and on the first teams in both hockey and netball. When the latter rule proved unpopular it was moderated only slightly to allow hockey players to join pick-up netball matches in the gymnasium.

Although the North London was a relatively large school and important matches occasioned considerable excitement, they failed to attract crowds as large as those elsewhere, nor were they overlaid with the number of rituals and symbols that gave public school sport its power as a mechanism of social control. Teams played fewer matches than did those at comparable schools; the school magazine paid them less attention; sports clubs were influenced more by staff and their membership was smaller; and students has to be reprimanded, on occasion, for being so casual about games that they did not bother to learn skills.

The ideal North London Collegiate School product was the 'new girl' described by the school magazine in 1900. She did not equate weakness with womanliness; she was willingly co-operative rather than passively obedient; she was rational rather than emotional, and moral, intelligent and good-humoured. She appreciated the dignity of work and could bear considerable discomfort; she loved fair play and evinced the spirit of corporate loyalty women were often accused of lacking. She could swim, cycle and play hockey; indeed, she could do virtually anything as a result of a 'true instinct of sport, a thing hitherto little accounted of in the feminine mind, but now at length aroused, and capable of producing . . . a great revolution'.[21] At the same time, however, she retained a sense of balance and, above all, her femininity.

The North London Collegiate School was the model for the schools of the Girls' Public Day School Company (GPDSC), which was founded in 1872 by the National Union for the Improvement of the Education of Women of All Classes Above the Elementary (1871). Its purpose was to provide the daughters of business and professional men with a reasonably priced education of the boys' public school type and at the same time to provide shareholders with a reasonable rate of return. As a preparation for further education and the practicalities of domestic or public life, GPDSC leaders determined to offer demanding training combining mental, moral and physical ingredients. Their schools thus offered classics, mathematics and science from the first; and because they considered bodily health a necessary precondition to mental and moral growth, they endeavoured to have hygiene and physical exercise incorporated as reputable and essential elements into curricula, and whenever possible, to appoint at least one staff member with gymnastic training.[22]

As at the North London, lessons were confined to the morning hours in order to leave the afternoon free for recreation. But for some time the extent of exercise depended on the proclivities of principals and the attitude of parents and teachers towards proper activities for young ladies. Early on students were not allowed swimming or hockey and other strenuous games because they were 'dangerous' or 'boyish'. It was 1884 before a GPDSC school — the Sheffield High School (1878) — acquired a gymnasium, and 1885 and 1888 before the foundation of games clubs by students at the Blackheath (1880) and Shrewsbury High Schools (1885) signalled the appearance of sport.

The schools of the GPDSC were often situated in middle-class residential areas and so had problems finding conveniently located sports fields. During the 1880s and 1890s, however, a number acquired spacious and discreetly secluded grounds; and they appointed mistresses whose university or teacher or physical training college experience had convinced them that a combination of Swedish gymnastics and athletic games improved health, character and academic performance.[23] Their games-playing example provided important models for students lacking prior sports experience. Outdoor sports began proliferating, and soon became encoded with the type of ritualistic processes and symbols that were a vital facet of male public school life.

Physical education was especially important to Florence Gadesden, late of Girton College, who was appointed principal of the Blackheath High School — the largest of the GPDSC schools — in 1886. Gadesden insisted that sports built character and were essential to mental and bodily health; and under her aegis, over the next 30 years, Blackheath developed a particularly proud reputation for athletic excellence, and an elaborate games machinery involving a wide variety of activities and types of competitions and supported by enthusiastic alumnae and extensive facilities and legitimating paraphernalia. Students, past and present, sang Gadesden's praises for allowing games to teach them 'the necessity of fair play, give and take, courtesy to opponents, endurance of hard knocks, and so on — things which in those days were a novel part of a girl's training'. More than giving them a taste of physical freedom, the perceptive realised, she was training them 'to manage [them]selves and others'.[24]

By the early-twentieth century, the 30-plus GPDSC schools differed markedly in enrolment and facilities. All, however, endeavoured to protect students' health through physical education, remedial exercise and games.[25] The company had an inspector of physical exercise; each school had trained physical educators and a playground; and most had playing fields, presented annual drill displays and provided medical inspection.

Tennis, fives, rounders, archery, badminton, athletic sports, netball, cricket, hockey, lacrosse, swimming and cycling were organised by games mistresses and/or games clubs run by older girls, and attracted as participants students, Old Students and teachers. Sporting rivalry between houses and forms within schools was fierce, while that between schools was encouraged by the London and suburban schools' organisation of a games association presided over by the indefatigable Florence Gadesden, within which were leagues for competition among 15 schools in tennis from 1893, among 14 schools in hockey from 1897 and among 12 schools in netball from 1904. Elsewhere in the country company schools affiliated with games associations in their own districts, which brought them out of isolation, raised standards of play and produced the *esprit* and competitive school spirit that were more difficult to arouse in day than boarding schools. While GPDSC schools became known for excellence in games as well as academics, however, they never lost sight of balance and the bounds of convention and of the danger of making exercise a fetish. Games were always optional and offered as adjuncts to intellectual training. Great care was taken to guard against over-exertion, which explains why hockey matches had 25-minute halves instead of the regulation 35, and girls were encouraged to play in a womanly manner.[26]

Boarding schools

Important as sport and exercise became at prominent day schools, they retained an element of spontaneity, for they were never as deliberate a part of policy as at the great girls' boarding schools where the games-playing phenomenon became a particularly infectious trend and reached its peak. St Leonards School in St Andrews, Fife and Roedean School in Brighton are prime examples.

The St Andrews School for Girls — later St Leonards — which opened to a middle-class clientele in 1877, was the first girls' school deliberately patterned after boys' public schools. Its founding principal, Louisa Lumsden, was a clever, forceful and sometimes erratic Scotswoman who had been one of the original students at Hitchin College and subsequently classics mistress at the Cheltenham Ladies' College.

Lumsden was determined to establish a veritable Eton for girls.

As a result, while she acknowledged the danger of overstrain from excessive mental effort and assured that ladylike accomplishments were not completely ignored, she centred St Leonards' first curriculum on demanding academic subjects and regular examinations. Because she had experienced the lack of games and exercise during her own education, and associated the harmonious development of physical powers with the development of character and intellect, she also made games and physical training an integral part of student life.

At a time when a playground and gymnasium in a girls' school were almost as incongruous as sewing classes in boys', Lumsden provided both from the start, albeit in cramped quarters. She appointed a drill mistress and required students to take one gymnastics lesson a week; and she began what quickly became a tradition of student independence in games by encouraging girls to play cricket, rounders, tennis, fives and goals, regardless of protests from townspeople against such 'masculine' activities. The discipline of the playground was of inestimable good, she said, in teaching boys to obey and command and 'to gain patience, good temper, toleration, and the power to stand a beating good humouredly and to fight for the side and not for self. It is training of this sort I wish to secure for girls'.[27]

For the typically Victorian reason that her mother was ill and needed her at home, Miss Lumsden resigned in 1882 just before the school moved to a spacious new building with a large playground and changed its name to St Leonards. Her successor was Jane Frances Dove, another Old Girtonian who held strong views on the value of open-air exercise, as her first prospectus clearly indicated. 'St Leonards School', it said,

> is intended to provide for Girls from all parts of the United Kingdom an education, which, while especially adapted to their requirements, is not less thorough than that given to their brothers at the great public schools . . . plenty of time for open-air exercise is given; and the use of the extensive playground is specially encouraged . . . The playground is immediately attached and has well-drained gravel tennis courts, etc. There is good and safe bathing, and swimming forms one of the chief recreations of the summer. A perfectly safe skating-pond is in the neighbourhood of the school.[28]

The house system, which for boys meant restraint from too much liberty, for girls meant escape from excessive gentility by providing unprecedented scope for independence and activity;[29] and by 1887 such a system was well established at St Leonards. About 120 girls, mostly boarders, were divided among seven houses headed by house mistresses and prefects, and each house developed its own societies and sports teams with an elaborate paraphernalia of legitimating rites and symbols.

To encourage regular practice in games, in 1888 the mistresses presented a handsome challenge shield for thrice-yearly house competitions in gymnastics, cricket and goals. Immediately the desire to gain the glory attached to the name of the shield winner 'added zest to play and great excitement among spectators'.[30] In an unusually bold if unsuccessful move, students protested that the mistresses' formation of a games committee, which proceeded to make elaborate regulations for carrying out the competitions, was 'tyrannical'; but in other respects the management of games was left largely in their hands.

When gymnastics proved unsuitable for inter-house competition because it failed to stimulate sufficient enthusiasm, the school *Gazette* invited suggestions for an outdoor game to replace it. Athletic sports and golf were proposed, but the decision was finally taken 'to award the shield on a competition in lacrosse'.[31] Lacrosse did not appear at other schools and university colleges until after the turn of the century, so St Leonards' adoption of the game in 1890 was very early indeed and made its girls the first in Britain to play the game.

In her autobiography Louisa Lumsden recalled having watched a lacrosse match between teams of Montrealers and local Indians while visiting New Hampshire in 1884, and, thinking the game graceful and beautiful, introduced it at the school.[32] Since she was no longer principal, however, a more likely explanation is that she recommended it to a receptive Jane Frances Dove. Whatever lacrosse's origin, the school magazine was soon reporting that 'the new game . . . is being carried on with vigour'.[33] During the next quarter century, lacrosse developed into the major sport at St Leonards, and was introduced into schools and colleges all over the country by former mistresses and students.

Because one of St Leonards' principles 'was always that games were harmless if those who played had already some physical training in the gymnasium',[34] Miss Dove superintended the opening of a fully equipped Swedish gymnasium in 1891, and appointed Esther Ida Carolina Schermanson, a graduate of the Central Gymnastics Institute, Stockholm, as gymnastics mistress.

Swedish drill was immediately introduced and made compulsory; and Schermanson was joined, in 1892 and 1893, by two other Swedish devotees who had been trained by Madame Bergman-Osterberg. One of these, a remarkable woman by the name of Josephine K. Stewart, was appointed games mistress and given particular responsibility for teaching fencing and superintending the playground. A former St Leonards day student, she was one of the first distinguished female athletes in Britain. A fine golfer, she also played hockey and lacrosse, and in 1900 and 1920 was founding vice-president of the Scottish Women's Hockey and Scottish Ladies' Lacrosse Associations. Seniors, as Old Girls were called, described her as combining elements of masculinity with womanly elegance, and providing students, particularly those in her house, with a powerful athletic role model.[35]

Although the *Gazette* occasionally complained of a 'lamentable want of interest and consequently stagnation in all games and outdoor pursuits' and too much 'loafing about',[36] opportunities for, and the inclination of, students to participate in a variety of physical recreations increased. During the 1890s three hours each afternoon were set aside for exercise; the playground was enlarged to 16 acres; the number of tennis courts was increased; and a nine-hole golf course was acquired.[37] Cricket was particularly encouraged for it was thought to teach one 'to trust one's fellow-workers' and 'to play one's part thoroughly in a subordinate position or a losing game' better than any other sport.[38] A professional coach was even hired briefly in 1891 to help girls to improve their technique and grasp the rules of the Marylebone Cricket Club.

Hockey finally replaced goals in shield competition in 1896, the same year that the house mistresses presented a challenge cup to be competed for in tennis, golf and fives. In the late 1890s away matches in hockey and lacrosse — hitherto infrequent because of the school's geographical isolation and head start in games — began to be played against ladies' clubs, St Andrews University and such schools as Roedean and Wycombe Abbey. In addition, students fenced, swam, ice-skated, rode horse-back and participated in gymnastics displays, annual athletic sports days and special bowling, batting and throwing competitions.

Seniors recollected that sports were a virtual passion at St Leonards by the turn of the century. Each girl without a medical excuse was expected to play at least once a week. Every house produced first and second teams in the three major sports; and match days, particularly house, shield and inter-school, created breathless anxiety and excitement. House and school songs were composed with the intention of inspiring emotion and great sporting deeds. The *Gazette* devoted far more space to games than any other subject, sometimes as much as a third of an issue, and it went into great detail on matches past and future, on batting and bowling averages, on style of play and ways to improve and on the strengths and weaknesses of individual players. Participants were urged to give their all for the sake of house and school, and spectators to turn out *en masse*, as if each match were a public contest that exposed moral fibre.[39]

The magazine's periodic denunciation of cheering opponents' mistakes and confusing rough with spirited play indicate that the single-mindedness and enthusiasm of players and spectators sometimes went to extremes. Numerous trophies and awards to teams and individuals were pursued in a grail-like quest that encouraged keenness and, more importantly, the perpetuation of school traditions and feelings of identification with an important community, particularly when they were presented at the annual prize days before the whole school. The ambitious girls who became school and house captains wielded considerable power, since they did much of the coaching and were responsible for inviting mistresses to play as well as ensuring that girls played neither too much nor too little; their names were inscribed for posterity on a board in the gymnasium. Distinguished players were lionised, and special brooches were awarded to the considerable number who played on the first teams in the three major sports.

A certain amount of group pressure and compulsion accompanied this enthusiasm which made life unpleasant for the unathletic and left little time for individuality.[40] But to most St Leonards students games-playing offered an unaccustomed degree of physical freedom and to the school's authorities it was one of the most valuable agents in the development of moral character. As the authors of the official history of the school observed:

> No mere physical enjoyment can explain the intensity of excitement in matches. The truth is that each team . . . is conscious of being put to a public test. Not only quickness and skill but staying power, combination, resource, the courage to play a losing game and the generosity to be a good winner, all those qualities once supposed to be untypical of girls are there.[41]

The Misses Lumsden and Dove lost no opportunity to bring these points home. In addresses to outside groups and during frequent visits back to the school, Lumsden extolled the virtues of games and insisted that they were as essential to the training of girls as of boys. St Leonards' experience proved, she asserted, that girls could play games without the loss of a particle of womanly gentleness. Games produced beauty, grace, mental lucidity, quickness, steady nerves and good health, and better than anything else, imparted self-control, endurance, patience, courage, resourcefulness, modesty, generosity, unselfishness and the ability to command and obey. Lumsden refuted the argument that girls were too intense and excitable to learn such lessons from games, and retorted that had it been true it would have been all the more reason for training them; and she inevitably recalled the opposite extremes that had existed in her youth:

> . . . the dreary 'crocodile' walk, that apology for healthy exer-
> cise, and the hours spent on the reclining board which were
> supposed to keep children's backs straight. [Only those who
> experienced them] can realise the change and the health and
> happiness which games have brought to girls — and more
> — what lessons in self-control, good temper, love of fair play,
> and service not for praise or gain but in some cause beyond
> self, are learned in the playground. It is on this side of the
> movement for reform of girls' schools . . . that St Leonards
> can justly claim to have led the way.[42]

Dove waxed even more rhapsodic, after the fashion of male athleticists. Agreeing that preparatory lessons as valuable as those taught in the classroom were learned on the playing field, she insisted that 'active games in the open air, are essential to a healthy existence, and that most of the qualities, if not all, that conduce to the supremacy of our country in so many quarters of the globe, are fostered, if not solely developed, by means of games'.[43]

St Leonards had a reputation as a 'games' school by the early-twentieth century, something about which successive headmistresses were extremely sensitive. Opposed to extremes, they endeavoured to ensure that health was a primary concern by providing regular medical inspection and the compilation of elaborate tables on students' height and weight. They also sought to make certain that enthusiasm for sport jeopardised neither femininity nor academic performance.

In the case of femininity, most girls spontaneously evinced a reluctance to bowl and serve cricket and tennis balls and play lacrosse overhand in the masculine fashion, or to protest a rule against raising hockey balls more than three feet even when shooting at goal. As for protecting academic performance, although hardly much of a limitation, students were forbidden to play in more than four matches a week; and somewhat belatedly in 1904 administrators decided that 'no Shield match shall be played on a day upon which a Certificate Examination is being held'.[44] They regularly pointed to the honours lists and the results of the Oxbridge higher certificate examinations as proof of the vigour of St Leonards' academic work in general and among sporting girls in particular.

Nevertheless, if one games-playing Senior is to be believed, academic standards were not particularly high and games did predominate; and because 'St Leonards gave girls the great boon of healthy and innocent interest for their recreation hours [it was] always connected in the minds of educators with success in athletics'.[45]

Games were even more important at the Wimbledon House School — better known as Roedean School — which opened to ten students in Brighton in 1885 under the joint principalship of three sisters — Penelope, Dorothy and Millicent Lawrence. Penelope, the eldest and most dominant, had attended Newnham College, Dorothy, Bedford College and Millicent, the Maria Grey Training College for Teachers. Like Frances Buss and Louisa Lumsden, the Lawrences were committed to a revolutionary crusade designed to reject the traditional image of female helplessness and prepare women to play a fuller role in aspects of life that hitherto had been monopolised by men. The school was thus intended 'to provide for the womanhood of the nation what the public school as an institution provides for the country's manhood'.[46]

The Lawrences were convinced of the value of academic learning, and also of the intimate connection between a vigorous, healthy body and a mind similarly endowed. Since they regarded physical training as the branch of female education most generally neglected, and the one most likely to develop trustworthiness and a sense of responsibility, they took the unprecedented step of announcing it as their top priority in the first prospectus, thereby signalling a major reorientation of educational priorities.

The aims of the school will be to give a thorough education, physical, intellectual, and moral [they said]. Special pains will be taken to guard against overwork; and from two to three hours daily will be allotted to outdoor exercise and games. Opportunities will be given for Swimming, Riding, Dancing and Gymnastics.[47]

Exercise was actually given somewhat less time; but from the first, despite hostility from parents and townspeople who were offended by the idea of schoolgirls playing boys' games, the Lawrences encouraged hockey and cricket as part of a full programme of physical activity that eventually included archery, tennis, fencing, swimming, water-polo, life-saving, diving, running, walking, drill, Swedish gymnastics, athletic sports, cycling, tennis, golf, rounders, fives, hockey, cricket, lacrosse and netball, and was accommodated by an 18-acre playground, eight tennis courts, a swimming pool and a cricket pavilion.

As soon as numbers permitted, the house system was introduced and inter-house sports competitions were inaugurated. By 1893, tennis, hockey, cricket and swimming clubs existed under the presidency of teachers, as did a games committee comprised of student representatives from each house which was responsible for scheduling practices and matches, assigning grounds, selecting teams, awarding colours and intimidating shirkers.

The school hockey team's only opponent at first was Newnham College, but opportunities for outside matches increased after 1895, when Roedean became the only school among the eight original members of the AEWHA, on the initiative of Christabel Lawrence — the games mistress and sister of the principals — and rules and equipment were standardised. Before long the school team could hold its own among the strongest clubs in the country and was recognised for producing some of the best players.

As games-playing spread among girls' schools, away fixtures in a variety of sports became increasingly frequent, culminating in a great rivalry with Wycombe Abbey, while intra- and inter-house matches abounded. In 1897, when the school moved to a large new building surrounded by spacious grounds just east of Brighton and changed its name to Roedean, a student population of about 100 supported eight cricket and ten hockey teams. Two hours a day in winter and three in summer were set aside for games and exercise. The school magazine, which began publishing in

1889 and was largely controlled by teachers, reported all school and house contests at great length and in a critical fashion designed to shame those whose play was irregular or unenergetic into striving to improve. Endlessly chronicling team membership, scores and batting and bowling averages, it enjoyed calling players 'men' and urging them to show 'grit and determination' before 'large and excited crowds'. At the same time, however, it reflected the Lawrences' desire that players display proper feminine images. Roedean may not yet have become the 'potting shed of the English rose', but the magazine regularly reminded readers that good players would never be hot, untidy, noisy or out of breath, or swing a stick more than two inches above the ground.[48]

In 1902 lacrosse joined the roster of major sports by resolution of the games committee. Since few students knew how to play, all started on an equal footing, a situation that stimulated particular enthusiasm. A St Leonards Senior was invited to teach basic skills, house matches were quickly arranged and school teams formed, with the result that by 1913 Roedean was known as the strongest of the lacrosse-playing schools in Britain and the one most responsible for the development of the game among post-secondary school women.

In other sporting areas, running practice was instituted in 1896, although care was taken to ensure that stamina was built up gradually because Penelope Lawrence felt that it put a strain on all organs. Soon after the advent of cycling in the mid-1890s, teachers accompanied students on tours of several days' duration. Students also fenced from the start as a result of encouragement by mistresses who felt that it cultivated grace and agility; and they swam, for recreational, safety and competitive purposes, first in the sea and the Brighton Baths and then from 1907 in their own pool.

Although the house system was less extensive at Roedean than at St Leonards, members of the hockey, cricket and lacrosse first house and school teams were heroes, particularly the several who played more than one major sport. The captains of drilling sections and major teams were listed with the school officers. Challenge cups and trophies sanctioned the activities for which they were awarded and inspired the composition of sporting poems and songs. Outside the school Old Students' teams were formed; and Roedeanians apparently did not relinquish the pleasure in games acquired in school on departure, for the Lawrences had ample opportunity to congratulate a good many who played hockey for county clubs or England.

As for physical training, drill was offered from the early days by one James Harvie who held the enlightened views that systems of physical education for boys and girls should be similar, and that games were but adjuncts to a complete course of training designed 'to give equal development and uniform excellence to every organ'.[49] A gymnasium — still in use in the 1980s — was included in the new building complex which opened in 1897, just before the retirement of Mr Harvie. In 1904 three graduates of Madame Bergman-Osterberg's Physical Training College were hired to teach Swedish gymnastics during a 40-minute period five mornings a week and in special remedial classes for girls who stooped or had weak backs. These new arrangements, the Lawrences felt, had the advantage of giving every girl daily attention from a trained expert and producing immediate improvement in carriage and general deportment.

In 1898 Penelope Lawrence made a lengthy submission to the Education Department which stands as a classic defence of female sport.[50] Intent upon explaining the philosophy, nature and results of physical education and games at Roedean, she began by observing that while it was generally accepted that exercise was important in the education of girls, differences of opinion remained on the proper type and amount. At her school, she said, a balanced and graduated system, combining drill, games and dancing, was adapted to the needs and abilities of each girl so as to make her 'owner of herself' by developing every muscle and organ equally. Training in gymnastics was rigorous, and resulted in half the upper school and many in the lower division being able to show their heads above a horizontal bar in a hanging position and nearly all students being able to go hand-over-hand up a 16-foot rope. But important as gymnastics were, Lawrence explained, games were the staple form of exercise because they had the advantage of requiring movements that were voluntary and could be performed outdoors year round.

Lawrence shared with Jane Frances Dove and devotees of male athleticism the extreme view that England's superior national character arose from the fact that games 'make us able to evolve and preserve free institutions, and make us law-abiding and moderate'.[51] In the case of girls' schools, she felt that they filled leisure periods with innocent and wholesome diversions and left little time for gossip and loafing. They improved *esprit* by promoting friendliness and mutual satisfaction among teachers and students. They combined healthy and pleasant exercise with training that produced skill and physical strength; and most importantly, they built character. Since the majority of girls had led restricted lives, even more than did boys they needed to be trained to look beyond themselves and to work for the common good. Games, she argued, provided the discipline which facilitated this, and they taught fortitude, persistence, self-control and judgement — precisely those elements which hitherto had been lacking in female education and which it was thus the responsibility of girls' schools to cultivate. Compulsory participation for everyone without a medical excuse she justified on the grounds that games provided many benefits and that the very girls who were likeliest to avoid them were the ones who needed them most.

To Lawrence games meant not tennis or rounders, however enjoyable they might be, but the great team games of hockey and cricket. Hockey she regarded as an admirable substitute for football, about whose inherent roughness and unsuitability for girls she had no doubt, while cricket admitted girls to a world far wider than their own and offered the best possible training in courtesy, good breeding, honour, obedience, magnanimity and organisation. To those who argued that cricket was beyond a girl's power, she retorted that practice could produce a respectable standard of play, and that in any event it was irrelevant to argue that a girl could never equal her brother's accomplishments, for if she learned to play well enough to make the game interesting to herself that was sufficient justification.

She conceded that games filled too large a place in the life of some schools, but denied this was the case at Roedean. Even though by 1914 Roedean had sports facilities second to none and a reputation as the most games-oriented of girls' schools, she insisted that the physical and intellectual were carefully balanced. Students were warned not to think of games merely as a means of acquiring strength, but as a key to health, happiness, mental acuity and moral virtue. Outside matches were limited to two or three a term, and games mistresses were always given duties apart from sport so they were not separated from the academic life of the school. In conclusion, Lawrence stated, Roedean's experience and examination results demonstrated that girls who showed earnestness and energy in games usually applied the same qualities to their scholastic endeavours, while those who neglected their studies would have done so regardless.

An exception to the games ethos was the most famous of all girls' public schools, the Cheltenham Ladies' College. Founded as a proprietary day school in 1853 to provide the daughters of professional and private gentlemen with an education similar to that received by their sons at the Cheltenham College for Boys, it anticipated as the typical student the girl who looked forward to a leisured life devoid of the necessity of working for a living. To her it aimed to afford,

> . . . on reasonable terms, an education based upon religious principles which, preserving the modesty and gentleness of the female character, should so far cultivate intellectual powers as to fit her for the discharge of those responsible duties which devolve upon her as a wife, mother, mistress and friend, the natural companion and helpmeet for man.[52]

Although its early curriculum included polite accomplishments and was far from pretentious, parents objected to the time spent on academic subjects and 'unfeminine' annual examinations, so the school languished. When Dorothea Beale became principal in 1858 it had few pupils or qualified teachers and little money or equipment. Beale quickly transformed things, and in the process made Cheltenham a great influence on the reform of female education and herself a legend.

Through adaptation rather than imitation, and without comparing the abilities of boys and girls, Beale aimed to apply the male public school system to the education of females, 'so that they may best perform the subordinate part in the world, to which . . . they have been called'.[53] She was convinced that women whose minds and bodies were fully developed were healthier and more womanly than those whose abilities were not, and she set out to furnish girls with a sound and balanced religious, intellectual and physical training in a way that would magnify their femininity. Beale had a conservative if elevated conception of dutiful womanhood, and while she de-emphasised accomplishments and introduced more demanding subjects, she delayed the introduction of mathematics and the classics until the late 1860s so as not to alienate too many parents, and then confined them to older students whose brains were sufficiently mature. She also abolished competitive examinations.

Cheltenham's prospectuses listed callisthenic exercises as part of the regular course of study, because Beale considered them an antidote to excessive brain work which could permanently damage constitutions. In 1864 she reported to the Schools Inquiry Commission:

> The vigorous exercise which boys get from cricket, etc., must be supplied in the case of girls by walking and callisthenic exercise, skipping, etc. We have a room specially fitted up with swings, etc. It is to be wished that croquet would be abolished; it gives no proper exercise, induces colds, and places the body in a crooked posture.[54]

About the same time she became concerned that students had insufficient opportunities for outdoor exercise, and despite parental protests she decided to terminate the school day at 12.55 p.m., thus, with Frances Buss, starting a trend in numerous other schools.

Over the years Beale endorsed a gradual improvement of exercise facilities. In 1876, three years after the opening of a new school building with ample accommodation for boarders, she provided a larger room for callisthenics and appointed teachers who conducted morning classes in a kind of musical drill that combined marching with a series of rhythmic ball exercises. In 1890 this routine was replaced by the full Swedish system, following the employment of a woman trained in Ling gymnastics who persuaded Beale to provide a gymnasium 'specially fitted with all needful appliances'.[55] By 1905 Cheltenham had six trained physical education mistresses who were responsible for superintending games and teaching gymnastics, fencing, swimming and remedial exercise.

Beale regarded competition by girls in any form as productive of too great a desire for success and incompatible with their unique emotional and intellectual needs and future family responsibilities. Sports competition she particularly deplored, equating it with masculinity and the tendency in boys' schools to make far too much of physical proficiency. It took all the persuasive powers of Louisa Lumsden, when she was classics mistress at Cheltenham in the mid-1870s, to persuade Beale to allow a small tennis court. Although numerous staff members strongly favoured giving more encouragement to games and exercise, for years thereafter the only other activities offered were walking, swimming, riding, occasional games of rounders and fives, and quiet recreation like nine-pins organised, from 1885, by a sports club.

Finally, in 1890, Beale ordered the rental of a piece of ground for experimental use as a playing field, apparently convinced that the introduction of games in some form was inevitable. As a few daring students joyously took up cricket and hockey, and parents looked on with trepidation, Beale determined that if there were going to be games at Cheltenham they should develop in harmony with her school's general purposes. Remaining true to her distrust of competition and the public excitement it engendered, she refused to allow matches against other schools for fear they would foster the emulation and overstrain she tried to avoid in the classroom; and for similar reasons, as well as a conviction that a good job done was its own reward, she refused to sanction conspicuous awards. Furthermore, she firmly rejected the idea of compulsory participation on the grounds that a variety of outdoor pursuits would best provide for the release of youthful energy.

This philosophy she elucidated in her report to the school council in the year 1893–4, the first in which she gave special mention to games and physical education.

> The Physical Education is much advanced and many take lessons in the Swedish Gymnasium . . . our 26 tennis grounds and our new playground, give facilities for outdoor games which are much appreciated, but, I am most anxious that our girls should not over-exert themselves, or become absorbed in athletic rivalries, and therefore we do not play against the other schools. I think it better for girls to learn to take an interest in botany, geology, etc., and to make country excursions.[56]

Paradoxically, considering her basic conservatism, at the age of 67 Beale learned to ride a tricycle. Despite failing hearing and sight, she replaced her life-long habit of taking a morning walk with a cycle ride; and she had no hesitation about permitting her staff and senior students to cycle.

During the 1890s Beale was gradually converted to the view, by then widely held, 'that the power of acting with others, or rapidly judging, is cultivated by the exercise of school games',[57] and she started to allow competitions within and among Cheltenham's 18 boarding houses and day students. The playing field was enlarged substantially, and by the turn of the century all the houses had cricket, tennis and hockey teams. The *Hockey Field* reported that it was common to find a dozen or more house hockey matches going on simultaneously on Saturday afternoons; that the assistance of staff members who had played at college and university elevated the quality of play; and that competition was so keen that the school could be aptly described as a 'hotbed of hockey'.[58]

This was a far cry from the situation only a few years earlier when Beale watched her first hockey match with a distinct lack of enthusiasm, and is reported to have exclaimed, 'The children will hurt themselves if they all run after one ball. Get some more balls at once!'[59] She continued to enforce the prohibition against prizes and outside matches, however. Just before her death in 1906 she yielded slightly and allowed hockey matches against Old Lady Cheltonians and the East Gloucester women's club; but her determination to go no further was manifested by her reassertion almost simultaneously that 'no games are played against other schools, as the strain and excitement are guarded against'.[60]

By the time Beale died, however, a number of former Cheltonians had gained prominence as sportswomen and there was scarcely a school in the country with better sports facilities. Cheltenham had 26 tennis courts in the gardens of the 18 boarding houses, two fives courts, a 16-acre playground and a Swedish gymnasium, and its prospectus boasted of dance, callisthenics, fencing, swimming, riding, Swedish drill and remedial classes as providing excellent opportunities for exercise. Games may have been less prominent than at other major public schools, but their gradual institution, despite Beale's deeply-rooted suspicions, indicates the inexorable growth of their influence and acceptance.

The conversion of Cheltenham's council to the games ethic was demonstrated by its choice of Miss Beale's successor. She was Lilian M. Faithfull, late of Somerville Hall, the Oxford High School for Girls, the Royal Holloway College and the King's College Ladies' Department. Well known in the world of women's sport, she was an avid golfer and tennis player and had only recently given up active participation in hockey. At the time of her Cheltenham appointment she was president of the AEWHA, a fact that positively influenced her selection and proved to be 'a far greater passport to the approval of the girls than any other honour [she] could have had'.[61]

As was predictable, under Faithfull sport received more encouragement, for she believed that certain invaluable lessons could be learned only on the playing field and that games improved the tone and character of a school and counteracted the tendency to spend too long over books. Greater organisation and trophies, colours and outside matches were soon introduced in hockey, tennis and cricket. A male hockey coach was hired, and the roster of games was expanded to include badminton and netball. The college magazine, a staff controlled journal directed primarily towards former students, began to report more fully on match results, although still not to the same extent as its counterparts elsewhere. A swimming pool was built — with a movable floor so the facility could double as a gymnasium — and Cheltenham became one of the first schools to adopt the Dalcroze system of eurythmic exercise to musical accompaniment. Further, the cautious advance made under Beale about 1905 towards medical inspection was followed four years later by the institution of compulsory inspection of each entering student and annual re-inspection by a female doctor, along with more scientific classes to remedy defects of carriage and posture.[62]

To the disappointment of some of the keener students, however, Faithfull was always careful to ensure that games were neither played to excess nor the objects of all-consuming interest. In addition, she subscribed to the progressive view that games mistresses should stimulate a general interest in exercise by devoting attention to ordinary and younger girls who badly needed instruction and encouragement, as well as to members of teams; and for coaching and playing purposes, she introduced a system of grading students and dividing them into groups.

Less progressive was her conviction that women were naturally inferior and subordinate to men. Despite her own distinguished career as an educator and sportswoman, she never challenged women's secondary role in public and private life. In a series of 'Saturday Talks' to her Cheltenham students she described boys positively and girls negatively, and opined that while school life would help to improve girls' moral, intellectual and physical powers, and thus their potential for leadership, it could never make them boys' equal. In particular she advised the athletic to avoid flaunting their physical prowess, 'because after all . . . girls cannot help being inferior to boys in games, and the girl who boasts of her play in games makes herself extremely ridiculous'.[63]

The situation by 1914

By 1914 not all schools for middle-class girls had adopted the games-playing ethic, and there remained considerable differences of opinion about the types and amount of exercise appropriate for pubescent girls, as well as variety in the degree of compulsion and time devoted to it.

The first issue of the *Girls' School Year Book* (1906) classified 119 schools as of the public type that catered to different castes within the middle class.[64] Enrolments ranged from about 80 to 650,[65] and opportunities for exercise from dancing only to almost every sport extant, while supervision of exercise, although usually in the hands of trained teachers, was sometimes still in those of academic mistresses and former military personnel. Numerous private ladies' academies still survived, largely unaffected by the movements for educational reform and women's rights, where 'young-ladyhood tinged with Christianity' was emphasised; students played, worked and slept in tight corsets; and parental permission was required for anything resembling games-playing.[66]

Nevertheless, the change in girls' schools away from the old routine of backboards, gentle callisthenics and crocodile walks was 'nothing less than a revolution'.[67] Whereas it would have been impossible for a school in 1860 to boast that 'outdoor games and physical culture play an important part in school life',[68] by the end of the century ignorance and narrow-mindedness had been overcome to the extent that it was generally recognised that girls required exercise year-round and that athletic games should form an important part of a school's curriculum. 'Most headmistresses [had become] keen on training muscles as well as minds and could not conceive of a girls' school without organised gymnastics and games.'[69] The prospectuses of schools with pretensions to excellence, whether day or boarding, boasted of playing fields and gymnasia, opportunities provided for games and physical education and trained physical educators and medical doctors on the staff. One to three hours of exercise a day had become common, as had a tradition of games-playing mistresses, many of whom, as in boys' schools, were Old Students;[70] and like boys' schools too, certain institutions for girls had gained reputations for excellence in particular sports and developed great inter-school rivalries, which gave them an influence far beyond mere numbers enrolled. Day schools in many parts of the country had even formed games leagues and associations for competition in tennis, swimming, hockey, lacrosse, netball and rounders, although the compulsory element in their physical education programmes was gymnastics rather than games until after the First World War because of the time involved in travelling.[71]

As in boys' schools, the rigid schedule of work and play in girls' was ill-suited to those of a non-conformist or unathletic nature. But if some students were unenthusiastic about exercise, most were games mad. Entire student bodies turned out for major form, house or school matches, during which they participated in many of the same type of socialising rituals that had come to be associated with male athleticism. Inspired by the relatively untrammelled freedom of the playing field, the hymn-like ballads of earlier days had turned into militant fight songs that were sung with religious fervour. School magazines disseminated the games ethic by stressing the building of character and the necessity for players to demonstrate pluck and selflessness. Students revelled in sporting paraphernalia, such as the trophies that were objects of intense devotion and the colours in the form of badges, ties and hatbands that were awarded to outstanding players who them-selves were virtually worshipped. Photographing of teams for posterity was an annual rite; and sporting language conjuring up masculine images was considered smart.

The section on 'Games for Girls' in *Girls' School Year Books* for the period 1906 to 1914 provides revealing information on actual attitudes to and the extent of sport. It credited games with making the term 'bluestocking' inapplicable to public school products, and with providing the perfect antidote to academic overwork and the means to produce valuable moral qualities. It identified and described the various sports played and the associations for competition. It explained how games were usually organised by a trained mistress who arranged matches and managed the finances of a games club, and that students played major roles in the actual running of games, particularly the captains of games for school, house or form whose role in selecting teams, awarding colours and providing instruction gave them considerable power and adula-tion. It noted too that while away matches were played regularly, they were limited ordinarily to three or four a term so as to distract as little as possible from internal play and study, and even more important were the house, form and scratch matches that gave students at various levels of proficiency an opportunity to join in. Finally, it indicated that at boarding schools participation was often compulsory for all but those with a medical exemption.

A few late Victorian educators, such as Dorothea Beale of Cheltenham, Sara Burstall of the North London Collegiate School and Manchester High School for Girls and Emily Davies of Girton College, eventually complained about the excessive zeal with which some schoolgirls pursued games. The fact that debates on whether athletics were over-done occurred regularly within and without schools, and that numerous Old Girls recalled the primacy of games over brains, indicates the seriousness of the concern and the probability that it was justified, at least in some instances. Athleticism, however, never acquired anything like the same hold on girls' schools that it did on boys'. Games were encouraged in both to improve moral standing, and they provided a ritualistic agent of socialisation that created cohesion and social control; but in the last analysis the two had different aims, ends and meanings.

Boys' schools may have had a marked influence on girls', and both may have separated children from various ranks within the business and professional classes from home, family and the opposite sex and put an imprint on their products that often lasted a lifetime. But they were basically separate systems with distinct functions, whose similarities only superficially obscured fundamental differences that were 'important indicators as to how within the same social class each gender [was] socially defined and culturally reproduced'.[72] The purpose of boys' public schools was to produce manly leaders of country and empire who conformed to the middle- and upper-class image of the 'decent chap', and who transmitted the loyalty and patriotism they developed at school to the regiment, the trading company or the diplomatic service. What Mangan calls the crude Darwinism and pretentiousness of the boys' school came out most clearly on the playing fields, where the physical and moral qualities of manliness were supposedly best developed in struggles which emphasised the idea that success in the endless battles of life went to the strong and the powerful, the brave and the true.[73] Far more was made of the relationship between games and moral health than between games and physical health; and the correlation between athletic and military warfare was stressed. In the outside world public school men were to form an easily identifiable community ready to fight the good fight, when and wherever the call came, with bats straight and upper lips stiff, for the honour and glory of crown, country and school.

Girls' schools, by contrast, had divided aims and continued to be influenced by very different values. They were intended, on the one hand, to educate thinking and socially useful women for careers other than marriage, by providing them with unprecedented opportunities for intellectual and physical development and independence while knocking the affectation and false sensibility out of them. At the same time, however, they remained essentially faithful to the demands of the traditional, domestic, female role and so trained students in femininity. Games were thus never worshipped in isolated splendour, but were always viewed as a part — albeit usually the most important part — of a systematic and quasi-social Darwinistic programme of measurement, medical inspection and physical training intended to make students healthier and so fitter for academic toil and ultimately motherhood. Their character-building propensities were certainly emphasised, but the Darwinistic significance of conflict and power was not, nor were unathletic and intellectual students despised, since it was never forgotten that the schools' primary purpose was to demonstrate the capacity of the female mind. Like those of boys', the rituals and symbols that became attached to girls' games encoded notions of hierarchy and transmitted and revivified the value system of the dominant classes in wider society, but not to the same extent; nor did they have such jingoistic overtones. The latter were not completely lacking in girls' schools. The supremacy of Great Britain lay behind the significance some proponents of games attached to preparing future mothers of the race and wives of empire-builders who were 'straight-forward, honest and self-reliant and able to co-operate with others to wage war on the side of right'.[74] This certainly had Darwinistic implications involving the survival of the fittest and the process of natural selection, as did converse arguments about games producing overstrain, but aggressive nationalism was never a dominant feature of female education.

Furthermore, girls' games were rarely defended as a disciplinary medium within schools, since the maintenance of order was not a problem. Although student-run activities such as games fostered in girls a degree of independence and accustomed them to act together in an organised fashion for a specific purpose, girls were generally inured to habits of obedience and conformity. Even 'heroic' girls such as prefects and games captains, had much less freedom, authority and privilege than their brothers. In girls' schools, too, there was never the slightest suggestion that games were a useful distraction from sexual irregularities; nor was the link between attendance at a public school and success in adult life comparable. While girls' schools broadened views of the female role to include work apart from family service, they continued to identify success with domesticity: their graduates may have become part of a distinctive network, but this network was so loose and impotent compared with the male equivalent as to make the 'old school tie', with its implications of power and patronage, virtually meaningless in a female context.

There was an important discontinuity between girls' schooling and what was realisable in adulthood. The academic and physical education girls received at public school may have made their sex's potential better appreciated, but that potential remained only incompletely attainable. The new curricula appeared to be a breakthrough into the staunchest of male domains and seemed to imply that women with an education similar to that of men should be able to lead similar lives; and by the end of the nineteenth century there were certainly an unprecedented number of independent and innovative young women in English society who were involved in a variety of unique enterprises. Yet public school women frequently found themselves in an ambiguous position. They might have been freed of many traditional trammels in their efforts to acquire knowledge, health and careers, but they remained restricted by social conventions relating to their class and gender and by the striking contradictions that were implicit in reformed ideas about the socialisation of women. Public school girls were encouraged to develop opposite sides of their personality at the same time. They were allowed to pursue academic study that was serious and goal-directed; they were encouraged to be ambitious and self-disciplined and to aspire to careers before marriage. They were taught that excellence, accuracy, thoroughness, achievement, courage and initiative were appropriate for ladies. They were permitted good health and physical stamina, and to bicycle and play tennis, hockey and lacrosse. Simultaneously, however, they were taught to be subservient and self-sacrificing; that their highest duty was to perform well as wives and mothers; and that they must accept obediently many of the limitations that society continued to impose on their sex. In other words, some of the characteristics prominent in the education and socialisation of middle-class males, which were also developed in women by sound intellectual and physical training, proved to be in conflict with those of the traditional lady, whose gifts were to be used in the private not the public sector.[75]

Manliness and womanliness remained very different concepts, the former conjuring up images involving physical strength and authority in a public setting, and the latter, those of mutual sharing and intimacy in a domestic one. While reforming educators were largely responsible for making sports a respectable activity for adolescent girls and encouraging them to be physically fit and to develop new ambitions and temperamental qualities, they remained committed to the preservation of many conventional Victorian values relating to family life and to conservative views about the dangers of overstrain during maturation. Whether their students were writing the Cambridge Higher Local Examinations or playing a strenuous game of hockey, they insisted on femininity in mental outlook and physical manner and on the avoidance of excess.

Although games-playing became increasingly widespread in girls' schools and valued for its physiological and social benefits during the late-nineteenth century, in conservative quarters there remained a strong feeling of unease about serious sports competition for females, particularly in rough and potentially unsexing games like hockey and cricket. While biological factors had become less absolute determinants of the way women were educated, people continued to worry about competitive athletics producing a dangerous amount of nervous excitement and physical overwork, and to argue that 'a sound mind and body is [sic] much more likely if the brain is rested, not by violent exercise, but by manual labour such as needlework'.[76] They continued to believe that girls were too intense and excitable to learn successfully from games the masculine lessons of self-control and steadfastness, and that it would be better if adolescent girls exercised privately and gently and so assumed graceful attitudes than if they took strenuous exercise that might well produce ungainliness.

The gradual acceptance of girls' school sport as compatible with femininity resulted from protracted negotiations and compromises that reconciled the apparent conflict between games and appropriate female behaviour. Many of the legendary head-mistresses who pioneered the reformation of female education may have extolled civic values and public spirit, but they were also anxious to avoid anything that might damage the reputation of their schools. They rejected the designation 'feminist' because it implied a broader commitment to womens' rights in general than they espoused or wished to communicate publicly, and they went to considerable lengths to adapt to the dominant value system. While they believed that excellence and achievement were appropriate ambitions in middle-class girls, they also accepted that men and women had different missions. At the same time as they encouraged increased physical activity among girls, they perceived games players as acting in a boyish manner, and communicated this view to their charges. So, like their university counterparts, the school games pioneers themselves contributed to the continued identification of vigorous physical activity with masculinity, and thus to its use as a powerful mechanism of gender-based social control.

To counteract sport's masculine image, they required students to dress and behave in a way that projected an image of moderation and girlishness. They accepted the notion of limited sports, that is, that certain sports and ways of playing were off-limits, such as those requiring physical contact, awkward positions and great endurance or strength; and in so far as was possible they eliminated painful and dangerous elements and the aggressive use of hands and feet. The introduction of new sports, like hockey, lacrosse and netball, that did not carry the stigma of overt masculinity, helped as well, as long as they were played under conditions that minimised threats to femininity. If these conditions — like special rules and time-limits — hindered skilful performance and perpetuated the view that girls' sport was 'only' play, that was the price that had to be paid to preserve modesty and gain acceptance.

On the sports field schoolgirls experienced a suspension of normal role-playing and the conventional image of female impotence. But because of limiting conditions and continuing scepticism about the extent of female physical competence, when girls' games were contrasted with boys', the image of female incompetence was partially reaffirmed. The upshot was that the sporting schoolgirl, like her college sister, simultaneously accommodated to and challenged traditional bourgeois mores. In addition, to 1914, opportunities for public schooling among middle-class girls remained limited, and for the majority — still educated partially at home and partially at less ambitious establishments — self-realisation through proper mental and physical development remained an unattainable concept.

Nevertheless, over the years the public school became an integral part of the educational experience of an increasing number of girls from the privileged ranks of society; and its encouragement of sport, however insulated from public view, extended the age up to which it was considered appropriate for girls to exercise and was most important to the general advancement of the female sex. The public schools were rarely overtly feminist, but they were an ideal locale for promoting women's rights, and battles almost as important as those fought in lecture and examination halls were played out on sports grounds and in gymnasia. The fact that it was girls of breeding who took up games-playing added a degree of respectability to their sporting activities, which was important too, for it facilitated the concession that physical exertion was suitable for young ladies. This in turn made possible the inclusion of games and physical training in the curricula of the best girls' secondary schools and made female sport more widely acceptable.

Public school sport may have had to compromise with Victorian concepts of femininity to gain acceptance, but it made a major contribution to redefining women's rights and abilities. The schools in general successfully refuted the accusation that sound intellectual and physical educations would produce defective creatures, uninterested in and incapable of motherhood and domesticity. Their student-athletes in particular presented females in non-traditional roles and contributed important modifications to the feminine ideal.

In every society the use of the physical body is constrained by the social body, and in that of Victorian England the physical rituals which appeared in girls' school games both reflected and generated changes in society at large. Whether they realised it or not, the reforming educators who argued that exercise was a necessary prerequisite to good health and successful schooling, and the first generations of games players at girls' public schools, were part of a broad movement for social reform. They were involved in nothing less than affirmative action on behalf of the sovereignty of the individual woman and the general worth of the female sex.

Notes

1. Reprints from *St Leonards School Gazette* (1901), pp. 16–17. See also Jane Francis Dove, 'Reminiscences dictated to Lady Stephen', 10 March 1925, in Wycombe Abbey School archives.

2. *St Leonards School Gazette* (October 1898), p. 327.

3. Mangan, *Athleticism*, pp. 22, 113–14.

4. Henry Newbolt, 'Vitaï Lampada' in *Heroes of Land and Sea* (Toronto, 1919), p. 161; Geoffrey Best, 'Militarism in the Victorian Public School' in Brian Simon and Ian Bradley (eds), *The Victorian Public School* (Dublin, 1975), pp. 129–46; Mangan, *Athleticism*, pp. 194–5, 202; Norman Vance, 'The Ideal of Manliness' in Simon and Bradley (eds),

Victorian Public School, p. 128.

5. J.A. Mangan, 'Social Darwinism and English Upper Class Education', paper presented at the meeting of the History of Education Society, Atlanta, Ga., 10 November 1985, p. 28.

6. Sara Delamont, 'The Contradictions in Ladies' Education' in Sara Delamont and Lorna Duffin (eds), *The Nineteenth-Century Woman* (London, 1978), pp. 140–1; Felicity Hunt, ' "Divided They Fall" ': The Educational Implications of Opposing Ideologies in Victorian Girls' Schooling 1850–1914', paper presented at the meeting of the History of Education Society, Atlanta, Ga., 9 November 1985, pp. 3–4.

7. Dove, 'Reminiscences'; *Girls' School Year Book* (1906), p. 389; Hargreaves, 'Playing Like Gentlemen', pp. 135–7.

8. Patricia Vertinsky, 'The Evolving Policy of Equal Curricular Opportunity in England: A Case Study of the Implementation of Sex Equality in Physical Education', *British Journal of Educational Studies*, vol. 31, no. 3 (1983), p. 240.

9. Association of Head Mistresses, Minutes (9–10 March 1877). See also (12 June 1880).

10. Royal Commission on School Education, *Report* (1868), vol. 5, p. 265.

11. North London Collegiate School, *Prize Day Report* (1866).

Information on exercise and sport at the North London Collegiate School was derived primarily from Josephine Kamm, *How Different From Us* (London, 1958); Mrs Roscoe Mullins, 'The North London Collegiate School for Girls', *Sylvia's Journal* (September 1898), pp. 498–505; Annie E. Ridley (ed.), *Frances Buss and her Work for Education* (London, 1895); Ruby M. Scrimgeour (ed.), *The North London Collegiate School 1850–1950* (Oxford, 1950); and from the following archival material: Governors' Minutes (1875–1910); Gymnastic Medical Notes (1882–6); Head Mistresses' Reports (1871–1914); Hockey, Netball and Tennis Clubs Minutes (1900–14); Mrs Hoggan's Notes (1882–5); *Our Magazine* (1875–1914); letters; photographs; Prize Day Reports (1850–1914); Staff Meeting Minutes (1885–1914); Swimming Club Minutes (1912–14).

12. North London Collegiate School, Prize Day Reports (1871), p. 3.

13. Ibid. (1885), pp. 90–2.

14. North London Collegiate School, Gymnastic Medical Notes (1882–6); Mrs Hoggan's Notes (1882–5).

15. North London Collegiate School, Prize Day Reports (1885), p. 92 and Staff Meeting Minutes (25 November 1889), p. 170, (16 February 1891), p. 212; *Our Magazine*, vol. 10 (July 1885), p. 82. To develop breathing prowess and expand the lungs, teachers suggested that students blow up air balls and blow darts at targets during the winter months.

16. *Our Magazine*, vol. 14 (July 1889), p. 54.

17. Former students established an Old North Londoners Athletic Club in 1903 to enable them to continue to participate in hockey, tennis, fives and netball, and in athletic and swimming sports days at the school. It proved difficult to get full teams together for practices and matches, however, for the same reasons that plagued university alumnae clubs.

18. A cricket club was contemplated, but failed to materialise because of fears that it would have insufficient practice time to compete

successfully against schools whose grounds were conveniently situated.

19. Sophie Bryant was the first woman in England to earn a doctorate (DSc., London University, 1884). She was an avid cyclist and encouraged students and teachers to ride; she also rowed on the Thames, was a great walker and even climbed the Matterhorn. Her unusual example of physical activity and academic achievement provided a compelling model for students to emulate.

20. For information on the powerful fillip given to dress reform by sport and exercise at the North London Collegiate School and other girls' schools, see Chapter 8.

21. North London Collegiate School, *Jubilee Magazine* (April 1900), pp. 40–4.

22. Emily Shirreff, *The Work of the National Union* (London, 1872), p. 47; Alfred Schofield, *The Physical Education of Girls* (London, 1898), p. 8; Edward W. Ellsworth, *Liberators of the Female Mind* (Westport, Cn., 1979), pp. 194–7; Josephine Kamm, *Indicative Past* (London, 1971), pp. 75–6; Girls' Public Day School Trust, *Norwich High School, 1875–1950* (Norwich, 1950), p. 39. (The GPDSC became a Trust in 1906, and after that date is referred to as the GPDST.)

23. The new girls' high schools needed a supply of adequately trained instructors. Some came from Oxbridge women's colleges, some from the training departments established in connection with several GPDSC schools, and some from the training colleges for female secondary school teachers that evolved from the 1870s. The first and most important of the latter, the Training College for Teachers in Middle and Higher Schools for Girls, was opened in London by National Union in 1878, and renamed the Maria Grey Training College, after one of the GPDSC's founders. Under the influence of the exercise movement, teacher training colleges quickly introduced Swedish drill and sports such as swimming, lawn tennis, rounders, netball, hockey and cricket. In the major games, matches were played against other normal schools, London University women's colleges, girls' day schools and private ladies' clubs, although the teacher trainees were handicapped by attending college only for a year and thus by having insufficient time to practise together. See *Maria Grey Training College Magazine* (1891–1914).

24. Mary C. Malim and Henrietta C. Escreet (eds), *The Book of the Blackheath High School* (London, 1927), pp. 109–11, 116. See also pp. 103–5, 108; Florence Gadesden, *The Education of Girls and the Development of Girls' High Schools* (1900), p. 21; Great Britain, Board of Education, *Report of Inspection, Blackheath High School* (30–31 March and 1 April 1903), p. 19; K.M. Watts, *A History of the Blackheath High School* (London, 1980), pp. 7–9.

25. Among other GPDSC schools noted for sports were the Oxford High School (1875), the Wimbledon High School (1880) and the Sutton High School (1884). At the Sheffield High School (1878) girls suspected by form mistresses of taking insufficient exercise were compelled to take more. The South Hampstead and Notting Hill High Schools (1876 and 1873) were the first to compete in swimming, and at the latter, as well as at the Brighton High School (1876), girls even played football briefly, until it was condemned as 'unsuitable'. See Faithfull, *In the House*, pp. 78–9; V.E. Stack (ed.), *Oxford High School, 1875–1960* (1963), pp. 7–9;

Evelyn Spence Weiss, *Report on Physical Training* (26 February 1903); E. Woodhouse, 'Physical Education at the Sheffield High School for Girls', Great Britain, Parliamentary Papers, Reports from Commissioners, Inspectors and Others. *Education Department, Special Reports on Educational Subjects* (1898), vol. 2, pp. 133–44.

26. Sara Burstall and M.A. Douglas (eds), *Public Schools for Girls* (London, 1911), p. 212; Gadesden, *Education*, pp. 20–1; *Report of Inspection, Blackheath High School* (20–23 October 1908), pp. 21–2; GPDST, *Norwich*, pp. 40, 44–5; *Girls' School Year Book* (1906), p. 82, (1911), p. 532; *Hockey Field* (26 February 1905), p. 296; E.M. Leaky, 'Some Educational Aims in a School for Girls', *Journal of Education* (April 1909), p. 288.

27. Louisa Lumsden, 'Discussion: What may be the Dangers of Educational Overwork for both Sexes', *Transactions, National Association for the Promotion of Social Science* (1880), p. 446.

Information on sport and exercise at St Leonards School was derived primarily from Julia M. Grant, Katherine McCutcheon and Ethel E. Sanders (eds), *St Leonards School, 1877–1927* (Oxford, 1927); Julia S.A. Macaulay (ed.), *St Leonards School 1877–1977* (Glasgow, 1977); and from the following archival material: Rules and Record of Challenge Shield Competitions (1888–1900); *St Leonards School Gazette* (1877–1914); school lists, register, photographs and songs.

Goals was a primitive form of hockey played with a weapon that was a cross between a heavy walking stick and a shepherd's crook.

28. St Leonards School, School List (August 1883), pp. 3–4.

29. Paul Atkinson, 'Fitness, Feminism and Schooling' in Delamont and Duffin (eds), *Nineteenth-Century Woman*, p. 115.

30. *St Leonards School Gazette*, vol. 1 (June 1888), p. 47.

31. St Leonards School, Rules . . . of the Challenge Shield Competition (January 1888–July 1900). See also Jane Claydon, 'Lacrosse at St Leonards School', *Lacrosse*, vol. 34 (Autumn 1980), p. 9.

32. Lumsden, *Yellow Leaves*, p. 81.

33. *St. Leonards School Gazette*, vol. 1 (February 1890), p. 115.

34. Dove, 'Reminiscences'.

35. Mary Butts, *The Crystal Cabinet* (London, 1937), p. 216; White interview.

36. *St Leonards School Gazette*, vol. 1 (June 1889), p. 81.

37. Golf had a chequered history at St Leonards. Student interest ebbed and flowed; but a number of Seniors distinguished themselves in championship competition. In 1907, for example, one was victorious in the Scottish Ladies' Golf Championship and nine of the 45 entrants had St Leonards backgrounds.

38. *St Leonards School Gazette*, vol. 4 (October 1898), p. 327.

39. Ibid., vol. 4 (November 1899), pp. 385–90; Celia Haddon, *Great Days and Jolly Days* (London, 1977), p. 54.

40. Butts, *Crystal Cabinet*, pp. 194–5.

41. Grant, McCutcheon and Sanders (eds), *St Leonards School*, p. 63.

42. Ibid., p. 151.

43. Jane Frances Dove, 'The Cultivation of the Body' in Dorothea Beale, Lucy H.M. Soulsby and Jane Frances Dove (eds), *Work and Play in Girls' Schools* (London, 1901), p. 397. Dove believed so completely

in the value of exercise that she had all students weighed on their return to school. Those below the average weight were required to study less and play games more.

In 1896 Dove became the first principal of a new school in Buckinghamshire, Wycombe Abbey School, which she made a virtual clone of St Leonards. At the Abbey her aim was to provide a wholesome balance of work and play, after the fashion at a great public schools for boys, and she particularly encouraged games as an important counterpoise to mental work and contributor to good health and moral fibre. Within three years of the school's foundation, it was recognised as one of the foremost in paying attention to games and physical training; and it offered students lawn tennis, fives, bowls, croquet, quoits, boating, golf, swimming, skating, archery, tobogganing, basketball, rounders, hockey, cricket and lacrosse. Dove, 'Cultivation of the Body', pp. 396–423; Peck, *A Little Learning*, pp. 113–14; *Wycombe Abbey School Gazette* (1896–1914).

44. *St Leonards School Gazette*, vol. 4 (November 1904), p. 673.

45. *Ladies' Field* (September 1911), p. 57. Also White interview.

46. *Queen* (16 July 1936), p. 23. See also L. Cope Cornford and F.R. Yerburg, *Roedean School* (London, 1927), p. 10.

47. Dorothy E. de Zouche, *Roedean School, 1885–1955* (Brighton, 1955), p. 27.

48. *Wimbledon House School News* (Michaelmas Term 1892), pp. 3–11, (Christmas Term 1893), pp. 6–8; *Roedean School News*, vol. 6 (Lent Term 1903), pp. 96–103; Linda Blandford, 'The Making of a Lady' in George M. Fraser (ed.), *The World of the Public School* (London, 1977), p. 198.

49. *Wimbledon House School News* (Summer Term 1895), p. 56.

50. Penelope Lawrence, 'Games and Athletics in Secondary Schools for Girls', *Education Department, Special Reports on Educational Subjects* (1898), vol. 2, pp. 145–58.

51. Ibid., p. 149.

52. Elizabeth Raikes, *Dorothea Beale of Cheltenham* (London, 1908), p. 87.

53. Blandford, 'Making of a Lady' in Fraser, *World of the Public School*, p. 200.

54. Royal Commission on School Education, *Report* (1868), vol. 5, p. 740. See also Raikes, *Dorothea Beale*, Appendix D.

Information on exercise and sport at the Cheltenham Ladies' College was derived primarily from Kamm, *How Different*; Raikes, *Dorothea Beale*; F. Cecily Steadman, *In the Days of Miss Beale* (London, 1931); and the following archival material: *Cheltenham Ladies' College Magazine* (1880–1914); Lady Principals' Reports (1880–1914); prospectuses.

55. *Cheltenham Ladies' College Magazine* (Spring 1895), p. 182.

56. Ibid.

57. Dorothea Beale, quoted in A.K. Clarke, *A History of the Cheltenham Ladies' College 1853–1979*, 3rd edn (Great Glenham, Suffolk, 1979), p. 82.

58. *Hockey Field* (17 October 1901), p. 7.

59. Kamm, *How Different*, pp. 21–2.

60. *Cheltenham Ladies' College Magazine* (Spring 1906), p. 94.

61. Faithfull, *In the House*, p. 134.

62. Cheltenham Ladies' College, Report of the Lady Principal

(1909–10 and 1913–14); Faithfull, *In the House*, p. 79. Faithfull's own hockey stick became the inter-house hockey trophy.

63. Lilian Faithfull, *You and I* (London, 1928), p. 52.

64. Social considerations involving class prevailed in the matter of who played whom. On the whole boarding schools were more up-market than day schools and usually played other boarding schools and university colleges, while day schools tended to play other schools and to be less sports oriented because students commuted, playing fields were often distant and games-playing was optional. It is worth noting too that the denominational or non-denominational character of schools, with the exception of Roman Catholic schools, does not appear to have affected the degree of games-playing to any extent, while the proclivities of mistresses and principals definitely did. Pauline C. Bell, 'A History of Physical Education in Girls' Public Schools, 1870–1921, with particular reference to the influence of Christianity', unpublished MEd thesis, University of Manchester, 1978, pp. 137–8.

65. There were approximately 40,000 girls in over 200 public second-ary schools by 1900, 70 per cent of whom were in boarding establishments. This represented less than one third of the total receiving secondary instruction. See Great Britain, Royal Commission on Second-ary Education, *Report* (1895), vol. 40, pp. 15, 76, 232–3, vol. 41, pp. 168–71; Hunt, '"Divided They Fall"', p. 21.

By 1914 the schools used as case studies had approximately the follow-ing enrolments:

North London Collegiate	350
Blackheath	400
St Leonards	380
Roedean	380
Cheltenham Ladies' College	650

66. Gwendolen Raverat, *Period Piece* (London, 1952), pp. 69–71.

67. 'Are Athletics Overdone', p. 247.

68. *Girls' School Year Book* (1906), pp. 28–9.

69. *Lancet* (19 March 1910), pp. 794–5.

70. The question of allowing mistresses to play on school teams was a vexing one for years. By the early-twentieth century, at the large schools, although they sometimes played in matches against ladies' clubs, they rarely did so in inter-school matches, their participation having been recognised as making students too dependent on them and usurping students' places on teams.

71. For example, the GPDSC Games Association (1893), the Midlands Games Association (1894), the East Anglian High School Games Association (1899), the Lancashire Girls' Schools Lawn Tennis League (1894), the Liverpool Girls' Schools Rounders League (1897), the Cheshire High School Hockey League (1897), the Northern Schools Basketball Association (1903) and the London Schools Swimming League (1903).

72. Judith Okely, 'Privileged, Schooled and Finished: Boarding Education for Girls' in Shirley Ardener (ed.), *Defining Females* (London, 1978), p. 136.

73. J.A. Mangan, 'Social Darwinism, Sport and English Upper-Class

Education', *Stadion*, vol. 7, no. 1 (1981), p. 99.

74. Bell, 'A History of Physical Education', p. 177. See also *Wycombe Abbey School Gazette*, vol. 3 (November 1907), pp. 161–4.

75. Burstall, *English High Schools*, pp. 90–1; Gathorne-Hardy, *Public School Phenomenon*, pp. 273–4; Gorham, *Victorian Girl*, pp. 105–18; Hargreaves, 'Playing Like Gentlemen', pp. 138–82; M. Felicity Hunt, 'Secondary Education for the Middle Class Girl: A Study of Ideology and Educational Practice, 1870–1940, with special reference to the Harpur Trust Girls' Schools, Bedford', unpublished PhD thesis, University of Cambridge, 1984, pp. 399–411.

76. Pleasaunce Unite, 'Disillusioned Daughters', *Fortnightly Review*, vol. 68 (1 November 1900), p. 854.

4

The Rise of the
Physical Training Mistress

The Anstey College Song

To Swedish Gymnastics now,
 Our youth and strength we bring
To build up healthy bodies
 After the Laws of Ling.
For we ourselves the sculptors are,
 And we ourselves the clay,
When mind and will and spirit
 United hold their sway.

Chorus: England! England!
 Home of our hearts so dear,
'Ling' makes thy daughters healthy,
 Their hearts bereft of fear,
Their spirits free and joyous,
 Their minds both strong and sane,
'Vis atque gratia harmoniaque,'
 This is our lofty aim.[1]

The highly organised system of games and sport that evolved at girls' public schools did little for the academic development of physical education. The serious study of physical training belonged to unique new institutions — specialist physical education colleges for women — and to the trained teachers of gymnastics and games that they produced.

In the nineteenth century three major and largely independent developments occurred in physical education in England: the growth of organised games in boys' public schools into a cult of athleticism; the introduction into state-aided elementary schools after 1870 of drill-like exercises designed to provide for large numbers of undisciplined lower-class children in poor facilities;

and the introduction of scientific gymnastics into progressive girls' secondary schools and their amalgamation with the athletic games that were already beginning to be played. Whereas in boys' schools sport was only rarely regarded as part of a wider system of physical education, in girls', games, drill and gymnastics were welded into just such a system through the efforts of an entirely new professional woman — the gymnastics and games mistress. The unusual result was that in the area of physical training girls' schools were considerably ahead of their male counterparts by 1914.[2]

The battle to secure systematic physical training for girls was in some ways even more difficult than that to improve the standards of intellectual attainment, for the subtle consequences of inadequate physiques were less obvious. Despite the protests of physicians and educational reformers, during much of the Victorian period what passed for exercise in many girls' schools was entirely unscientific. Its supervision was monopolised by dancing mistresses and drill sergeants who were ignorant of anatomy, physiology and their charges' requirements, and it was geared more to the production of ladylike deportment than genuine vigour and vitality. Gradually, however, a need was recognised for something more systematic, for instructors qualified to provide it and for institutions to train them. The solution to the problem came ultimately from abroad.

In Germany and Sweden quasi-scientific systems of physical education evolved in the late-eighteenth and early-nineteenth centuries out of a concern for health, patriotism and military capability. The German system, which was developed by J.C.F. Guts Muths and Ludwig Jahn, the famous *Turnvater*, emphasised strength, and included marching, singing, free exercise to music with wands, dumb bells and clubs, and apparatus work on the vaulting horse, ropes, rings, ladders and bars.

The Swedish system, on the other hand, stressed style and precision, the cure and treatment of diseases and the harmonious development of the whole body. Its creator, Per Henrik Ling considered mind and body a unit. On the basis of 'exact' anatomical and physiological knowledge, he developed an elaborate system of free-standing movements intended to produce the highest degree of health and physical culture and to elevate morally its practitioners and make them more independent. Ling prepared extensive tables of exercises designed to cultivate all parts of the body in an ordered, almost ritualistic way by gradually progressing from simple and gentle movements to more difficult and complicated ones. His teaching approach emphasised discipline, the identification of individuals with a group and the repetition of identical movements. Excessively regimented, it gave little thought to individual or imaginative ways of moving, or to the idea that exercise should be enjoyable. Considering the general neglect of women at the time, however, it was to Ling's credit that, although he believed women's physical make-up required less robust handling than men's, he was concerned with the health of females because of its implications for that of future generations.[3]

Prompted by Ling's work, the Swedish government opened the Royal Central Gymnastics Institute in Stockholm in 1814 to train men and women to teach the Ling system.

When the system appeared in England about 30 years later it attracted very little interest. To the English gentleman who was devoted to field sports, gymnastics were completely irrelevant, while to the muscular Christian of the public school type they were unmanly and off-puttingly foreign. The result was that, until late in the century, gymnastics developed outside the educational and athletic mainstream, despite efforts to popularise them and convince educational authorities of the need for a national system of physical training.

A particularly persistent devotee was Mathias Roth, a Hungarian medical doctor who took refuge in London from the revolutions of 1848. In 1853 Roth opened a private institution for the treatment of disease through Swedish exercise; and for the next quarter-century, in the face of opposition and apathy, he waged a solitary crusade to have physical education made compulsory in the nation's elementary schools and taught in all teachers' training colleges and schools for middle-class boys and girls. The resulting increase in the population's physical, mental and moral power, he argued, would greatly improve England's military strength, productive work and racial quality.[4]

Roth's main competitor was Archibald MacLaren, a disciple of the German system, who opened a fencing school and gymnasium for men in Oxford in the late 1850s after having studied fencing and gymnastics in Paris. Like Roth, MacLaren believed that gymnastics were a higher form of exercise than games and better for developing the whole body, and he zealously promoted the reform of gymnastics along scientific lines and their introduction as a standard part of educational curricula. Like Roth too, MacLaren rejected the view that girls were naturally weak and would be coarsened by vigorous exercise, although in practice he virtually ignored them.[5]

Proponents of each system damned the other as too likely to develop bulging muscles in females and too exhausting. For business and ideological reasons, and in response to the growing national interest in bodily health, both factions established private gymnasia and health clinics in major urban centres. Some welcomed female clients, and gradually replaced the dancing academies that from the 1840s had offered instruction to gentlewomen in callisthenics as well as fashionable dances. Among the earliest were the Institution for the Treatment of Spinal and Other Deformities, by Movements, Water, Etc. according to the Ling system started in London by one Franz Bernard about 1860;[6] the Birmingham Athletic Club which offered classes in gymnastics and callisthenics to properly chaperoned women and girls twice a week from the 1860s; and Madame Brenner's German gymnasium in Berkeley Square, London. The latter's patrons included a number of middle-class ladies whom Madame Brenner attempted to protect from charges of 'tom-boyism' by arguing moralistically that she

> . . . in no way . . . desires to pass those lines of separation between the sexes which all well-ordered minds must ever wish to see strictly preserved . . . Gymnastic Practice, carried out by the Educated, and in the spirit of refinement and conscientiousness, can never be objectionable to the feelings and habits of the True Lady.[7]

At all the establishments production of healthy women was a primary concern, not for any feminist reasons involving rights to self-development, but so they would produce healthier children and better 'cheer and sweeten the manifold cares and labours of stern and striving men'.[8]

Examples of gymnastic diversity later in the century were Stempel's Scientific Physical Training [German] Institute, Gymnasium and Academy of Fencing and Boxing, Regent's Park, London, which had a fashionable clientele of both sexes; Mr and Mrs Alexander Alexander's Southport Gymnasium [Swedish] in Birkdale, Lancashire;[9] and the Alexandra House Gymnasium [German] in Kensington, which was run by the Misses Beatrice and Evelyn Bear for wealthy and socially prominent patrons, and aimed to produce, without undue fatigue, 'ease of carriage, grace of motion, and the development of the physique, with an eye to the fate of future generations and the general physique of girls'.[10] By the Edwardian era, these had been joined by a profusion of physical culture and gymnastic clubs and societies, run by people with widely varying qualifications who were out to exploit the commercial possibilities of exercise. Most were for men, but a number catered to women who were eager to cultivate health as well as beauty.[11]

Some private gymnasia offered courses and certification in physical training, but on the whole they are memorable in the context of this study only as interesting aberrations. The professionalisation of physical training occurred elsewhere.

In 1870 Forster's Education Act finally created a state system of elementary schools. It failed to make gymnastic exercise compulsory, but a revised code soon provided that participation in drill could be counted as part of school attendance and supported by a financial grant. Since the drill was dull and monotonous, and usually only for boys, Mathias Roth continued to campaign for a more scientific and elevated approach to the subject and for the provision of exercise to children of both sexes. His conversion of Mrs Alice Westlake, a member of the London School Board, to a belief in the therapeutic benefits of Swedish gymnastics for girls, marked a watershed, for she in turn persuaded the board to create a new position — Superintendent of Physical Education in Girls' Schools.

Because no English women possessed the requisite training and qualifications, Concordia Löfving, a graduate of the Central Gymnastics Institute, Stockholm, was appointed in 1879. This was an event of the utmost importance, for it marked the beginning of systematic physical education in state elementary schools and the rise to dominance of the Swedish system. More importantly, it signalled the beginning of the exceptional influence of women in the development of physical education.[12]

When Löfving resigned in 1881, she was succeeded by another Swede, Martina Bergman-Osterberg. A woman of remarkable energy and determination, Bergman-Osterberg possessed tremendous self-confidence and an almost fanatical desire to popularise the Swedish system.

I never for one minute doubted I should succeed [she observed]. The idea of training the body as carefully as we do the mind is too good to fail; our means for this training, as provided by Ling's system, are too excellent not to overcome the opposition, and finally — you English love nothing better than success — you are yourselves experts in this difficult art, and you are always ready to support those who with tenacity of purpose stake everything for the sake of succeeding.[13]

Bergman-Osterberg's initial tasks were to conduct courses in gymnastics, anatomy and physiology for female teachers in board schools and to certify competence. Within five years she had trained over 1,300 and laid the foundations of a national system of physical training by introducing Ling gymnastics into all board girls' schools and departments. She also helped awaken public interest in physical education by having students stage large displays at such places as the Crystal Palace, and found time to establish physical training courses at several teacher training colleges and to give evidence on the physical training of girls before the Cross Royal Commission on Elementary Education.

Soon, however, she began to turn her back on elementary schooling. A concern about improving the quality of the race and a conviction that this could be best accomplished by women of the middle ranks led her to contemplate the wisdom of training such women as teachers of scientific gymnastics in girls' public schools. To this end, in the autumn of 1885, she opened the Hampstead Physical Training College and Gymnasium, the first institution in Britain to have a fully equipped Swedish gymnasium and to provide a specialist course in the theory and practice of physical education. Two years later — Hampstead having won her mind and heart — she resigned her position with the London School Board.

Because the Hampstead enterprise was unique and personal, Bergman-Osterberg enjoyed complete freedom of action. At first she offered private instruction for healthy women and children and remedial exercise and massage for those with defects.[14] But it was the training of teachers that interested her most. At a time when women's attempts to penetrate male professions were meeting only limited success, Bergman-Osterberg envisaged nothing less than the creation of an entirely new, exclusively female profession, and the introduction of 'scientific' physical education into schools and colleges for middle-class females, as an essential subject of instruction and the ideal counterpoise to the 'scientific' opposition to academic education.

The course she developed was modelled on that at the Swedish Central Institute. Spread over two years, it included anatomy, animal physiology, chemistry, physics, hygiene, theory of movement, dancing and Swedish gymnastics, which was at the heart of the training because Bergman-Osterberg considered it the best means of developing, quickly and fully, an individual's mental, moral and physical capacity. In addition, while Bergman-Osterberg never really understood or became proficient in English games, she appreciated their value as a complement to gymnastics and academics that taught an 'appreciation of space and time; discipline, reason, quickness, and unselfishness'.[15] She appreciated too that games were becoming important in girls' schools, and that if her students were to penetrate the public school world they would have to present themselves as games as well as gymnastic specialists. As a result, her earliest students received instruction in the theory and practice of such sports as tennis, cricket, hockey, fencing and swimming.

Initially 'Madame' (as students called her) did most of the lecturing herself, with the help of an unqualified assistant; and then, as they became available, she took the incestuous but common route of hiring back her own graduates.

Only four students entered the first year and two the second, but the little college got a good deal of favourable publicity, particularly when students put on impressive public demonstrations; and as its reputation grew so did enrolment. At a time when rewarding and well-paying careers for middle-class women were still relatively few, and the demand for physical training instructors greatly exceeded the supply, candidates were attracted by the virtual guarantee of employment at the relatively handsome salary of at least £100 a year. Within six years 28 students were packed into the cramped Hampstead quarters.

In 1895, in the face of a shortage of space and Hampstead's imminent demolition to make way for a railway line, Bergman-Osterberg purchased 'Kingsfield', a large country house which stood amidst 14 acres near Dartford, Kent. At the renamed Bergman-Osterberg Physical Training College — hereafter called Dartford, its modern name — the course hardened into a pattern that lasted for several generations. Swedish gymnastics, performed indoors and in a unique outdoor gymnasium, remained the core of a curriculum that included scientific subjects — anatomy, physiology and pathology — massage, remedial exercises and dancing. Students received useful practice-teaching experience giving classes in massage and medical and educational gymnastics to local adults and children in nearby board schools; and since much more scope for outdoor sport was provided by Dartford's spacious grounds, students were encouraged to make the most of the opportunity. Over the years a quarter-mile running and cycling track — a rare facility at the time — was laid out, as were tennis courts and grounds for hockey, lacrosse and cricket. The great athletic all-rounder, C.B. Fry, was hired to coach cricket; and Dartford students played a leading role in refining the game of netball, which Madame Bergman-Osterberg informally introduced from America in 1895 to meet the need for an outdoor winter game that could be played in a small space and would develop both sides of the body, and which was regularised in 1901 when a group of Dartfordians drafted a formal set of rules that were widely adopted. As the quality of games-playing improved, matches in various sports were arranged against private clubs, university colleges and prominent day schools. Before long Dartford graduates were conspicuous at the highest levels of women's sport in the country; indeed several were key figures in establishing national governing bodies for women in hockey (1895), lacrosse (1913) and netball (1926).

Bergman-Osterberg strongly advocated practical dress for ordinary wear and exercise.[16] She deliberately kept fees high and enrolment low as a result of the conviction that the fewer the students the easier it would be to establish and maintain the college's reputation.[17] Similarly, the selection process and training programme remained extremely exacting, to the point sometimes of cruelty. Bergman-Osterberg believed that physical education could only be established as a respectable career for middle-class women, and her graduates could only meet their colleagues in the public schools on terms of equality, if students were recruited from among the best and brightest in the middle ranks — from those with above-average intelligence and education, an aptitude for natural science, a sound constitution and character, a pleasing appearance and considerable zeal and devotion. At least 50 per cent of applicants were rejected, while the successful had to submit to discipline strict to the point of abuse and to live with the knowledge that if they did not measure up they could be expelled at any moment. They also had to endure a residential life that was made austere in the extreme by stringent rules about ordinary dress and lights-out and against students visiting each other's rooms; and they were allowed only occasional weekend leaves, and even had to tolerate Madame's censorship of their mail.

It was no wonder that Bergman-Osterberg was nick-named 'Napoleon'. A natural dictator and uncompromising perfectionist, she would not tolerate slackness or insincerity or anything smacking of weakness, such as illness and fatigue. She had an extremely sharp tongue which was slow to praise and quick to criticise in a hurtful way. The quintessential authoritarian, she refused to allow any student self-government, thus contradicting her own aim to produce independent women. Nevertheless, she was substantially correct in attributing her success to the thoroughness and strictness of Dartford's training and discipline. Although a few students protested by resigning or orchestrating their own expulsion, the majority viewed their principal with a mixture of respect, gratitude and loyalty. They appreciated that she wanted the best for them, and accepted her argument that severity was necessary because of the limited time available to train them for the 'grave responsibilities' they would have as teachers, mothers and citizens. Genuinely inspired by Bergman-Osterberg's sense of mission, many left Dartford for posts throughout Britain and the Empire as highly disciplined crusaders for a 'noble cause' who were proud of the designation 'Madame's girls'.

Bergman-Osterberg's domination of Dartford was so complete that she felt no necessity to participate in the organisation and development of the gymnastics profession at large or to maintain contact with educational matters in general. While Dartford could not meet the demand for physical educators that she herself was largely responsible for creating, she strongly disapproved of the establishment of other colleges, particularly by her own students. Similarly, she was infuriated when a group of former students — manifesting the growing professional consciousness evident in other fields, and recognising the need to facilitate revision of their work through the interchange of ideas and to elevate physical education's status by permitting only the qualified to teach — resolved in 1899 'That an Association [the Ling Association] be formed, admitting as members all women holding a certificate from Madame Bergman-Osterberg or from the Royal Central Institute, Stockholm', to unite trained gymnastics teachers; protect and improve their salaries and status; start a register of those qualified to teach Swedish gymnastics; give massage, and arrange meetings and holiday courses. Bergman-Osterberg brusquely rejected an invitation to head it on the grounds that it would lower standards, but in reality because the idea was not hers. Not to be outdone, she forbade Dartford instructors to join, and the next year established a rival group, the Bergman-Osterberg Union of Trained Gymnastic Teachers, to facilitate the circulation of news among Dartford graduates and instigate a benefit fund.[18]

Unattractive though posterity might find Bergman-Osterberg's domineering and self-righteous personality, she deserves credit for establishing the physical education profession in England and profoundly influencing its development. By the time she died, in 1915, the physical education syllabus in state elementary schools was Swedish; Swedish gymnastics had been adopted by the army and navy and by a few exclusive boys' schools; and it was even spreading to the colonies. The 500 students Bergman-Osterberg trained had fanned out across the country and abroad to teach in physical education and teacher training colleges and girls' secondary schools; to coach in university colleges; and to work for educational authorities and private health clinics. Dartford was recognised as the leading physical education institution in the country; and although Bergman-Osterberg disliked the competition and failed to appreciate its furtherance of her own work, it had inspired the development of a whole system of specialist women's physical education colleges. Most importantly, Bergman-Osterberg had accomplished so well her double task of training physical education teachers who had a sound general education and special training in Swedish gymnastics and games, and convincing public school headmistresses of the need to hire them, that virtually all the best girls' schools employed physical education mistresses — preferably from Dartford — and had coherent physical education programmes centred on the Ling system; and the prejudice that physical education was suited mainly for girls who lacked 'an overdose of brains' and would make them unladylike and unmarriageable had been eroded substantially.[19]

A committed feminist who laboured throughout her life to remove barriers to women's progress, Bergman-Osterberg was proudest of her achievements' contribution to the liberation of women. She was a traditionalist to the extent that she believed pubescent and adult females were naturally weaker than males, and that, because of their importance to 'the regeneration of the race', care must be taken to avoid overstrain and permanent 'evil effects' by assuring that movements were modified. But she regarded feminism and physical training as inextricably linked. In order to raise the status of their sex and take charge of their own salvation by acquiring the economic independence essential for true emancipation, she argued, women had to be healthy and strong, to which end a sound physical education was indispensable.[20]

An unshakeable faith in womanhood gave Martina Bergman-Osterberg's work a kind of spiritual force; and in this she was not alone.

By the time the first edition of the *Girls' School Year Book* appeared, 'Drill and Games Teaching' was so extensive as to warrant a special section; and the number of colleges providing special training in physical education to women was said to be increasing so quickly that it was impossible to give an 'exhaustive list'.[21] Among them were the Physical Training College for Women, South-Western Polytechnic, Chelsea, the Anstey College of Physical Training and Hygiene for Women Teachers and the Bedford College of Physical Training.

The Chelsea College, like Dartford, was founded and dominated by an enterprising and determined foreign woman. Dorette Wilke arrived in England from Bavaria in 1886 at the age of 18, and almost immediately undertook a two-year course in German gymnastics at Stempel's Gymnasium, Regent's Park, London. After qualifying she remained on for a year in order to repay the remission of tuition fees, before moving as an assistant to the Misses Bear at the Alexandra House Gymnasium, and then to the Battersea Polytechnic. When the latter's authorities rejected her proposal of a plan for training specialist teachers of physical education, she accepted an appointment at the South-Western Polytechnic which promised her free rein.

In 1898 the Chelsea College of Physical Training opened its doors to six students; and within a few years it had a sound reputation and its own personality and characteristics. An eclectic two-year course was centred on German gymnastics, but included Swedish exercises under the supervision of a Danish woman and the English system of military drill supervised by a sergeant from the Grenadier Guards. Special teachers provided instruction in anatomy, physiology, massage, histology, household chemistry, hygiene, logic, elocution, dancing, singing, ambulance and sick nursing, plus teaching practice. Such games and sports as fencing, swimming, netball, lacrosse, tennis, cricket and hockey were also encouraged, and, as with English gymnastics, Wilke occasionally compromised her view that girls should be taught only by women by employing male professional coaches.[22]

Facilities were never as good as at Dartford — students played games in Battersea Park and swam in the Chelsea Baths — but within a few years they included a new gymnasium and a number of residential rooms for the minority of students who did not live at home. Numbers rose steadily, reaching about 32 in 1907, the year Wilke bowed to current orthodoxy, and the necessity of supplying the insatiable demand for teachers trained in the Swedish system, and went over completely to Ling. Two years later, having already considered the possibility of gaining university recognition for the physical training profession, Wilke made Chelsea the first physical education college with a three-year course on the grounds that this would bring it into line with the undergraduate curriculum and produce better qualified and more mature students.[23]

Wilke was a contrast with the public image of 'the hygienic dowdily inclined lady who usually advocates physical culture for women'.[24] An unconventional person who encouraged unconventionality in her students, she moved in the world of art and folk dance. Like Martina Bergman-Osterberg she was outspoken and pointed in her criticism, but she was much less dogmatic and harsh. She had a good sense of humour and a cheerful, friendly demeanour; and she allowed her artistic streak to manifest itself in a colourful style of dress.

Unlike Bergman-Osterberg, Wilke was actively involved in the development of the physical training profession beyond her college. Adaptability and openness were among her most attractive and useful qualities; and they moved her to become connected with the British College of Physical Education (1891), the National Society of Physical Education (1897) and the Gymnastic Teachers' Institute (1897), and with the first serious physical education journal, the *Journal of Scientific Physical Training* (1908), which was dedicated to pushing forward 'those methods which have proved to be good in the educational service of the race'.[25]

Like Bergman-Osterberg, however, Wilke was a convinced feminist who had considerable confidence in her sex. She supported votes for women; encouraged staff and students to join the Gymnastic Teachers' Suffrage Society (1909); and regarded a sound education and good health as prerequisites to the independence and adaptability women needed to be good citizens, good workers and good mothers of strong children. She believed, too, with a fervour approaching the religious, that scientific physical training was essential for sound mental and moral development, and that the combination of gymnastics and athletic games produced qualities fundamental to a successful fight in the battle of life:

> A body as hard as steel — to work hard, to work well and bear up under many difficulties; a mind clear as crystal to see and understand all that is good and noble and beautiful in the world, and also to distinguish the true from the false; a heart as warm as sunshine, so that we feel and sympathise with the joys and troubles of our fellow creatures.[26]

Wilke also shared with Bergman-Osterberg a revulsion at women's appalling ignorance of their own bodies, at the remnants of the feminine predilection to cultivate enervating weakness and at the idea that physically active girls were in any way unfeminine. Wilke took offence at the implications that girls who undertook physical training lacked the intelligence for success in anything else and that physical education colleges developed muscles to the detriment of brains. She too thus appreciated the propaganda value of public gymnastic displays which revealed students to be the epitome of elegance and grace, and of the college's prospectus identifying refined and gentle birth, a well-formed figure and a cheerful disposition as qualities required of a successful physical educator.

Wilke and Bergman-Osterberg parted company on the subject of woman's most desirable fate, however. While Wilke worked hard to equip women to face the world and turn physical education teaching into a respectable new profession, her feminism had limits. Her confession — 'although I love training them . . . I hope my girls may never have to teach in the end; I want them all to marry and be as happy as they can be'[27] — is a startling revelation of the durability of tradition. Here was an independent and highly successful single woman, who had great confidence in and ambitions for her sex, asserting that marriage meant ultimate happiness and was infinitely superior to the career which she devoted her life to establishing.

Since Dorette Wilke was not one of 'Madame's girls', Bergman-Osterberg's displeasure at the opening of Chelsea College was much less acute than when her own students were 'disloyal'.

One such student was Rhoda Anstey. While at Hampstead College from 1893 to 1895, Anstey became aware of the career possibilities that physical education held for educated women of character and ability, particularly those thoroughly trained in Ling gymnastics. In 1897 she opened her own college and health clinic — the Anstey College of Physical Training and Hygiene for Women Teachers — in a rambling country house set amidst 16 acres near Halesowen, Worcestershire. There it thrived for ten years before moving to the Birmingham suburb of Erdington, a more central location offering better opportunities for practice teaching and remedial work in nearby orphanages, factories, state schools and working girls' clubs. Initially Bergman-Osterberg was livid; but her determination to fight Anstey 'tooth and nail' was hopeless, for physical education training — as she would have been the first to argue — was an idea whose time had come.[28]

Rhoda Anstey was an intense and eccentric woman who dressed in sandals and an arab-style djibbah, ate no meat and was so devoted to astrology that she was inclined to admit any Sagittarian. Like her Swedish mistress, she was blunt in manner, dogmatic and outspoken in speech and slow to praise, although she had a compassionate side that came out in benevolence to poor students. Like Bergman-Osterberg and Wilke she was totally dedicated to creating a centre where the qualities of a successful physical educator — a good education, clear voice, healthy body, refined manner, cheerful disposition, industry and enthusiasm — would be cultivated, and where women could study the human body and how best to train it in preparation for spreading their knowledge among others, particularly in girls' secondary schools, upon the health of whose products depended the moral and physical well-being of the race. As the college prospectus stated, Anstey aimed

> . . . to send out women, trained in mind and character as well as in body, to spread a knowledge of physiology and the laws of health; to work in schools for the advancement of physical education and for prevention of deformity and imperfect bodily development, which often arise out of the conditions of school life, as well as to cure ailments and deformities where they exist.[29]

Until 1918, when it was lengthened to three, the Anstey course lasted two years. Uncompromising in its determination to serve the nation through the pursuit of physical culture, its core was the Ling system. To Rhoda Anstey the body was 'the instrument of the mind and the habitation of the spirit',[30] and it required improvement and harmonious development through a wide range of theoretical and practical training that emphasised grace and harmony rather than muscular strength.[31] Students were instructed in educational and medical gymnastics, massage, anatomy, physiology, hygiene, artistic and folk dancing, voice culture and teaching practice; and unlike their contemporaries elsewhere, they sat the examinations of the St John's Ambulance Society, the Royal Sanitary Institute and Birmingham University. For purist reasons, they were not permitted competitive gymnastics, but they regularly put on displays and demonstrations in schools and clubs. They were also taught how to play outdoor games such as hockey, cricket, lacrosse, netball and tennis, and were encouraged to compete against local ladies' teams, although small enrolment resulted in outsiders and patients resident in the remedial clinic sometimes being recruited to complete sides; and in cricket and lacrosse it proved difficult to locate adequate competition in the Birmingham area.

The Anstey community was small and closely-knit, and its life was strictly regulated and formal. Fees of 100 guineas a year before 1907, and 35 guineas a term for six terms after that, guaranteed an affluent, middle-class clientele. Enrolment was kept low deliberately, starting with three students in 1897 and averaging only eight in each year between 1899 and 1910 and eleven between 1911 and the end of the First World War. The permanent staff complement was small as well, rising from three initially to only nine in 1911. All students and staff, apart from the occasional visiting lecturer, were required to live in college, and deliberately encouraged 'to identify with an institutionalised value system not far removed from the Girls' Public Schools, but tempered by the progressive spirit which was harnessed to the establishment of a new profession for women'.[32] Staff and senior students took their meals at a high table; late-comers to meals were reprimanded; vegetarianism was encouraged; and all students were required to rest in their rooms for an hour every day after lunch regardless of need or inclination.

Rhoda Anstey fully appreciated the power of rituals and symbols in developing a collegiate identity and shared goals and obligations. Her passion for mottoes resulted in the adoption of one for the college that summarised her aims — *Vis Atque Gratia, Harmoniaque* [strength, grace, harmony] — and for inspirational purposes the posting of it and others all over the premises. A patriotic college song was written; a magazine, whose object was to keep students in touch with the college and each other after graduation, was published from 1904; summer schools, that brought former students back for refresher courses and a transfusion of the Anstey way, were run from 1905; a much-prized silver brooch became the college badge in 1909; and an Old Students' Association, which sponsored regular reunions, was founded in 1911.

The ordered pattern of existence was accepted by both staff and students without complaint as essential to the nature and success of the work being undertaken. Old Students indicated that, despite restraints on behaviour and activities, they had had a good deal of fun while at Anstey as the result of the relatively well-balanced social life permitted by a miscellany of clubs.

All Rhoda Anstey's work was permeated by a profound commitment to feminism. An ardent belief in the rights of women, and in the necessity to train them to be independent so they would not have to depend solely on marriage for support, underlay her desire to establish an attractive, well-paying profession. It also underlay her views on physical education, which she equated with strengthening and liberating women's minds, characters and bodies and preparing them for citizenship. As do modern feminists, Anstey drew a parallel between body control and social control, for she understood fully that the woman who controlled her body was likely to control her destiny.[33] In addition she was the only head of a physical education college to campaign actively for the vote. She was a founder of the Gymnastic Teacher's Suffrage Society; and in June 1910 and 1911, with some of her staff and students, she marched with a contingent from the society in great suffrage demonstrations in London, good-naturedly handling cat-calls and remarks like 'Here come the elastic teachers. Let's see their biceps.'[34] With Anstey's encouragement, stirring accounts of such events appeared in the college magazine, while a general sympathy with 'the cause' was demonstrated in college by pro-suffrage meetings addressed by members of the Women's Social and Political Union (WSPU), the raising of money for the WSPU through suffrage garden parties and theatrical performances and the recruitment into the union of a dozen Anstey members.

Conversely, one can imagine no circumstances under which Margaret Stansfeld, however feminist her sympathies, would have allowed her college to become a forum for suffrage agitation or her students and staff to join the WSPU or march in suffrage demonstrations.

Margaret Stansfeld was the second Bergman-Osterberg product to commit treason by establishing her own physical training college. She first encountered Ling gymnastics in 1881 when, as a board school teacher, she took Bergman-Osterberg's courses. After Hampstead opened, Stansfeld was recruited as an instructor, a position she retained until she moved on to teach physical education at the Bedford High School for Girls, to conduct private remedial classes, to give lessons at the Cambridge Training College for Women Teachers, the Froebel Institute in London and to the children of Cambridge dons. In 1903 she took the fateful step of purchasing a house in Lansdowne Road, Bedford, and opening it to 13 students as the Bedford Physical Training College.[35]

While Stansfeld cannot be called a snob, Bedford was certainly the most isolated and elitist of the physical training colleges. High fees kept undesirables from even applying, and prior to 1914 enrolment was never allowed to exceed 50. Like the Oxbridge women's colleges, students came largely from such schools as St Leonards, the Cheltenham Ladies' College, the Bedford High School and those of the GPDSC; and their practice-teaching experience involved the working classes less frequently than elsewhere.

A thoroughly professional woman, Stansfeld was a severe, commanding figure who was married to her ideals and work. Forceful and forthright, she was so determined to achieve what she thought was best for her college that she used almost any means. There were generous and humble sides to her nature, and she hated affectation and pretension. But she found it difficult to show affection or accept approbation; and one of her favourite teaching devices was criticism, which often started with the interview preceding admission, to cut the over-confident down to size, and continued throughout the two-year course. She not only rarely praised students, but regularly insulted and publicly humiliated them in a manner that was downright cruel and made some absolutely desperate for even the faintest expression of approval. Thus the face she presented to the world was that of an austere and single-minded despot.

The regime at Bedford was entirely oriented towards physical education and only occasionally allowed a little time for play or relaxation. Mornings were devoted to lectures in anatomy, physiology, hygiene, remedial and educational gymnastics, teaching methods, first aid and elocution, afternoons to gymnastic practice, sport and games and teaching practice and evenings to more lectures or study. Students learned to swim in the River Ouse; they had male cricket and fencing coaches; and before long a number of students became distinguished in hockey and lacrosse on the national level.

The atmosphere in the college was described by Old Students as nunnery-like and familial, strict and narrow. Discipline and regimentation were watchwords. Students were expected to be honest, hard-working and thorough, to do their best at all times and to pass on the value of behaving thus to their future charges. Because they were expected to look and act like ladies, they were required to wear hats and long skirts over their gymnastic tunics when they covered the few yards between the two houses comprising the college — an inconvenience they lamented at the time and years later. No quarter was given to pain or illness. Meals had to be taken together and the best table manners exhibited, and after the evening one Stansfeld often played the role of matriarch, reading or talking to groups, or visiting individuals in their rooms before lights-out at 10.30 p.m. The first and second years were divided into 'Sets', between which relations were very formal, as were relations between staff and students and staff and Miss Stansfeld. Students were not allowed to have dates or male visitors, and even staff members had a curfew and were required to get the principal's permission to accept invitations from men. Staff were also required to be single and live in college. Miss Stansfeld even personally selected students' first jobs, and literally ordered to stay on or return home those whom she wanted for her own college.[36]

An Old Students' Association, formed in 1909, proved an important mechanism for communicating and perpetuating a sense of common identity. Its original aim — to form a 'bond of union between all students trained in the Bedford Physical Training College' — was fulfilled very well, for into their old age Bedfordians in considerable numbers returned to the college during a 'holiday week' each July for what was ostensibly a refresher course but was more akin to a family reunion. There obeisance was paid to Miss Stansfeld, the head of the family and president-for-life of the association, to whose influence alone many attributed 'anything that one has been able to do since leaving college'.[37]

The whole Bedford system now seems incredibly regimented and juvenile, but the impressions left by Old Bedfordians is of college days that were essentially happy. Rather then resenting Stansfeld's sharp tongue and frighteningly authoritarian manner, most students appear to have idolised her and accepted her autocracy as essential to the achievement of near perfection. Just as Stansfeld intended, the prodigious work load and high standards developed in Bedfordians a tremendous pride in themselves, their college and their profession, and a profound sense of gratitude for having had the privilege of being 'Stanny's Stues'.[38]

Stansfeld helped to found the Ling Association and was its president from 1910 to 1920, but unlike Bergman-Osterberg, Wilke and Anstey, she disliked publicity and wrote and spoke in public very little. She was also less philosophically and aesthetically inclined than they, although her students certainly were indoctrinated with the view that their work had a moral value and was a service to the race that could best be accomplished if they remained single. Within ten years of her college's foundation, Stansfeld had produced over 125 students, the majority of whom were employed as teachers in girls' secondary schools. As were their contemporaries from other colleges, some also were employed as private clinicians, teachers in board and domestic science schools, physical training colleges and schools abroad, and by the Board of Education as inspectors responsible for developing physical training programmes for large numbers of working-class children.

When Martina Bergman-Osterberg opened her little college in Hampstead games and scientific gymnastics were in their infancy in even the best schools.

> Both the drill and games were more or less in the charge of the regular staff, who had no special knowledge of the laws of health and physiology, and who were so much taken up with the regular work of the school that the additional burden this imposed on them was often too great a strain.[39]

Within two decades, because of the increasingly important place given in schools to games and physical education, and in the nation to female health, a tight specialist empire of six physical training colleges offered 'a career with many possibilities for an enterprising woman, who delights in physical exercise and has initiative enough, if opportunity arises, to strike out a line of her own'.[40] All but Chelsea were private enterprises supported by students' fees; all were disciples of Ling; and all were committed to opening a new profession for middle-class women by providing suitably trained physical education and health mistresses for girls' secondary schools. The colleges had different origins, and took their identity from the ideas and characters of their indomitable founders, a diverse and unorthodox lot in the Buss-Beale tradition of extraordinary headmistresses. But they shared common values and aims, demanding curricula and an important role in the general movement to reform women's education.

As Sheila Fletcher demonstrates convincingly in *Women First: The Female Tradition in English Physical Education 1880–1980*, 'By comparison with everything else in the history of women's education, [physical training] was notably, if not uniquely, promoted, institutionalised and authorised by women.'[41] Whereas women's university colleges and girls' public schools were islands in a sea of masculinity and deliberately patterned on male models, the women's physical training colleges, and the skilled and dedicated specialists they produced, formed the nucleus of a specifically female tradition. This tradition was created, developed and sustained at exclusively female institutions in which women controlled the sources of power and determined standards of excellence on the basis of wholly female norms; and it was greatly facilitated by the fact that, unlike other aspects of education, it was largely unrivalled and unresisted by men until the late 1940s because physical education was a new and comparatively asexual subject in which men had no established stake.[42]

There was actually a greater degree of continuity between the old and new provisions for female physical education than Bergman-Osterberg and company would have cared to admit. The physical training colleges reflected important aspects of the structure and values of Victorian society. They were run by bourgeois women with bourgeois values for bourgeois students who got posts in bourgeois schools. All were concerned with winning the approbation of middle-class parents and headmistresses, which meant that physical training practice continued to be guided by traditional perceptions of true womanliness and the importance of maternity. Scientific gymnastics had little in common with the genteel callisthenics that characterised physical training at mid-century, and their emphasis on the production of physical and moral health was to women's distinct advantage. But in building their faith around an exercise system that stressed racial progress and regeneration, deportment and graceful movement, and regimentation rather than individuality and initiative, the physical training colleges supported the principles of obedience and social control, and so modified rather than fundamentally transformed orthodox cultural constructs.[43]

To counteract the public image of the gymnastics mistress as a 'physical strainer' — a mannish, acidic and homely spinster[44] — as well as to establish and protect the good name of their colleges, the physical training pioneers imposed strict rules governing dress and behaviour. They played down the development of aggressive characteristics which would diminish students' claims to usefulness and contradict the best traditions of the female sex. They created college life-styles that combined the values of the gymnasium and drawing room, and espoused the conventional view that one of their discipline's highest purposes was to serve the race by producing noble mates and mothers.

According to Fletcher, the female tradition in physical education does not fit neatly into the conventional patterns of women's history for it involved neither opposites nor inequality, nor the idea of separate but equal.[45] Nevertheless, physical education and feminism had an important reciprocal influence. Bergman-Osterberg, Wilke, Anstey and Stansfeld were all convinced feminists whose strictly professional aims were combined with a strong desire to elevate and emancipate their sex. While a minority of their students viewed physical education as little more than healthy recreation and a means of developing character, most were mission-oriented. 'They treated the female body as a field for cultural intervention, rather than as a passive field of naturally determined processes.'[46] They regarded their training as part of a radical doctrine of physical emancipation and were convinced that they themselves would never have been able to 'do' physical education without the women's movement's achievements. When the physical training colleges were being established women were breaking free of some of the restrictive elements of the Victorian code of behaviour, and the feminist movement was being strongly motivated by the need to provide fit employment for respectable women whose choice of occupation was severely limited. By opening up a new career the physical training colleges played a successful part in a larger effort to draw an increasing number of middle-class women into the public sphere. 'In a sense', Fletcher says, 'the gymnasts were responding to the same call which led women to sit on School Boards or undertake a professional involvement in philanthropy.'[47]

Although by 1914 the world of women's physical education was small and rather closed, and inbred and resistant to change, its success was nothing short of spectacular. Physical training had become well-established as a suitable, enjoyable and remunerative occupation. While most educators of boys clung stubbornly to games and a form of military drill, a few exceptional women had brought a combination of energy and enthusiasm, integrity and single-mindedness to the spread of knowledge about health and fitness among girls. By creating an institutional complex in which teaching was 'scientific', they repudiated the idea that it was enough for a physical educator to have been good at games, and conveyed the view that physical education was a serious subject. At the same time, they did so remarkable a job of convincing the heads of girls' secondary schools of the necessity of therapeutic gymnastics to the production of health and beauty — and thus of hiring their own products — that physical education based on Swedish gymnastics had become an integral and important aspect of the secondary school curriculum.

Women such as Martina Bergman-Osterberg and Margaret Stansfeld may not have been ideal role models. Their autocracy and rigidity were at odds with their averred liberalism; and in attempting to mediate role changes that marked the transition in girls from dependent ladies into responsible women they themselves became almost sexless. Furthermore, while their pioneering work gave the physical education profession its impetus, it isolated it from the mainstream of educational and academic thought and ignored the essential dullness of the Ling system and the need for change and flexibility. It also ordained the separation of the sexes that characterised the history of physical education in Britain for over half a century and that, when it began to break down, resulted in the female specialists losing their head start and positions of responsibility. All thing considered, however, the increasing attention paid to physical education was one of the important changes affecting the lives of women in the late-nineteenth century. The rise of the physical education mistress and institutions to train her represented the concession to women of a right to a degree of body control and to a respectable, well-paying career. The physical education profession attracted intelligent and idealistic women who were enterprising and plucky enough to seek training in a vocation for which there was no precedent and which ran counter to a number of conventions of the time. It provided powerful examples to generations of English schoolgirls who idolised their 'gym' mistresses; and it offered its practitioners a combination of economic and physical emancipation which heightened their own and the public's consciousness of the dignity and potential of the female sex.

Notes

1. *Anstey Physical Training College Magazine* (Christmas 1907), pp. 29–30.

2. McIntosh, *Physical Education*, pp. 11–12, 140–1.

3. Oswald Holmberg, *Per Henrik Ling* (c. 1922), pp. 12–13.

4. Mathias Roth, *The Prevention and Cure of Many Chronic Diseases by Movement* (London, 1851), pp. v–xvi; T.J. Surridge, 'Mathias Roth — Spokesman for Ling's Gymnastic System', *Physical Education Year Book* (1973–4), pp. 10–11. Roth served as an advisor to the Girls' Public Day School Company.

5. Archibald MacLaren, 'Girls' Schools', *Macmillan's Magazine*, vol. 10 (September 1864), pp. 414–15; Archibald MacLaren, *A System of Physical Education, Theoretical and Practical* (Oxford, 1869), pp. 36–8, 77.

6. Franz Bernard, *The Physical Education of Young Ladies* (London, 1860).

7. Lucie Brenner, *Gymnastics for Ladies* (London, 1870).

8. James Chiosso, *Gymnastics, An Essential Branch of National Education, Both Public and Private* (London, 1854), pp. 33–4.

9. Alexander Alexander, *Healthful Exercise for Girls*, 5th edn (London, 1896); Alexander Alexander and Mrs Alexander, *British Physical Education for Girls* (London, c. 1907); Nicholas A. Parry, 'Pioneers of Physical Education in the Nineteenth Century: Mr. Alexander Alexander', *Physical Education Review*, vol. 2, no. 1 (1979), pp. 11–24.

10. Mrs Stuart Snell, 'Gymnastics for Girls: Their Use and Abuse', *Journal of Education* (1 November 1892), pp. 577–8. See also 'Gymnastics and Musical Drill at Alexandra House', *Journal of Education* (1 April 1889), p. 209.

11. One such was Sandow's Gymnasium in London, the proprietor of which, Eugene Sandow, was a professional gymnast and physical culture faddist, who promoted a system of exercise emphasising chest and abdominal development for purposes of child-bearing. See *Physical Culture* (1898–1901).

12. Fletcher, *Women First*, pp. 19–20.

13. Madame Bergman-Osterberg, quoted in *Woman's Herald* (20 June 1891), p. 547.

Information on Martina Bergman-Osterberg and her physical training colleges was derived primarily from 'Life and Work of Madame Osterberg', *Journal of Scientific Physical Training*, vol. 8 (Autumn 1915), pp. 14–17; 'Madame Bergman-Osterberg's Physical Training College', *Educational Review* (November 1896), pp. 24–6; Sybil C. Mitford, 'A

Physical Culture College in Kent', *Girl's Realm*, vol. 1 (April 1899), pp. 55–60; Arthur Montefiore, 'The Physical Education of Girls', *Educational Review* (March 1892), pp. 280–6; Fletcher, *Women First*, pp. 20–41; McIntosh, *Physical Education*, pp. 288–93; Jonathan May, *Madame Bergman-Osterberg* (London, 1969); and from the following archival material: Kingsfield Book of Remembrance; miscellaneous addresses and publications by Martina Bergman-Osterberg; prospectuses and reports (1895–1914); Scrapbook of College History (1881–1915).

14. Bergman-Osterberg believed a supervised regime of Swedish exercise could relieve anaemia , chronic constipation, dyspepsia, emphysema, foot deformities, heart disease, joint infections, knock knees, nervous diseases, paralysis, rheumatism, spinal curvature and writer's cramp.

15. Martina Bergman-Osterberg, 'Gymnastics and Games', *Teachers' Encyclopaedia* (1911), pp. 215–16.

16. For information on dress at Dartford and other physical training colleges see Chapter 8.

17. Fees were 33 guineas per term for residents and 10 guineas for non-residents. In 1898 the enrolment was about 30, and in 1915, about 65, while fees by 1914 were 108 guineas a year, which was comparable with those at Girton and Newnham.

18. Fletcher, *Women First*, pp. 51–4; May, *Bergman-Osterberg*, pp. 77–8; J.H. Wickstead, 'The Early Days and Development of the Ling Physical Education Association', *Journal of Physical Education and School Hygiene*, vol. 29 (1937), p. 156.

For several decades the Ling Association guarded the purity of Swedish gymnastics and assured that members of the physical training profession would be strictly recruited. Graduates of other physical education colleges were soon admitted, providing their training had been purely Swedish; and in 1904 the association began conducting examinations and issuing diplomas. Dartford students could not join until 1919.

19. Bergman-Osterberg Physical Training College, Reports of Trustees (1915–17); 'Life and Work', *Journal of Scientific Physical Training* (Autumn 1915), pp. 14–17; May, *Bergman-Osterberg*, pp. 110–11.

20. Martina Bergman-Osterberg, 'Women in Education', report presented to the International Conference of Women (1899), p. 188; Bergman-Osterberg, 'Gymnastics and Games', *Teachers' Encyclopaedia* (1911), pp. 211–14; Madame Bergman-Osterberg, *On Physical Training as a Profession* (London, 1899), p. vi; Martina Bergman-Osterberg, 'The Training of Teachers in Methods of Physical Education' (n.d), pp. 1–13; 'A Chat with Madame Bergman-Osterberg', *Spinning Wheel* (24 February 1894), p. 404; *Woman's Herald* (20 June 1892), p. 547.

Bergman-Osterberg's conservatism on the subject of overstrain was demonstrated by the fact that Dartford — like the other physical training colleges — reduced the length of hockey matches from 35 minute halves to 25–30 minutes as a result of a fear that exhaustion could have permanent 'evil effects'.

Her feminism was manifested by her unusual marriage. In 1886 Martina Bergman married Dr Edwin Osterberg, a professor at the University of Uppsala and later the head of a secondary school. She took her husband's name only in a hyphenated combination with her own, and during most of their married life the two lived and worked apart. With regard to the question of the vote, she was not active in the suffrage campaign in England, but contributed generously to that in Sweden.

21. *Girls' School Year Book* (1906), p. 262.

22. Information on the Chelsea College of Physical Training was derived primarily from Ida Webb, 'The History of Chelsea College of Physical Education', unpublished PhD thesis, University of Leicester, 1977, and from the following archival material: *Chelsea College of Physical Training, 1898–1958* (1958); miscellaneous addresses and articles by and about Dorette Wilke and about the Chelsea Physical Training College.

Dorette Wilke was known as 'Fraulein' until 1914, when anti-German feeling aroused by war prompted her to become a British citizen and change her name to Wilkie, after which she was called 'Domina'.

23. The fees in 1902 were twelve guineas a term for day students, which was sufficient to guarantee a middle-class clientele but of lower status than at Dartford. Chelsea, in fact, was the least socially exclusive of the physical training colleges, and even had students with Cockney accents who Wilke advised to arrange elocution lessons as soon as possible.

Wilke died in 1930, three years before the first diplomas in the theory and practice of physical education were awarded by London University. The first degree course in physical education began at Birmingham University in 1946.

24. *Woman at Home*, vol. 9 (April–September 1900), p. 778.

25. *Journal of Scientific Physical Training*, vol. 1 (October 1908), quoted in Sheila Fletcher, 'The Making and Breaking of a Female Tradition: Women's Physical Education in England 1880–1980', *British Journal of Sports History*, vol. 2, no. 1 (1985), p. 34.

The British College, the Gymnastic Teachers' Institute and the National Society were rival organisations that trained or examined mainly board school teachers. They aimed to develop a British system of gymnastics, but were actually German oriented. The *Journal of Scientific Physical Training* propagated the Swedish faith in preference to any other, and gave a forum for discussion to the men and women who taught physical education without the training of the new female specialists. Its first editor was Mrs E. Adair Impey, a Dartford graduate who was an instructor at Chelsea. McIntosh, *Physical Education*, pp. 163–4.

26. Dorette Wilke, 'The Effect and Influence of Physical Training', an address to the English Educational Exhibition, London (27 January 1900).

27. 'Interview with Fraulein Wilke on Gymnastic Teachers' Training Colleges', *Women at Home* (n.d.).

28. *Anstey Physical Training College Magazine* (Christmas 1907), p. 3; Rhoda Anstey, 'Anstey College for Physical Training and Hygiene', *Child* (July 1912), p. 875.

29. *Anstey Physical Training College Magazine* (1904), p. 3. See also Colin Crunden, *A History of Anstey College of Physical Education 1897–1972* (Birmingham, 1974), p. 8.

30. *Anstey Physical Training College Magazine* (Summer Term 1905), p. 3.

31. Anstey shared the Lingian confidence in Swedish gymnastics' remedial value in treating everything from spinal curvature, round shoulders, flat chests, chronic bronchitis, neurasthenia, chronic

constipation, obesity and intercostal neuralgia, to asthma, emphysema and 'imperfect development'. Because a greater emphasis was placed on medical gymnastics and massage than at the other physical training colleges, Anstey graduates were particularly inclined to start their own remedial clinics.

32. Crunden, *Anstey College*, p. 5.

33. *Anstey Physical Training College Magazine* (Summer Term 1905), pp. 3, 21; Crunden, *Anstey College*, p. 7.

34. *Anstey Physical Training College Magazine* (Christmas 1910), pp. 10–11.

35. Information on the Bedford Physical Training College was derived from Fletcher, *Women First*, pp. 42–73, and from the following archival material: Students' Association Minutes and Reports (1910–14); taped and written reminiscences of Old Students; *Margaret Stansfeld* (Bedford, 1953).

36. Molly Evans (1904–6), Ida Hadley (1903–5), Freda Colwill Holroyd (1913–15), D.P. Payne (1902–5), Phyllis Spafford (1908–10), taped and written reminiscences.

37. H.M. Neild (1905–7), written reminiscences. See also Bedford Physical Training College Students' Association, Report (1911), p. 2 and Minutes (4 August 1910).

38. Freda Young (1902–5), written reminiscences; Fletcher, *Women First*, pp. 56–7, 67.

39. *Girls' School Year Book* (1906), p. 262.

40. Ibid., p. 264. In addition to Dartford, Chelsea, Anstey and Bedford, there were physical training colleges in Liverpool and Dunfermline, Scotland. The former was founded in 1900 by Irene Marsh who trained in German gymnastics at the Southport Physical Training College, Birkdale, Lancashire, in the 1890s under Alexander Alexander. The Liverpool curriculum included musical drill, but was basically Swedish; and at a cost of 60 guineas a year it involved a two year course designed to supply teachers for girls' schools and clubs. Marsh shared with her contemporaries a dictatorial streak and a missionary-like desire to develop not only physical prowess but personality, character and creativity. Dunfermline was established by the Carnegie Trust in 1905 under the direction of a Chelsea Old Student who soon gave way to a Dartfordian. A small men's section was introduced in 1908, and the college eventually split into two single sex institutions.

Besides the men's section at Dunfermline, from 1908 to 1912 there was a one year course for men at the South-Western Polytechnic, Chelsea, and that was all until 1933 when the first men's physical training college opened in Leeds. J.G. Dixon, P.C. McIntosh, A.D. Munrow and F.F. Willetts, *Landmarks in the History of Physical Education* (London, 1957), pp. 198, 206; Fletcher, *Women First*, pp. 4, 40, 54.

41. Fletcher, *Women First*, p. 5. See also Fletcher, 'Making and Breaking', pp. 29–39.

42. Ibid., pp. 4–5; May, *Bergman-Osterberg*, p. 127.

43. Atkinson, 'Fitness . . . and Schooling', p. 98; A.E. Hendry, 'Social Influences upon the Early Development at Physical Education in England', *Journal of Physical Education*, vol. 61, no. 183 (1969), pp. 18–19.

44. *Punch* (11 April 1906), p. 261.

45. Fletcher, *Women First*, pp. 155–6.

46. Paul Atkinson, 'Strong Minds and Weak Bodies: Sports, Gymnastics and the Medicalization of Women's Education', *British Journal of Sports History*, vol. 2, no. 1 (1985), p. 70.

47. Fletcher, *Women First*, p. 55. See also Holroyd, taped reminiscences; Crunden, *Anstey College*, pp. 60–1.

5

For the Sake of the Team: Hockey, Lacrosse and Cricket

Tell me not in falt'ring accents
   'Hockey's but a game for men',
True enough, 'twould shock our grand-dames,
   But ideas have changed since then.[1]

The legitimation of physical activities for schoolgirls and college women was a major factor in the development of women's sport in the late-nineteenth century. 'But the acceptance of games playing by adult women was not so easily achieved.'[2] It was acceptable for females to play games at school, but after school they were expected to 'become true graceful women ready to be good wives and mothers — not existing merely for the next hockey match'.[3] In the adult environment, cultural patterns regarding appropriate gender-specific activities were more rigorously enforced, and this meant considerable disapproval of women's playing team games on several grounds: they were 'seldom wholesome and always unbecoming'; they were 'freakish' and frivolous; they would deplete the energy required for 'racial regeneration', particularly of women employed outside the home; and they were potentially subversive to the integrity of sport and women's proper sphere. The result was that most women left their playing days behind them upon completion of their education. Indeed, most probably never even realised that they had a choice.

At the same time, however, middle-class women were urged with increasing frequency to abandon idleness and to use their leisure time constructively; and as the number of sporting pursuits available to them expanded, they and public opinion in general became prepared to accept their doing so in physically active ways.

A prominent characteristic of English gentlemen was the retention of an interest in sport after leaving school or university, and the formation of clubs to facilitate continued play and associations within deliberately restricted social and spatial zones. Likewise, albeit to a much lesser extent, from the 1880s a number of women refused to forego the pleasure of continuing to play games when their school days were over; and despite the male conviction that women lacked the ability to form, run or enjoy clubs, they began to emulate male models and to participate in the organisational process that characterised sport in general, by establishing sports clubs of their own through which they hoped to enjoy healthy exercise and congenial companionship. The first such clubs were for hockey.

Hockey began to assume its modern form in the 1880s with the establishment of a number of men's clubs and the creation of a national governing body — the Hockey Association (1886) — which quickly organised and regularised the game under a definitive code of rules, but failed to develop it into a major male activity. At public schools hockey was often regarded as effeminate and fit only for malingerers, so it never acquired the grandeur or overt masculinity of cricket and football. Thus, when women took it up, they were not perceived necessarily as trespassing on a sacred manly preserve.

The first private women's hockey club — the Molesey Ladies' Hockey Club — was founded in 1887. Why and by whom remain a mystery, as does the identity of the club's opponents, for the game was not yet played seriously at colleges or public schools. During the 1888–9 season clubs also appeared in Ealing and Wimbledon; and in the years immediately thereafter, while no more private clubs were formed, hockey spread rapidly in educational institutions. Simultaneously a playful form, involving mixed teams with light sticks and tennis balls, became fashionable as a country-house and holiday game played on private grounds.[4]

Meanwhile, the game was progressing among women in Ireland. In 1892 a club started at Alexandra College, Dublin, and two years later its members boldly formed an Irish Ladies' Hockey Union. Later the same year the Alexandra ladies invited a team of Newnhamites to play in Ireland during the Christmas holidays; and although the English women failed to win a single match, they returned home eager to form an association of their own and an England team for official international competition. Contacts with private and college clubs produced a lukewarm response on the grounds that the proposals were too bold, but they went ahead anyway and attempted to assemble as good a national team as possible. In March 1895 try-outs were held on the ground of Madame Bergman-Osterberg's Hampstead Physical Training College at Neasden, following which the possibility of an association was discussed informally. Two weeks later 'England' played Ireland to a scoreless draw on a ground in Brighton.

Afterwards those players who favoured a national organisation met in a local tea-shop and proceeded to elect a provisional slate of officers and adopt the rules of the Hockey Association. The following November representatives of Roedean School, Girton, Newnham, Somerville, Royal Holloway and Bedford Colleges, and the East Molesey, Columbines and Croft Ladies' Clubs convened the first formal meeting of what they called the Ladies' Hockey Association (LHA) in the Westminster Town Hall. When Eleanor Sidgwick of Newnham refused the presidency, Lilian Faithfull, at the time head of the Ladies' Department, King's College, London, was elected. Christabel Lawrence of Roedean became the first secretary and E.G. Johnson of the Molesey Ladies the first England captain despite the fact that a genuine national team did not yet exist.[5]

Though it was little more than a company of friends, the LHA, with all the audacity and naivety of extreme youth, immediately applied to the Hockey Association for affiliation. The latter's curt and disdainful refusal, on the grounds that its interest was solely in men's clubs, was fateful, for it meant that women's hockey would develop entirely on the initiative of women. Deeply wounded by the men's rebuff, the hockey pioneers resolved to push ahead on their own and established a principle still extant — that no man could hold an executive office in the LHA or any of its affiliates. The following year, in a controversial move designed to emphasise seriousness of purpose, they dropped the term 'Ladies' from their association's name in favour of a new designation — the All England Women's Hockey Association.[6]

Under the leadership of the AEWHA, women's hockey made rapid strides and developed a structure that endured. School and college teams, the association's early backbone, were joined by more and more private ladies' clubs; and the association immediately got involved in setting standards, making rules, establishing regulations about membership in the association and its council, fixing subscription fees, selecting an England team, setting international match dates, compiling fixture lists, selling tickets, trying to solve the problem of cancellation of games and practices because players failed to show up, and much more. An initial reluctance to get involved in county hockey was quickly overcome by a desire to retain initiative and to control every aspect of the women's game. When county clubs not only formed but moved towards creating their own association, the AEWHA intervened in 1898 and formulated regulations for the creation of county and territorial associations and for county matches that immediately proved to be the most exciting form of hockey and the one inspiring the keenest competition for team places. And hockey took on a genuinely British dimension when national associations were established in Wales (1898) and Scotland (1900).

During the next 15 years the AEWHA continued to expand into an extensive and efficient network of five territorial and 36 county associations, over 300 school, college and private clubs, and matches at every level including the international.[7] It even established an official journal, in response to arguments that a medium of communication was needed to link the national organisation with its members, encourage competition at all levels, facilitate an exchange of views and chronicle activities.

The inaugural issue of the *Hockey Field*, the first periodical devoted entirely to women's sport, appeared in October 1901, declaring as its aim 'to promote the best interests of the game and bring lady players into closer contact, by providing them with interesting, instructive and amusing reading'.[8] The latter included fixture lists, match results, correspondence, reports from the association, territories, counties and clubs, reports on distinguished players, hockey poems and advertisements for physical training colleges, gymnasia and sports equipment. The journal was an immediate success, and earned a well-deserved reputation for promoting unity and increasing *esprit de corps* and good fellowship.

Most of the AEWHA's operations were suspended for the duration of the First World War, but clubs continued to play and the *Hockey Field* continued to publish a truncated, morale-boosting version in which readers were encouraged to tackle with fortitude all available war work, work for which 'hockey [had] been instrumental in producing a vast supply of women in the best of condition'.[9]

The phenomenal growth of hockey was one of the major success stories in the early history of women's sport. But it did not occur without considerable controversy, much of it related to the perennial issues of femininity, propriety and female capacities.

The charge — rejected by the AEWHA — that hockey was too rough a game for ladies endured for years. Roughness was not unknown in the women's game, however, particularly in highly competitive situations, and this brought 'grave discredit' on organisation and players. To minimise it the AEWHA stressed the importance of etiquette; urged players to avoid all rude behaviour; and discouraged them from abusing umpires and from shouting and deliberately shooting at and knocking down opponents. On occasion when bounds were overstepped, it sent players stiff letters of reprimand and even suspended some.

The question of rules is another example of the clash between liberty and feminine norms. From the first the AEWHA was determined to observe those of the Hockey Association in so far as possible, because it realised that only thus would women's hockey be taken seriously and accorded respect. Not until after the war were rules revised to fit the conception of hockey as a women's game, but before that there were occasional adjustments. The first came in 1907, when, after prolonged discussion, the AEWHA council decided to counter charges that hockey was unladylike and dangerous, and to emulate the example of its Scottish and Irish counterparts, by ruling that 'there shall be no hooking nor striking at sticks'.[10] A storm of controversy immediately developed between those who feared that the prohibition represented the thin end of a softening wedge and an admission that hockey as played by men was unsuitable for women, and their opponents who argued that there was no reason why the rules of the men's and women's games should be identical and that the change would make the latter less rough and risky and more open and quick.

The fears of the strict constructionalists were fuelled further by questions about whether the duration of women's games should be shortened and grounds reduced in size. Revisionists favoured smaller grounds and a reduction in full time from 70 to 60 or even 50 minutes to avoid overtaxing female constitutions to the point that reproductive development and the health of future generations might be jeopardised; and they carried the day at most physical training colleges and schools. The AEWHA on the other hand clung tenaciously to full-sized grounds and full-length matches of two, 35-minute halves, arguing that neither involved the risk of undue strain so long as players were in good condition.

Other controversial areas involved dress,[11] publicity, gate receipts, prizes and sexually and socially mixed play.

Shortly after the AEWHA's foundation, the *Field*, a prominent sportsmen's magazine, offered to publicise women's hockey by printing fixture lists. The respectability of publicity, along with that of playing international matches in public before a paying audience, became extremely controversial when the first international played in England (1897) was not only advertised in advance but supported by spectators' admission fees. The strong negative reaction against the 'unsexed creatures' who had the audacity to play hockey in public prompted the AEWHA to announce that it did not 'countenance advertising by posters in public places, or in newspapers', and would take 'no further steps to facilitate particular journalists in writing about women's hockey'.[12] After Royal Holloway College's continued dissatisfaction with the association's handling of the advertising and gate receipts issues resulted in its resignation in the autumn of 1898, the AEWHA attempted to restrict the gate, to the point of virtually picking and choosing spectators, by resolving

> . . . [in order] to protect the game from 'roughs' and other undesirable spectators, that tickets for international matches be obtained by members free beforehand from secretaries of clubs, non-members obtaining tickets before the day paying one shilling only if their application is accompanied by a member's card, and two shillings and six pence at the gate only if accompanied by a ticket holder or on the production of the card of a member.[13]

The resolution was probably unnecessary since the attitude of male spectators was changing quickly from antagonistic to curious to quietly interested; but it had the desired effect of assuaging the feelings of most conservatives and ensuring — without reducing their size — that crowds were primarily female.[14]

The publicity issue was also behind the AEWHA's prohibition against members engaging in cup and prize competitions. The subject arose in 1898 when the *Ladies' Field*, a popular magazine highly supportive of women's sport, offered a challenge cup worth 20 guineas to be competed for annually at the discretion of the association. Although not all clubs agreed, the association considered such competition demeaning and likely to provoke resignations. Players, it believed, should seek rewards only in maintaining standards of play and their positions on a first XI. It thus not only rejected the offer but confirmed its antipathy to 'pot-hunting' by resolving that any affiliated association or club — apart from those in schools and colleges — competing for cups or in prize competitions would be deemed guilty of misconduct and expelled.

The debate on publicity continued for years. Critics insisted that it was not 'nice' for ladies to make a public spectacle of themselves by playing athletic games before large crowds; that this was contrary to the true spirit of recreation; that no woman looked good playing hockey; and that journalistic reports would confirm people's prejudices. Supporters, on the other hand, recognised publicity's potential to help women's hockey become first class by promoting a healthy public interest in the game, preventing abuses and encouraging improved play.

Still another contentious issue was the propriety of mixed hockey, by sex and class, even though there was little of either. Matches involving both sexes were played occasionally, in rural districts where there were insufficient men and women for single-sex teams, mostly for fun on country-house lawns and by a handful of mixed clubs. Proponents of a serious version held that men were useful to women as coaches and that mixed hockey would lead to a higher standard, for it would make men play more scientifically and women with greater speed, pluck and endurance. The AEWHA officially discouraged the mixed game, however, arguing along with other opponents that each sex played better alone; that mixed hockey put women at risk for men could run much faster and hit much harder; that women who played with men were much more concerned with their appearance than performance and with matrimonial rather than hockey goals; and that the mixed game was but a burlesque of the real thing.

As for social mixing, prior to 1914 most female hockey players, like women in sport in general, came from the affluent middle classes. Practices and matches were during the day in mid-week, which excluded working women; and club subscription fees and the cost of uniforms and travel to matches were an additional guarantee of class distinction. When the AEWHA was founded, clubs were snobbish and socially exclusive. There were no businesswomen's or working-girls' clubs of any kind; and while there was nothing in the AEWHA constitution regarding social differentiation, for years it made little effort to breach class barriers. A letter to the *Hockey Field* in 1907 recalled an attempt to introduce into a ladies' club a skilled player whose father had been in trade, that failed because several members thought themselves above playing with a tradesman's daughter.[15]

By then, however, there were signs that 'the game was passing from a sociable pastime for those with plenty of leisure to be an enterprise, a recreation and an enthusiasm for those working for a living',[16] for it was beginning to be played in schools for less well-to-do girls and by clubs formed in factories and offices in Midland and northern communities. In areas where there were insufficient players to support separate clubs of different social standing, the question of amalgamation arose. The *Hockey Field* recommended union, and spoke of hockey's power to mix women of all sorts by providing them with a common interest. But among ladies' clubs the idea received a cool reception despite assurances that players need not socialise off the field. Working-class clubs, most of which were organised by men, thus went their own way.

In 1910 a Ladies' Hockey League was created in Oldham, which provided regular matches on Saturday afternoons for the points and cups that were taboo to the AEWHA. Within three years it had 36 teams and four divisions; and despite its disavowing a desire to interfere with the older association, the AEWHA became worried and made belated and unsuccessful attempts to persuade working-girls' clubs to affiliate and its own members to accept them. A match between Lancashire of the AEWHA and the Ladies' Hockey League's premier team in 1914 produced an easy Lancashire victory, and served only to confirm the older association's condescending conviction that working girls had much to learn about hockey — as about life — from their social superiors.[17]

Thanks largely to the efforts of the AEWHA, hockey was the paramount winter team game for adult middle-class women by 1914; and it was considered of sufficient importance to warrant occasional coverage in *The Times*. But the 'hockey girl' remained so modern a product that the public still did not know quite what to make of her or whether hockey was safe and genteel. With a few notable exceptions — such as Mrs Lambert Chambers, the tennis champion who played hockey for Ealing and Middlesex, and Mrs Somerville and Mrs Heron Maxwell, who were presidents of the AEWHA from 1910 to 1912 and 1912 to 1923 respectively — the vast majority of players and administrators were single. Most women, however skilled and enthusiastic, relinquished the pleasures of hockey upon engagement or marriage, for as a team game it was considered incompatible with the traditional images and duties of a respectable matron. The letter from a Miss Chamberlain to the AEWHA in April 1899 announcing her marriage and consequent retirement from hockey and the AEWHA council spoke volumes.[18]

Long after women were playing hockey by the thousands the question of whether their doing so was ladylike and safe remained an issue. In the early days the pioneers had to tolerate being called 'unsexed Amazons' and told that hockey was too dangerous for females by people who had never even seen a match; and their successors had to endure similar criticisms from 'old fogies', such as G.K. Chesterton, who remarked sardonically, 'Let women play violent and confused games if you think it will do them any good to be violent and confused.'[19]

The arguments were repeated for years, by members of both sexes, that hockey was so violent and exhausting that it would damage women emotionally, physically and morally, that its

> . . . strenuous nature . . . as in all cases where keen physical rivalry takes place, produces angularities, hardens sinews, abnormally develops certain parts of the body, causes abrasions, and at times disfigurement. It thus destroys the symmetry of mould and beauty of form, produces large feet and hard, coarse hands. Its fierce excitement destroys the serene, tranquil beauty of the features, and its spasmodic climax is most injurious to the fine, keen nervous temperament of women.[20]

It was a woman who asserted that 'only the few square, squat, and burly outdoor porter type of girls should play . . . [the] rough, competitive' game of hockey, which, 'with its muddy field, rush and excitement, for the unformed, untrained or nervous girl is surely unadulterated lunacy';[21] and it was a schoolgirl who observed that hockey made women 'mannish' and neglectful of their domestic duties and just the 'detestable' sort likely to become suffragettes.[22]

Fortunately for the future of women's hockey, criticisms were vastly outnumbered by expressions of support. Proponents argued that it made little sense to assert that hockey was unfitted for women when thousands had taken it up without physical or psychological damage. Females needed wholesome, healthy recreation as much as males, and hockey playing was a natural way to acquire it, they insisted. If rules were observed and proper care taken, the risk of injury was slight, and in any event taking a few knocks and bruises provided good training in co-operation, endurance and self-reliance, and developed in players a range of desirable traits that would contribute to a general improvement of the national character.

> To sink one's identity, become a docile unit in a composite whole; to wear a uniform, obey orders unhesitatingly, accept reproofs becomingly and praise modestly, to be diligent in practice, careful in health, punctual in attendance — all constitute a discipline which if pursued, will be found useful in many affairs of life of even greater importance than hockey . . . for hockey like all our national sports and pastimes is much more than a mere form of general exercise.[23]

Rather than masculinising women, supporters argued, hockey produced splendid specimens of English womanhood, who were beautiful in form and graceful in movement and possessed of the qualities necessary in a helpful wife and prudent, discerning mother.

Considering women's 'total ignorance of any other game of combination',[24] they picked up hockey with surprising quickness. By 1914 women's hockey had established its right to an honourable place in the history of the sport, and it was acknowledged, even in male circles, to have far outstripped the growth of the game among men. The sport had changed greatly from a game in which players were criticised quite rightly for dribbling too much, passing too little, moving too slowly, shooting too feebly, playing too timidly, being short on initiative and tactics and using their skirts to stop balls. As experience was gained, coaching and grounds improved and dress rationalised, the women's game became more rapid and tactical. The view remained general that it was inferior to the men's, because 'no girl can expect to rival men in pace, clean hitting and clever stick work'.[25] But there were some quarters in which it was actually considered more accurate, scientific and interesting to watch, and in which it was argued that a first-class women's XI was very little if at all inferior to a men's. More importantly, some even expressed the real wisdom that the sex's differences in temperament and physique made it inevitable that the two games would be different, and hence should not be compared.

By emphasising the grace and femininity of female hockey players, supporters compromised with social norms; and these norms seemed to be confirmed by women's pronounced reluctance to become involved in coaching and umpiring, perhaps because, at the same time as they were confident of their ability to play a man's game and run their own organisation, they still hesitated to challenge too far his right to monopolise decision-making positions and those involving judgement. Simultaneously, however, the very existence of female players represented defiance and rebellion.

To call women's hockey a feminist activity would be to distort the truth, for pioneers played the game for its own sake, not for any cause. Hockey nevertheless had a powerful feminist dimension. 'Born on the crest of a wave of female rebellion and release from restrictions',[26] hockey was recognised at the time as 'part of the great movement in the direction of increased freedom for women to live their own lives'.[27] Hockey was a form of self-expression for early players, some of whom rejoiced in the opportunities the game provided for emancipation from ancient strictures, and saw it as a symbol of the larger game they were playing in the arena of social change. The AEWHA may not have sponsored matches to raise money for suffrage activities or sent delegations to march in suffrage parades, but in the stance it took on rules and on running its own affairs, and in the efficiency and success with which it did so, the association — and women's hockey generally — struck a blow for equality and freedom.

The only game that presented any sort of challenge to hockey was lacrosse, a sport that also began among men but was largely taken over by women and girls.

Lacrosse came to England from Canada about 1867. The first men's clubs were formed in the Manchester, Leeds, Bristol and London areas in 1876 following a series of exhibition matches by touring sides from the Montreal Lacrosse Club and the Caughnawaga Indian Reservation. In 1879 and 1880 several formed the North and South of England Lacrosse Associations; and in 1892, to co-ordinate their activities, they established the English Lacrosse Union. To the distinct advantage of women, however, men's lacrosse failed to become popular.

By the turn of the century lacrosse was beginning to become the major autumn sport at a number of girls' schools. In 1902 the *Hockey Field* recognised it as an excellent game for females, but doubted that it would be played by adult women since it was 'pre-eminently a game for the young'.[28] The first (and for seven years the only) club in England, the Southern Ladies' Lacrosse Club, was formed in London in 1905 by Old Students from Wycombe Abbey, Roedean and Prior's Field Schools. Its chief opponents were schools such as Roedean and St Leonards, to whom it usually lost. The club's prime mover and captain was Audrey Beaton, an Old Roedeanian who collected the names and addresses of women who wanted to continue to play lacrosse, in an effort to keep them in touch with the game and encourage them to establish clubs throughout the country. By 1912 the only concrete result was the formation of a club in Edinburgh; but as a result of the Southern Ladies' growth to 50 members, two teams and a professional instructor, Beaton's ambitions remained strong.

In April 1912, on the initiative of Beaton and the Southern Ladies' Club, a Ladies' Lacrosse Association (LLA) was launched, involving schools, physical training colleges and polytechnics as well as the ladies' club. Roedeanians were particularly prominent. Penelope Lawrence, the headmistress of Roedean, was chosen president; Margaret Stansfeld of the Bedford Physical Training College was vice-president and Audrey Beaton, honorary secretary. A further meeting the following July established administrative procedures and powers, and audaciously, considering the dearth of clubs, discussed rules for international, territorial and county matches. In addition it restricted membership in the association to schools and clubs composed entirely of amateurs, an amateur being defined as 'one who does not play for money or who is not directly interested in the sale of athletic implements or outfits';[29] and, after the fashion of the AEWHA, it ruled that no members of the LLA were to participate in any prize competitions except those connected with educational institutions.

The formation of the LLA provided an immediate impetus to a growth of interest in the game, and by the end of the first season membership had risen from 20 to 70 schools and colleges plus seven clubs.[30] In March 1913, 31 aspirants, most of whom were school games mistresses, tried out for the first England team; and the following month the team easily defeated Scotland and Wales in the first international series, which was played at the Richmond cricket ground before a crowd of over 100 comprised mainly of women players. The next year the same result occurred in the same place before 400 'eager and excited' spectators, including large parties from the Dartford and Bedford Physical Training Colleges. Press reports credited the internationals with increasing the popularity of lacrosse and demonstrating that, although lacrosse as a women's sport was still in its infancy, it was a dignified endeavour in which many women were becoming proficient.

By 1914, although clubs were few and there were still no county or territorial matches or associations, the LLA listed 100 schools and colleges playing the game. It took considerable satisfaction from the fact that a few schools such as Wycombe Abbey had completely dropped hockey in lacrosse's favour, and that the association's efforts to arrange matches, encourage new clubs, help Old Girls to play after school and bring lacrosse players together in different districts were having considerable success.

From the first, the history of women's lacrosse differed somewhat from that of hockey. Unlike hockey, which spread from colleges to schools, lacrosse started in schools and spread upward and outward. Unlike hockey, too, the men's and women's lacrosse associations quickly established cordial relations. Female lacrosse players had no hesitation in crediting 'men players [with having] done much to encourage ladies to take up the game and their coaching [with having] raised the standard of play'.[31] The honorary secretary of the English Lacrosse Union helped the LLA draw up the first standardised set of rules for women's play, which, unlike those of hockey, assured a much milder form of the game than was played by men. The ladies' field was smaller, although how much smaller was not immediately specified; their game was limited to 30- rather than 45-minute halves; body contact and checking were almost entirely outlawed as unsuitable for ladies; goal crease shooting was banned in order to allow goalies more freedom from attack in their own territory; and to stop attackers barging through their opponents' defence by dint of sheer weight, guarding of crosses with arms was prohibited.

A number of women played both hockey and lacrosse at school and college, and a number, such as E.R. Clarke, a mistress at Roedean and then Dartford, pursued both sports afterwards at the club and international level. Some people insisted that hockey and lacrosse were fine, robust games that could be played side by side by women. But just as there were major differences in the attitudes and activities of the governing bodies of the two sports, there were major differences of opinion among each game's supporters as to which was the superior, and there were suspicions that each group intended to woo away the other sport's players.

This was particularly true among hockeyists, whose fears that the novelty of lacrosse would usurp hockey's pride of place as the favourite game of English schoolgirls — and thus of adult women — were fuelled when a few schools abandoned hockey completely. In defence they insisted that hockey was much the superior game because it was safer and more interesting to watch, while lacrosse was innately dull, too strenuous, more dangerous and more difficult to play well.

For their part lacrosse enthusiasts, including some physicians, asserted the opposite: that lacrosse was a superior game for women because its rules were simpler; it was faster, freer, more varied, more beautiful, more skilful, better for deportment, of greater moral value, and healthier and less strenuous and rough since action was almost continuous and the work-load for players was more evenly distributed. Better than any other game, lacrosse stimulated the mind, developed quick judgement and perception and cultivated self-control and unselfishness. Perhaps most important of all, lacrosse required attractive movements and upright posture rather than stooping and slouching, and thus provided exercise which developed all the muscles equally, 'to the advantage not the expense of womanly grace'.[32] In short, as Jane Frances Dove explained:

> Lacrosse is a game which requires the qualities of combination, obedience, courage, individual unselfishness, for the sake of a side . . . and is full of interest on account of the various kinds of skill required, fleetness of foot, quickness of eye, strength of wrist, a great deal of judgement and knack. The game of lacrosse is full of grace and ability. The skill required, moreover, is so great that the attempt to acquire it is a splendid training in courage and perseverance.[33]

What most supporters of lacrosse rarely admitted was that hockey had prepared the way for them. As the older game, it had attracted and successfully resisted the opprobrium of opponents of women's sport. Lacrosse may also have been spared some of the antipathy directed against hockey by the facts that there was no question of mixed lacrosse, even for fun, and that the game's supporters went out of their way to stress its gracefulness, beauty and respectability, and to call their organisation the Ladies' — not the Women's — Lacrosse Association.

By 1914 women's lacrosse was still in its infancy and no serious rival to hockey. The number of clubs for adults remained small and socially exclusive, despite a few efforts to cater for those without free time during the week by arranging matches in London on Saturdays; and the game had yet to become popular in day schools. It was, however, played extensively at boarding schools and physical training colleges and increasingly so in universities; it had a growing number of ladies' clubs and an effective national organisation; it received occasional coverage in the daily papers; and its quality was such that a few supporters who were tied to male standards asserted that some women played a game junior men's teams would find hard to beat.[34]

Unlike hockey and lacrosse, women's cricket had a history that pre-dated the nineteenth century. The first recorded game occurred in 1745 between 'eleven maids of Bramley and eleven maids of Hambleton [who] bowled, batted, ran and catched as well as most men'.[35] For over half a century matches involving females of the rustic set flourished in Sussex, Hampshire and Surrey and were reported on regularly in newspapers and sporting magazines. They usually offered an entertaining spectacle for both participants and the substantial crowds who turned out to watch, and welcome opportunities for betting and to win prizes of cakes, ale and lace.

Village women's cricket continued to be played until the late 1830s, but the good humour with which it had been greeted initially diminished during the early years of the new century. The time and space requirements of the factory system and an increasingly strict moral attitude among the 'better classes', who regarded games-playing among the lower orders as frivolous, non-improving and morally suspect, militated against working-class sport of any kind. In 1838 two teams of Hampshire hay-makers played the last game of cricket for several decades in which women are known to have taken part.

Ladies of the higher classes also were attracted to cricket in the late-eighteenth century, and their matches appear to have been great social occasions. Few were reported publicly, but in 1777 the *Morning Post* commented on a notable one

. . . between the Countess of Derby and some other Ladies of quality and fashion, at the Oaks in Surrey, the rural and enchanting retreat of her ladyship, [during which] Miss

141

> Elizabeth Ann Burrell, sister of [the] first Baron Gwydyr
> . . . achieved undying fame [by getting] more notches . . .
> than any Lady in the game, and Diana-like, creating [so]
> irresistible [an] impression . . . that the eighth Duke of
> Hamilton fell in love with her on the spot and married her
> before the next cricket season.[36]

Afterwards one of the spectators, the third Duke of Dorset, penned the first apologia for women's cricket in which he asked, 'What is human life but a game of cricket? and if so, why should not ladies play it as well as we?', and went on to urge ladies not to worry about hurting their 'delicate hands' or about the 'dreadful apprehensions of demi-men', and to:

> Let your sex go on and assert your right to every pursuit that
> does not debase the mind. Go on, and attach yourselves to
> the athletic, and by that [prove] how worthy you are of being
> considered the wives of plain, generous, and native
> Englishmen![37]

Considering the elegant long dresses, high-heeled shoes and large hats adorned with millinery in which ladies of quality played, their style was much less energetic than that of their socially inferior sisters. Nevertheless, ladies' cricket too disappeared in the early-nineteenth century, since even it was discordant with the evolving ideal of helpless and fragile femininity.

Women's cricket of all sorts thus entered a prolonged slump from which it did not re-emerge until late in the century.

All the while men's cricket was undergoing a metamorphosis, involving changes in equipment and technique, the foundation of clubs, standardisation of rules and establishment of an organisational network of local and county teams — centred on the Marylebone Cricket Club and Lord's Ground — that made it the first major organised sport in England.[38] Furthermore, its evolution at public schools and universities made it much more than a 'mere game' and gave it an almost sacred mystique. Cricket became the sport most closely connected with athleticism and manly virtues. Its rules became synonymous in elite circles with the gentlemen's code of honour, with 'manliness, self-dominion and modesty' and beyond that even with England's racial and imperial supremacy, which explains why, when women took up cricket, they were viewed as trespassing on sanctified territory.

The beginnings of the renaissance of women's cricket date from the 1860s, when occasional references were made to a primitive form of cricket-playing in girl's schools. The first, in 1868 — that 'in a ladies' school near Frome the pupils are allowed to play cricket, and the best cricketers are said to be the best scholars'[39] — accords with a fictionalised account of her own schooldays at the Chantry School, Frome, by Helen Mathers. Her novel, *Comin' Thro' the Rye* (1875), gave a delightful picture of the joy with which schoolgirls took up cricket after having been introduced to it by a local parson. The heroine, Helen Adair, described the blissful feeling of shedding ribbons, gowns and crinolines in favour of knickerbockers and blouses, 'for a time at least, emancipated . . . from the slavish thraldom of our petticoats, and [able to] stretch our limbs and use them'.[40] About the same time girls at a school in Brighton apparently enjoyed games of cricket behind the high walls of their playground, and those from a Clergy Orphans' School, a match at Lord's on Ascension Day in 1876.[41] In the decades thereafter the game was taken up at major girls' schools and at women's university and physical training colleges.

Outside the groves of academe too, from the 1870s there were occasional reports of amusing forms of ladies' and mixed cricket played, as a fashionable and informal garden-party entertainment, among family and friends in the discreet obscurity of country house lawns. Mixed matches offered wonderful opportunities for encounters with the opposite sex, and ladies were advised to 'Get yourself bowled first ball so that you can spend the rest of the time at tea and flirtation with the five fielders who have been withdrawn from the field to give the ladies a chance.'[42] Since the men involved usually played left-handed with broomsticks, and the women were made fun of for such things as their ignorance of the rules, not concentrating, running at the wrong times, throwing wildly and stopping the ball by any means possible, such matches had no serious value and served only to confirm prejudices about women's ignorance and lack of ability.

The all-female version was at first no more serious, but it quickly attracted male attention and stimulated men's innate suspicion of sportswomen in general. Witness Mr Punch's comment, in 1873, on 'Pretty Batswomen':

IRREPRESSIBLE Woman is again in the field. 'Ladies Cricket' is advertised, to be followed, there is every reason to apprehend, by Ladies' Fives, Ladies' Football, Ladies' Golf, etc. It is all over with men. They had better make up their minds to rest contented with croquet, and afternoon tea, and sewing machines, and perhaps an occasional game at drawing-room billiards.[43]

In a similar vein five years later, G.J. Whyte-Melville sarcastically described women's cricket as the thin end of the wedge, and predicted ominously that, 'although in the game of cricket the Graces have as yet been male, at no distant day we may expect to see the best batsman at the Oval bowled out, or perhaps caught by a woman'.[44] Even observers were ridiculed in various journalistic commentaries on the 'hilarious' conversations about cricket supposedly held by female spectators at Lord's.[45] Nevertheless, 'at country houses the ladies' cricket match [became] quite an institution. It is not harder work than lawn tennis, it gives an opportunity for the wearing of some very pretty costumes, and it amuses the other sex'.[46]

It was country-house cricket that changed women's cricket from an amusing spectacle into something more serious and that gave birth, in 1887, to the first female cricket club in England. The White Heather Club — which survived until 1957 — was founded at Nun Appleton in Yorkshire by eight ladies from prominent families, who thought it 'advisable to start a club in consequence of the large amount of cricket at Normanhurst, Glynde and Eridge'.[47] By 1891 it had 50 members – some married, some single and all of independent means and gentle birth – and a uniform consisting of white shirt blouse, long white flannel skirt, pink, white and green tie and boater hat; and by 1895 *Cricket* (the sport's official journal) was able to report, 'The New Woman is taking up cricket, evidently with the same energy which has characterised her in other and more important spheres of life.'[48]

During the next two decades a number of other women's clubs came and went, their members largely being unmarried women from the leisured classes who had learned cricket from their fathers and brothers or perhaps at school and college. At one time or another there were clubs in Shanklin, Southsea, Southport, South Wiltshire, Uxbridge and Clifton, and clubs which went by names like Miss Wetherall's XI and Miss Tuke's XI and the Nausicaa, Tottenham House and St Quentin's Ladies' Cricket Clubs. The latter was connected with the St Quentin's Ladies' Hockey Club, London, and in 1908 it had 14 matches against teams from

Cambridge and London Universities, physical training colleges and other clubs.[49]

In the early-twentieth century women's cricket had a devoted but small following. The game could in no way be called popular, since it was confined primarily to educational institutions where it had fewer adherents than hockey and lacrosse. For every 50 ladies' hockey clubs there was only one cricket club, and there was no county, territorial or national competition or organisation. A proposal for the formation of a women's cricket association as early as 1902 was greeted as premature.[50] In women's cricket even more than in hockey and lacrosse the emphasis remained on preserving as genteel and feminine an air as possible in order to legitimise the intrusion into the most manly of games. On the whole the gentlewomen who played cricket considered it more a healthy break from routine than anything else, and they deliberately reinforced the separate nature of the women's game in order to preserve womanly images.

Paradoxically, however, while their clothing emphasised femininity, equipment and rules were mostly those of men. In 1893 one Richard Daft, who was dubious about women's cricket but willing to give it the benefit of the doubt, advocated a lighter ball, smaller bat and shorter pitch, so 'the game might be played to advantage [and] more wrist and elbow work . . . seen in . . . batting'. Four years later Gamages began making a five-ounce ball especially for ladies, but it did not catch on; and bats remained cumbersome and the pitch often full-size for another three decades.[51]

The most interesting — if aberrational — event in the late-Victorian history of women's cricket was the formation of two teams of lady professionals in 1890, the first such teams in any sport. They were the brainchild of a group of male entrepreneurs, styled the English Cricket and Athletic Association, who anticipated that the growing popularity of women's cricket might be turned to profit, and who, shortly after advertising for players in a number of London newspapers, were able to announce:

> With the object of proving the suitability of the National Game as a pastime for the fair sex in preference to Lawn Tennis and other less scientific games, the English Cricket and Athletic Association Ltd. have organised two complete elevens of female players under the title of 'The Original English Lady Cricketers'.[52]

They went on to give assurances that players would be 'elegantly and appropriately attired', and that every effort would be made to keep the venture 'in all respects select and refined' by hiring a matron to accompany each eleven to all engagements.

The two teams were equipped and dressed by Lillywhite, Frowd and Company, and were known as the Reds and the Blues because of their costumes. Players were 'enterprising and decent' young women from the lower-middle classes, who were likely motivated by a desire to earn some money in an unconventional way and reassured that their reputations were safe by a requirement that they assume pseudonyms. They practised privately on grounds in the London area under the tutelage of two leading male professionals, and then toured the country playing exhibition matches against each other on major grounds before large crowds undoubtedly attracted by the novelty of the spectacle. On the Police Athletic Ground, Liverpool, 15,000 people turned up at a match at Easter to watch a style of play that involved overhand bowling — unusual for women at the time — and was described later by former players as decorous, dignified, serious and of a reasonable standard.

The promoters intended to follow the English tour with one to Australia, but players' parents were unenthusiastic, and in fact the teams disbanded at the end of the first season when the managers absconded with the profits. Thereafter women's cricket was strictly amateur, and so escaped the conflict between amateur and professional that characterised the men's game.

The Original English Lady Cricketers did little to popularise women's cricket. They were looked down upon by the highly respectable lady amateurs, and the whole enterprise was generally regarded as a stunt. As one wag remarked, they might be original and English, but they were neither ladies nor cricketers. On the other hand, although *Cricket* disdainfully ignored them, press comment was surprisingly favourable. The *Illustrated London News* called the Original English Lady Cricketers 'a social novelty illustrative of the disputed notion that women can, may and will do everything quite as well as men'.[53] The *Cricketer's Annual* remarked that, while ladies could never expect to challenge men on anything like equal terms, cricket was not a severe or dangerous exercise and there was no reason why women should not play; and the *Buckinghamshire Examiner*, Chesham, noted that the professional lady cricketers' 'dress has been designed with all possible regard to freedom of movement, and is by no means unbecoming', and that by their steady fielding and precise bowling, both round arm and underhand, they demonstrated that ladies could play cricket very well.[54]

On the whole, however, while opinion on the subject of cricket's suitability for women varied from strongly positive to strongly negative, the latter carried the day.

Proponents of women's cricket, including some male cricketers who took an active interest in the development of the ladies' game, usually assumed that women's physical and emotional disabilities prevented them from ever playing cricket as well as males, but they branded the conviction that females were incapable of performing scientifically and well as unreasonable. They argued that cricket required grace, balance and quickness rather than great strength, that it was less physically damaging than hockey and less morally dangerous than flirtation, and that it would train women's nerves, muscles and character better than any other sport. Even some in the medical profession conceded that cricket need not damage women, were the game and equipment suitably modified.[55]

Positive views notwithstanding, however, it was more common for women's cricket to face strong disapproval. Women on the cricket pitch were laughed at and portrayed as 'freaks' or monstrosities. They were told that cricket 'is absolutely unsuited to the fair sex owing to the number of purely masculine qualities essential to a good cricketer',[56] and that they should stick to games they could play well. They were warned that the structure of the female shoulder blade prevented their bowling overarm properly. They were instructed that their game was a travesty of a noble sport, and that their only legitimate connection with cricket was in the passive capacity of decorative presences who added style and fashion to a crowd of spectators, or as positive influences on their menfolk behind the scenes.[57]

When a case was made at a meeting of the Birmingham Teachers' Association in 1881 for allowing girls to play cricket, the *Birmingham Daily Mail* insisted that women who played men's games would jeopardise their femininity and physical and moral health. In irrational language similar to that used to denounce the idea of a female electorate, it asserted that there were sports which,

. . . though harmless in themselves, are unsuitable for girls. Cricket is essentially a masculine game. It can never be played properly in petticoats . . . If cricket is to become a recognised game at ladies' schools, we can expect football to be introduced, and then single-stick, and no doubt the dear damsels will finish up with boxing . . . the girls of the future will be horney-handed, wide-shouldered, deep-voiced . . . and with biceps like a blacksmith's . . . Let our women remain women instead of entering their insane physical rivalry with men. They can get all the exercise that is necessary for them in games far more suitable to their strength, and far more in accordance with feminine tastes. The line must be drawn somewhere, and it might just as well be drawn this side of those violent athletic pursuits which have hitherto been considered fit only for strong and active young men.[58]

Several years later, after a few women managed to play cricket in a Birmingham suburb, another paper denigrated their efforts as a 'pretty little burlesque', and warned that if they were allowed to continue 'the man of the future will be the stocking-mender, and the children's nurse'.[59] And the *Lancet*, apparently fearing threats to cricket's virile image, began to caution ladies to avoid cricket and to be content with methods of physical improvement in which the dangers of sudden muscular strain and malignancy-producing blows to the breasts were avoided.[60]

Whereas in lacrosse and in hockey — despite the efforts of the AEWHA — the men's and women's games were recognised as of two different kinds, there was only one kind of cricket, that of Lord's and the Oval. The fact that women made no claim to penetrate these meccas was ignored. Cricket was the ultimate national game, and women's efforts to play seriously were regarded as a foolish parody of the real thing that threatened it with desanctification, and more importantly, threatened men's natural right to monopolise athletic power and privilege. Women cricketers were thus instructed that their place was in the home, that games-playing was the special province of men and that it was against their best interests to take up manly games.

If women in substantial numbers were allowed to play most team sports without restriction, it was feared that the sports would be feminised and players masculined, for team activities were thought to develop character traits normally reserved for men.[61] A team game such as netball was highly approved of because it was played only by girls and involved neither body contact nor male participation, and so could be encouraged without 'dangerous' social consequences.[62] On the other hand, hockey and particularly cricket, played by females especially outside sheltered educational settings, were perceived frequently as threats to the separation of the spheres of men and women that predominated in society at large and protected the 'purity' of men's sport.

Just as female university students were regarded as threats to the integrity of the 'learned craft' and the survival of the race, just as a female electorate was portrayed as the thin end of a wedge that would lead to female judges, generals and bishops, so female hockey players and cricketers were presented as degraders of sport and precursors of the intolerable — female boxers and footballers.[63] Although the playing of team games by women had come a long way by 1914, this was the result of compromises with the social system that limited invasions of men's sacred turf and reinforced the separate nature of women's sport in order to preserve feminine and masculine images. Public opinion continued to have grave reservations about the efficacy and femininity of team sports for women and to suspect female players of unwomanly ambitions in other spheres.

Strictly speaking the latter was not the case. The adult women who insisted on playing team games usually were uninterested in feminism, and lacked an expansive vision of the emancipation of women through sport or of themselves as soldiers of 'the cause'. A few women persisted in playing, in the face of familial and public disapprobation, because they realised that it was a form of self-determination and liberation from conventional restrictions, but most did so for the simple reason that games-playing was enjoyable, and they failed to see why they should give it up on leaving school. Whatever their motivations, like their counterparts at schools and colleges, the adult players of hockey, lacrosse and cricket were women who ventured beyond traditional boundaries. They transgressed the image of the dependent female and demonstrated abilities and qualities that mere females had not been suspected of possessing.

Notes

1. *Hockey Field* (22 January, 1903), p. 215.
2. Marie Pointon, 'The Feminine Image' in David McNair and

Nicholas A. Parry (eds), *Readings in the History of Physical Education* (Hamburg, 1981), p. 23.

3. *Hockey Field* (8 December, 1904), p. 117.

4. The Molesey and Ealing Clubs disbanded in the early-twentieth century, but the Wimbledon Club is still in existence and is the oldest women's club in the world. For a number of years some women joined several clubs, an action that was discouraged; and clubs often came and went quickly.

5. *Hockey Field* (6 February, 1902), pp. 264–5; *Ladies' Field* Handbooks, *Hockey Annual* (1900–1), pp. 44–7; Ladies' Hockey Association, Minutes (10 April 1895), (23 November 1895).

The main sources of information on hockey were *Ladies' Field* (1898–1914); J. Nicholson Smith and Philip A. Robson (eds), *Hockey, Historical and Practical* (London, 1899); Edith Thompson, *Hockey as a Game for Women* (London, 1904); Eustace White, *The Complete Hockey Player* (London, 1909); All England Women's Hockey Association, *Women's Hockey from Village Green to Wembley Stadium* (London, 1954); Marjorie Pollard, *Fifty Years of Women's Hockey* (London, 1946); Marjorie Pollard, *Your Book of Hockey* (London, 1959); and the following archival material: *Hockey Field* (1901–14); Ladies' Hockey Association and All England Women's Hockey Association, Minutes (1895–1901).

The first official women's international, between England and Ireland in Dublin, was played in 1896, only a year after the first men's international. In 1902, following considerable discussion, a team comprised largely of members of the King's College (London) Women's Department Hockey Club accepted an invitation from the Haarlem Club to play in Holland. In 1914 an England team went to Australia and New Zealand on its first major tour. In the midst of great success war broke out, and it had a good deal of difficulty getting home.

6. AEWHA, Minutes (20 September, 1896).

7. There were only about half as many men's clubs.

8. *Hockey Field* (17 October, 1901), p. 1. See also AEWHA, Minutes (26 April 1901); Thompson, *Hockey*, pp. 6–7. See also Chapter 9.

9. *Hockey Field* (4 March, 1915), p. 308. See also (22 October, 1914), p. 4.

10. Ibid. (24 October, 1907), pp. 5–6. See also AEWHA, Minutes (23 May 1900).

11. The subject of dress for hockey, lacrosse and cricket is discussed in Chapter 8.

12. AEWHA, Minutes (2 April 1897), (29 April 1898).

13. Ibid. (4 November 1898). See also (8 September 1898).

14. The *Hockey Field* noted that *The Times* estimated — probably overestimated — that a crowd of 5,000–6,000, among which female players and students from girls' schools in the London area predominated, watched England play Scotland at Richmond in 1908. *Hockey Field* (26 March 1908), p. 359.

15. *Hockey Field* (10 January 1907), p. 189.

16. AEWHA, *Women's Hockey*, p. 7.

17. *Hockey Field* (11 January 1912), p. 195, (23 October 1912), p. 12, (8 January 1914), p. 179.

Plate 1: Croquet players, All-England Croquet Club, Wimbledon, 1870 (by permission of the Wimbledon Lawn Tennis Museum)

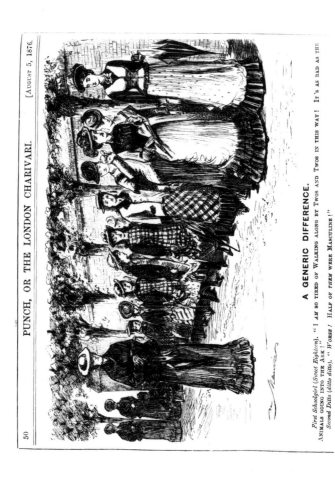

A GENERIC DIFFERENCE.

First Schoolgirl (Sweet Eighteen). "I AM SO TIRED OF WALKING ALONG BY TWOS AND TWOS IN THIS WAY! IT's AS BAD AS THE ANIMALS GOING INTO THE ARK!"

Second Ditto (ditto ditto). "WORSE! HALF OF *THEM* WERE MASCULINE!"

Plate 2: The Crocodile Walk: 'A Generic Difference', 1876 (by permission of *Punch*)

AMENITIES OF THE TENNIS-LAWN.

She. "YOURS OR MINE, SIR CHARLES?"   *He.* "YOURS—AW'FLY YOURS!"   OCTOBER 13, 1883.

Plate 3: 'Amenities of the Tennis-Lawn', 1883 (by permission of *Punch*)

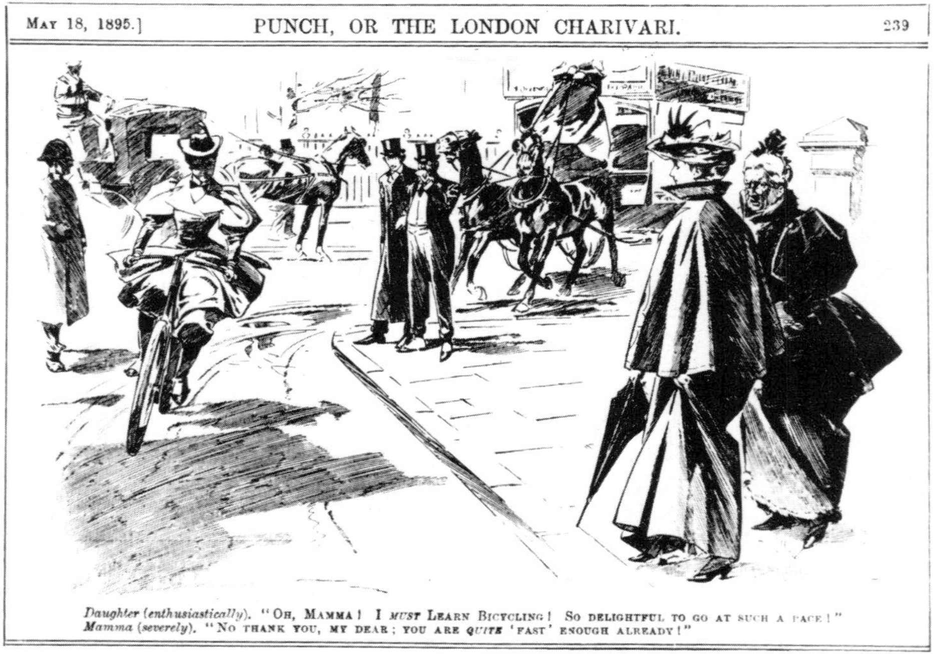
May 18, 1895.]
PUNCH, OR THE LONDON CHARIVARI.
239
Daughter (enthusiastically). "Oh, Mamma! I must Learn Bicycling! So delightful to go at such a pace!"
Mamma (severely). "No thank you, my dear; you are quite 'fast' enough already!"

Plate 4: 'Fast' Lady Cyclist, 1895 (by permission of *Punch*)

Plate 5: 'Past and Present', 1891 (by permission of *Punch*)

Plate 6: The Original English Lady Cricketers, 1890 (by permission of the *Illustrated London News* and Netta Rheinberg)

Plate 7: The East Molesey Ladies' Hockey Club, 1891 (by permission of Marjorie Pollard Publications)

Plate 8: Punting on the River Cherwell, Lady Margaret Hall, c. 1896 (by permission of the Governing Body, Lady Margaret Hall)

Plate 13: Lacrosse match at Lord's, Oxford versus Cambridge, 1914 (by permission of the Governing Body, Lady Margaret Hall)

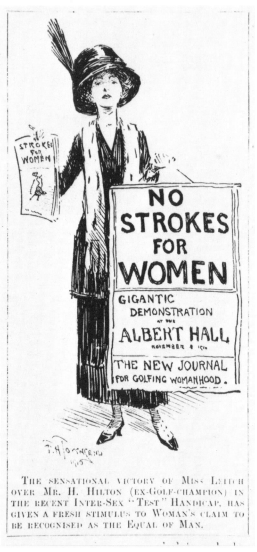

Plate 14: Golf and Votes for Women: 'No Strokes for Women', 1910 (by permission of *Punch*)

The **J.B.** Athletic Girl

THE object of all exercise and athletics for women should be to ensure correct deportment, poise and grace of movement. Moreover, the object of the corset should be to define and interpret these graces.

Model 511. Half-Guinea

Regd. **J.B** SIDE · SPRING
CORSETS

flexible, light, and exquisitely moulded—awaken every grace and charm of motion; they are the complement of form and grace.

¶ *The J.B. Athletic Girl scores artistically.*

OF LEADING DRAPERS EVERYWHERE
J.B. Corset Factories, 15 Fore Street, London, E.C.
SEND FOR STYLE BOOK—POST FREE

SCOTCH-KNITTED
SPORTING
COATS

The "Moray"

NEW SCOTCH KNITTED COAT of "Silkoria," a material with the rich finish of pure silk, but much more durable and less expensive. The coat is well shaped and prettily finished, and can be had in white and all fashionable shades.

Price

35/6

Illustrated Catalogue of Scotch Knitted Coats, priced from 8/11 to 13/6, sent post free on request.

JENNER'S PAY CARRIAGE

JENNER'S
PRINCES STREET EDINBURGH

Plate 15: Advertisements for sporting corsets and coats, 1912 (by permission of the British Library)

18. AEWHA, Minutes (28 April 1899). See also *Hockey* (13 March 1913), p. 444. An awareness of the difficulty attracting married players caused the AEWHA on occasion to sponsor married v. single matches.

19. *Hockey Field* (5 December 1912), p. 116. See also (2 January 1901), p. 191.

20. *Hockey* (13 March 1913), p. 444.

21. *Physical Education*, vol. 2 (October 1905), p. 1.

22. *Hockey Field* (18 February 1909), p. 323.

23. Smith and Robson (eds), *Hockey*, pp. 313, 321.

24. H.F.P. Battersby, *Hockey* (London, 1895), pp. 121–2.

25. *Hockey Field* (5 November 1908), p. 55.

26. Pollard, *Fifty Years*, p. 11.

27. *Hockey Field* (2 January 1902), p. 185. See also Smith and Robson (eds), *Hockey*, p. 313.

28. *Hockey Field* (11 December 1902) p. 115.

Information on lacrosse was derived primarily from *Hockey Field* (1909–14); *Ladies' Field* (1912–14); Kathleen Waldron, 'Lacrosse for Girls', *Girl's Realm*, vol. 5 (November 1902–October 1903), pp. 980–4; and from the following archival material: Ladies' Lacrosse Association, Council Minute Books; newspaper cutting record book.

29. LLA, Minutes (17 July 1912). Martina Bergman-Osterberg became vice-president in 1913. The question of professionalism was premature since there were no professional players at the time. It seems to have arisen because of the possibility of professional coaches and their wanting to play with amateurs.

30. Clubs included Cheltenham, Clifton, Oxfordshire, Manchester, Edinburgh and the Southern Ladies.

The introduction, around the time of the LLA's formation, of short, loosely-strung crosses, instead of the old, heavy, cumbersome models, also facilitated the spread of the game.

31. *Field* (26 April 1913).

32. Ibid. See also C.E. Thomas (ed.), *Athletic Training for Girls* (London, 1912), pp. 72–4.

33. Dove, 'Cultivation of the Body', p. 405.

34. *Hockey Field* (6 February 1913), p. 262; *Pall Mall Gazette* (14 December 1912).

35. *Reading Mercury* (1745), quoted in Nancy Joy, *Maiden Over* (London, 1950), p. 14.

36. *Morning Post* (22 January 1778), quoted in Joy, *Maiden Over*, p. 18.

Information on the history of women's cricket was derived primarily from *Notes and Queries*, 10th series, vol. 11 (15 May 1909), pp. 386–7, vol. 167 (8 September 1934), p. 169; *Sporting Magazine*, vol. 22 (April 1803), p. 13, vol. 39 (October 1811), pp. 3–4; Rachael Heyhoe Flint and Netta Rheinberg, *Fair Play* (London, 1976); J. Ford, *Cricket* (Newton Abbot, 1972); Joy, *Maiden Over*; Reekie, 'History of Sport', pp. 35–53, 122–33; Netta Rheinberg, unpublished articles in personal collection; *Women's Cricket*, vol. 1. (August 1930), p. 48, vol. 4 (August 1933), pp. 66–70, vol. 17 (8 August and 19 September 1952), pp. 116, 119, 148–49.

37. *Ladies' and Gentlemen's Magazine* (August 1777), quoted in Joy, *Maiden Over*, pp. 18–19.

38. In the early-nineteenth century the introduction of round-arm bowling represented a major advance in technique. There are several variations on a similar theme that attribute the development to women, the most common, that about John Willes, a Kentish squire and keen cricketer who, while convalescing from an illness in 1807, asked his sister to toss cricket balls at him. The story goes that Christina Willes, on finding that her voluminous skirts severely impeded underarm delivery, threw the ball in an overhand style and so effectively that brother John adopted it himself and spent the next two decades fighting to get it legalised. Other versions involve a Mrs Lambert, similarly encumbered by dress, bowling overhand to her husband, and the daughters of William Lillywhite, the famous sportsman, bowling to their father during the winter, to keep his game sharp, with extended arms to circumvent their shawls; and when the startled father found that they often took his wicket he began to imitate them, and in time others copied him. P.H. Ditchfield, *Old English Sports, Pastimes and Customs* (London, 1891), pp. 64–5; Flint and Rheinberg, *Fair Play*, p. 21; Ford, *Cricket*, p. 158; Joy, *Maiden Over*, p. 23.

39. *Shepton Mallet Journal* (1868), quoted in Turner, *Equality for Some*, p. 137.

40. Helen B. Mathers, *Comin' Thro' the Rye* (3 vols, London, 1875), vol. 1, p. 217. See also p. 214.

41. *Women's Cricket*, vol. 4 (August 1933), pp. 64–5.

42. Alison Adburgham, *A Punch History of Manners and Modes 1841–1940* (London, 1961), p. 171.

43. *Punch* (10 May 1873), p. 195. See also *Cricket*, vol. 7 (20 September 1888), p. 428; *Englishwoman's Review* (15 September 1887), pp. 429–30; *Ludgate*, vol. 7 (February 1899), pp. 314–18; *Pastime* (15 August 1888), p. 127.

44. George John Whyte-Melville, *Riding Recollections* (London, 1878), p. 123. See also J.M. Barrie, *The Greenwood Hat* (Edinburgh, 1930), pp. 100–3; *Cricket*, vol. 6 (24 November 1887), p. 460, vol. 20 (12 September 1901), p. 407.

45. *Cricket*, vol. 6 (15 September 1887), p. 406.

46. *Graphic* (June 1890). See also (18 August 1888).

47. *Queen* (6 July 1895), p. 45. The ladies were Lady Idina Nevill, Lady Henry Nevill, Lady Milner, the Honourable Maud Lawrence, the Honourable M. and B. Brassey, Miss Chandos Pole and Miss Street. Eridge was the family seat of the Nevills and Normanhurst of the Brasseys.

The club's most celebrated member was Lucy Ridsdale, the daughter of the Royal Mint's Assay Master and from 1892 the wife of Stanley Baldwin, who did not miss a university match in 40 years and held a meeting of the club at Downing Street during the General Strike of 1926. Flint and Rheinberg, *Fair Play*, p. 24.

48. *Women's Cricket*, vol. 17 (19 September 1952), p. 148.

49. *Cricket* vol. 1 (28 September 1912), p. 527; *Hockey Field* (21 May 1908), p. 110, (20 August 1908), p. 317; Margaret H. Elsworth, 'Women's Participation in Physical Recreation in the Nineteenth Century with Particular Reference to North-West England' in McNair and Parry (eds), *Readings*, p. 91.

Women's cricket was particularly popular in Derbyshire, South Wales and the Cotswolds-Severn Valley area. Bessie Grace, the daughter of the legendary W.G., was a member of the Clifton Club and enjoyed a reputation as a great hitter. Clifton and other clubs occasionally played against boys' schools.

50. *Hockey Field* (20 and 27 March 1902), pp. 369, 389. A Women's Cricket Association was not established until 1926, and then with only ten clubs.

51. Flint and Rheinberg, *Fair Play*, p. 29.

52. Ibid., p. 25.

53. *Illustrated London News* (24 May 1890) p. 655.

54. *Women's Cricket*, vol. 1 (July 1930), p. 31; *Buckinghamshire Examiner*, quoted in *Women's Cricket* (August 1930), p. 48.

55. *C.B. Fry's Magazine*, vol. 1 (July 1904), pp. 401–8; *Hockey Field* (25 June 1908), pp. 188–9, (8 April 1909), p. 438; *Lancet* (4 July 1885), p. 30; Eustace Miles, *Cassell's Physical Educator* (London, 1904), pp. 657–61; Haddon, *Great Days*, p. 60.

56. *Ladies' Field* (12 July 1902), p. 192.

57. *Women's Cricket*, vol. 30 (14 May 1965), p. 3. Examples were women such as Mrs Martha Grace, the mother of W.G., the importance of whose encouragement was acknowledged by her famous son, and earlier, Mrs Jane Walker who in the 1820s was instrumental in founding the Lascelles Hall Cricket Club, a club that became the nursery of Yorkshire Cricket.

58. *Birmingham Daily Mail* (1881), quoted in D.D. Molyneux, 'Early Excursions by Birmingham Women into Games and Sports', *Journal of Physical Education*, vol. 51, no. 153 (1959), pp. 47–8.

59. Molyneux, 'Early Excursions', p. 48.

60. *Lancet* (28 June 1890), pp. 1446–7, (5 July 1890), p. 37.

61. *Daily Mail*, 19 November 1904.

62. Okely, 'Privileged . . . and Finished', p. 133. For information on netball see *Girls' School Year Book* (1906), p. 393; *Hockey Field* (11 December 1902), p. 115, (12 December 1907), p. 119; Sara Burstall and M.A. Douglas (eds), *Public Schools for Girls* (London, 1911), pp. 212–13.

63. Football was the single most popular team sport in Britain by 1914, particularly among the working classes whose womenfolk attended matches in limited numbers. But even the most ardent advocates of freedom recommended against women playing, because football was too violent, masculine and dangerous. Apart from the odd reference to students occasionally kicking footballs at girls' schools, the game was not a part of the evolution of middle-class women's sport. A British Ladies' Football Club, which apparently played a few matches in 1895 amidst heckling and censure in the press, was an exception that proved the rule. *British Medical Journal* (8 December 1894), p. 1323; *Hockey Field* (2 January 1902), p. 183; *Lancet* (21 September 1901), p. 772; *Punch* (2 February 1895), p. 49; *School World*, vol. 9 (February 1909), p. 67; *Sketch* (6 February 1895), pp. 60–1, (27 March 1895), pp. 444–5; Fletcher, *Women First*, p. 162; Tony Mason, *Association Football 1863–1915* (Brighton, 1980), pp. 40–1, 144–5, 152–3, 159, 162, 171–2; Helene Roberts, 'The Exquisite Slave: The Role of Clothes in the Making of the Victorian Woman', *Signs*, vol. 2. no. 3 (1977), p. 567; David Rubinstein, *Before the Suffragettes* (Brighton, 1986), pp. 212–13, 228.

6

Individual Sports:
Lawn Tennis, Golf and Cycling

When lovely woman stoops to wheeling,
And finds too late that bikes betray,
Beauty, grace and finer feeling
She'll see her sex has chucked away.[1]

Women had a much easier time winning public approval of their participation in individual sports than in team games. Relatively speaking, at least some individual sports had a longer history of female participation; and in the nineteenth century many required membership in socially exclusive clubs, thus seeming much more conducive to the production of aesthetically pleasing images and much less competitive and overtly masculine.

Prior to the 1870s the few physical activities in which adult women could participate involved recreational, non-competitive and ruleless activities such as horse-back riding; and, although a good many ladies of the landed classes disagreed, for a time even riding fell out of favour with the arbiters of gentility. Exceptions were archery and croquet.

From the late-eighteenth century onwards, archery was considered appropriate for gentlewomen for it did not demand excessive strength or unwomanly movements and clothing. Country-house lawns provided the perfect setting for the tournaments sponsored by the clubs which popped up all over the country and welcomed female members. Pierce Egan, England's first sporting journalist, remarked in 1828 that:

Archery is equally open to the fair sex, and has for these last thirty years, been the favourite recreation of a great part of the female nobility, the only field diversion they can enjoy without incurring the censure of being thought masculine.[2]

154

The following year a *Young Lady's Book* . . . *of Elegant Recreations, Exercises and Pursuits* noted that meetings of noble archers of both sexes occurred frequently, and commended archery to young ladies as the most healthful and agreeable pastime in which propriety permitted them to indulge, for:

> The attitude of an accomplished female archer . . . at the moment of bending the bow, is particularly graceful; all the actions and positions tend at once to produce a proper degree of strength in the limbs, and to impart a general elegance to the deportment.[3]

In 1845, the year after the first Grand National Archery Meeting was held in York, eleven ladies responded to an invitation to women to participate in separate competitions. Over the next several decades, the increase in the number of clubs and entrants to regional and national competitions signified that archery was becoming well established as a sport for upper- and upper-middle-class ladies; and in acknowledgement of this, the Grand National Archery Society (1861) ran female national championships from 1880. Although the popularity of archery declined in the late-nineteenth century, as more exciting sporting alternatives presented themselves, a few women continued to draw the bow competitively and with increasing skill, secure in the knowledge that archery was indisputably genteel. Female archers were unconcerned about achieving male standards, and so were never perceived as a threat to male bowmen. Men and women always shot at different targets, with the women shooting fewer arrows shorter distances, with bows whose stringing was reduced to suit their limited strength.

The revolution in individual sports for women originated not with archery but with the game of croquet, which appeared in England in the 1850s and quickly became the rage in fashionable society. At first it was played by both sexes for amusement on vicarage and country-house lawns without set rules and with large, irregular hoops and a light mallet; but it soon became more scientific, as tactics and rules developed, equipment was improved and standardised and clubs began to form. The first championship tournament for men was held at Evesham, Worcestershire, in 1867, and the first for women two years later. In 1870 both championships transferred to the All-England Croquet Club, Wimbledon (1868), and in 1871 they came under the aegis of a new governing body, the National Croquet Club.

To women of all ages in polite society, croquet provided unprecedented opportunities to combine light, elegant outdoor exercise with flirtation and romance. *Punch* had a field-day poking fun at those whose pretty ankles peeped enticingly from below their fashionable dresses and who coyly used their crinolines and cages to reposition balls 'accidentally', and at those who suddenly discovered that, although too delicate to walk a mile, they could play croquet in mixed company for two or even three consecutive hours. Only the occasional pessimist cautioned against croquet for ladies because it 'involves too much unwholesome stooping'.[4]

While necessitating neither strenuous exertion nor an immediate reform of female dress or images, croquet was more than a charming leisure activity. Played well the game required a good deal of skill; and it was of considerable importance to the physical emancipation of women, for it effected a major change in the relationship of women to sport.

> When croquet made its appearance, it was a new experience for women to be able to compete with men on tolerably even terms, and for sisters to partake in the amusements of their brothers with a fair chance of holding their own in the struggle.[5]

Furthermore, croquet signalled the entrance of women into organised, competitive sport and gave them their first taste of its delights. These delights they refused to renounce when lawn tennis replaced croquet in the affections of the affluent classes.[6]

Lawn tennis, a combination of the old games of real tennis and rackets, adapted to the conditions of outdoor play, achieved sudden popularity in the 1870s, partly as the result of a desire among youthful croquet enthusiasts for more active exercise. Like croquet, lawn tennis was the prerogative of the leisured elite from its emergence until 1914, for only they had the time and facilities to play — first among family and friends on the lawns of country houses and suburban villas and then in exclusive private clubs. In its early form, tennis was considered a genteel kind of outdoor parlour game providing good-natured fun rather than serious exercise to members of the smart set of both sexes. Mixed doubles had a particularly strong appeal as a possible matrimonial agency at a time when there was a surplus of women and social intercourse between ladies and gentlemen remained difficult.

Sceptics occasionally represented that no woman would be able to understand tennis scoring or play seriously, because the game was too taxing, the ball too heavy, the court too big and the dangers of strained hand muscles and blows to the eye too great. Others argued that by introducing an element of frivolity women ruined lawn tennis, just as they ruined all men's games in which they participated; that tennis diminished women's beauty by making them flushed and dishevelled; that tournament play in public was inappropriate and too tiring for ladies; and that if care were not taken those who played regularly were likely to develop lateral curvatures owing to the continuous use of one arm. But on the whole tennis was judged eminently suitable to ladies, because it harmonised with ladylike images and 'exactly' supplied 'the want of physical recreation' and opportunities for approved social encounters 'so keenly felt by many'.[7] Tennis also had the advantage of being only a minor, not completely manly, sport at boys' public schools.

The majority of the first generation of female players offered no threat to the male ego, aspiring neither to excellence nor competence. They viewed tennis as a social asset providing training in graceful and charming movements. They never expected actually to run for the ball, but rather just to reach for it and pat it gently across the net. They knew nothing of hard overhand serves, back-court drives or smashes at the net. In mixed matches they expected gentlemen to behave considerately, allowing them to stand for service as near the net as they liked and not provoking them to too much exertion by serving or hitting hard.

Had ladies aspired to perform more energetically they would have found it almost impossible. Until shops began selling special tennis costumes in the 1880s they played tennis in the same long dresses they wore for garden parties; and although the first special tennis costumes were an improvement they were still hardly conducive to vigorous movement. Nevertheless, tennis seemed a fast and thrilling game after the languors of croquet; and as it grew in popularity *Punch* took great delight in lampooning ladies who popped balls across garden nets, and journalists and umpires who had a hard time deciding whether to be gallant and uncritical or to record accurately 'all those faults'.[8]

Increasingly formal organisation and competition inspired a relatively rapid change and then standardisation of rules that altered men's style of play; and they stimulated the development of elaborate rituals and rules of etiquette that guaranteed courtesy and social segregation. Private clubs were formed all over the country, often with mixed membership and in conjunction with existing croquet clubs. The most famous dates from 1877 when the All-England Croquet Club changed its name to the All-England Croquet and Lawn Tennis Club in the hopes that the addition of the more exciting and mobile new game would stimulate its flagging fortunes.

The All-England Club immediately organised a men's singles championship in which 22 gentlemen competed for a trophy worth 25 guineas before a mixed crowd of 200 in an atmosphere very like that of a garden party. It declined to offer a cup for ladies' singles competition, however, so the Irish had the distinction of pioneering championship tennis for women when a mixed and singles event was staged in Dublin in 1879. Bath (1881), the Northern Association (1882) and Cheltenham (1883) all held events for women before the All-England Club deigned to bestow on them the honour of a championship at Wimbledon in 1884.

During its first six years the Wimbledon club banned female members. As no committee minutes survive prior to 1883, it cannot be determined whether women's admission was a controversial issue before that, but given their participation in other clubs it seems likely that it was. In April 1883 the governing committee passed motions allowing women to join but denying them access to positions of authority and to the ground after 2.00 p.m. on Saturdays when it was much in demand by men. The following year, apparently because of a fear of losing control of championship tennis to another tournament, the club instituted a 'Ladies Championship, to be played for on the All-England Lawn Tennis Club ground at Wimbledon annually' following the gentlemen's singles and during the four-hand championship which moved from Oxford (1879) to Wimbledon that year.[9]

The committee determined that the entry fee for women would be half the guinea paid by men; that a women's match should not last beyond three sets as opposed to five in men's tennis; and that prizes worth 20 and ten guineas would go to the lady champion and runner-up. The committee also agreed to furnish the 'ladies' room' more comfortably and 'to send each lady competitor a complimentary ticket of admission for her chaperon or friend'.[10]

Thirteen women, five of them married, competed before a crowd of about 450; and Maud Watson, the daughter of an Anglican clergyman and a croquet-playing mother, defeated her elder sister, Lilian, in the final. As a result of practising against the Cambridge undergraduates her father tutored and playing in various club competitions, Maud had

> . . . developed an all-round game which had no apparent weaknesses. She had an ideal temperament and her cool, quiet concentration often upset her more excitable opponents. Her over-arm service gave her an edge over most opponents, who were wary of her volleying and driving ability. Her judgement was excellent for she was able to discover her opponent's weak points very early and take advantage of these to the utmost, while her behaviour on the court was an example to all.[11]

Several months later the committee reported to the annual general meeting 'that the success of the Ladies' championship is sure'.[12] Ironically, considering the view in some quarters that tournament play was too tiring for ladies, until 1886 the men's champion got a bye into the final round while the representative of the supposedly weaker sex had to play through.

In 1886, too, the All-England Club yielded to pressure and agreed to elevate the status of the ladies' championship by presenting the winner with the ultimate symbol of sporting legitimacy, a challenge cup; for, as one critic had put it, it was

> . . . ungallant to the fair sex to treat their champion as inferior, one not worthy of the dignity of a challenge trophy. If the contest is worthy of the dignity of a place at such an important meeting these invidious distinctions should not be allowed to exist.[13]

In the early years of the championship first-class players were scarce, and the final was fought between a few enterprising and exceptional ones who were used to competing against each other in tournaments around the country. Maud Watson successfully defended her title in 1885 against a promising young woman, Blanche Bingley, a sports all-rounder, and, it was noted, played in far more open competitions that year than the men's champion. The following year Bingley won the first of the remarkable string of six championships she was to accumulate by 1900, first as Miss Bingley and then as Mrs G.W. Hillyard. What gave her game distinction was competitiveness, a remarkably hard forehand and the ability to cover the court better than most. When Hillyard was in her prime, however, it was still considered questionable 'whether any lady can volley, and bear the exertion entailed by volleying, sufficiently well to make it pay', for even superior players like Hillyard were 'not cultivated in the art of volleying to any great extent' and had backhands that were 'weak and laboured'.[14]

While the majority of players at all levels were single, a sizeable minority were married, since tennis was recognised as a social asset regardless of marital status, and husbands and wives could interact at clubs. In Blanche Bingley Hillyard's case there was no question of her husband disapproving of her playing tennis even after she became a mother: for years Mr Hillyard was general secretary of the All-England Club, they had conducted their court-ship largely on the court, and both played tennis competitively on their honeymoon.

Hillyard's greatest rival was Charlotte Dod, the first prodigy of women's tennis and indeed of women's sport. Born in Cheshire in 1871 into a wealthy middle-class family with sporting inclina-tions, Lottie Dod began playing tennis at the age of nine, and when only eleven won the consolation doubles championship at the Northern Tournament in partnership with her sister. In 1885 and 1886 she won a number of remarkable victories in singles, doubles and mixed doubles, including the West of England championship over Maud Watson. At the age of only 15 Dod was ready for Wimbledon, where she dispatched a stunned Miss Bingley with remarkable ease.

A tall, athletic-looking girl, Lottie Dod was by far the best female tennis player of her day. She repeatedly bested her nearest rivals, and her style, consciously modelled on that of the best men, helped to revolutionise ladies' play. Instead of merely striding after the ball, she ran hard all over the court, which she was able to do because she was young enough to wear a dress much shorter than the full-length ones fashion dictated as essential for her adult opponents. She volleyed with great strength and accuracy thanks to an unusually powerful forehand drive, and through diligent practice she turned a suspect backhand into one of her strongest strokes.

Commentators repeatedly observed that Dod's play brought speed and agility to women's tennis and was much more varied than was usual. They described her attacking net play and smashes; and they remarked approvingly that she played 'overhand strokes with a grace and ease unequalled by any other lady player'; that she used 'her shoulders with a freedom not noted in other ladies'; that her anticipation was so good that she never appeared hurried; and that she did all of these things without losing her composure or womanly grace. Somewhat surprisingly considering the innovative nature of her game, Dod always served underhand, viewing the overhand style as no more difficult to receive and a waste of precious energy.[15]

Dod won the All-England championship in 1887 and 1888; then, to the disappointment and annoyance of her supporters, she sat out for two years in favour of yachting off the coast of Scotland. Women's tennis needed Dod, as the feeble entry of four in the 1890 championship indicated; and her reappearance in public competitions prompted the leading tennis journal to predict that it 'will encourage ladies' lawn tennis . . . by showing what a pitch of perfection can be attained without sacrifice (or rather with considerable enhancement) of their natural grace and dignity'.[16] Dod proceeded to win the All-England championship in 1891, 1892 and 1893 before retiring for good, aged only 22, with the enviable record of never having been defeated at Wimbledon and losing only five times in open singles anywhere. Thereafter, her association with tennis was as an occasional participant in exhibition matches and as a writer of articles on women's play. She went on, however, to achieve a unique and still unequalled record of distinction in a remarkable number of other sports without — as a contemporary commentator observed — the neglect of womanly accomplishments.[17]

The greatest of all the early tennis champions was another all-round athlete who was encouraged by her family and improved her game by practising against men. She was Dorothea Katherine Douglass (Mrs Robert Lambert Chambers), a parsons daughter born in 1878. Mrs Lambert Chambers, as she preferred to be called, was a keen golfer and badminton player and a long-time member of the Ealing Ladies' Hockey Club which she represented on the Middlesex county team. Between 1903 and 1914 she won the Olympic singles tennis competition and seven Wimbledon championships. She was runner-up in the 1920 championship at the age of 42 and in 1924 reached the semi-finals of the two doubles events. Lambert Chambers was known as an excellent backcourt player with a keen tennis brain, and she was given credit even by men for her sound judgement and great resourcefulness.[18]

Champions such as Blanche Hillyard, Lottie Dod and Dorothea Lambert Chambers were, of course, exceptions to the casual play of the thousands of ordinary club members whose primary motives were to combine healthy exercise with pleasant social encounters. But they are important because they demonstrated in public the 'inexhaustible scope and charm' of tennis and women's ability to play well and gracefully, and their invaluable examples to other women and to society in general of female sporting achievement stimulated interest in the ladies' game.

For years the only championship events at Wimbledon were the men's and women's singles and the men's doubles. The governing committee rejected a proposal to institute a ladies' four-handed championship in 1885 on the grounds that it would not represent serious competitive tennis; and even the best female players agreed that, as then played, ladies' doubles was no more than a boring and interminable form of pat-ball that would improve only if ladies became better at volleying and fought on the service line instead of playing at the back of the court. In club tournaments the event was none the less quite common, and from 1885 the Northern Championships, which alternated between Manchester and Liverpool, included a ladies' doubles contest styled 'the championship of England'.

In 1899, despite protests that it would bring an element of farce to the otherwise serious proceedings and prolong the meeting indefinitely, a non-championship event was added to the Wimbledon programme. After the 1907 championships, however, to the apparent relief of the referee, the committee thought better of its earlier decision and ruled that henceforth 'no ladies' doubles [would] be played during the championships'.[19] In turn, as a result of pressure from the Lawn Tennis Association (1888) and an improvement in the quality of play and increase in spectator interest, the All-England Club quietly restored ladies' doubles in 1913, this time on an official basis.

Mixed doubles had a similarly chequered history at Wimbledon.

One of the reasons tennis had become popular in the first place was because mixed foursomes allowed men and women rare opportunities to play together, albeit not particularly seriously. Garden party 'fours' were the bulwark of tennis throughout the nineteenth century, while in clubs the mixed game was the favourite type of competition with lady members who considered it interesting to spectators and players, less fatiguing than singles and more exciting than doubles. For years, however, the female mixed-doubles player was derided publicly as helpless, hopelessly unskilled and more interested in flirting than actually playing.

To the serious male player the mixed game was often more trouble than it was worth, for he was constantly torn between politeness and expediency when determining how many balls he should take himself and how many he dared hit full strength at his female opposite number. Commentators often portrayed male mixed players as chivalrous, long-suffering individuals who had to endure their partners' constant errors and concentration-disturbing chatter; and they reminded lady players that it was their duty to inspire and admire their menfolk and to encourage and give them sympathy when they erred. In a sense mixed doubles symbolised the traditional marriage relationship in which woman, as helpmeet, played a supportive role. Even after it shed its social image, mixed play continued to stress the strength of the male and the secondary role of the female, who was expected to use her skill and intelligence to supplement his efforts within a smaller area of their common half of the court.[20]

The All-England Club first considered 'lady and gentleman pairs' competition in 1887, but rejected the idea on the grounds that it would disfigure the championships since men dominated play and etiquette was a tricky problem. The more innovative Northern Association Tournament introduced an 'All England Mixed Doubles Championship' in 1888, and mixed matches became fixtures at tournaments and club competitions around the country. Wimbledon finally moved in a mixed direction in 1900, but until 1913 only unofficially; and no matter how many championship players competed, the stigma of frivolity was difficult to erase.

Although lawn tennis was one of the few sports that was readily accepted as befitting ladies — both married and single — the early players had to contend with prejudice concerning their abilities, seriousness and styles of play. The views that ladies were drawn to tennis primarily because of the opportunities it provided to exhibit social charms and indulge in flirtations, and that they must look attractive and elegant on the court, dogged women's tennis for years. Descriptions of female play and players used such terms as 'pretty', 'graceful', 'neat', 'charming', 'amusing', 'fair damsels' and 'fair sex', all of which belied vigorous competition and destined the women's game to be judged by standards quite apart from its intrinsic quality.

Ironically, while physical and social considerations were assumed to prevent the calibre of female play ever approaching that of men, as early as the inaugural women's championship the unfortunate habit appeared — among men and women alike — of comparing it with the men's game rather than that of other women. Naturally the conclusion was reached that 'even considering the handicap of dress, men's greater strength and activity will ever give them a very decided superiority over any woman'.[21] So intriguing was the prospect of testing the athletic disparities between the sexes that a private match was arranged in June 1888 between two of the game's premier players, Blanche Hillyard and Ernest Renshaw. Renshaw gave away a point and Mrs Hillyard played to her maximum capacity, but the results demonstrated 'how immensely superior the play of men is to that of the ladies'.[22] Two months later, when Renshaw met Lottie Dod at a difference of 30, Dod won the first set 6-2 and reportedly kept Renshaw on the run 'about as much as any first rate player of his own sex' before tiring and losing the second and third sets by scores of 7-5.[23] Such matches continued from time to time, and served no purpose other than to provide a 'spectacle' that confirmed female inferiority. No matter how able, the woman inevitably lost. If she took a game or set her success was attributed not to her skill but to her opponent's gallantry before he settled down to the business of proving his own and his sex's superiority.

Women's tennis at every level was considered much less serious and important than the male version, both on and off the court. Only a few women were thought responsible enough to umpire, to be instructors or to serve as honorary secretaries and committee members of clubs, and even fewer to manage tournaments. There was no question of lady professionals; and although the quality of play gradually improved, for years the number of first-class players remained small. In ordinary club play women tended to favour the doubles over the singles game because it was less energetic; and they were slow to change their techniques, since clothing inhibited movement and unusual strength and agility continued to be perceived as threatening to health and feminine reputations.[24]

Nevertheless, contemporaries felt that athletically minded women should give thanks to lawn tennis for advancing their sex's emancipation. As tennis evolved from an amusement into a form of genuine exercise, some credited it with improving women's health and strength and developing swiftness of movement, accuracy of judgement and aim, presence of mind and rapidity of thought. Some argued that women's participation demonstrated that females were not, after all, naturally incapable of playing all the games practised by men, and that 'the physique of the fair sex must be a great deal stronger than generally supposed'.[25] Women who survived matches lasting several hours in considerable heat clearly contradicted the stereotype of female frailty.

Few of the early tennis champions were feminists in the cause-oriented sense, but by their deeds and words several revealed a belief that participation in sport advanced the position of women. Blanche Bingley Hillyard, for example, thought that 'in tennis our sex can compete with a certain amount of equality with the "lords of creation"', for playing developed the self-confidence, 'coolness of head and judgement which we are so often taunted with lacking'.[26]

Lottie Dod perceived women as functioning in tennis as the weaker sex, and encouraged them to improve their play in mixed doubles so as not to spoil the sport for men, as if men's enjoyment was the paramount concern. But she applauded tennis for providing 'delightful and healthy exercise . . . and healthy rivalry, of which ladies had long felt the want'.[27] If women played as hard as possible, they would discover that many balls, seemingly out of reach, could be returned easily; and they would prove that tennis was a pastime of which they as well as men were worthy, and that the disparagement of ladies' play was unwarranted, Dod insisted.

Dorothea Lambert Chambers went even further. She defended the modern woman's right and need to take exercise and dismissed as ludicrous the charge that sport marred the female appearance. While conceding that players should always try to look as neat and attractive as possible, she reasoned that it was impossible to be 'just so' every second, and that it was much more interesting to see them in genuine action than delicately immobile with every hair in place. To the argument that vigorous exercise was injurious to health and womanliness, she replied that it had actually done wonders for women's moral, mental, and physical well-being and that damage to femininity depended on how the term was defined. The claim that strength was masculine and frailty feminine she branded as ridiculous on the grounds that endurance, nerve and physical vitality produced by strenuous games were admirable in both sexes. Sports in general, and lawn tennis in particular, she asserted, provided women with the skills and qualities necessary to deal successfully with life's varied experiences. Lambert Chambers always viewed woman as man's helpmeet and thought that 'man's stronger physique, naturally great activity and severer strokes [gave] him an advantage' in tennis that woman could never hope to overcome. But she was convinced at the same time that tennis was one of the few athletic pursuits in which women could combine with and compete against men without spoiling the game, and that if they made an effort they could excel.[28]

Because women on the tennis court could display 'the studied grace of athleticism' while continuing to appear fashionable and attractive, because most were members of the respectable classes and of exclusive clubs, and so could hardly be considered 'rough' or 'unsexed', and because tennis-playing never quite shed its garden-party legacy as a sexually integrating force, tennis was accepted as a charming social accomplishment, as 'a most desirable enjoyment with which to fill the idle hours of budding womanhood'.[29] As a result it was one of the first real sports in which adult women were allowed to participate in considerable numbers, and it paved the way for their admission to others. From the 1890s almost every book and article on tennis included a section on the women's game and used women in illustrations; and by 1914 there was a secure place in tennis for both the competitive lady player who took her game seriously and practised every day and the type who preferred the opportunities for entertainment and socialising the pat-ball style offered. Scarcely a town or village in England did not have a tennis club with lady members and a tennis tournament with lady participants; and the most skilled devotees could compete at the championship and international levels.

The great rival of tennis was golf, a game whose history can be traced back to 1457 when, during a war against the English, the parliament of King James II of Scotland declared it illegal because it was interfering with the archery practices of the citizen army. Isolated references reveal that women showed an early if not continuous interest in the game. In 1513 Catherine of Aragon wrote to the future Cardinal Wolsey, 'I thank God to be busy with golf . . . my heart is very good to it, and I am horribly busy making standards, banners, and bagets'[30]. Unbecomingly soon after the suspicious death of her husband in 1567, Mary Queen of

Scots played golf in the fields near Seton Castle; and in the late-seventeenth century, the Countess of Stair, the inspiration for the unpleasant Lady Ashton in 'The Bride of Lammermoor', was reputed to be a witch who defeated her golfing opponents by converting herself into her opponents' ball and then deliberately rolling out of line on the green or into the deepest bunker.[31]

A hundred years later the Statistical Account of Scotland, Inveresk, recorded that at Musselburgh in 1792, 'as women do the work of men, their manners are masculine, and their strength and activity is equal to their work. Their amusements are of the masculine kind. On holidays they frequently play at golf'.[32] In 1810, as a result of such activities among women of the lower orders, the Royal Musselburgh Golf club resolved

> . . . to present by Subscription a new Creel and 'shull', with consolation prizes of two of the best Barcelona silk handkerchiefs, to the best female golfer who plays on the annual occasion of the next January 1 to be intimated to the Fish ladies by the officer of the Club.[33]

When the first consistent records of women's golf appeared a half century later, however, the players involved were of a higher rank.

The first golf club in Great Britain, the St Andrew's Club (renamed the Royal and Ancient in 1834), was organised in 1754 by 22 'noblemen and gentlemen', and around the same time clubs were formed in Edinburgh and Musselburgh. The first outside Scotland, the Blackheath Golf Club, was established near London in 1766. In 1850 it remained the sole club in England, and in 1880 there were still only a dozen. During the late-Victorian period, however, golf became the most popular of all sports among middle-class men. It offered year-round activity to people of various ages who preferred to play alone against themselves or in company against others; and through a hierarchical ordering of clubs and quasi-rural settings it reinforced social exclusivity and zoning.[34]

Initially golf clubs had no female members, but around 1860 a few Scottish women decided they wanted more to do with the game than merely spectating. A Mrs Robert Boothby, whose husband was a member of the Royal and Ancient Club, and a few friends began to play golf on some vacant ground near the St Andrews railway station, and in 1867, after having found a more congenial location near the men's clubhouse, they boldly decided to form their own club and hold an open putting competition on 'a miniature edition of the regular golf course'.[35] The president and committee members of the new club were women, but, as was to become common in women's golf, the secretary-treasurer was a man.

The Royal and Ancient offered no impediments since the 'gentler sex's enthusiastic wielding of the club assumed a mild form . . . [not] extending beyond the simple stroke of the putting green'.[36] Before long St Andrews men were describing the ladies' green as a charming feature, the skill of the 'fair competitors' on their own ground as considerable, and the ladies' club's spring and autumn meetings as regular and attractive events. By the 1880s the St Andrews Ladies' Golf Club had 500 members; but since the Scots perceived golf as in essence a man's game, the impetus for the widespread development of women's golf came largely from England.

The first English women's club, the Westward Ho! and North Devon Ladies' Golf Club, was formed in 1868 by 47 women with 23 men from the Royal North Devon Golf Club who controlled the affairs of the women's club and laid out a small course where ladies could putt fortnightly on Saturdays from May through October. Four years later the Ladies' London Scottish — later the Wimbledon Ladies' Club — was established as a branch of a men's club, and once again men were put in charge. They were automatically honorary members of, and exercised general supervision over, the ladies' club and had two seats on its governing committee; and although women's matches involved only putting, men were allowed to play, albeit ineligible for prizes.

Two types of ladies' clubs gradually emerged. A few were independent, with all-female or mixed committees and their own clubhouses and nine-hole 'hen runs'. Most were adjuncts of men's clubs upon whose tolerance they subsisted. They had male-controlled committees and competitions, short, hazardless and often unkempt courses that retarded the development of skill, and inadequate quarters in huts or cottages separate from the main clubhouse which they were either forbidden to enter or restricted to the use of a side entrance. For years women usually were permitted to play only at inconvenient weekday times and never when male competitions were in progress. They were expected to give way to men on the greens, and to accept the argument that since they paid lower subscription fees they deserved fewer privileges and the contradiction of few privileges even when they paid the same. Suggestions about equalising privileges almost inevitably produced stormy meetings of men's club committees and negative results.[37]

Eventually this situation improved. The tight male grip gradually relaxed as younger female club members fought successfully for their own committees. By 1914, although only a few ladies' clubs were fully managed by women, a number had developed into respected sections of men's clubs and had been given accommodation in the main clubhouse and the right to play on the full course, albeit at restricted times. On the whole, however, women's golf grew in the face of the usual male objections: women's place was in the home; their proper sporting role was to watch and applaud men; their anatomy precluded proper golf swings and could not stand the strain; they would neglect graceful bodily positions and become masculinised; they were temperamentally unfitted for serious competition; they lacked the ability to achieve anything worthwhile as players and administrators; and, although this was not articulated, they might one day challenge men.

When they dared to extend their game beyond the putting green by taking longer and bolder strokes, their efforts were greeted with a mixture of mild amusement, scorn and outright hostility. It is little wonder that years passed before women progressed beyond the discreet and ladylike movements associated with putting, chipping and half swings. In the words of Mabel Stringer, the first female sports journalist, it was 'amazing women learned to play at all considering what they had to contend with and the little inducement there was for them to persevere and practise'.[38]

In the *Badminton Library* volume on golf Lord Wellwood discussed the women's game in a tone of friendly banter. He conceded that women had the strength to hit more than 70 or 80 yards if they took full swing, but advised against this, since the club would have to be raised above the shoulder, with 'postures and gestures . . . not particularly graceful when a player is clad in female dress'. He expressed reservations about women golfing on men's courses at times other than 'when the male golfers are feeding or resting', for they got in the way if they were in front and were a distraction if they played with the men. He even decried the presence of women as score-keepers and spectators, because they would likely make mistakes, talk too much and wear dresses that cast unsettling shadows on greens.[39]

Like most men Lord Wellwood did not dream that women's golf would ever remotely resemble the male game or that it would become a force to be reckoned with in its own right, for at the time he wrote there were only about 2,000 female golfers in the entire United Kingdom, and in England about 20 women's clubs, each with an average of less than 50 members. He was in for a shock, however, for despite the impediments of discrimination, convention and fashion, a number of determined women developed golfing ambitions and skills beyond their proper sphere.

The watershed in the history of women's golf came in 1893. In that year, having failed to organise a national golf association and a standardised system of handicapping for men, Mr Laidlaw Purves and some associates from the Wimbledon Golf Club threw their support behind Issette Pearson, of the Wimbledon Ladies' Golf Club, when she determined to apply the scheme to women. Under Purves's guidance Pearson invited ladies' clubs around the country to send representatives to a meeting at the Wimbledon Club in April to discuss the idea of a ladies' golf union and championship. Thirty-two delegates from 15 of the largest clubs appeared.

After denying that 'woman is incapable of a mature and seasoned interest in golf',[40] Purves claimed a union would represent all the ladies' clubs, stimulate the growth of ladies' golf by drawing lady golfers together, arrange inter-club, championship and international matches, and formulate uniform rules and a system of handicapping. So persuasive was he that the delegates immediately voted to create a Ladies' Golf Union (LGU) run by a council comprised of representatives from affiliated clubs and a seven-person executive, and to elect executive officers. Unlike the AEWHA, the lady golfers felt neither the desire nor capacity to run the new organisation on their own, so men were made eligible for the executive from the start. Purves and three other men were chosen as vice-presidents; Blanche Hulton became honorary treasurer and Issette Pearson, honorary secretary, a post she retained until 1919. Finally, a sub-committee, also including men, was chosen to draw up rules and regulations and arrange the first championship.[41]

A general meeting three weeks later adopted the committee's recommendations for a ladies' championship and the design of a championship cup worth £50. Problems could have arisen since, by the time the LGU was established, the Lytham and St Anne's Club in Lancashire had already announced plans to hold such a competition to stimulate ladies' play; but they were avoided by an amicable compromise under which the LGU agreed to hold its first championship at Lytham and pay for the trophy the club had intended to provide.

The inaugural contest, held from 13 to 15 June — and 33 years after the first men's open championship — was a rather casual affair not unlike an everyday match. Male members of the host club served on the organising committee and as officials. Play was by match over 18 holes. Registration in advance was not required, and the course — only nine holes and 2,132 yards long, and containing a longest hole of only 337 yards — included no formidable hazards and was not a severe test even for those days.

Thirty-eight women — most of them single — from England, Ireland and France entered; and in the final Lady Margaret Scott, who had played golf from childhood with her brothers and father on a private course on the family estate, defeated Issette Pearson for a gold championship medal. The fact that the winner was the daughter of a peer, and that her dress, demeanour and swing epitomised grace and femininity, helped to quash criticism about competitive golf being unbecoming for ladies and added a touch of glamour that helped to make the game fashionable and respectable. The next year Scott took on a field of 68 in the second championship which was played from shortened tees over the full-sized men's course at Littlestone, and once again she defeated Issette Pearson in the final. A third title followed in 1895 when Scott bested 84 opponents at Portrush in Ireland on a men's course slightly altered for the occasion. She then retired, perhaps, one author speculates, so as not to appear too competitive and hence unladylike; and although she participated occasionally in club matches she never played in public again.[42]

The entry in the first championship was small and the spectators few and largely motivated by curiosity about how women could play, but the contest was deemed so successful by a male writer in the *Golfing Annual* that he described golf

> . . . as a game . . . played even amid the distracting surroundings of public criticism . . . probably more suited than any other form of outdoor sport for ladies . . . As a general rule, women's enjoyments are restricted to a tolerably well-defined and narrow area, but the introduction of golf has opened up a fresh field of enjoyment to them, and its possibilities for good to the sex may not be estimated off-

hand. The game takes women into the sunlight and open air, it makes their complection and physique the envy of the womankind of European nations; it is the enemy of hatless dawdle and formal dress parades.[43]

However, progress was not completely smooth thereafter. For several years there was little serious golf apart from the championship and a few open meetings and inter-club matches; and only slowly did women graduate from special nine-hole courses to men's links and develop genuine skill. On the other hand, from the foundation of the LGU, women's golf made definite advances. The quality of the game improved as the number of players increased, particularly those with a diversity of strokes and the inclination to play seriously and competitively. By 1899, although only two had their own 18-hole courses, there were about 220 women's clubs in Britain, and all sorts of competitions ranging from private ones, to mixed and ladies' foursomes, to married versus single competitions, to intra- and inter-club contests, to the Open championship.

Despite predictions that women would never be efficient and businesslike in running their organisation and championship and that they were bound to squabble with each other, and despite occasional challenges to its sole right to govern women's golf, the LGU, with its mixed executive, enjoyed remarkable success and did much to propagate the idea that golf was a suitable game for women. The field in the Open rose to 127 in 1913, including women from France, the United States and all parts of the United Kingdom. The final round was increased to 36 holes, after the fashion of men; play was conducted over long courses; and an improvement in quality was demonstrated by lower handicaps and the longer distances and lower scores achieved in the driving and stroke competitions that preceded championship play.

In addition, the number of affiliated clubs and players grew from 11 and 500 respectively to over 400 and 20,000, and there were dozens of unattached clubs and hundreds of unattached players. The variety of serious competitions also increased. County golf was introduced unofficially in 1896 and officially in 1900, by which time there were 14 county teams. By 1905 there was a territorial championship, national championships in Ireland (1894), Scotland (1903) and Wales (1905) and a home international championship (1905), and there was even an unofficial contest between the representatives of Britain and the United

States. The most important development was the LGU's establishment, within only ten years of the union's foundation, of a national system of handicapping that was sound, workable and reasonably reliable from club to club, while men struggled along without one for another three decades.

Although a number of men gave their time and experience as players, businessmen and administrators to further the interests of women's golf, even after women became serious about playing and improving their skills and demonstrated their ability to run clubs and competitions, they had to tolerate the jibes of captious male critics, who resented the encroachments of the 'opposite sex' and feared that, just as they demanded to share the vote, women would eventually want to compete in male events. Women continued to be told that golf was too serious and complicated a game for females; that they would have difficulty counting strokes, learning rules and remembering to replace divots; that it would ruin their complexions and enlarge their shapely hands and feet; that it required unladylike attitudes and too much exertion; that they played too slowly and laughed and talked too much; that their dresses blew distractingly in the wind; that their primary interest lay in flirting rather than playing; and that they were generally a nuisance on the links.[44]

A breakthrough of sorts occurred in 1908 when the ladies' championship was played for the first time, seven years after permission was originally requested, on the Old Course at St Andrew's, before what was described as the largest and most boisterous crowd ever assembled there. Royal and Ancient members, overcoming their distrust of innovation and their prejudice against women, were courteous and helpful. They provided referees and stewards, allowed the LGU flag to be flown on their masthead and even invited the lady players to tour the sacred clubhouse and inspect historic trophies. But the competitors had to use hotels and boarding houses for changing and eating, a situation that endured until 1974 when the club finally risked contamination by opening its locker rooms and lounge to women on championship occasions.[45]

The sensation of the championship was the play of Cecil Leitch, one of the semi-finalists. The 17-year-old Leitch was the daughter of a doctor in Silloth, Cumberland, whose encouragement of his children to play competitive games resulted in Cecil starting to golf at the age of nine on the links of the local club. Whereas the other championship golfers of the day played like ladies, Leitch played in a way described by amazed spectators as 'rugged', 'powerful' and 'vigorous'. She abandoned a ladylike swing, played her iron shots crisply and adopted a wide stance, a strong grip and the habit of playing the ball well away from herself, demonstrating that there was no reason why a woman could not play powerful as well as graceful shots. She also dressed in an uncommonly practical fashion. In 1914, when she won the first of four Open championships, she wore an ankle-length skirt and soft-collared blouse in the interests of free movement.[46]

Leitch often played against and defeated male opponents, which raised the thorny questions of the quality of women's play in comparison to men's, and whether, since golf was a game of skill more than power and pace, it was possible that the golfing ability of women might actually approach that of men. Horace Hutchinson, a prominent sports writer, opined that while 'woman . . . has justified her claim to equality with man on the links, and the sooner he can be brought to understand it the better for the comfort of both sexes', she could not drive beyond about 75 yards, and until she could, should be confined to short links.[47] But he later changed his mind, having become convinced that male and female golfers were about equal if the latter were given half-a-stroke per hole.

The half-a-stroke theory was tested in 1910 when Eustace White, another well-known sports writer, arranged a match between Cecil Leitch and the famous amateur, Harold Hilton, over 72 holes from the men's tees at the Walton Heath and Sunningdale courses. An excited crowd of 300, including numerous journalists, was on hand for what was billed as a 'battle of the sexes' directly bearing on the women's suffrage question which was at its height at the time. Leitch, who was given nine shots per 18-hole round, was behind by five holes with 15 to play, but she kept calm and rallied to win on the 71st hole.[48] The result caused a momentary sensation, but in terms of determining the comparative strength of men's and women's golf it did nothing. Leitch was an exceptionally good golfer; yet she won only by being given an advantage, and would have been soundly defeated — 78 strokes to 90 per 18 holes — had strokes been counted.

Among both men and women a consensus prevailed that women would always be at a disadvantage because of their slighter physiques and lesser muscular strength. Even a golfing feminist like Mabel Stringer admitted what appeared to be the obvious, that men were 'immensely superior at golf to women not only in the length of hits but in cunning, finesse and accuracy',[49] despite occasional predictions that the day might come when women would compete successfully with men and even when the amateur champion would be a handsome, strapping English girl.[50]

What was important, of course, was not whether women could play golf as well as men or defeat men in head-on competition, but rather that over the years the number of female players and their level of proficiency increased markedly. Although the majority of women in competitions and on club rosters were single, golf as an individual and fashionable sport had the advantage of appealing to married as well as single women and to those of all ages; and with the handicapping system it had the advantage of being one of the few major sports the sexes could play together, although mixed foursomes were never as frequent as in tennis.

By 1914 women's golf had undergone a metamorphosis akin to that of women's tennis, and one that inspired a male commentator to conclude that 'women on the links have made greater strides than in any other section of womanhood'.[51] The putting game, the golfing equivalent of pat-ball, had become rare, as had short courses suitable only for neat iron or mashie play. Instead, facilitated by stronger physiques, more rational dress, better equipment and an improved understanding of the game, women golfers displayed seriousness of purpose, long, full-swinged drives and skilled shot-making on full-length links with no loss of modesty. Commenting on the progress made by women's golf in a relatively short time, May Hezlet, the Open and Irish champion on several occasions and a frequent writer on women's golf, remarked that:

> Even 20 years ago a woman walking in a London street, attired in short tweed coat and skirt, thick boots and carrying her bag of clubs, attracted much undesirable attention; but nowadays a whole team could walk down Bond Street or Regent Street, and no notice would be taken.[52]

Notwithstanding Hezlet's additional observation that on the links people of all ranks met, made friends and forgot about class distinctions, women's golf was socially exclusive. It was recommended as eminently suitable for ladies because it provided not only exercise that was healthier than tennis and less violent than hockey, but also interest, amusement and respectable social encounters for countless women whose otherwise monotonous existences could make them neurotic. It was confined largely to the affluent, for only they had the means to afford club fees, equipment and proper garb as well as the time to play, particularly during awkward mid-week hours, and to migrate to the fashionable resorts where golf was available. The women who took their golf seriously enough to compete conducted their meets along the lines of country-house parties. Everyone knew everyone else, and following a day on the course players would adjourn for tea and musical evenings, and shortly thereafter would read reports of their activities in society journals. There may have been working men's clubs before the war, but predictions of similar clubs for working girls proved misplaced. The contact with golf of women on a lower social rung was limited to the few female caddies and professionals.[53]

Women golfers and the LGU epitomised propriety and were rarely overtly feminist. A few marched in suffrage processions, but 'on the whole lady golfers don't show much interest in the battle for the vote and seem indifferent to it'.[54] Observers realised at the time, however, that golfing women were of considerable importance to the cause of female emancipation and were its products, at least indirectly; and they perceptively equated the ladies' championship with women disputing men's superiority in other spheres and invading other 'men's provinces' such as medicine and the universities.

Some questioned how far the emancipation of women from the rule of etiquette that forbade their general participation in the sports and pastimes of men was beneficial, and predicted that male games like golf would be overdone by emancipated women — since it was a female characteristic to go to extremes — to the detriment of both feminine accomplishments and the communal good. Others, more positive, argued that golf taught women self-control, courage under adversity and judgement; that women's participation in golf, as in any sporting activity, changed attitudes of and to women for the better and contributed to recognition of their right to lead their own lives; and that men must be very weakly constituted if they could not bear the smallest movement or lightest whisper by women on a golf course.[55]

Looking back over the recent history of women and of golf in the first issue of *Ladies' Golf*, Blanche Hulton concluded:

The whole-hearted adoption by women of the Royal and Ancient Game marks an epoch in the history of the sex, and without unduly straining a point, it may be said that golf has been a factor of no small importance in the mental, as well as the physical development of the modern girl . . . None of [their] pre-golf pastimes led their devotees far afield or brought them together in such numbers as golf has done.[56]

Furthermore, she claimed, the success of women's golf clubs and of the LGU demonstrated the female capacity for organisation, management and detail, and allowed them to unite and enjoy each other's company in a candid and tolerant manner formerly undreamed of and considered 'the prerogative of the superior masculine mind' in the pre-golf era.

From the 1860s to 1914 women worked with such vigour, diligence and seriousness to secure for their sex a respected position in the game of golf that the women's game became not only respected but highly popular. The female relatives of military officers, medical doctors, lawyers and members of both houses of parliament organised their own golfing associations in the years before the war; and, with an ever-vigilant eye on opportunities to increase profits, manufacturers of equipment, clothing and miscellaneous products, such as Bovril, recognised the potential of women's golf, as did railway companies who began to provide lady golfers with special fares and facilities.

In August 1914, in a burst of patriotic enthusiasm, *Ladies' Golf* credited golf with playing a major part in changing the attitudes of the public to women and of women to themselves, and in demonstrating that women were both entitled and qualified to share in the nation's work.[57]

Whatever the liberating potential of lawn tennis and golf, it was bicycling — not a sport at all in the competitive sense — that provided women with their most significant experience of physical exercise and did more than any other activity to break down conservative restrictions.

The bicycle evolved from wheeled contraptions developed in the eighteenth century. In the early-nineteenth century, for the exclusive use of ladies, a London coachmaker produced a crude machine called a 'hobby-horse', but, since it weighed more than 60 pounds and required riders to spend most of their time walking, it never became popular, nor did devices that spared ladies the problem of riding astride. The first machine to be propelled by pedalling appeared in 1839 and led in due course to the development of the penny-farthing and the tricycle. Because their clothing made mounting the seat perched high atop the large front wheel virtually impossible, women did not ride the former. From the 1870s, however, they evinced considerable interest in tricycles as a new and relatively rapid means of locomotion and amusement, particularly after it became known that Queen Victoria had ordered machines for herself and her daughters and granddaughters to ride at Osborne. It was not long before journalists began to comment on the number of lady riders and the ability of some to cover distances of many miles without much fatigue, and to pose awkward questions about admitting the claims of 'strong-minded women' to a 'mount'.

Technical innovations in the 1880s, specifically the invention of the drop-frame, chain-driven safety bicycle and the pneumatic tyre, did more than anything else to admit women to the world of cycling by greatly increasing comfort, safety and ease of propulsion. Women's cycles were being manufactured by the early 1890s; by 1894 cycling was a widespread pastime among members of both sexes; by 1895 it was a national passion; and by 1900, as prices dropped dramatically, the bicycle was accepted as a utilitarian form of personal transport for women of all classes who wished to pedal their way to freedom.

Cycling brought to a head most of the usual issues surrounding women's participation in sporting activities, for by its very nature it required muscular exertion and encouraged physical freedom. As with other social innovations involving women, the first sight of large numbers of lady cyclists occasioned amazement and antagonism in arbiters of feminine behaviour. Because of its public nature cycling was scrutinised closely, and, according to the dictates of conventional protocol, branded ungainly, fast, indecorous, conspicuous, unsexing and dangerous. The problems of whether women should ride and, if so, how, in what clothing and with whom, became major preoccupations. Sceptics predicted that the bicycle would undermine morality by introducing an intolerable degree of permissiveness and familiarity in relations between the sexes; that it would destroy the 'sweet simplicity' of the female nature; and that it would provide women with another means of escape from the domestic circle. Mrs Lynn Linton, the well-known critic of the 'girl of the period', opined that 'the chief of all dangers attending this new development of feminine freedom is the intoxication which comes with unfettered liberty'; and she described cycling as 'a queer cross between the treadmill and the tight-rope . . . demanding constant strain of attention to keep balance, and such a monotonous and restricted action of the limbs as to render it a work of penance rather than pleasure'.[58] To Linton the lady cyclist was the embodiment of the New Woman she despised for neglecting her home, disobeying her parents and reading improper novels, and in whom 'there is not left the faintest remnant of that spirit of allurement which, conscious or unconscious, is woman's supreme attraction'.[59] *Punch* and other journals revelled in depicting lady cyclists as mannish, rationally dressed 'wild women of the usual unprepossessing pioneer type'.[60]

In the earliest days of the safety bicycle it took considerable courage and adventurism to defy such disapprobation and to endure being stared and jeered at and sometimes pelted with missiles. Dame Ethel Smyth, the composer, recalled that when she decided to buy a bicycle around 1890 most of her female relations were horrified by her 'indelicacy'; and Helena Swanwick, the author, recollected that, about the same time, as she and her husband cycled around Manchester, she was harassed by mill hands, bus drivers and cabmen whose normal deference to women of her class disappeared in the face of her 'boldness'.[61]

There was also negative medical opinion to contend with.

Although cycling had no medical history, physicians and others claiming medical expertise did not hesitate to give advice that initially at least discouraged cycling as dangerous to female health. They insisted that no one should cycle without first undergoing a physical examination, and bombarded the reading public with advice on when, how far and how fast to cycle, and what to eat and not eat before and after riding. They predicted a derangement of the body's framework through the production of deformed arms, hands, legs and feet and curvatures called 'cyclists' humps', especially if the machine were adjusted incorrectly. They warned of cycling producing bowleggedness and unnaturally large lower leg muscles and so an 'indifferent gait' or 'bicycle walk', and ruining complexions as a result of over-exposure to the elements. They forecast that the anxiety of learning to ride and to avoid accidents would produce the 'bicycle face', a visage with a permanently tense and careworn expression. They pointed out that cycling women would develop the muscles of prize fighters, and that the use of the high gear, because it involved extravagant and strenuous action of the legs and feet, was likely to endanger the heart and produce varicose veins. They warned that women should not ride if they suffered from tuberculosis, hardening of the arteries, emphysema, insomnia, asthma, anaemia, epilepsy, rheumatism, obesity or pelvic disease, and if they were pubescent, menstruating, pregnant or post-partum; and they anticipated cycling causing exhaustion, nasal disorders, headache, lassitude, depression, palpitation, lack of appetite and amenorrhea. In addition they cautioned that sudden deaths could occur while riding up hill, and that over-fatigue 'could bring on severe cases of nervous prostration . . . in a very short time, while the cure of it often covers many years in such cases as do not terminate fatally'.[62]

Finally, and most importantly, they made ominous predictions about cycling robbing women of their womanly charm, jeopardising morality and producing unspecified gynaecological problems that would threaten the birth rate. They forecast, for example, that if the pedals were too far from the seat 'grave consequences' would ensue from the pelvis being dangerously inclined; that uterine displacement was likely to occur as a result of jarring, jolting or vibrations; that difficult parturition would result from the 'pelvic compression and rigidity' caused by a tightening of the pelvic muscles and the decrease in the size of the birth canal; and worst of all that if the saddle were tilted in a certain way the genitalia would be stimulated and the habit of masturbation fostered.[63]

Social and medical Grundyism seems to have had little effect on aspiring cyclists, however. Some parents undoubtedly forbade their daughters to ride, but tens of thousands of women found cycling so utterly delightful a pastime that they allowed their common sense to convince them they were quite as entitled to enjoy it as men. By simply ignoring the scorn and predictions of physical and moral breakdown, they manifested a degree of independence unknown in any other physical activity. Cycling became not only popular but highly fashionable for a time, an essential social accomplishment among all the 'best' women, who eagerly enrolled in the cycling schools that were established to teach affluent beginners the art of balancing and to test their proficiency. The fact that royal women, aristocratic and highly respectable upper-middle-class women became avid cyclists helped to lay the spectre of indelicacy to rest and created an example ordinary women sought to emulate. After all, cycling could hardly be vulgar or dangerous when all the 'right' people rode.

Faced with a *fait accompli*, medical and social authorities soon changed their tune in order to preserve their credibility. Some went to the opposite extreme and made extravagant claims about cycling being the most potent activity yet discovered for creating and retaining good health, and for treating gout, uterine maladies, constipation, anaemia, obesity, constipation, chlorosis, neurasthenia, hysteria, dysmenorrhea, rheumatism, indigestion, alcholism, liver trouble, dyspepsia, haemorrhoids, diabetes, insomnia, neuralgia, headache, asthma and the ordeal of childbirth. The more temperate majority decided that women did not have to be extraordinarily muscular or robust to cycle safely after all. And they became convinced that cycling provided a wonderful release from domestic imprisonment for corseted women who had been forced to dress unhygienically, and healthy, exhilarating exercise for normal women and those who were nervous, over-wrought and bored — if taken prudently and avoided 'at certain times of life'. In the words of an anonymous writer in the *Lady Cyclist*, 'Cycling fulfils its best purposes, from a pleasurable and health-giving standpoint, when kept well within the limits of the rider's strength.'[64]

One of the most cogent statements on cycling for women was produced by W.H. Fenton, a Harley Street physician. Fenton condemned his profession's vague mutterings about the 'grave consequences' that would attend cycling females as based on no practical experience with the pastime. Insisting that women had less physical endurance than men only because they were debarred from the benefits of physical recreation, he identified cycling as the ideal exercise for them since those unaccustomed to exertion could condition themselves gradually and the amount of effort could be regulated exactly to the powers of the individual. He concluded, therefore, that if growing girls and adult women avoided excess and cycled for pleasure and health on common-sense terms their muscles, hearts and lungs would be strengthened to the benefit of themselves and the community at large.[65]

Although most cycling by both sexes was unorganised, given the human instinct to form groups, it is not surprising that as early as the 1870s bicycle clubs were formed to promote tours and arrange meets and races. The largest, most important and one of the oldest was the Cyclists' Touring Club (CTC), which was formed in 1878 to assist town dwellers of the 'better sort' to venture into the countryside. In 1880 it took the unusual step of admitting women, and so established a pattern that became common throughout the cycling world of mixed clubs with women as full or honorary members or members of special ladies' sections.

A kind of Automobile Association for cyclists, the CTC established branches all over the country which it encouraged to provide special facilities for lady visitors; it appointed representatives in each town along major cycling routes and published a list of hotels that provided reduced rates to members. From 1882 it also published the *CTC Gazette* which soon featured women on its cover and included a regular 'Ladies' Column'. The CTC had no hesitation about encouraging women to go on mixed runs and lengthy tours of Britain and the Continent, but its relative liberalism did not extend to their participation in organised competitions. Like the whole cycling world, the club refused to countenance ladies' racing as this would have posed too serious a challenge to propriety and the strength of the female body; and not until 1916 did it sponsor its first ladies' rally. Women were also denied major roles in administering the club. In 1899 an enquiry about whether a female might serve on the council received a positive response, but the first woman was not returned until 1907.[66]

Despite 'the old superstition on the part of the other sex that women can neither form clubs nor enjoy them',[67] and that, as a rule, they were unfitted for club life because they were 'not so broad-minded as men' and were 'apt to be arbitrary and tyrannical when in authority',[68] and despite the argument that organisations were unnecessary since most ladies rode with relatives and friends, it was predictable that once cycling became fashionable a demand would grow, as in other sports, for exclusively female clubs. From the 1890s women's cycling organisations proliferated.

Among the first were the Coventry Lady Cyclists' Club and the Trafalgar Club in London, 'a charming homelike little residence where tea and scandal are served daily throughout the season and the elite practise [riding cycles] on a covered track and in a neighbouring square'.[69] There was even a Chaperon Cyclists' Association (1896) to conduct timid and conventional gentlewomen on tours and excursions. The most important, however, was the Lady Cyclists' Association, which was founded in 1895 'to organise the control of cycling for women and the development of the cause'[70] and presided over for some years by Susan, Countess of Malmesbury. It published a monthly *Gazette* to facilitate communication among members and established branches in most large towns that provided women with the opportunity to become expert riders and see remote parts of their land. It also demonstrated that women were as good at working in associations as men.[71]

The social impact of the bicycle in the late-nineteenth century is difficult to exaggerate. To hundreds of thousands of people of both sexes and of all ages and classes the cycle was much more than an amusing toy. It was a revolutionary form of personal transport and recreation, which helped to destroy the barriers between town and country and provided opportunities to conquer space and time.[72] By enabling women to escape from chaperons and the physical bounds of home, it brought the sexes together on equal terms more completely than any other sport or pastime.

Because of its public nature and wide popularity, cycling focused attention on women's right, desire and need to participate in healthy, outdoor exercise; it symbolised their growing determination to cast social controls aside and to play a fuller role in the life of the nation. The New Woman, pedalling her way to freedom, was a sign of dramatically changing times. Her ability to ride 50 miles a day and repair her own machine belied the traditional image of female helplessness and frailty, and conveyed a new one of strength, vigour and self-sufficiency. Awheel on the open road, she appeared every inch an independent being who could think, say and do what she liked, who deserved to be taken seriously, and who rejected the sartorial and ideological corsets of the past.[73]

As with other sportswomen, the cycling pioneers were rarely active feminists, for despite their defiant dress and behaviour they sought to preserve their standing as ladies. But perhaps more clearly than in any other sport they realised they had a choice between liberty and confinement. Basic conventionality notwithstanding, they opted *en masse* for freedom because the delights and advantages of the cycle were irresistible. Reminiscing years later, a number of early cyclists recalled that it was 'always the fashion in England to be horrified at the participation of women in any exercise hitherto the monopoly of men',[74] and that men objected to women entering domains like cycling out of a fear that they would outdistance them. They remarked on 'how difficult it was for the modern woman, driving her motor car or steering her aeroplane, as naturally and easily as her grandmother walked in the garden',[75] to realise that delicacy was once considered interesting and robustness unattractive, or to appreciate the sudden sense of emancipation that cycling provided to women who were in their prime in the 1890s. In short, said Sara Burstall, 'We could buy a machine, go about and take care of ourselves and with a few pounds in our pocket see something of the world.'[76]

Even more enthusiastic contemporaries called the bicycle one of the greatest boons to women in all of history, and their most significant emancipator during the Victorian age, for it broadened 'woman's mind as well as her chest measure', and achieved more for her than all the activities of politicians and journalists combined. Equating mastery of the bicycle with mastery of self, they related cycling to consciousness-raising among women, and to their ability 'to take a long-sighted and large-minded view of their true interests'.[77] And they were convinced that female cyclists' courageous defiance of tradition and opprobrium went hand-in-hand with women's demands for equality and liberation in other areas, and gave the feminist movement a powerful fillip at an important stage in its development.

In conclusion, then, the cycling phenomenon, like other aspects of women's sport, was an important part of an intricate pattern of wider change, at a time when values were altering rapidly and powerful conventions and stereotypes so far as women were concerned were passing away. Behind it were potent social forces connected with the late-Victorian desire for novelty, greater personal and social mobility and a relaxation of relations between the sexes. The bicycle rage coincided with the first movement for the emancipation of women, with an increase in the popularity of active forms of recreation among women, with the beginning of women's recognition as physically competent beings and capable sportspersons, and with a readiness on the part of middle-class women to adopt 'a mechanical device which gave them independence physically, as their education had given many of them some measure of mental independence and self-control'.[78]

Bicycling reached all sorts of women and encouraged many who otherwise were sedentary and unathletic to do something physical. While only a few could play hockey, tennis or golf, almost all women could ride. Unlike other women's sports, which were class specific and effected gradual reform, cycling transcended class barriers and brought about revolutionary changes in social behaviour and perceptions. Tradition and propriety were compelled to give way at least partially to the lady cyclist who had taken a stand, and 'by so doing . . . vastly improved the chances of taking her true position as man's equal'.[79]

Women's invasion of the world of individual sport in the late-nineteenth century did not stop at the activities discussed above. They also played badminton, swam, rowed, fenced, bowled, rode horses, hunted, shot, fished, yachted, skiied, tobogganed, snow-shoed, ice- and roller-skated, fell-walked and climbed mountains. Indeed there were few sports in which women did not participate to some extent.

This was the case because most individual sports accorded much more with social and cultural images of womanhood than did team games, and thus inspired less controversy. Because many involved aesthetically pleasing images but not body contact or 'excessive' strength, because many were not typed as overtly male, because competitions were usually sex-segregated and not particularly intense, and because the women involved made compromises that emphasised femininity and muted claims to equality, they were perceived as little real threat to male athletic supremacy. In addition, with exceptions, participation in individual sports involved membership in socially but not necessarily sexually segregated clubs which provided facilities and organised competitions and activities. This meant considerable expenditure on club fees as well as equipment, clothing and travel, so that participants were almost always women of the affluent classes whose womanliness was unquestionable and inclined to rub off on their activities. Whole families could join in, which helps to explain why individual sports were considered much more acceptable for married women than those involving teams. Furthermore, the institution of clubs and competitions often involved men as organisers or advisers, and this too helped to gain approval and buffer criticism.[80]

To the conventional Victorian mind, however, sport was still sport. In individual as in team sport it considered men's participation much more serious, valuable and legitimate than women's, and that it was essential for the good of women and the good of the game that women go only so far and that a line separating the sexes be maintained. Long after thousands of women were cycling, golfing and playing tennis, the question of whether their doing so was ladylike was still discussed. Consequently, individual sports, on the one hand, confirmed notions about femininity and female inferiority. On the other hand, they were important emancipators, for the women who bicycled and played tennis and golf and all the other individual sports available to them confounded stereotypes of womanly weakness and inactivity, and provided models for their sisters to emulate.

Notes

1. *Punch*, quoted in Catherine Carr (ed.), *The Spinning Wheel* (Cardiff, 1955), p.10.

2. Pierce Egan, *The Finish to the Adventures of Tom, Jerry and Logic* (London, 1869), p. 251.

3. *Young Lady's Book*, pp. 420–1.

4. Charles Kingsley, *Health and Education* (London, 1874), p. 44. See also *Punch* (17 August 1861), p. 66, (30 April 1864), p. 177, (1 July 1865), p. 261, (14 October 1865), p. 152.

5. Duke of Beaufort and Alfred E.T. Watson (eds), *The Badminton Library of Sports and Pastimes* (19 vols , London, 1885–1902), vol. 12: *Tennis, Lawn Tennis, Rackets, and Fives*, by J.M. Heathcote, C.G. Heathcote, E.O.P. Bouverie and A.C. Ainger (4th edn, 1897), p. 132.

6. Competitive croquet revived in the 1890s, and in 1897 the British Croquet Association (1896) resumed a national championship which included an open section involving both men and women. In 1901, and for several years thereafter, a most extraordinary thing happened. A woman — Miss Lily Gower — emerged victorious from 'the strongest field of combatants ever known'.

7. *Pastime* (12 June 1889), p. 379.

8. *Punch* (12 September 1874), p. 105, (10 October 1874), p. 148, (7 July 1877), p. 302, (17 August 1878), p. 66, (5 October 1878), p. 150, (23 November 1878), p. 239, (19 July 1879), p. 23, (13 September 1879), p. 112. Sarcastic suggestions that, because of their lack of strength, women should be permitted to allow the ball to bounce twice and serve closer to the net were never formalised.

9. All-England Lawn Tennis Club (AELTC), Committee Minutes (21 June 1884), in the Kenneth Ritchie Wimbledon Library. See also AELTC, Committee Minutes (1 and 26 February and 12 April 1883). In 1882 Croquet was expunged from the name of the All-England Club, but was reincluded, in 1902, after Lawn Tennis.

Women were excluded from administrative roles in the AELTC until December 1982 when Virginia Wade was appointed to the Committee of Management.

10. AELTC, Committee Minutes (28 June 1884). For years at Wimbledon and other tournaments women's dressing rooms were a constant problem, because more often than not they were small, shabby, drafty and short of lavatories, showers and hot water. Dorothea Katherine Lambert Chambers, *Lawn Tennis for Ladies* (London, 1910), pp. 81–2.

11. Alan Little, *Maud Watson* (London, 1983), p. 3. As a permanent momento of her victory Maud received a silver flower basket, and her sister a mirror and brush.

12. AELTC Committee, Report to Annual General Meeting (1884). Neither the men's nor the women's championship entries grew steadily until after 1900. The men's reached 61 in 1880 but dropped to only 17 in 1887, while between 1885 and 1897 the ladies' field ranged from a high of only eleven to a low of four. In 1914 103 men and 50 women competed. Lance Tingay, *100 Years of Wimbledon* (Enfield, Middlesex, 1977), p. 223.

13. *Pastime* (22 July 1885), p. 65.

14. Ibid. (23 August 1893), pp. 115–16. See also *Lawn Tennis* (4 August 1897), p. 212.

15. Lottie Dod, 'Ladies' Lawn Tennis' in Heathcote *et al., Tennis, Lawn Tennis*, p. 313; *Pastime* (1 July 1885), p. 5, (29 June 1887), p. 441, (13 July 1887), pp. 29–30, (15 July 1891), p. 43, (13 July 1892), p. 21, (3 May 1893), p. 272.

16. *Pastime* (10 June 1891), p. 355.

17. Ibid. (3 May 1893), p. 272; *Hockey Field* (2 July 1908), p. 195; Alan Little, *Lottie Dod* (London, 1983), p. 13.

Dod once remarked that 'the great joy of games is the hard work entailed in learning them' (Little, *Lottie Dod*, p. 23), and she certainly practised what she preached. After her retirement from competitive tennis she captained the England hockey team in 1899 and 1900; she won the Ladies' Open Golf Championship in 1904; she passed her diamond test at figure skating; she won a silver medal in archery at the 1908 Olympic Games; she was an active member of the Ladies' Alpine Club; and she was an ardent cyclist and an excellent billiards player, rower, sculler and horse-back rider.

18. Alan Little, *Dorothea Chambers* (London, 1985), pp. 1–30.

Over the protests of the Baron de Coubertin, whose Olympic ideal was infused by the English public school cult of manliness, lawn tennis and golf were introduced in 1900 as the first sports for women in the modern Olympic Games. Golf was replaced by archery in 1904; figure-skating and swimming were added in 1908 and 1912, respectively. Among the few female competitors British women were a small minority. For information on women in the Olympics see Joanna Davenport, 'The Women's Movement into the Olympic Games', *Journal of Physical Education and Recreation*, vol. 49, no. 3 (1978), pp. 58–60; Sheila Mitchell, 'Women's Participation in the Olympic Games, 1900–1926', *Journal of Sport History*, vol. 4, no. 2 (1977), pp. 208–28; Uriel Simri, 'The Development of Female Participation in the Modern Olympic Games', *Stadion*, vol. 6 (1980), pp. 187–216.

19. AELTC, Committee Minutes (4 November 1907).

20. *Pastime* (28 May 1884), p. 343, (12 June 1889), p. 379, (2 September 1891), p. 166; *Lawn Tennis* (25 May 1911), p. 184, (23 May 1912), p. 277, (27 June 1912), p. 405, (27 November 1913), p. 57; Chambers, *Lawn Tennis*, p. 51; Dod, 'Ladies' Lawn Tennis' in Heathcote *et al., Tennis, Lawn Tennis*, p. 312; Eleanor Metheny, 'Sports and the Feminine Image', *International Olympic Academy* (August 1964), p. 103.

21. Miss Toupie Lowther, 'Ladies' Play' in R.F. and H.L. Doherty (eds), *Lawn Tennis* (London 1903), p. 66.

22. *Pastime* (29 June 1888), p. 389.

23. Ibid. (15 August 1888), p. 127.

24. *Lawn Tennis* (6 July 1904), p. 179; M. Marshall, 'Lawn Tennis' in Frances E. Slaughter (ed.), *The Sportswoman's Library* (2 vols , London, 1898), vol. 2, pp. 341–2.

25. *Pastime* (27 July 1887), p. 67. See also (5 September 1888), p. 178; *Lawn Tennis* (2 July 1902), p. 197; *Physical Culture*, vol. 1 (September 1898), p. 170.

26. *Young Woman*, vol. 2 (October 1893–September 1894), p. 370.

27. Dod, 'Ladies' Lawn Tennis' in Heathcote *et al.*, *Tennis, Lawn Tennis*, pp. 307–9. See also p. 311.

28. Chambers, *Lawn Tennis*, pp. 1–13.

29. Ibid., p. 174.

30. Amy Bennet Pascoe, 'Ladies' Golf' in Garden Smith, W.J. MacGeagh, W.G. vanT. Sutphen and Amy Pascoe, *The World of Golf* (London, 1898), p. 279.

31. *Ladies' Golf*, vol, 1 (April 1912), p. 16. See also Charles Price, *The World of Golf* (London, 1962), p. 10.

32. *Ladies' Golf* (April 1912), p. 16.

33. Robert Browning, *A History of Golf* (London, 1955), pp. 121–2. See also G. Cousins, *Golf in Britain* (London, 1975), p. 55. A creel was a large wicker fish basket and a shull, an attached smaller one.

34. John R. Lowerson, 'English Middle-Class Sport, 1880–1914', *Proceedings of the Inaugural Conference of the British Society of Sport History, 20–21 March 1982* (Liverpool, 1982), pp. 10–12; John R. Lowerson, 'Scottish Croquet; The English Golf Boom, 1880–1914', *History Today*, vol. 33, no. 5 (1983), pp. 25–30.

35. May Hezlet, *Ladies' Golf*, 2nd edn (London, 1907), pp. 14–15.

36. *St Andrews Gazette and Fifeshire News* (21 August 1872), quoted in Bernard Darwin *et al.*, *A History of Golf in Britain* (London, 1952) pp. 22–3.

37. Mabel E. Stringer, *Golfing Reminiscences* (London, 1924), pp. 21–3; *Hockey Field* (10 September 1908), p. 360; *Ladies' Golf* (7 May 1914), p. 13.

38. *Ladies' Golf*, vol. 2 (January 1913), p. 14. See also Anne O'Hagan, 'The Athletic Girl', *Munsey's Magazine*, vol. 25 (August 1901), p. 737.

39. Beaufort and Watson (eds), *Badminton Library*, vol. 11: *Golf* (1890), by Horace G. Hutchinson, pp. 51–2.

40. Hezlet, *Ladies' Golf*, p. 16.

41. Ibid., pp. 16–20; Stringer, *Golfing Reminiscences*, pp. 238–40. By 1902 the LGU had nine vice-presidents, all men, and a male honorary treasurer and honorary auditor. The honorary secretary and assistant honorary secretary were women, as was the president. *Ladies' Golf Union Year Book* (1902), p. 4.

42. *Golfing Annual*, vol. 7 (1893–4), pp. 10, 28; Hezlet, *Ladies' Golf*, pp. 16–20; *Ladies' Golf*, vol. 1 (September 1912), p. 39; Enid Wilson, *A Gallery of Women Golfers* (London, 1961), pp. 14–15; Enid Wilson, 'Women's Golf' in Darwin *et al.*, *History of Golf*, pp. 223–4. None of the entrants in the first championship was from Scotland where the putting game still dominated.

43. *Golfing Annual* (1893–4), p. 38.

44. Ibid., vol. 10 (1896–7), p. 22; Mrs Ross [May Hezlet], 'From the Ladies' Point of View' in Horace G. Hutchinson (ed.), *The New Book of Golf* (London, 1912), p. 355; Stringer, *Golfing Reminiscences*, pp. 33–4, 238.

45. *Golfing Annual*, vol. 11 (1908–9), p. 36; *Hockey Field* (28 May 1908), p. 119.

46. Cecil Leitch, *Golf* (London, 1922), pp. 13–18, 39. An interest in golf, as in tennis, seemed to run in families. There were three Hezlets and five Leitches in the 1912 Open championship.

47. Horace G. Hutchinson, *The Book of Golf and Golfers* (London, 1919), p. 165; Horace G. Hutchinson, *Fifty Years of Golf* (London, 1919), p. 165.

48. Stringer, *Golfing Reminiscences*, pp. 199–200; *The Times*, 12 October 1910.

49. Stringer, *Golfing Reminiscences*, p. 202. See also Issette Pearson, 'Introductory' in Louis Mackern and M. Boys (eds), *Our Lady of the Green* (London, 1899), p. 6.

50. *Golfing Annual*, vol. 4 (1890–1), pp. 24–5, (1893–4), p. 38; *Sunday Times*, 26 April 1914.

51. *Ladies' Golf*, vol. 2 (April 1913), p. 35.

52. Ross [Hezlet], 'Ladies' Point of View' in Hutchinson (ed.), *New Book*, p. 267.

53. The abundance of hyphenated names on club membership lists is a clear indication of social class. Classic examples are 'Auntie' and 'Niecie' Tyrwhitt-Drake, who were members of nearly every ladies' club in the south of England in the 1890s.
Apart from a handful of golf professionals, women's sport was entirely amateur. The former, who were not considered 'ladies', were hired at a few women's clubs in recognition of the advantages to women of being taught by other women, especially when male professionals often regarded females as hopeless and thus gave only half-hearted instruction. Another way for a woman to make a living from golf was to become a paid secretary of a golf club, in which case she could retain her amateur standing. Hezlet, *Ladies' Golf*, pp. 8–9, 66; *Hockey Field* (18 June 1908), p. 164; *Ladies' Golf* (July 1912), p. 23, (30 October 1913), p. 8; *Queen* (23 August 1913), p. 353; Wilson, 'Women's Golf' in Darwin *et al.*, *History of Golf*, p. 225; Wilson, *Gallery*, pp. 11–12.

54. *Hockey Field* (25 January 1908), p. 179.

55. *Golfing Annual* (1890–1), p. 24, (1893–4), p. 38; *Golf Monthly* (December 1912), pp. 747–50; Hezlet, *Ladies' Golf*, pp. 1–8; *Ladies' Golf*, vol. 1 (March 1912), p. 36, (April 1913), p. 35; Cecil Leitch, *Golf for Girls* (London, 1911), p. 4; *Pastime* (11 May 1892), p. 304.

56. *Ladies' Golf*, vol. 1 (March 1912), p. 21.

57. Ibid. (6 August 1914), p. 5.

58. Eliza Lynn Linton, 'Cranks and Crazes', *North American Review*, vol. 161 (December 1895), pp. 671–2. See also *Lady Cyclist*, vol. 1, no. 1 (1895), pp. 46–7; S.H. Aronson, 'The Sociology of the Bicycle', *Social Forces*, vol. 30, no. 3 (1952), p. 308; David Rubinstein, 'Cycling Eighty Years Ago', *History Today*, vol. 28, no. 8 (1978), p. 546; Roderick Watson and Martin Grey, *The Penguin Book of the Bicycle* (Harmondsworth, 1978), p. 133.

59. Eliza Lynn Linton, quoted in James T. Lightwood, *The Cyclists' Touring Club* (London, 1928), p. 201. See also Frank Bowden, *Points for Cyclists* (Leicester, 1891), pp. 35–6; Lillias Campbell Davidson, *Handbook for Lady Cyclists* (London, 1896), p. 10; David Rubinstein, 'Cycling in the 1890s', *Victorian Studies*, vol. 21, no. 1 (1977), p.62.

60. See, for example, *Punch* (18 May 1895), p. 239, (3 August 1896), p. 59, (13 June 1896), p. 282, (11 September 1897), p. 110, (6 September 1899), p. 114.

61. Ethel Smyth, *Impressions that Remained* (2 vols , London, 1919), vol.

2, pp. 230–1; Helena Swanwick, *I Have Been Young* (London, 1935), pp. 163, 239.

62. *Idler*, vol. 8 (August 1895), p. 74. See also *Lady Cyclist*, vol. 1, no. 4 (1895), p. 158; *Lawn Tennis* (26 August 1896), p. 159; *Review of Reviews*, vol. 1 (January–June 1890), pp. 287–8.

63. *Humanitarian*, vol. 17 (August 1900), p. 144.

64. *Lady Cyclist* (1 May 1897), p. 907. See also *Badminton Magazine of Sports and Pastimes*, vol. 1 (August–December 1895), p. 413; *British Medical Journal* (7 July 1894), p. 35, (19 January 1895), pp. 139–40, (25 May 1895), p. 1168, (21 December 1895), pp. 1582–3, (11 January 1896), pp. 115–16, (16 May 1896), pp. 1211–12, (30 May 1896), pp. 1336–7, (6 June 1896), p. 1399, (20 June 1896), p. 1510, (4 July 1896) pp. 38–9, (11 July 1896), pp. 98–9, (25 July 1896), p. 203, (12 September 1896), p. 681, (1 October 1898), p. 994; *Lady Cyclist*, vol. 1, no. 2 (1895), p. 66; Davidson, *Handbook*, pp. 85, 87–88; F.J. Erskine *Bicycling for Ladies* (London, 1896), p. 14; F.J. Erskine, *Lady Cycling* (London, 1897), p. 131; Oscar Jennings, *Cycling and Health* (London, 1890), pp. 88–9; *Lancet* (16 May 1896), pp. 1369–70, (24 July 1897), pp. 221–2, (24 December 1898), p. 1717, (9 December 1899), p. 1583, (10 October 1903), p. 1966; Susan, Countess of Malmesbury, 'Bicycling for Women' in H. Graves, G.L. Hillier and Susan, Countess of Malmesbury, *Cycling* (London, 1898), pp. 91–2; *Review of Reviews*, vol. 7 (January–June 1893), p. 524, vol. 14 (1896), pp. 161, 440.

65. W.H. Fenton, 'A Medical View of Cycling for Women', *Nineteenth Century*, vol. 39 (May 1896), p. 798.

66. Davidson, *Handbook*, p. 95; Erskine, *Lady Cycling*, pp. 7–8, 85; Malmesbury, 'Bicycling for Women' in Graves, Hillier and Malmesbury, *Cycling*, p. 94; Lightwood, *Cyclists' Touring Club*, p. 176. There were occasional newspaper accounts of women acrobats — definitely not ladies — participating in races around banked tracks during public cycling shows, and of young gentlemen in the audience denouncing these as 'degrading', 'revolting' and 'bizarre' exhibitions despite finding them so fascinating that they returned day after day. *Weekly Telegraph* (Sheffield), 21 December 1895.

67. Davidson, *Handbook*, p. 107.

68. Erskine, *Lady Cycling*, pp. 137–8.

69. A.C. Pemberton, Mrs Harcourt Williamson, C.P. Sisley and G. Floyd, *The Complete Cyclist* (London, 1897), pp. 55–6.

70. *Lady Cyclist*, vol. 1, no. 1 (1895), p. 44.

71. Ibid.; *Lady Cyclist* (27 March 1897), pp. 664–6; Malmesbury, 'Bicycling for Women' in Graves, Hillier and Malmesbury, *Cycling*, p. 95.

72. Meller, *Leisure and the Changing City*, p. 227; Rubinstein, 'Cycling in the 1890s', pp. 47–8; Watson and Grey, *Penguin Book*, p. 126.

73. Carr (ed.), *Spinning Wheel*, p. 11; Rubinstein, 'Cycling Eighty Years Ago', p. 544; Rubinstein, 'Cycling in the 1890s', p. 68.

74. *Badminton Magazine of Sports and Pastimes* (August–December 1895), p. 407.

75. Sara A. Burstall, *Retrospect and Prospect* (London, 1933), p. 131.

76. Ibid. See also Elizabeth S. Haldane, *From One Century to Another*

(London, 1937), p. 145.

77. *Lady Cyclist*, vol. 1, no. 1 (1895), p. 11, (27 March 1897), p. 665. See also M. Ann Hall, 'The Role of the Safety Bicycle in the Emancipation of Women', *Proceedings of the Second World Symposium on the History of Sport and Physical Education* (Banff, Al., 1971), p. 245; Rubinstein, 'Cycling Eighty Years Ago', p. 546.

78. Burstall, *Retrospect*, p. 131.

79. *Northern Wheeler* (1893), quoted in James Walvin, *Leisure and Society 1830–1950* (London, 1978), p. 97.

80. June A. Kennard, 'Women, Sport and Society in Victorian England', unpublished PhD dissertation, University of North Carolina, Greensboro, 1974, p. 176; Albert D. Munrow, *Physical Education* (London, 1972), p. 162.

7

The Medical and Scientific Debate on Women's Sport

> There are some women whose physical and intellectual powers are alike great; but these form the exception and they are generally as remarkable for the masculine qualities of their bodies as for those of their minds.[1]

As Peter McIntosh observes, 'sport . . . is so intimately associated with the human body and with bodily function and activity that different attitudes towards the body and the physical have inevitably affected or been reflected in attitudes to sport'.[2] This was certainly true from 1870 to 1914 when much of the controversy about women in sport concerned the question of female bodies and their capacities, even though relatively little was known about women's biology and less about how it related to physical activity.

From time immemorial patriarchy has had a 'powerful hold through its successful habit of passing itself off as nature';[3] and the roles assigned to women have generated elaborate scientific justifications. In the nineteenth century, when the intellectual standing and popularity of science increased tremendously, the virtually exclusively male medical and scientific establishment offered supposedly scientific arguments to rationalise and legitimate various aspects of English life, particularly those that were under stress from powerful forces of economic and social change. Yet in attempting to move to science from myths based on prejudice and superstition, scientists and physicians actually created a series of new myths to explain and justify social judgements, which they passed off as empirical 'truths'.

Nowhere did this pattern operate more frequently and successfully than when cultural values were presented as biological

192

factors to counteract the women's rights movement's apparent threat to social stability and men's monopolies and prerogatives. Since the authority of male experts in diverse areas was increasingly acknowledged and rarely questioned, scientists and doctors were in an especially effective position to attack feminist theories and activities, to shore up traditional female roles and to dictate what were safe and legitimate uses of the female body; and in support of the negative side of the woman question they distorted and magnified the biological differences between the sexes and showed a remarkable willingness to grasp at any alleged fact of physiology or anatomy.

Most physicians sincerely believed that a woman's biology was her destiny — which was not their attitude to men, the male body being considered the standard and the supposed physical weakness of the female, a cause for indulgent contempt. Their thesis was that the sexes should occupy separate spheres because women's reproductive functions, absolute physical inferiority and propensity to illness inevitably disqualified them from sharing men's privileges in the political, educational, economic and sporting arenas. They simultaneously praised the female body for the 'weaker' sex's elevation to the transcendent calling of motherhood and blamed it for its uncleanness and uselessness during and after menstruation and menopause. They insisted that women were very different from men, that women were physically more fragile, and that biological differences in the brains of the sexes meant that female nervous systems were more irritable; and they argued that women possessed only a limited amount of energy and that adolescent girls should get plenty of rest, avoid intellectual overstrain and take moderate exercise in the open air. The rub was that they formulated all of this in the most impeccably scientific language, when their positions had much more to do with social attitudes and codes than with genetics and systematic investigation.[4]

Recent studies of symbolic culture have shown that things which violate a society's sense of order are usually seen as threatening, nasty, disorderly or wrong,[5] and this was clearly evident in the late-nineteenth century. One is struck by the continuing coincidence between social developments and the critiques of higher education offered by a series of eminent physicians who defined women almost exclusively in terms of their reproductive capacity and ability to be good companions to men, and who represented activities and characteristics considered to detract from this as unnecessary, unattractive and unnatural.

Medical men such as Edward Clarke and Henry Maudsley wrote their biological criticisms of women's higher education in the 1870s in response to social developments — in Clarke's case, pressure on Harvard University to open its facilities to women, and in Maudsley's, the foundation of the campaign to gain university education for women in England and the opening of Girton College — rather than to developments within scientific theory. But their professional reputations guaranteed that their views would offer a 'sound' physiological basis for the conservative defence of the Victorian ideal of womanhood and opposition to equal educational opportunity.

Despite overwhelming evidence to the contrary, and despite their gradual development of more genuinely scientific views of the body, many doctors insisted for years thereafter that the failure to tailor education to the realities of female inferiority 'in every organ and tissue', and to the need for rest during puberty, could ruin minds and bodies forever. Mental competition with men they styled 'Amazonian ambition' which atrophied the organs of reproduction and produced repulsively sexless creatures incapable of giving birth to normal, healthy children. It was thus, they argued, a dereliction of 'true duties' and counter to the best interests of women and the English race.[6]

Female physicians ordinarily did not share their male colleagues' alarm about the physiological dangers of over-education. They often used biology conversely to support the idea that rather than being natural, physical and mental weakness in most women was the result of enervating habits and a complex process of socialisation and sex-role stereotyping. They thus got involved in the nature versus nurture debate that was critical to the controversy over women's rights and duties and central to the issue of whether women could safely and legitimately participate in sport. Physical fitness was one of their frequent themes, for they were much more enthusiastic about preventive medicine than men. Furthermore it had feminist overtones, for they described good health as a necessary precondition for the pursuit of various rights, and they promoted its acquisition through good nutrition, dress reform and exercise.

Elizabeth Blackwell, the first woman on the British Medical Register, may have identified the improvement of the race as woman's sacred duty, but she described the system in force in boarding schools as 'ruinous' to mind and body and the daily crocodile walk as a 'melancholy spectacle'. With remarkable insight, she recommended running, sliding, jumping, gymnastics and every active sport for girls, on the grounds that 'bodies that can move in dignity, in grace, in airy lightness, or conscious strength, bodies erect and firm, energetic and active bodies are truly sovereign in their presence, are expressions of a sovereign nature'.[7] Elizabeth Garrett Anderson exhibited the same sort of progressive conservatism when she supported sound academic training for girls, identified lack of exercise as the chief cause of illness and recommended a regular course of physical activity — including walking, dancing, sports and gymnastics — as productive of health, strength, grace and self-mastery, if it were interspersed with periods of rest.[8] The views of 'lady doctors' were often discounted by medical and public opinion, however, for female physicians were not numerous enough to make much of an impact and were long resented as interlopers and aberrations.

On the whole, the medical establishment was far more open-minded on the subject of female physical education than mental. If intellectual achievement among women had little appeal, physical — at least within limits prescribed by ideological assumptions about the female body and the roles and characteristics of women — definitely did, but because of its perceived reproductive, rather than emancipatory, benefits.

As was indicated in the Introduction, from the early years of the nineteenth century advocates of exercise for women used medical arguments to support their case, and doctors certainly considered female ill-health a major problem, with real and psychosomatic causes. Despite the deficiencies of their scientific knowledge — the limited energy theory has been discredited completely — they were correct in criticising the sedentary lifestyle, inadequate diet and confining clothing of middle-class females. Further, the boredom and confinement of the lives of many women fostered a sense of invalidism and hypochondria. There is evidence that some women actually cultivated or feigned illness to give themselves something to do and to gain attention and psychological control at a time when they had very little political, economic or social influence. Whatever the causes of illness, the medical profession was virtually unanimous in its estimate of women as physically inferior to men, and in its concern about excessive female debility because of the implications for the future of the race. Doctors thus concluded that moderate types and amounts of exercise would have a rejuvenating effect on women, and by making them healthier would improve their child-bearing capacity.

At first the potentially high energy demands of exercise caused little concern in comparison to the 'dangers' emanating from excessive mental training, partly because physical training and open-air games gave at least some consideration to the rules of health. But as women's sports grew increasingly vigorous and competitive — and thus more masculine — barriers to physical exercise similar to those against mental began to be imposed by some members of the medical community.[9]

An examination of the two premier medical journals, the *British Medical Journal* and the *Lancet*, is useful in illuminating changes in medical attitudes to women's bodies and to women's sport and exercise in the late-nineteenth century, 'for both covered a spectrum far beyond . . . immediate medical aspects' and gave a high priority to social considerations.[10]

In 1858 an article in the *British Medical Journal* on 'Physical Education' attributed the greatness of the English race to its masculinity and the superior qualities of courage, self-reliance, endurance and pluck that were developed through manly games and field sports. No mention was made of women apart from the unsubstantiated claim that they were in better physical condition than their American sisters. During the 1860s and 1870s the journal dealt with the subject of physical education and exercise for either sex only occasionally, although it went so far as to publish, in 1863, an unusual piece supportive of ladies riding horses astride. In 1868 it included a letter to the editor condoning the opportunities for exercise provided to young ladies by the Liverpool Gymnasium, because of the moral, social and physiological benefits, and in 1873 and 1874, articles supporting physical education in the new state elementary schools and physical recreation as part of the programme at women's university colleges.[11]

The 1880s found the *British Medical Journal* manifesting a growing, although never great, interest in gymnastics in board schools, games and exercise in girls', which it favoured to obviate race degeneration, and athletics in boys' public schools, which it supported as a counter-weight to the development of 'filthy habits' so long as they did not occupy too large a place in the curriculum. An 1884 article condemned as 'absurd' the view that active play was unladylike, and went on, in the same breath, to encourage cricket and tennis for schoolgirls but warn that really 'violent' exercise could damage health. Another, in 1888, urged girls' schools to pay more attention to teaching the laws of physiology and health, and women's colleges, more attention to physical culture to reduce the danger of collapse produced by prolonged study during puberty.[12]

Although, from 1894 until the turn of the century, the *British Medical Journal's* primary sporting preoccupation was cycling, it also considered the state of the national physique, exercise in state schools, the effects of severe muscular exertion on male adolescents, the value of sports to schoolboys and the effects of sports on the health of girls. On the latter subject, writers acknowledged the benefits to girls' health of swimming, hockey, cycling and tennis. Indeed, one said,

> . . . the improvement in the physique of women has been very noticeable since the development among them of a taste for cycling, lawn tennis, hockey and other forms of outdoor exercise, which would have been thought very unladylike in the early days of the Victorian Era when girls lay on boards to straighten their spines, and were in all respects compelled to follow what may be called the 'prunes and prisms' system of life.[13]

At the same time, however, the *British Medical Journal's* general view was that girls could overdo sports and should not continue athletic participation much past school age, for reasons that were so obvious as not to need explaining.[14]

Over the years, the other major medical journal, the *Lancet*, had more to say about female exercise and sport. Its first remarks on the subject were made in 1869 in an editorial response to John Stuart Mill's *The Subjection of Women*. As was predictable, the *Lancet* disagreed with Mill on women's physical and intellectual powers, and opined that women with unusual strength in either quarter were generally masculine. If they were to remain true to their real nature, girls must be given an education that allowed for the differences between the sexes, it said. At the same time, however, it attributed

> . . . much of that subsequent delicacy, feeble health, and proclivity to hysteria to which the female sex is relatively so liable [to] the absence of proper physical training and healthful out-door exercises, as a relief to the close and stuffy school-room in which girls are too often confined, [and it

argued that] every girls' school should have its playground and gymnasium.[15]

In a similar vein, an article on gymnastics later the same year noted that there was

. . . stronger reason for judicious and systematic exercise of the bodily frame in the case of the softer than rougher sex. Ladies, particularly in the middle ranks, have neither the compulsory exertion of the lower, nor the open-air pastimes of the upper classes. Their life on the whole, particularly in cities, is too sedentary for vigorous development and health.[16]

It went on to applaud the opportunities for physical training available to young ladies at the Liverpool Gymnasium and the Bruton Street Gymnasium in London, and to lend support to undertakings conducive to the 'bodily health' and 'symmetrical development' of the girls of the period.

In the 1870s *Lancet* authors, almost all medical doctors, favoured introducing a system of physical education into every boys' school in the country, defended athleticism at public schools as producing no antagonism with mental work, and even supported systematic physical training for girls, because of its positive effects on their figures and bearing, as long as discretion was the watchword and strain avoided.[17] Then, towards the end of the decade, they began to evince a more sustained interest in female exercise and games.

On the whole the *Lancet*'s contributors, like those of the *British Medical Journal*, supported the limited energy theory, and predicted that higher education would have negative medical effects on women; and they regarded all females as 'lower in the scale of human development than males' and as destined for 'subordinate roles' within the domestic sphere.[18] But they generally agreed that

. . . in these days when so many women are engaging in intellectual pursuits, and even desire to compete with men in the cares and anxieties of professional life, the question of their physical training ought to receive more attention than it has hitherto done.[19]

They regretted that healthy exercise for girls, after about the age of nine, was sacrificed to the bondage of genteel deportment, tight lacing and perceptions of femininity, and they commended the health-giving benefits of swimming, fives, rackets and tennis, although, they hastened to add, 'girls should [not] emulate their brothers in the cricket field' nor should 'female athleticism become the vogue'.[20] As one writer observed in 1883, the movement concerning girls' exercise was in the right direction as long as the importance of grace and womanly bearing was recognised and activities were kept within reasonable limits.[21]

By the middle of the 1880s *Lancet* writers advocated moderate exercise as forming 'the co-efficient of healthy scholastic training' and healthy motherhood,[22] and they observed with approval that increasing attention was being paid to the physical training of growing girls in schools for the better classes. They noted the advantages to be gained by the introduction of a well-regulated and moderate athleticism in the form of healthy games and athletic pursuits — like Swedish gymnastics, swimming, tennis, golf, rowing and riding — that were still too often limited to boys and which had formerly been completely proscribed by timid mothers and prudish schoolmistresses; and they predicted that the 'thorough development of the female frame which such exercise would induce, would . . . do much to diminish the tendency towards the special diseases which so many women suffer from in after life'.[23] At the same time, however, they opined that the extension of competitive sports to girls' schools would be a great mistake, because, to be conducive to well-being and health, the exercise of females had to be limited in time and degree since their frames could not be unduly taxed without great harm ensuing.[24]

As female sport became more competitive, serious, skilled and extensive, and thus apparently more masculine and threatening to the male monopoly, some members of the medical profession took increasingly conservative positions on the subject and began to apply the limited energy theory to sport and to issue ominous warnings about sport's production of 'womb irritation', 'pelvic disturbances' and muscular and skeletal damage. They stressed particularly that a woman's whole system was disrupted during menstruation, that during the monthly period a woman was ill and especially susceptible to pathological conditions of the physiological and nervous systems; so menstruating women must rest for a minimum of two days and at all costs avoid vigorous exercise lest the reproductive organs be displaced, the development of the womb retarded and years of suffering inaugurated.

In 1911, for example, in a letter to the editor of the *Lancet* which inspired responses varying from complete rejection to complete endorsement, one Robert Jones denounced the lack of opportunity in the crowded timetable of the average girls' school for rest and real recreation, and the idea in some that exercise could be an end in itself instead of a mere adjunct to the cultivation of the mind. With little regard for factual evidence, he asserted that violent games, like hockey, football, cricket and golf, were carried to excess, and that 'the moment classes are over a girl is driven compulsorily to the playing field to practise games which do not in themselves sufficiently supply a training for all the muscles of the body'. The 'undue, wicked devotion to pointless athleticism', he went on, produced 'gregariousness rather than self-reliance' and the neglect of domestic responsibilities, and tended 'to make the body a motor machine rather than the expression of a healthy and refined mind'.[25]

While Jones chastised teachers for failing to differentiate between the biologies of males and females, his own case rested much more on traditional and anti-feminist prejudices than on anatomical and physiological investigation. When he damned excessive devotion to games, particularly the more intense and energetic ones, it was because they 'caused' mental restlessness and nervous debility and 'lukewarmness' towards housekeeping and child care, and produced unfeminine postures like the 'cricket stoop', 'hockey walk', 'golf stride' and 'football roll' that implied a change in mental as well as physical characteristics and 'doomed' the gentleness and aesthetic beauty of women and the refinement of home life.

Periodically, as indicated in Chapters 5 and 6, the medical journals commented on particular sports, often without the benefit of firsthand experience, and they sometimes offered strikingly different opinions.

Cricket was described on one occasion as well-suited to girls as long as the risk of blows to the breast was obviated by the wearing of well-padded corsets; but it was usually discouraged because of the likelihood of sudden muscular strain, malignancy if a ball struck a breast, and dislocated shoulders from throwing balls with force since the female shoulder joint was more shallow than the male. The real reason, however, was simply that 'we do not wish to see them too boldly imitating their brothers in all their games and physical accomplishments'.[26]

A few doctors condoned riding horses astride, but the common medical view was that women who habitually rode thus courted physical disaster because the position strained and displaced vital organs and fostered prolapse, and was dangerously insecure, since 'women's thighs, being round and fat, cannot grip the saddle like the long flat ones of men'.[27] In addition, in a distinctly unscientific fashion, the medical journals described the cross-saddle style as 'aesthetically unappealing'.

Tennis was generally recommended as long as lateral curvatures from the continuous use of one arm were guarded against. Football, on the other hand, was damned out of hand as dangerous to the reproductive organs and breasts because of sudden jerks, twists and blows. Competitive rowing and swimming were condemned as bad for the heart. Swimming when overheated was blamed for turning hair snow-white. And bicycling, the sport which attracted the most medical attention, was described contradictorily as producing and curing an amazing array of physical and psychological maladies and as offensive to the qualities of true womanliness and productive of such if moderation were observed.[28]

In the eyes of many conservative medical men, 'an ideal pastime for ladies' must

> . . . be capable of yielding exhilaration without unduly taxing the muscular power and nervous energy. It should provide gentle exercise in the open air and act as a mild stimulant to respiration, circulation, and other organic functions, combined with an agreeable variety to excite and keep up interest.[29]

Physicians also had opinions on dress, and when they supported female sport they often mentioned approvingly its inevitably positive effects on dress reform. Doctors over several decades were virtually unanimous in their conviction that the unnatural constriction of vital organs by tightly-laced corsets was a dangerous abomination particularly during games and exercise. Few doctors had had much opportunity to observe the corset's actual effects, because respect for the dictates of Victorian prudery in the consulting room meant that women patients were rarely asked to undress. In this instance, however, the doctors' lack of scientific method might be at least partially forgiven, because for once their criticisms made eminent good sense, as did their prediction that the increasing participation of girls and women in games and physical training would lead to the introduction of sensible, looser and shorter costumes. Convention and conservatism prevented their going as far as supporting rational dress, however.[30]

The conclusions to be drawn from the medical literature are that male physicians, despite being influenced much more by social ideology than empirical investigation, unhesitatingly presented themselves as experts on the female organism; and they used what passed for the authority of science to protect traditional values concerning women's roles and functions rather than to alter them in accordance with changing scientific and social realities. In other words, whether advocating or opposing exercise for reasons of health, they did everything possible to keep females from the intense involvement with their own bodies that inevitably accompanied serious sporting activities.

In the face of feminist attacks on the sexual *status quo*, and the disturbing tendency of an increasing number of women to demonstrate an unfeminine interest in so-called masculine activities, a good many natural scientists and social theorists emulated the medical profession's unscientific inclination to follow popular opinion about women's nature. The theories of Charles Darwin, for example, had a tremendous ideological impact on the nineteenth century by shattering the notion of stability and lack of change in nature. According to Darwin differences of sex were grounded in evolutionary history, and since women were less completely evolved than men they were mentally and physically inferior. In the prehistoric past both sex and natural selection favoured such 'masculine' qualities as courage, energy, reason, invention and imagination, he argued. Women's minds could be improved through education, but they could never equal men's, for some of the traits which characterised them were typical of lower forms of life and states of civilisation.[31]

Darwin's contemporaries were more than willing to use evolution to explain culturally acquired characteristics without questioning the assumption that they were heritable. Despite increasing evidence to the contrary, they cited differences in brain size and capacity as reasons for sexual inequality; and they passed judgements about the strengths and weaknesses of the female sex and its natural domestic and maternal role being the necessary continuation of an evolutionary trend visible in the higher and lower animals, on the basis of simple observation of women's traditional activities and reproductive capacity.[32]

In a time of rapid social change when age-old supports of the social order were being undermined, the idea that there was social as well as natural science had considerable appeal, as did the notion that human societies were kept in balance by the fittest surviving. A number of Victorians thus became convinced that natural laws could be applied to all sorts of social and moral phenomena; and they used Darwinian theories of natural causation to defend the social order and competitive, *laissez-faire* capitalism. These so-called social scientists took the biologist as their guide, for he could make conceptions of the social order appear rational and scientific and create a kind of moral universe in which nature and society reflected each other and in which the question of authority was fundamental. One of the results was that by the 1880s some of the arguments of supporters of the limited energy theory and women's traditional role had been rephrased in characteristic Social Darwinistic terms, Social Darwinism being the name loosely given to the application to society of Darwinian and related biological concepts such as the struggle for existence and survival of the fittest.[33]

Some Social Darwinists demonstrated that the Victorian ideal of family and womanhood was not necessarily natural but rather only one of various possibilities. Yet their work supported conventional wisdom, for they used ideas of order and hierarchy similar to those in biological evolution in a social context, specifically in their search for a 'natural underpinning' to the social system and a theory of the individual's obligation to respect it. Social Darwinism removed a deity and substituted natural processes like evolution as the guarantor of social stability. It ultimately became a means of explaining current social arrangements, such as the differences between classes, races and sexes, in a manner quite distinct from pure Darwinism, but which presented them as the culmination of the human race's long and difficult evolution from savagery to civilisation. It thus provided apparently solid justification, as well as moral support, for traditional arguments about woman's inferiority, proper sphere and 'highest function' as the guardian of the quality of the race.[34]

Herbert Spencer, one of the fathers of Social Darwinism, posited that sex and gender roles were not historical accidents, but rather were prescribed by evolution — by natural selection for purposes of survival. Therefore they were permanent. By the

1870s his initial support for improvements in female education had given way to fears about the effects of excessive mental labour, and thus to arguments that normal women gloried in their domestic duties, while intellectual women were abnormal creatures with flat chests and no capacity to bear or suckle children. Concern about the production of healthy mothers and children, however, prompted him to urge that 'sportive activities' involving competition and play be made an intrinsic part of female educational and cultural life.[35]

Spencer's particular brand of evolutionism was very influential, and was used by anti-feminists for years to condemn the women's movement for threatening the natural evolutionary process. Other Darwinians introduced their own variations. For example, George J. Romanes, the physiologist and comparative psychologist who exerted considerable influence on popular and scientific opinion and to whom Darwin bequeathed his psychological papers, argued in 1887 that men and women were different physiological and psychological species. A process of natural and sexual selection — not limited social and educational opportunities — had given women less mental and physical strength than men, and destined them to be men's complements rather than equals. On the other hand, Romanes actually encouraged higher education as important to women's duties as wives and mothers, and he was unconvinced that serious study would cause breakdown. He also advocated exercise such as riding, rowing, skating and tennis as graceful, conducive to good spirits, useful for tempering the strain of book-learning, and most importantly as a protector and improver of maternal capacities. But he held no genuinely advanced views on women's right to unrestricted development; and his fear that women would seek to outstrip men and evolve in an undesirable direction threw him back on nature as the ultimate guarantor of the *status quo*.[36]

From the 1880s, and particularly after the turn of the century, both advocates and critics of women's sport and physical training took increasing account of Social Darwinistic arguments. Some, concerned with questions of 'national efficiency', told women that the highest function of womanhood was maternity, and that to have a full and perfect life, and to do their duty to the cause of racial improvement, they must become mothers. Women's participation in sports and physical education, it was argued, would result in an upgrading of maternal and racial quality; and this view underlay at least partly the introduction of exercise and medical inspection in girls' public schools. Witness Sara Burstall's statement that,

> . . . important as are bodily vigour and active strength . . . in the men of the country who may have to endure the supreme test of physical fitness in war, the vitality and passive strength — potential energy — of its women are even more important, since Nature has ordained women to be the mothers of the race.[37]

Others, however, criticised exercise — especially that from which the 'painful' and 'dangerous' elements had not been eliminated — as productive of mannish Amazons who were physiologically and psychologically unfit for motherhood. Burstall herself warned:

> The pendulum has probably swung too far in the direction of over-exertion . . . [among] wealthier girls, who belong to the social classes in which men and boys care so much for games and sport that national efficiency is actually being impaired by their pre-occupation.[38]

Young women had come to enjoy games so much, she lamented, that they were disregarding their sacred duties and expending too much of the vital force these duties required.

This argument was echoed by eugenists, those Social Darwinists — followers of Francis Galton — who aimed to prevent racial deterioration and to improve the characteristics of future generations by making reproductive considerations the primary determinant of human behaviour.[39]

In addition to fanning the fears of unchecked reproduction by the lower classes, a number of eugenists warned against feminism and its apparent threat to women's natural and crucial role as mothers of the race. The growing independence of women alarmed them, so they presented women's self-fulfilment as contrary to racial progress, and the 'fatal' principle of sex equality as responsible for the degeneration of the political and social systems. Male norms, they said, must be adapted in the case of women to take account of femininity. Women's willingness and capacity to bear children they described as a duty to God, husbands and the English race. If a woman pursued 'unhealthy' modes of life involving too much education and competitive sport, her vital energy would be depleted and she was likely to become sterile or capable of bearing only defective offspring. This, they insisted, was a particular danger among women of the superior classes who, by getting carried away with a concern for women's rights — and women's sports — threatened to leave inferior women of the lower orders to perpetuate the species.[40]

By no means all eugenists were cranks or crackpots. At a time when the birth rate among the middle ranks was dropping, eugenic theories made a good deal of sense to at least a minority of politicians, scientists, physicians and educators, and influenced their attitudes to women's education, work and activities.[41]

Although only a minority of doctors were eugenists, and several of the leading medical journals, including the *British Medical Journal*, were consistently hostile, a number of devotees of eugenics held medical degrees. Ironically, the most strident of eugenic writers on the subject of women was a woman herself, one Dr Arabella Kenealy, who was convinced that the type of intellectual and physical education received by middle-class girls was calculated to induce critical imbalances.

In several articles that were classic anti-feminist and anti-athletic statements, Kenealy supported the expansion of women's educational and employment opportunities and criticised the frivolous ideal of ladyhood. But she accused the women's movement of seeking to replace feminine women with sexless creatures by giving them a masculine mental and physical training which would destroy the delicate emotional organisation of their minds and the grace and beauty of their bodies. Upon women, she said, the conditions of evolution were absolutely dependent, and if their energy were not conserved for motherhood, good health would yield to 'morbid pathology' and the race would degenerate.[42]

Describing 'womanhood' as 'a beautiful achievement of evolution which it is a crime to deface',[43] Dr Kenealy conceded that exercise was essential to health. But excessive exercise masculinised women, unfitting them for their womanly duties by diverting energy from vital areas to the muscular system. 'One cannot possess all the delicately evolved qualities of woman together with the muscular and mental energies of man', she said.[44] Rather than characteristics of which to be proud, 'augmented sinews' and muscular capacity were symptomatic of atrophied emotions, physical degeneracy and a lack of feminine attributes.

Kenealy repeated frequently that the production of children was a woman's highest duty and greatest satisfaction, and urged women, for the sake of the race, to conserve their energy and guard against overstrain by opting for repose rather than vigorous exercise. As the strength of athletic women increased, they grew coarse and mannish. Although they might be adept games players, they lacked the qualities of true womanhood and were destined to produce either no or else defective children, and so to fail as human creatures. As long as women retained their special character they would be inferior to men in physical and mental achievement, despite every effort at improvement, but they would be fit to perform their own special work. By taking women out of their proper sphere, Kenealy concluded, feminists and athleticists threatened to destroy their noblest attributes and undo all the progress achieved by the noble women of the past.[45]

Kenealy struck her *coup de grace* against the women's movement in a book on *Feminism and Sex-Extinction*, which was conceived earlier but not published until 1920, at a time when 'wartime losses had added a new dimension to anxiety about the falling birth rate'.[46]

The modern feminist invasion of schools, colleges, politics, commerce and sport was misleading women into thinking that they would be happier and more useful if emancipated, she said, when in fact emancipation would only unsex them, weaken their sons, threaten the natural dominance of men and destroy the supremacy of England. Women must be made to realise, she asserted, that they were the custodians of life, and that because the race depended on them, and because they suffered periodically from constitutional and nervous stress and debility, the nation had a right to restrict their liberty and protect them from too much education or sport.[47]

Using dubious medical and scientific evidence, Kenealy blasted feminism as unnatural and productive of racial decline, because it made no concessions to the differences of sex that had resulted from the evolutionary process of natural selection and ignored the fact that woman's basic function was motherhood. The militant feminist movement she described as 'an explosion of suppressed muscularity in young women deprived of other outlets for accumulated muscle-steam . . . an ebullition of masculine mentality on the part of its leaders'.[48]

Sex extinction, she argued, was acutely visible in modern girls who were unsexed by the male type of mental and physical training they received at 'progressive' schools and colleges which made a speciality of sport. Obsessively preoccupied with athletic girls' physical appearance, Kenealy described their grim, heavy faces and muscular physiques, and made the ominous prediction that in evening gowns joints that had been adroitly hidden would be obvious. She condemned their knickerbockers, cropped hair and rough manners and language for belying their femininity and making them barely distinguishable from males. Women who fenced or played hockey and other competitive games during girlhood developed a sterile glint in their eyes and, as a result of the overuse of limbs and muscles, suffered from degenerative atrophy of the mammary glands and reproductive organs that incapacitated them for childbirth and lactation, Kenealy insisted. Furthermore, they were prone to nervosity, heart disease and premature ageing, and were essentially passionless and sexless. The spectacle of the young sportswoman — assertive, combative, with set jaw, eyes straining and limbs in ungainly positions — was appallingly ugly, she said, and proof positive of the baleful effects of competitive sport.

For emphasis, she cited the examples of a woman who grew deaf from walking ten miles a day, and of

> . . . a well-known Girls' College which makes pre-eminently for the cult of mannishness . . . Here are seen, absorbed in fierce contests during the exhausting heat of summer afternoons, grim-visaged maidens of sinewy build, hard and tough and set as working women in the forties; some with brawny throats, square shoulders and stern loins that would do credit to a prize ring. All of which masculine developments are stigmata of abnormal sex transformation, precisely similar in origin to male antlers in female deer; namely deterioration of important sex-glands, with consequent obliteration of the secondary sex-characteristics arising normally out of the functional efficiency of these.[49]

Games, Kenealy concluded, might develop habits of co-operation, but they usually stifled individualism and initiative and contracted the mind, and they destroyed a woman's natural sense of beauty and love of art and nature. Commonplace household chores, not sport, were the proper exercise for women.

Although not all eugenists agreed with Kenealy, several supported her view that aspects of the women's movement, especially the 'excessive' interest in physical exercise and sport, were 'even more harmful [to race progress] than too close an application to intellectual pursuits'.[50] They warned, for example, that an over-emphasis on hockey endangered players' ability to suckle their infants and indeed to give birth at all.

Another doctor, Caleb W. Saleeby, a founder of the Eugenic Society and perhaps the best-known propagandist and populariser of eugenics for over two decades, on the other hand, supported votes for women. He believed that females were capable of combining to 'play the game' in the true spirit of sportsmanship and should be free to do so, for games improved health and developed useful moral qualities. He also believed, however, that differences of sex were natural not nurtural, and that because women were the custodians of the welfare of the race those of superior physique and intelligence had a duty to reproduce and to avoid anything which would damage their capacity to do so. Because women were weaker than men, he argued, exercise had to be taken cautiously, particularly during puberty and menstrual periods. Only activities that would facilitate pregnancy and involved fun rather that competition and risk were advisable.[51]

Dr Mary Scharlieb, of the London School of Medicine for Women and a prominent suffragist and anti-birth controller, epitomised those eugenists who were consumed by England's manifest destiny to civilise the world, and who concluded, 'that we may be worthy of it behoves us to perfect the spirit, mind, and body of every man and woman of our imperial people'.[52] Scharlieb believed that healthy minds and bodies went together in women as well as men, and that proper physical exercise was even more necessary for women because of the peculiar demands their maternal duty imposed upon their bodies. Gymnastics and games she identified as useful for the production of improved health and character. But limited energy meant that great care had to be taken, through special rules and a de-emphasis of the competitive element, to assure that the fatigue and overstrain productive of permanent injury and 'disastrous consequences' were avoided. Girls who were excessively devoted to athletics and victory she described as having flat chests, narrow hips, poor health and irregular menstrual periods, and being thoroughly unfitted for motherhood.

Finally, there was Havelock Ellis, a eugenist and trained but non-practising medical doctor who pioneered the systematic study of sex psychology. Despite arguing that the respective fitness of men and women for any kind of work could be ascertained only by experiment, and suggesting that women's natural characteristics were reinforced by convention, repression and environment, and thus could be partly modified, he also chastised feminists for stressing the resemblance of the sexes, and insisted that women's primary sexual characteristics and reproductive functions made it impossible for them to equal men 'in the highest psychic processes'.[53] He claimed further that women's unique physiologies and mentalities were nearer than those of men to the infantile type on the evolutionary ladder, and warned women that, while their activities need not be oriented to reproduction alone, they should be aware that the active athletic life of some of their sisters led to difficulties at parturition dangerous to infant lives.[54]

Eugenists, then, obviously disagreed among themselves on the degree to which environment and heredity determined the roles of women, and on the degree of exercise that was safe. But whatever their views they generally centred on the progress of the race and ignored that of women themselves in any independent sense. Even though their influence was limited, they represented the mind-set of thousands to whom the actual discipline of eugenics was unknown.

An examination of medical and scientific attitudes towards women illuminates how profound change both caused and reflected tensions surrounding formal definitions of sex and gender roles. During the years between 1870 and 1914, fundamental social and economic developments appeared to threaten the stability of society and the traditional relationship between the sexes. Inevitably those alarmed by the rapidity of change sought in domestic constancy the sense of security and continuity that was increasingly difficult to find in the world at large, which meant preserving the family and the roles of its members in as nearly unchanged a form as possible.

It was no coincidence that just when women became more effective in the public sphere, medical and scientific opinion undertook a wholesale re-evaluation of sexual mores,[55] and transformed biological differences between the sexes into the social inferiority of one. When women began to challenge men intellectually it made a strong case against their higher education. When the women's movement made 'extravagant' claims about women's rights and abilities, it condemned them as contrary to the evolutionary progress of the female sex, and indeed the whole Anglo-Saxon race. When women began to take vigorous exercise and play men's games seriously, it made a similar case against their overdoing physical education and sports. Male domination and women's traditional inferiority and roles, as well as the whole social order, it attributed to biological determination. The progress of the race and the self-fulfilment of women it thus presented, on the basis of 'scientific' evidence, as completely contradictory.

At the same time, attitudes towards the human body and the importance attached to its health experienced a marked change as the result of a number of interrelated social forces ranging from the revolutionary doctrines about humanity and nature propounded by Darwin and Spencer, to acknowledgement of the problem of public health and the spread of sanitary and medical knowledge that characterised efforts to improve it. The late Victorians, in fact, became extraordinarily preoccupied with health and with a perception of the body as the temple of the soul, and this preoccupation was closely connected with the debate on women's sport and women's rights.[56]

Although it can be argued that medical issues influenced women's sport and exercise in an affirmative way, it should be noted that health reformers ordinarily justified their demands for women's physical education and sport not in terms of freeing women from traditional restrictions on bodily movement but rather of improving their contributions as mothers.[57] In other words, the selfless image of ideal womanhood was perpetuated. Furthermore, when women passed the point of exercising in moderation and primarily for health reasons, and started to compete vigorously in masculine sports like cricket for the sheer joy of so doing, science and medicine increasingly mobilised in defence of the social and athletic *status quo*, arguing against really strenuous activity lest it injure delicate female organs, and thus cause a decrease in fertility, or even harm the feminine mind through the emotional strain of competition.

The picture was certainly not all black. At various stages of the period some physicians who were not especially pro-feminist pronounced 'a sound body in the full swing of its naturalness [as] . . . the foremost of all the rights of women'.[58] Some learned, and said so, that women were not as fragile as conventional wisdom made out, and that the perception of female physiology was more limiting than the actuality. All things considered, however, 'The interplay of biological and social factors in sport as in many other fields of human endeavour [was] subtle, complex, and very profound;'[59] and in the last analysis the attitudes of the natural and social scientific communities were based essentially on ideologically conservative views of society rather than on empirical revelations. While games and exercise were considered beneficial to health, disposition and character, like activity of the brain they were perceived as safe only if pains were taken to avoid excess and to cultivate femininity. It therefore seemed eminently reasonable to restrict women's sporting opportunities.

Implicit in all of this was the understanding that women themselves had no say in determining what was acceptable, what was muscular and graceful, what was masculine and feminine, and what was excessive and moderate. That was all up to the mainly male arbiters of science and behaviour. The tyranny of medical ignorance and social sentiment dogged the sportswoman for years. Myths that sport was unladylike and would have negative effects on sexuality and childbirth proved remarkably influential and durable, and probably kept many from serious participation. Arguments about women's inferior biologies, grounded in opinion, old wives' tales, fear of social change, stereotypical views about women's traditional roles and a lack of reliable medical evidence, continued to perpetuate the view well into the twentieth century that strenuous exercise, particularly during menstrual periods, was bad for females and their unborn children, and that women therefore required 'protection'. The female athlete was viewed 'not only as socially deviant but flying in the face of biological reality and predestination'.[60] It took generations for sporting women to prove by their actions that no harm would befall them.

Notes

1. *Lancet* (9 October 1869), p. 511.
2. Peter C. McIntosh, *Sport in Society* (London, 1963), p. 13.
3. Kate Millett, *Sexual Politics* (New York, 1971), p. 58.
4. Brian Harrison, 'Women's Health and the Women's Movement in Britain: 1840–1940' in Charles Webster (ed.), *Biology, Medicine and Society 1840–1940* (Cambridge, 1981), pp. 18–31; Susan Sleeth Mosedale, 'Science Corrupted: Victorian Biologists Consider ''The Woman Question'' ', *Journal of the History of Biology*, vol. 11, no. 1 (1978), pp. 1–3; Janet Sayers, *Biological Politics: Feminist and Anti-Feminist Perspectives* (London, 1982), p. 1; Nancy Theberge, 'Toward a Feminist Alternative to Sport as a Male Preserve', *Quest*, vol. 37 (1985), pp. 196, 201.
5. Michele Z. Rosaldo, 'Woman, Culture and Society: A Theoretical

Overview' in Michele Z. Rosaldo and Louise Lamphere (eds), *Woman, Culture and Society* (Stanford, 1974), p. 31.

6. *British Medical Journal* (14 August 1886), pp. 295–9; *Lancet* (7 May 1892), pp. 1011–15, (14 August 1886), pp. 314–15; James Thorburn, *Female Education from the Physiological Point of View* (Manchester, 1884); Sayers, *Biological Politics*, pp. 7–11.

7. *English Woman's Journal*, vol. 1, no. 6 (1858), pp. 189–90. See also Elizabeth Blackwell, *The Laws of Life* (London, 1859), pp. 8–165.

8. *Victoria Magazine*, vol. 11 (June 1868), pp. 151–2.

9. *Lancet* (7 May 1892), pp. 1011–15; Gorham, *Victorian Girl*, pp. 68, 97.

10. Marie Pointon, 'The Growth of Women's Sport in Late Victorian Society as Reflected in Contemporary Literature', unpublished MEd thesis, University of Manchester, 1978, p. 18.

11. *British Medical Journal* (30 January 1858), pp. 91–2, (15 November 1863), p. 539, (29 February 1868), p. 212, (8 March 1873), p. 260, (18 April 1874), p. 531.

12. Ibid. (22 March 1884), p. 574, (23 August 1884), pp. 74–5, (16 January 1886), p. 129, (21 July 1888), p. 136, (7 July 1894), p. 53.

13. Ibid. (8 June 1901), p. 1426.

14. Ibid. (16 February 1901), pp. 383–6.

15. *Lancet* (9 October 1869), pp. 510–11.

16. Ibid. (11 December 1869), p. 817.

17. Ibid. (4 June 1870), pp. 815–16, (24 December 1870), p. 914.

18. Ibid. (1 October 1881), p. 599.

19. Ibid. (2 February 1878), p. 179.

20. Ibid. See also (6 January 1882), p. 20, (16 September 1882), pp. 431–3.

21. Ibid. (8 December 1883), p. 1004.

22. Ibid. (12 July 1884), p. 73.

23. Ibid. (5 July 1885), p. 30. See also (15 June 1889), p. 1179; *Medical Magazine*, vol. 1 (April 1893), pp. 930–40.

24. *Lancet* (8 December 1883), p. 1004, (1 March 1884), pp. 401–2, (16 August 1884), pp. 286–7, (8 October 1892), p. 861, (19 March 1910), pp. 794–5.

25. Ibid. (4 February 1911), p. 329. See also (11 February 1911), p. 398, (25 February 1911), p. 54.

26. Ibid. (5 July 1890), p. 37. See also (4 July 1885), p. 30, (28 June 1890), pp. 1446–7, (21 September 1901), pp. 771–4.

27. Ibid. (4 April 1914), p. 1005. See also (19 May 1883), p. 879, (21 March 1914), p. 839.

28. Ibid. (5 July 1890), p. 37; *British Medical Journal* (8 December 1894), p. 1323.

29. *Lady Cyclist*, vol. 1, no. 2 (1895), p. 66.

30. *British Medical Journal* (8 April 1882), p. 526; *Lancet* (18 February 1871), p. 256, (2 December 1882), p. 951, (15 June 1889), p. 1179. See also David Kunzle, *Fashion and Fetishism* (Totowa, N.J., 1982), pp. 161–73.

31. Charles Darwin, *The Descent of Man*, 2nd edn (Akron, Oh., 1874), pp. 575–7.

32. Hargreaves, 'Playing Like Gentlemen', p. 27; Mosedale, 'Science Corrupted', pp. 4–5.

33. Robert C. Bannister, *Social Darwinism* (Philadelphia, Pa., 1979), p. 5.

34. Carol Dyhouse, 'Social Darwinistic Ideas and the Development of Women's Education in England, 1880–1920', *History of Education*, vol. 5, no. 1 (1976), pp. 41–7, 54–5; Elizabeth Fee, 'The Sexual Politics of Victorian Social Anthropology' in Mary Hartman and Lois Banner (eds), *Clio's Consciousness Raised* (New York, 1974), p. 87; Jennifer A. Hargreaves, '"Playing Like Gentlemen While Behaving Like Ladies": Contradictory Features of the Formative Years of Women's Sport', *British Journal of Sports History*, vol. 2, no. 1 (1985), pp. 41, 44–5; Greta Jones, *Social Darwinism and English Thought* (Brighton, 1980), pp. xiii, 157.

35. Spencer, *Essays on Education*, pp. 136–7, 150–1; Spencer, *Principles of Biology*, vol. 2, pp. 512–13. See also Atkinson, 'Fitness . . . and Schooling', pp. 124–5; Dyhouse, 'Social Darwinistic Ideas', p. 43; Mosedale, 'Science Corrupted', pp. 9–10; Sayers, *Biological Politics*, pp. 32–6.

36. George J. Romanes, 'Mental Differences between Men and Women', *Nineteenth Century*, vol. 21 (May 1887), pp. 654–72; George J. Romanes, 'Recreation', *Nineteenth Century*, vol. 6 (September 1879), pp. 401–24. See also Mosedale, 'Science Corrupted', pp. 16–20.

37. Burstall, *English High Schools*, p. 90.

38. Ibid., p. 98.

39. *Anstey Physical Training College Magazine* (Spring 1914), p. 3; Michael Freeden, 'Eugenics and Progressive Thought: A Study in Ideological Affinity', *Historical Journal*, vol. 22, no. 3 (1979), pp. 645, 652, 655; Harrison, 'Women's Health', pp. 61–2; Jones, *Social Darwinism*, pp. 97–115; G.R. Searle, 'Eugenics and Class' in Webster (ed.), *Biology, Medicine and Society*, p. 217.

Leonard Darwin, Charles Darwin's fourth son, was president of the Eugenic Society for years.

40. *British Medical Journal* (5 November 1910), pp. 1469–70.

41. Prominent female educators, Lilian Faithfull of the Cheltenham Ladies' College, Margaret Tuke of Bedford College (London) and Rhoda Anstey of the Anstey Physical Training College, espoused eugenic views.

42. *British Medical Journal* (15 October 1910), pp. 1172–3; Arabella Kenealy, 'The Worship of Masculinity', *Gentleman's Magazine*, vol. 265 (July–December 1888), pp. 354–69.

43. Arabella Kenealy, 'Woman as an Athlete', *Nineteenth Century*, vol. 45 (April 1899), p. 643.

44. Ibid., p. 644.

45. Arabella Kenealy, 'Woman as an Athlete: a rejoinder', *Nineteenth Century*, vol. 45 (June 1899), pp. 915–29.

46. Fletcher, *Women First*, p. 75.

47. Arabella Kenealy, *Feminism and Sex-Extinction* (London, 1920), pp. 227–8, 249–52.

48. Ibid., p. 141.

49. Ibid., p. 139.

50. R. Murray Leslie, 'Women's Progress in Relation to Eugenics', *Eugenics Review*, vol. 2 (April 1910–January 1911), p. 294. See also

pp. 283, 287, 291–4.

51. Saleeby, *Woman*, pp. 14–15, 114–22, 150, 347. See also V. Volkhowsky, review of *Woman and Womanhood*, by C.W. Saleeby, in *Journal of Scientific Physical Training*, vol. 5 (Spring 1913), pp. 49–54.

52. Mary Scharlieb, 'Recreational Activities of Girls During Adolescence', *Child*, vol. 1 (April 1911), p. 586. See also pp. 571–86; Mary Scharlieb, 'Athletics and School Life', *Child*, vol. 1 (March 1911), pp. 519–21; Mary Scharlieb, 'Adolescent Girlhood Under Modern Conditions, with Special Reference to Motherhood', *Eugenics Review*, vol. 1 (April 1909–January 1910), pp. 174–83.

53. Havelock Ellis, *Man and Woman* (London, 1894), p. 26.

54. Havelock Ellis, *The Task of Social Hygiene*, 2nd edn (Boston, Mass., 1927), p. 310. See also Ellis, *Man and Woman*, pp. 385–6, 390, 397.

55. Vicinus, '"One Life"', p. 622.

56. Colin Crunden, 'The Concept of the Body' in McNair and Parry (eds), *Readings*, pp. 14–19; Pointon, 'The Growth of Women's Sport', p. 161.

Brian Harrison makes the interesting point that, while the feminist movement did not have a direct impact on women's health, it had a positive effect through its interest in providing women with a greater knowledge of health and sex, more rational dress, a better diet and regular exercise. Keeping fit was an important feminist theme, for an improvement in women's health was seen as central to real achievement and emancipation. Some satisfaction, too, could be derived from the fact that the image of female beauty changed from one of sickly delicacy and weak nerves to one of good health and high spirits. Harrison, 'Women's Health', pp. 16–60.

57. Carroll Smith-Rosenberg and Charles Rosenberg, 'The Female Animal: Medical and Biological Views of Woman and her Role in Nineteenth-Century America', *Journal of American History*, vol. 60, no. 2 (1973), p. 342.

58. W. Wright Wilson, quoted in Molyneux, 'Early Excursions', p. 48.

59. K.F. Dyer, *Catching Up the Men* (London, 1982), p. 33.

60. Ibid., pp. 5–6.

8

Women's Sport and Dress Reform

> The object of all exercise and athletics for women should be to
> ensure deportment, poise and grace of movement. Moreover the
> object of the corset should be to define and interpret these graces.[1]

Fashion is no isolated phenomenon. Rather it is a product and
expression of socio-cultural systems and the operation within them
of inertia, continuity and change; it is also an important indicator
of class and gender relationships. From time immemorial clothing
has been a powerful symbol of women's roles and status, and has
given them identity, recognition and degrees of approval. The
clothes a woman wore reflected aesthetic rules and social
constraints, and communicated to the world the functions she was
expected to perform. They reminded her and society of women's
rights, responsibilities and limitations; and they played a
pervasive and sometimes insidious part in determining her
behaviour and conditioning her to accept restrictions. They also
reflected social and political tensions and changing attitudes
towards woman's place in the community.[2] It is not surprising
then that the development of special clothing for sport, which
allowed women greater physical freedom, was a major area of
controversy.

Stylistic changes in women's dress are complicated, and neither
completely random nor deterministic. When the roles of the sexes
have diverged widely — as during the Victorian age — their clothing has usually done the same. While styles changed through the
nineteenth century, on the whole men's clothes were dark, plain
and loose enough to allow movement, and implied seriousness,
strength and activity. Women's, on the other hand, emphasised
light colours, soft contours and ornamentation to project the

appearance of delicacy, submissiveness and immobility.

Since Victorian society judged women much more than men according to their attractiveness to the opposite sex and the attention they paid to their personal appearance, physical comfort was not a prime consideration. As the image of ideal womanhood became increasingly 'sacred', dress designers — almost exclusively male — deliberately sought to check unladylike activities and to compel women to conform to the passive life-style that was the hallmark of gentility. The design of female clothing thus became more confining and discordant with anatomical realities, and permitted women only a distant acquaintanceship with their own bodies. Rapid motion, ample waists and the raising of arms above the head were considered unfeminine, so sleeves were cut to inhibit the latter, corsets became tighter and petticoats got more voluminous. Helene Roberts describes the mid-Victorian lady, trapped into inactivity by layers of under-garments, encumbered by ruffles, lace and bows and 15 to 20 pounds of material hanging to the ground from a constricted waist, and encased in a portable prison of tight corsets, as an 'exquisite slave' in bondage to a 'submissive-masochistic pattern'.[3] Slaves or not, women's clothing made them unable to engage in any activity more rigorous than a sedate stroll.

The wire cage and crinoline introduced in the mid-1850s made walking in long skirts somewhat easier, but expanding circumferences, sometimes to as much as 5 yards, impeded ease of motion and continued to hide the fact that women were bipeds. The dresses of the 1870s and 1880s, with tied-back skirts and bustles, had a smaller circumference, but also a train that swept the ground and leg-of-mutton sleeves that restricted arm movement. In the 1890s, although daytime clothing was reduced in weight and complexity, ordinary skirts remained long, and 'sensible' walking costumes were 3.5 yards wide and hung to the ankle. Then, during the Edwardian period, the reaction against the New Woman and her unconventional attitudes and activities produced one of the most shackled fashions of all time, the hobble skirt, whose exaggerated narrowness at the knee barely permitted a normal step and more than offset the advantage of a slightly raised hemline.

Head- and foot-wear, under- and outer-clothing and hair-styles also inhibited movement. But the garment that best exemplified women's restricted activities and sphere and their forced submission to and dependence upon men was the corset.

Designed to shape the body to the configurations of the feminine ideal, corsets magnified and distorted the differences between the male and female anatomy by constricting waists and enlarging busts and hips. They also dictated the habits of body in which girls were instructed from infancy, for they were manufactured for babies, little girls and adolescents as well as adults. Eventually there were even corsets for sleeping women, pregnant women and sportswomen.

The invention of the metal eyelet allowed greater force to be exerted and inaugurated the custom of tight lacing that was almost universal in polite society from the 1830s to the 1890s. Its extent and degree may have been over-stated, but historians of costume agree that most women above the working classes probably laced themselves sufficiently tightly to experience discomfort, fatigue and sometimes physical debility. Even moderate pressure impeded breathing while extreme tightness could produce lassitude and feebleness. Both made ordinary activities — standing, sitting, walking and bending — difficult, and those that required rapid and vigorous movement a virtual impossibility. Nevertheless, women showed a remarkable reluctance to reduce the pressure on their bodies, in defiance of a spirited campaign against tight lacing by physicians and dress reformers, a defiance which David Kunzle provocatively but unconvincingly attributes to self-assertiveness.[4]

Members of the medical community had no interest in reforming dress in order to increase female freedom, but they blamed the corset for producing the low vitality, fainting fits and mysterious indispositions that so frequently plagued the lives of Victorian ladies. Tight lacing they implicated in an amazing array of physical and psychological disorders from hepatitis, to cancer, consumption, stomach ulcers, diarrhoea, constipation, floating kidneys, slit livers, lung and heart disease, nervous diseases, wrinkles, uterine prolapse, infertility and even death. The *Lancet* cited cases of women who courted death by wearing corsets during gymnastic exercise and pregnant women who had to be advised to loosen their stays and when in labour to remove them. One doctor so despaired of women ever giving up tight lacing that he exclaimed in frustration, 'There is no need to adopt artificial measures for the repression of female brains!'[5]

The link between ill health and tight lacing was never scientifically proven; but given the respect accorded the medical profession, it is surprising that women paid the anti-tight lacing campaign little heed, until one considers the enormous pressure on them to conform to the submissive ideal and what appeared to be stylistic necessity. Many women's primary desire was to be attractive to men, and they considered the corset vital to the type of small-waisted feminine 'beauty' that would improve marital chances. In addition, tight laces and the ornamental costumes that overlay them performed the useful function of displaying status and affluence. Female dress that was expensive and impractical for productive labour testified to a woman's economic dependence on a male protector and to his (and thus her) social class; and it ensured that women would be fit only for the decorative, indolent roles that gentility dictated. Furthermore, the corset was laden with sexual symbolism. Its wearing seems to have become a hallmark of virtue, the implication being that the woman with loose stays, or, worse, none at all, was likely to have loose morals — hence the term 'strait-laced'.[6]

It is difficult now to appreciate fully the extent to which clothing affected the physical activities of Victorian women. Tightly laced corsets, tight-fitting bodices, tight sleeves and arm holes, and long, heavy, flowing skirts severely restricted movement of the chest, abdomen, arms and legs, and seemed purposely designed to prevent participation in any form of genuine exercise. If females had to wait years for permission to really exert themselves, they had to wait even longer for costumes that would enable them to do so effectively; and, being much more enslaved by fashions and definitions of propriety than men, they were slow to demand special sporting apparel combining style and comfort.

So-called walking dresses were part of the fashionable lady's wardrobe from the early-nineteenth century, but their design permitted only the most leisurely of paces. In mid-century, when outdoor exercise began to be recognised as healthy, women still wore ordinary clothing that interfered badly. To play croquet ladies dressed in fashionable, flowing dresses with skirts that could be used 'innocently' to relocate a ball but more frequently got in the way. Women also wore ordinary garb in the early days of tennis and golf, since the pat-ball and putting games were more social than physical activities and required little vigour or rapid movement.

The struggle to reduce the weight of women's clothing and to free their legs for exercise was carried on intermittently throughout the second half of the nineteenth century, a long conditioning process being necessary before more functional attire could be widely adopted. In the early 1850s, for example, an American woman, Mrs Amelia Bloomer, tried to persuade the English that beauty and utility in dress were not incompatible, and to adopt a form of Turkish trousers worn beneath a knee-length skirt. The bloomer costume was far too revolutionary for the time, however, and the few bold women who wore bloomers in public were ridiculed and denounced. Efforts to devise suitable walking dresses during the 1860s and 1870s were also largely ineffectual; and as late as 1885 some arbiters of fashion still insisted that 'there is no need for a woman to be able to do more than use her limbs in a feminine fashion'.[7]

One of the first defences of reformed dress for sports appeared in 1876 in a dietary manual by one Thomas Chambers:

> Ladies who are going to try training for athletic purposes will find some attention to costume expedient. If stays are worn (and there is no objection to them if well-fitted and not too tight) they should have no shoulder straps. The drawers should not be tied below the knees. The best defences to the lower extremities in rough ground are stout Alpine shoes, and light leather gaiters half way up the knee supporting the long socks without garters. A light woollen jersey should be worn next to the skin. The skirt of the dress should be short and narrow, and the best materials are serge and homespun. Besides these the less drapery is worn the better.[8]

However, an organised campaign for dress reform did not begin in earnest until the 1880s, by which time many women were showing an interest in taking active exercise and playing athletic games. A number of dress reform societies were founded alongside those for sanitation and health reform, women's rights, aestheticism and eugenics. Although their primary concern was to educate women to sensible habits of everyday dress for reasons of health, they also considered sportswomen's need for less restrictive fashions.

The best known was the Rational Dress Society which was founded in 1881 by a redoubtable noblewoman, the Viscountess Florence Harberton, 'to promote the adoption, according to individual taste and convenience, of a style of dress based on considerations of health, comfort, and beauty'.[9] The Rational Dress Society lamented that robust health and bodily strength were not objects for which women were ready to make a sacrifice, and it condemned the current 'bad system of dress' for making it virtually impossible for women to walk properly, never mind take genuine exercise. It never tried to persuade women to dress like men, but it did equate rational dress with women's advance towards greater equality, and argued that 'if women had the strength of character to adopt some form of clothing which they knew was best for themselves, they would find their actual position as much benefited as that which they would acquire in public estimation'.[10]

The Rational Dress Society attacked high-heeled and narrow-toed shoes, tight corsets, heavy skirts and garments that impeded arm movements as especially unhealthy and disfunctional. Instead it recommended a warm, light and loose bifurcated garment, consisting of knee-length trousers and a mid-calf skirt worn over a rational system of underclothing, as attractive, modest and practical, particularly for walking, skating, boating, cycling and mountain climbing. When rational dressers appeared proudly in public, however, their costume was condemned out of hand by fashion consultants and general opinion as ridiculous, monstrous, outrageous, unnatural, unwomanly, unhealthy, immoral and ugly, and by some doctors who warned, vaguely, that trousers would cause a dangerous increase in bodily heat and threaten health and morals.[11]

The Victorian mind associated trousers with the authority of men, and with attempts by women to usurp that authority, and it associated skirts with women's special roles as 'mysterious priestesses' and 'angels in the house'. The ordinary women whom the Rational Dress Society hoped to convert to rational dress always considered it unattractive and unsexing and so threatening to chances of marital happiness. Even those who yearned for physical freedom were deterred from dressing rationally by tradition and hostile criticism.

The question of dress reform in general and for sport in particular was extremely controversial, and attracted a diversity of opinion that confounds simple designation as liberal or conservative.

Rational dressers and physical culturists formed one wing of the campaign to persuade women to discard corsets and heavy, constricting garments in favour of common-sense ones that would facilitate active exercise and improved health. On the opposite wing were eugenists, such as Arabella Kenealy, whose views on sportswomen were reactionary but who advocated a purge of corsets because they caused sickliness, suffering and premature death. In between were reformers like Ada Ballin and Gertrude

Douglas, who favoured dress reform in general and for sports in particular and urged women to think for themselves on the subject as long as they avoided offending public opinion.

Ballin aimed to produce healthy women for the good of the female sex and the state. She attacked 'outmoded' and 'tyrannical' ideas about dress; and in relating health to dress and physical exercise and in outlining the consequences of following fashion at the expense of health and safety, she recounted the story of

> . . . a Gentleman of scientific frame of mind, who determined to make the experiment of walking in petticoats in order to estimate the disadvantage under which women laboured in regard to dress. He walked for a mile up a hill; but was so exhausted by the endeavour that he gave up with the remark that women must be stronger than men or they would never be able to stand it.[12]

Sporting costume should be simple, warm, light and loose, and short enough — ankle-length — to permit free movement, she said. But while she conceded that divided skirts were very comfortable, Ballin considered them far from absolutely necessary, for 'almost all sports and games can be enjoyed without making great changes in dress'.[13]

Several years later, in a highly popular book of dress for gentlewomen, Mrs Gertrude Douglas credited the rational dress movement with effecting great improvements in female underclothing, but producing singularly masculine and unattractive outer garments. Douglas went into considerable detail on what she considered to be appropriate, warm, comfortable and healthy costumes for various sports. Stays, she said, should be loose enough for health and tight enough for neatness and support. Divided skirts and trousers, however, she deemed unbeautiful and destructive of women's own good, except for cycling and 'country wear'.[14]

As for feminists, they spent less time on dress reform than on larger issues, although they were usually sympathetic in principle, and the subject was an important if minor theme in the women's movement. They often deliberately appeared in the latest fashions, however, to avoid committing the heresy of dressing rationally that would have damned their causes further. Lydia Becker, one of the leaders of the suffragist campaign, rejected tight lacing as injurious but urged ladies to 'Stick to [their] stays . . . and triumph over the other sex', since elastic ones, comfortably laced, provided warmth and support to the bosom and back and made dresses look more agreeable;[15] which prompted Lady Harberton to respond that women did not need props to support their bodies, and that not until they freed themselves from the 'monstrous defects' of dress could they hope to take their proper place in the civilised world.[16]

Gradually, as women's causes made progress and as women began to participate in sport and to view themselves in a different light, modifications occurred in clothing which mirrored important changes in the feminine ideal and in the types of sports and ways in which women participated. The problem was that although women's admission to each new sport signalled the passage of a milestone along the road to physical emancipation, their liberation from the tyrannies of fashion did not keep pace. Dress reform was not always linear and progressive, for while the principle was conceded that if women were to participate in sports — even as dilettantes — they required special costumes, contradictions remained between the sartorial requirements of a sport and those of a society with conservative views on womanliness.

A philosophy of health and freedom found practical expression in utilitarian dress for exercise at all the physical training colleges.

Madame Bergman-Osterberg forbade corsets and required functional dress for ordinary wear and exercise. At first, for gymnastics her students wore long-sleeved, knee-length, blue merino dresses over knickers and stockings. After 1892 these were superseded by a revolutionary new costume, designed by a student named Mary Tait, which totally defied convention and fashion and was soon used for games as well. This was a sleeveless, knee-length tunic with three box pleats in front and back, worn with knickers and woollen stockings and over a long-sleeved knitted jersey in winter and cotton blouse in summer. Old Students recalled that the first tunic-wearers had to contend not only with parental disapproval, but, while in transit to and from matches, with being called 'those dreadful girls' by 'men who don't know how troublesome skirts are and by women who don't know how delicious it is to be free of them'.[17] The tunic had little immediate effect on adult fashion; but it eventually became the standard uniform for gymnastics and games all over Great Britain and the

English-speaking world, for it made wearers loath to return to restrictive clothing for sports in adulthood, and provided just the right combination of utility and sexlessness. The tunic costume covered the wearer's whole body, and with its barrel shape and deep pleats, that hid breast, waist, hips and buttocks, it gave freedom of movement without contour.[18]

Chelsea College students wore academic gowns over a long, navy serge skirt, a blouse with turned-down collar, a white piqué tie, navy serge knickers that buttoned on to the blouse, a belt, white canvas shoes and a white boater hat with a heavy band and the college badge. The gown and skirt were removed for gymnastics, and for games were replaced by a skirt about four inches from the ground. About 1902 a knee-length tunic designed by Fraulein Wilke became the gymnastics costume, with a games tunic on the same pattern but reaching to within eight inches of the ground. Corsets were absolutely *verboten*.[19]

At Anstey College, Rhoda Anstey practised her own form of rational dress, and preached regularly to students on the dangers of high-heeled shoes and tightly-laced corsets and the necessity for neat, comfortable clothes. For all physical activity she required students to wear a loosely fitting tunic to just above the knee, a long-sleeved white blouse and black stockings. Apparently they reacted shyly to the unusual sight of their own legs at first, but were quickly captivated by a 'delightful sense of freedom' that made them reluctant to change into ordinary costume.[20]

Physical training mistresses who had become used to more practical dress at college took their 'advanced' ideas into the outside world — especially into schools where a reform of dress was already underway.

Games and exercise at public schools helped to bring younger girls out of restrictive clothing. In the early years special dresses, that permitted freedom of movement without exciting attention by displaying overt non-conformity, were worn only for gymnastics lessons, while games were played in ordinary apparel, which, though not standardised, had to be the 'right sort', i.e. plain. When games costumes were first introduced they varied considerably; but gradually they were regularised, and in fact heralded the sports and school uniforms that were to be crucial to the process of affiliation.

At the North London Collegiate School from the outset Frances Mary Buss opposed tight clothing that inhibited free movement, and she attempted to modify parents' attitudes towards their daughters' dress. Throughout her long career she agitated for simplicity and neatness on the grounds that fashionable wear impeded health and physical activity; and although for several decades gymnastics were performed in ordinary garments, Buss insisted that they be loose and light. She imposed no uniformity until around 1892, however, when a costume was adopted for gymnastics and sports days consisting of a knee-length, dark blue, serge or flannel skirt, dark stockings and a loose white blouse, loosely tied at the waist by a sash in the school colours of yellow and blue, over which a regular skirt could be buttoned on at the waist for wear outside the gymnasium. Under Sophie Bryant, a stickler for conformity in dress, dark blue belts, light blue hair ribbons and regulation ties and shoes were added; and teachers obeyed orders to ensure that every detail was correct with such vigilance that students fussed excessively over the exactness of skirt length and ribbon width. In due course the costume evolved into the school uniform. Ordinary attire continued to be worn for games until the late 1890s, when shirt blouses, ties and caps in the form of a tam-o-shanter topped by a knob in the school colours were adopted, along with a skirt of calf- and later knee-length.[21]

The subject of dress was behind one of the most interesting sporting contests in the history of the North London. During the winter of 1890, in an attempt to determine the efficacy of wearing stays, Mrs Bryant sponsored a competition between 16 loosely-laced corset- and 16 non-corset-wearers, all of whom had been pronounced fit by the school medical inspector. Each group was compared according to the results of high and long jumping, endurance running and a tug-of-war. Somewhat surprisingly, the corset-wearers triumphed in the high jumping, but otherwise the non-corseted group had the best of things, with the result that Bryant recommended the discontinuation of corset-wearing; and observers outside, such as the sex psychologist Havelock Ellis, concluded that corseted females were obviously inferior in muscle power and physical endurance.[22]

Louisa Lumsden of St Leonards School regarded uniforms as a means of promoting corporate spirit and freedom for gymnastics and games. She detested crinolines, starched petticoats and tight laces; and, in imitation of her experience as a student at a school in Belgium, she produced a special costume for gymnastics as soon as the school gymnasium was ready — a blue serge, loosely-belted tunic worn over knickers or short trousers. Enterprising girls also wore the costume in the playground, after the fashion of several games-playing mistresses; but although they rejoiced in the unaccustomed sensation of liberty and comfort, for a time they had to tolerate the scorn of more conservative students who preferred to play in ordinary dresses, despite being hampered by long skirts and tight bodices. From the mid-1890s, however, students commonly played games in gymnastics dresses embellished by house colours; and over the years the costume for all physical activities evolved into a knee-length tunic and bloomers of dark blue serge, a dark blue fisherman's jersey with a soft white collar and long sleeves, a silk handkerchief in school or house colours that was worn round the neck in cold weather, dark stockings and a distinctive broad belt of leather and then dark blue webbing, a costume that one Old Student recalled was very uncomfortable. Eventually members of the school hockey, lacrosse and cricket teams earned special colours — a red sash or scarf, red stockings and a blue band with the school crest at the side on the regulation school hat.[23]

Special costumes were slower to evolve at the Cheltenham Ladies' College than elsewhere because Dorothea Beale disapproved as much of uniforms as of competitive sports. For years long dresses with bustles, tightly-fitted bodices and tightly-laced corsets were worn even for exercise. Around 1890, when Swedish gymnastics were introduced, dresses were replaced by more functional, loose skirts and blouses, but for outdoor games there was still no regulation garb. Players abandoned hats during the 1890s but continued to wear full-length dresses. After 1906, under Lilian Faithfull, different costumes for different sports became standardised: white shirts, ties and dark, mid-calf skirts for tennis, for example, the same in white for cricket, and with dark knee-length skirts for hockey.[24]

A delicate related issue involved facilities for changing clothes, which varied widely from school to school. At first they were non-existent, and although by 1914 larger establishments such as Roedean usually provided dressing rooms, smaller ones most certainly did not. Gwen Raverat recalled that at her small private boarding school around 1901, when girls came in steaming hot after a 'ferocious' game of hockey, they had to go straight to class without having time to change or wash or comb their hair and so were susceptible to chills.[25] On the basis of the experience of sports clubs, it is reasonable to conclude that the relative slowness of girls' schools to adopt the boys' custom of providing dressing rooms for changing out of damp clothes after games was probably connected with uncertainty about the propriety and morality of young ladies changing in front of each other; but the school records are silent on the subject.[26]

The adoption of special costumes for gymnastics and games in schools was not always achieved easily. Headmistresses sometimes had to use all their powers to persuade parents to allow their daughters to wear them, for many were afraid the new attire would make girls careless about their appearance. Furthermore, at some schools the reluctance of students themselves to adopt the costumes for fear of jeopardising modesty — despite the obvious freedom they offered and despite their confinement to the privacy of school playing fields — was long the bane of physical training mistresses' existences.

Nevertheless, dress reform in the direction of bringing comfort and ease into fashion was one of the best results of the school games movement. The majority of students probably would have agreed with Winifred Peck that:

> Part of the fun [of games-playing] came from the games dress — short tunics and baggy bloomers with tam-o-shanters which always fell off . . . what freedom, what glory, to scamper about after one ball or another in sun or rain or wind as one of a team, as part of the school, on an equality . . . with . . . brothers at last.[27]

On the other hand, as Paul Atkinson indicates:

> The adoption of gymnastics suits and later the pleated gymslip . . . had a number of unintended consequences. The physical similarity thus imposed paralleled the social uniformity and regimentation which was promoted by the Swedish system [of gymnastics] as well as the physical freedom of the games field. Arguably the young ladies had escaped the confines of stays and skirts, only to encounter the institutional control manifested in the gym mistress and her uniform. At the same time, the reform of school dress was part of a process whereby the 'young ladies' of earlier years became 'schoolgirls'. A break with the dictates of fashion and ladylike comportment were symptomatic of more fundamental discontinuities — although it remained necessary for the schools to preserve strict limits of propriety.[28]

It should also be noted that while sports costumes included a number of overtly masculine items — shirts, ties in school and house colours, tie pins, and hats and caps with identifying badges and bands — they had little significance once school-days were over. The 'old school tie', signifying power and connection, was meaningless for females in the outside world. Upon leaving school young ladies were expected to drop 'masculine' attire and activities for ladylike dress and behaviour patterns.

At the Oxbridge women's colleges, dons and students adopted a plain, austere style of ordinary dress to demonstrate their professionalism and seriousness of purpose, and this was worn at first for games. Only gradually were modifications incorporated to accommodate greater physical activity, and these were far from radical. The Girton College hockey team, for example, was dressed in much the same way in 1904 as in 1894 — in tailored shirts and ties and dark, ankle-length skirts that permitted but still impeded running. At Newnham, hockey players wore navy-blue serge skirts deliberately designed to hide the legs as far as possible and so only about eight inches off the ground; and even these were regarded in some quarters as immodest. Shirts, ties and hats completed the ensemble. For tennis at both colleges skirts changed from dark blue to white over the years, and were worn slightly longer and with somewhat dressier white blouses than for hockey. Only after the turn of the century were the boater hats that prevailed in both sports abandoned; and only just before the outbreak of war was the way pointed to a more genuinely liberated future when the Cambridge university and college lacrosse and cricket teams began to play in knee-length gymnastics tunics.

The style of games dress at Oxford was much the same. In hockey and tennis hats were gradually abandoned and skirts shortened slightly. But 1914 found the college and university teams still attired in ankle-length skirts, and the university lacrosse team vying with its tunic-clad Cambridge opponent in old-fashioned mid-calf uniforms. For boating, Oxford women continued to wear long stockings, boater hats and full-length skirts which the more energetic anchored below the knees with strong rubber bands. College women, after all, were ladies, and were expected to behave and dress as such no matter what their activity.

The adoption of gymnastics and games dress within public schools and university and physical training colleges epitomised the spirit of emancipation that inspired women to break free of some of the more restrictive elements of the Victorian code of femininity in a variety of areas, at the same time as its limitations symbolised the lingering strength of tradition and propriety. This was true as well of reforms in the costumes worn by sportswomen outside educational settings.

In women's hockey the thorny question of dress caused a prolonged and heated debate, behind which lay the necessity for players to 'be able to bend, swing, stoop, and breathe with absolute ease', and at the same time look neat, smart and ladylike.[29]

Despite relatively advanced views on the role of women in sport, the AEWHA could only partly support the idea that:

> For the time being a player is no longer a lady whose social position is suitably expressed in attire. She is a workman in a particular field, whose one object it should be to subordinate everything to the efficient performance of her duties.[30]

It hesitated to defy too many conventions and risk charges of immodesty and unwomanliness; so over the years it condemned 'unsightly garments', 'heavy boots' and 'unaccustomed cuts'.

To prevent injury the association prohibited wearing 'sailor, or other hard brimmed hats, or hatpins' during matches; and, on the principle that every player 'must maintain a womanly standard', it developed as the official uniform of the All England XI a white canvas shirt, a white silk tie and a long, cardinal serge skirt lined in the front with silk to facilitate running and diminish 'riding-up', and when travelling a sailor hat with a cardinal serge band and the association badge. The rose of England appeared on the pocket of the skirt and the peak of the cap.[31]

The question of skirts was perennially vexing. There was general agreement that ones of ordinary weight, length and volume impeded running and led to overheating and exhaustion, and that their tendency to be used to stop balls and to droop in the back and drag along muddy fields was unsportsmanlike and ungraceful. In 1899 the AEWHA passed a rule that skirts must be six inches off the ground and the same length all round, but this was not rigidly enforced, as witness complaints that members of county teams were exposing themselves to charges of immodesty by playing in gym slips barely covering their knees and arguments that skirts should be no shorter than seven to eight inches. The association responded by redefining the ideal length as at least eight inches; and, although refusing to set an upper limit, it made clear its disapproval of tunics, particularly during the furore created in 1910 by the appearance on the Kent team of a player wearing her Dartford tunic.[32]

A few advanced souls considered it odd that women wanted to play hockey under the same rules as men yet insisted on doing so in disfunctional long skirts when tunics were more sensible, comfortable and neat, and permitted faster, more skilful play; and they argued further that the simple act of playing in a tunic was unlikely to unsex a young woman and make her careless of her appearance. Conversely, some of the more conservative insisted that, while tunics might be wonderfully comfortable and acceptable for girls in the seclusion of school grounds, they were shockingly unsuitable for public display by adults. Some clung to long skirts because of their advantage in stopping the ball. Most supported the attitude of the chauvinistic fiancé of a county player, who, in the aftermath of the Kent controversy, told his betrothed that 'if there is any chance of your wearing kit like that, my foot comes down bang, and you have no more hockey'.[33]

By 1914, although club players wore functional boots with studs or bars on the soles to prevent slipping, and spats and shin guards to prevent injury, they remained handicapped by skirts that hung midway between the knee and ankle and even by corsets. Despite the commonly held views that corsets were 'the most formidable barrier to easy, graceful and efficient play'[34] and to arm and body movements and respiration, and that they were even potentially productive of heart strain, some people continued to argue against the abandonment of stays, since they came in 'many excellent patterns, specially adapted for athletes'.[35]

Also unresolved was the need to change from hockey kit after matches. There was general agreement that this was desirable in order to avoid stares, ridicule and colds, and in the long run it was certainly encouraged in women by the development of team uniforms and the general habit of changing clothes for different activities. But by 1914 only a few clubs had dressing rooms. Victorian prudery being what it was, there was a strong though infrequently articulated feeling that 'you cannot expect eleven ladies to disrobe in one room'.[36]

Dress was the only area in which women's lacrosse was more innovative than hockey, perhaps because the game was newer and thus less encumbered by traditions. In 1910, the year of the commotion over the Kent hockey player's tunic, the Southern Ladies boldly adopted green tunics as becoming and practical.

The LLA followed suit, and, while allowing some flexibility, strongly encouraged the wearing of tunics of 'regulation length — one inch off the ground when kneeling'; and it chose as the uniform of the first All England team a golden brown tunic, shoes and stockings to match, and a cream blouse cut square at the neck.[37]

For cricket in the eighteenth century, whatever a player's class her dress accorded with prevailing fashions, the only concession to utility being slightly shortened skirts. John Collet's portrait of the elegant Miss Wicket, in her corsets, ground-length gown with long, tight sleeves and large ornamented hat, makes one wonder how she ever managed to swing a bat or field a ball. When cricket reappeared among the country-house set in the late-Victorian period, ladies played in long skirts sometimes with bustles, tight-fitting, high-necked blouses and large hats, which prompted Lady Milner of the White Heather Club to make an impassioned plea for the abandonment of corsets, and to chastise players for their lack of grace and sportsmanship in using their petticoats to stop balls.[38]

Cricket clubs adopted boater hats and then caps, before abandoning hats altogether around the turn of the century because of the dilemma they caused players who had to choose whether to run after the ball or try to keep their hats on; and they made other modifications in a moderately utilitarian direction to allow greater freedom of movement. But since they aimed to look as feminine as possible in order to legitimate their playing the king of mens' games, they stuck to long skirts, shirts and ties. Only the very odd lady cricketer dared to appear in a gymnastics tunic.[39]

The 'elegantly and appropriately attired' Original English Lady Cricketers wore attractive and effective, if somewhat heavy, outfits including loose shirts of white flannel with a sailor collar trimmed in red or blue opening in front to show a jersey embroidered with the letters OELC and a large blue or red bow to keep the sailor collar in place; fullish skirts of the same material fell to the shockingly short length of about 14 inches from the ground and had three coloured stripes around the bottom. Stockings, sashes and the trim on the shirts and skirts were in the colours of the side. A white cap like a man's, with a coloured bow above the peak, was worn, as were ordinary lace-up white cricket boots.[40] Like the lady cricketers themselves, the garb was considered eccentric and unladylike, and did not catch on.

In the world of individual sports, tunics and short skirts had a similar lack of success.

Since lawn tennis was a new and fashionable activity without precedents, in the early days women dressed as stylishly as possible for tennis parties. This meant they wore ordinary garden-party dress: 'Elaborate flounced, ground-length [frocks] with ornamental sleeves, high neck and cinched waist made from wool or silk and worn with a comparably elaborate hat'.[41] During the 1870s tight dresses with trains and bustles and voluminous sleeves were found on tennis courts — all, of course, worn over steel-boned corsets, several petticoats and long drawers. Lottie Dod claimed that it was not uncommon to see a lady sally forth to play in mid-summer in black velvet, long, black kid gloves, and large, wide-brimmed and befeathered or beflowered hats, or to see a player holding her racquet in one gloved hand and picking up her long skirt with the other.[42] Thus encumbered, the wonder is not that players moved slowly, but that they moved at all.

From the 1870s Mr Punch expressed concern about the difficulties caused on court by feminine costumes, and on one occasion he suggested that men should experience the handicaps women took for granted by playing with scarves tied round their knees.[43] But since the primary object of tennis was to socialise, and 'proper' style demanded little action, for some time cumbersome dress was not considered a major impediment. Finally in the 1880s, as improved skills led to increased movement, the unsuitability of ordinary clothing for even leisurely play dawned on players and fashion designers alike. The result was that tennis became one of the first sports for which special ladies' costumes were produced. They continued to imitate the style popular in fashionable drawing rooms; but their long skirts were fuller, allowing greater mobility, and began to be tied back by aprons with pockets to hold spare balls. All-white outfits which looked neat and camouflaged unladylike perspiration stains also became *de rigueur*. Maud Watson won the first Wimbledon ladies' championship attired in a white, two-piece costume with a bustle, and a straw boater hat rather than the elaborate headgear still worn by most lady players.

Over the years bustles and hats disappeared; dresses gave way to blouses with choker collars and ties and then softer lace jabots; and skirts became looser and slightly shorter. White plimsolls, which Mrs Hillyard said were to be avoided as 'they made the feet look large',[44] replaced high-heeled black boots. But few women had the courage or inclination to emulate the example of Lady Archibald Campbell, who in 1883 adopted a divided skirt. *Fin de siècle* tennis dress was basically an all-white version of contemporary summer fashions. Edwardians relaxed their corsets only slightly and wore skirts that were still almost ground-length and bolstered by several petticoats; these became narrower following the fashion in everyday wear.

Mrs Fenwick, a player of championship calibre, in 1908 wore a white skirt that swept just clear of the grass on ordinary shots and brushed the ground when she stooped, and a blouse with sleeves so long that they almost concealed her hands. Mrs Sterry, the All-England champion that year, thought skirts two inches off the ground were quite short enough. Dorothea Lambert Chambers won the 1912 championship wearing several stiff petticoats; and Elizabeth Ryan, who earned her first title in 1914, recalled seeing blood stains on players' stays. The most daring costumes worn at Wimbledon before 1914 were those of Lottie Dod, whose calf-length skirts and peaked cap were accepted only because of her tender age, and May Sutton, the first American champion, who in 1905 boldly rolled back her cuffs to reveal bare wrists because the sleeves of her blouse were too long and hot.[45]

Discussion of what could and should be worn by lady players occurred regularly in club rooms and tennis and fashion journals. Contributors to *Pastime* discussed the subject frequently, an unusually perspicacious one remarking,

> . . . that if ladies are to play lawn tennis at all, they should be allowed to play with ease and comfort, and this would seem to require a radical modification in the present style of dress. The difficult part of the question is . . . the mode in which this is to be effected. In spite of all the improvement that has been made of late years . . . ladies' costume is still most unfavourable to athletic exercise, being generally speaking tight where it should be loose, and loose where it should be tight. In particular, it is the long loose skirt on which dress reformers concentrate all their attacking forces; but this is also the precise detail on which fashion is most tenacious. Few persons are so little fettered by usage and conventionality as to contemplate without alarm the abandonment of what is looked upon as the essentially feminine garment.[46]

When Moorish trousers, gathered at the ankle and covered by a knee-length skirt, were advocated for serious players in a letter to *Pastime*'s editor in the mid-1880s, the suggestion was dismissed with a warning that, however acute the need for modifications in tennis skirts, if any of the leading players adopted trousers their bad taste and masculinity would deal a death-blow to lawn tennis for women in public.[47]

Not surprisingly, the question of dress reform was of more concern to the best players than to ordinary club types. Mrs Hillyard reported having seen ladies at tournaments who preferred smartness to agility to such an extent that they wore skirts so long they could not run backwards; and she attributed the improved quality of women's play to the abolition of the trailing, tight-sleeved gowns of her early youth. She was no revolutionary, however, her modest aim being to see ladies playing in ordinary cotton or flannel shirts, white sailor hats and a serge or white duck skirt.[48] Lottie Dod considered dress 'a matter for grave consideration', and asked how women could 'ever hope to play a sound game when their costume impeded the free movement of every limb'.[49] Her ideal was a pretty but practical costume that did not impede breathing and was loose and short enough to allow sudden movements in all directions, a full sweep of the racket and long strides. Dod's great successor, Dorothea Lambert Chambers, commended the marked improvement in the attire worn by experienced players, but lamented that the inexperienced still appeared in trailing skirts, dressy blouses and trimmed hats. She advised the abandonment of hats entirely, the adoption of a plain, white gored skirt four or five inches off the ground, a plain white shirt with collar and tie, and white shoes and stockings.[50]

Over the years modifications in tennis dress were necessitated by, and themselves facilitated, improved skills. By freeing the limbs they allowed new strokes, quicker execution and a faster pace; but their limitations simultaneously played a retarding role. As long as lady players wore corsets and skirts approaching the ground, the degree of proficiency achievable remained limited — a fact that was often conveniently forgotten when the innate superiority of the male game was extolled. To 1914 tennis dress and tennis players were caught in a familiar double bind involving convenience and display. Even reformers eschewed radical changes that might have involved a drastic shortening of skirts and the display of bare skin, for tennis remained a game of the fashionable classes in private clubs where the social aspect was strong and players' clothing and behaviour were rigidly controlled by protocol. It is thus hardly surprising that the majority of women, who played tennis primarily for social and recreational purposes, continued to consider the way a costume looked more important than its contribution to ease of play.

Not until the First World War swept away the nineteenth-century world and many of its conventions, and Suzanne Lenglen of France sent shockwaves through the staid world of Wimbledon by appearing on centre court in 1920 in a pleated skirt shortened to mid-calf, was a genuine revolution inspired in tennis dress.

In the game of golf, too, prevailing fashions seemed purposely designed to prevent women from performing athletically. Those who took up the putting game in the 1860s wore ordinary finery; and for years thereafter, even when women began to play on long courses, their golfing attire closely emulated the standard patterns for street dress: tightly-laced corsets, big hats over inappropriate hair-styles which caused no end of difficulty in wind and rain, and uncomfortable long dresses that impeded the swing. Only slowly did it occur to designers and players that a costume suitable to a fuller swing could be devised, rather than swings accommodated to the restrictions of clothing.[51]

Lady Margaret Scott won the first Open championship in a dazzlingly beautiful costume consisting of a sailor hat, blouse with voluminous sleeves, starched collar and wasp-waisted skirt that swept the fairways. About the same time Gertrude Douglas advised that the only modifications necessary for comfort when playing golf were 'to have the skirt a trifle shorter and the sleeves and bodice a bit looser than usual to ensure freedom of stroke'.[52] Three decades later Mabel Stringer gave a moving account of the torture of playing in the early days in a sailor hat that was almost impossible to keep on, in a high starched collar that made her neck raw, and in a ground-length skirt, worn over two petticoats and with a stiff, tight belt, that was extremely heavy and cumbersome. She also recollected seeing players slip elastic bands around their knees, and straps around their left arm to restrict the circumference of voluminous sleeves when addressing a ball, so that they could see it.[53]

When golfers started to demand clothing more appropriate to serious play, manufacturers began to appreciate the commercial possibilities of women's golf and to produce a whole line of golf attire, advertisements for which emphasised the combination of functionality and femininity. The preservation of a feminine appearance was considered of paramount importance to the acceptance of the ladies' game and to counteracting the notion of the 'golfing girl' as an eccentric creature who wore extraordinary garments and strode the fairways in an unbecomingly self-possessed manner.[54] After Amy Pascoe won the Open in 1896 clad in less than fashionable apparel, she was taken in hand and remodelled so as not to harm the game's image.

Gradually, more comfortable blouses of silk, flannel or cotton replaced starched collars and ties. Jackets became shorter in the Norfolk style, and for spring and summer wear were made of a lighter material or replaced by knitted jerseys and loose, woollen cardigans. Boater hats gave way to tam-o-shanters, or motor caps with voluminous veils that kept long hair out of the eyes but were unattractive and stuffy; and in the years before the war some players even copied the American fashion of playing hatless, despite warnings that they risked headaches or sunstroke. Skirts too were modified for the ordinary type was untidy, dirtied easily and

> . . . in wet weather . . . hampers every movement . . . and is very tiring to drag about. A short skirt — really short, not simply a couple of inches off the ground — looks infinitely nicer and more workman-like, and makes an inestimable difference in comfort.[55]

Designers raised hems to the dizzying height of six to eight inches off the ground and made skirts slightly wider than ordinary walking garb, which in turn inspired smarter, more practical footwear with flat heels and studs for traction.

Corsets were adapted rather than discarded for golfing purposes. The makers of the Royal Worcester Boneless Sports Corset, for example, advertised by sponsoring a golf tournament, predicting that their product would be worth at least three strokes a round and that uncorseted golfers risked losing control of their hips. The rival J & B Athletic Girl Corset was extolled for encouraging the poise and grace that it was the object of golf to develop.[56]

May Hezlet warned golfers against the mistake of considering indifference to clothes a sign of strength of mind. She advised them to combine comfort, grace and elegance and to take as much trouble over selecting golf costumes as any other part of the wardrobe, since one unkempt player could cast a slur on the whole society of lady golfers. Her ideal costume — plain, neat and well-cut — consisted of a blouse made from a soft material, a tweed or serge skirt six inches off the ground with a coat to match or a woollen or silk jersey, neat stockings and good-looking but sturdy shoes with square heels.[57]

When Cecil Leitch won the Open in 1914 her utilitarian, ankle-length skirt and soft-collared blouse were in marked contrast to the highly fashionable attire of Lady Margaret Scott 20 years earlier. On the whole by that time the clothing worn by women golfers above the waist was relatively practical — a soft-collared shirt or blouse or a jersey and knitted cardigan for protection on cold days; but below the waist, despite cautious shortening, skirts were still cumbersome, and restricted the degree to which the quality of play could improve.[58]

All the team and individual sports contributed in some degree to modifications in dress, but the most important single factor was the bicycle, for it converted the lady into a biped.

From the first the question of what the lady cyclist should wear troubled moralists and fashion designers, and engendered heated controversy. Cycling and normal clothing obviously were incompatible: stiff, tightly-laced corsets and long, trailing skirts could be worn neither comfortably nor safely. But what was the alternative? The problem was to devise attire that was functional, fashionable and feminine, which necessitated reducing the amplitude of skirts for the sake of safety yet not so much as to jeopardise respectability by exposing to a curious public too much ankle and leg.

In the days of tricycling the arbiters of fashion and behaviour agreed that the lady rider should avoid 'making herself offensive to the general public by dressing in a style to excite undue notice',[59] for:

> The advantage of quiet dress is immunity. It impresses those whose support the cyclist desires. A lady, if she dresses quietly on and off her machine, will meet with respect and attention, where a gaudily-dressed, fast girl will be treated differently, besides creating strong prejudice against 'women riding those tricycles'.[60]

The advocacy of rational costume for tricycling by Mrs E.M. King, one of the early members of the Cyclists' Touring Club and secretary of the Rational Dress Society, achieved nothing.

When the bicycle craze struck in the mid-1890s, some ladies mounted their iron steeds in large hats that flew off, full capes that ballooned outward in the wind, and dresses or blouses with large, constricting sleeves and long skirts that made pedalling difficult and got caught in moving parts. A few even attempted to carry parasols to protect their delicate complexions from the elements.[61]

To rational dressers comfort and safety awheel lay in rather full, knee-length knickers, long gaiters buttoning to the knee, a stiff-collared shirt, a tie and a hip-length jacket. The appearance of a few cyclists thus clad shocked the public, however, and inspired condemnations as indecent, immodest, incompatible with womanly elegance and grace, representative of an unacceptable degree of permissiveness, contrary to women's best interests and utterly ugly. The *Review of Reviews*'s observation, in 1894, that 'a lady can cycle all over Britain alone attired in neat and simple knickers, without attracting attention',[62] was far too optimistic. Women who persisted in wearing rationals were lampooned in the press and harassed by stares, jeers and even missiles. During the 1880s a mistress at the Swansea High School for Girls was dismissed for riding through a respectable neighbourhood in bloomers. There was even a legal case involving cycling dress. In 1889 while out cycling, Lady Florence Harberton was refused admission to the coffee room of a Surrey hotel on the grounds that she was wearing rational dress. Harberton persuaded the somewhat reluctant Cyclists' Touring Club to bring the proprietor to court, but amidst strong feeling and considerable publicity she lost on a technicality.[63]

Some women argued that, although rational costume was not very becoming, ladies, particularly those who went on long cycling tours, should be able to exercise freedom of choice in dress without having their femininity impugned. They suggested as a compromise the divided skirt which allowed freedom of movement but kept the figure gracefully and modestly shrouded. It looked 'better' than rationals, but it too failed to win acceptance by cyclists from the better classes who went in for moderate speed and distances. Torn between a desire to enlarge their horizons yet not offend propriety, they preferred to ride in modified skirts because they were more ladylike.[64]

The lady cyclist was warned that if she wore dowdy and eccentric attire, if she appeared before her large public audience looking anything other than neat, stylish and womanly, both mounted and dismounted, she would discredit not only her own womanliness but that of all cycling ladyhood. The whole secret of looking well was perceived to lie in the cut of the skirt, for the well-cut skirt would hang in such a way as to conceal the 'ugly action of the knees and legs', and, if fastened down by elastic straps and not too long or wide, need cause no danger.

The costume most often recommended for cycling included the essential elements of looseness, lightness, warmth, comfort and practicality along with attractiveness and inconspicuousness. It was of the basic walking style, worn with gaiters and over knicker-bockers instead of petticoats, with a skirt three to six inches above the ground, gored, loosely-fitting around the hips, and 2.5 yards wide. Ingenious methods were devised to prevent the skirt from blowing up and exposing legs, such as weighting hems with pieces of lead and sewing loops of elastic to both sides of the hem and slipping the feet through the loops before placing them on the pedals. Above the waist, tight lacing was avoided, but corsets themselves were not since they 'give great support and protect vital parts from chills'.[65] Over them shirts, ties and jackets with unconstraining arm holes were worn, and the whole ensemble was topped with neat and secure headgear.

For a number of years cycling manuals and women's magazines were filled with elaborate lists detailing every article of the lady cyclist's garb, from jacket and skirt, to hat, muffler, corset, boots and gloves. Designers struggled to develop the perfect costume, and devotees described dressing for cycling as a fine art involving as much expense and faultless tailoring as the preparation of a horse-back riding habit.[66] Only after the turn of the century, when cycling lost its fashionable appeal, did the dress issue fade.

Bicycling did not revolutionise women's dress, but it certainly contributed more than any other physical activity to the development of practical forms. Although the majority of cyclists rejected knickerbockers and really short or bifurcated skirts, a considerable number of perfectly respectable young women did adopt them, and by doing so provided a public demonstration of the utility of more rational dress. The thrilling and delightful sense of independence and power that women experienced cycling with limbs unfettered they were loath to sacrifice in other spheres. Ordinary cycling dress may not have been completely practical by 1914, but the cycling women of all sorts, who loosened their laces and demanded and got more comfortable attire, provided a catalyst for further dress reforms and struck an important blow for their sex's physical liberation.

Clothing has always profoundly affected sport from a variety of perspectives, including its psychological impact on self, team and opponents, its practical impact on the way activities are performed and its effect on the level of public acceptability.[67] The converse of course is also true, that sport can have a powerful influence on dress not just for sports performance but for ordinary wear as well. Both were clearly the case with virtually every sport in which women participated between 1870 and 1914.

When English women began to take part in sport during the second half of the nineteenth century, they did so in conventional dress because there was nothing else for them to wear, and because their motives were more social than athletic and they were afraid of offending propriety. It gradually became obvious, however, that even a casual interest in sport required more sensible garb; and from the 1880s clothing manufacturers and retailers began to appreciate — some would say exploit — the sportswoman as a commercial commodity and to produce costumes designed specifically for physical activity that permitted greater swiftness and power. By the turn of the century there were outfits for sports of all sorts, and ladies had come to consider them essential parts of their wardrobe, symbolic of their status as members of leisured society. On the whole they were plainer, slightly shorter, looser and less bulky than before. None was entirely practical or comfortable, however, since functionality remained a contentious issue and designs were still adapted more to the main lines of contemporary dress and social mores than to the requirements of performance.[68]

What this meant in practice was that most sports clothing continued to suggest restricted motion and the 'naturalness' of female anatomical — and therefore athletic — shortcomings, which in turn reaffirmed the innate superiority of the male. The exposure of arms and legs that would have facilitated physical competence and unimpeded movement had not progressed very far, while corsets were retained, albeit more loosely strung and made from softer material,[69] and uncomfortable items of male attire — masculine-looking jackets, shirts, stiff collars and ties — were incorporated in a kind of contradictory tribute and challenge to the male world that was being invaded.

Below the waist, the length of hemlines continued to be

considered a barometer of public morality, and thus a critical ethical issue. The retention of the skirt — the most inefficient but essentially feminine of garments — albeit elevated by a lofty six to eight inches, signified that sportswomen did not intend, and were not going to be allowed, to challenge seriously the authority of men or societal definitions of femininity. Women may have been permitted to use their legs more and even to wear knickers, but long skirts denied the existence of both. The year 1914 found women skiing and ice-skating in ankle-length skirts, hiking and climbing mountains in ankle-length skirts, riding horses and bicycles in ankle-length skirts, yachting and rowing in ankle-length skirts, and playing tennis, golf, cricket and hockey in ankle-length skirts. 'The uneasy marriage of a masculine top half with a feminine lower half was the inhibiting circumstance which dominated all female sports wear until World War I freed women physically and mentally from many of the clothes and conventions of past ages.'[70]

The psychologist J.C. Flugel argues that to become popular a fashion has to appeal in some way to a large number of people and accord with current ideals. Women, he says, must see in a new style a symbol of an ideal that is before them, even if they do not consciously realise its true significance; and they only accept major changes when there is a corresponding idealistic change. The failure of rational dress he attributes to the conservative reaction against threats to the Victorian social system which was perceived to be under assault on all fronts, and to the symbolic association of trousers with manhood which was apparently threatened by feminists and aesthetes.[71] Flugel's theories help to explain why sportswomen demanded and got more functional costumes, and yet why the skirt, although recognised as the greatest sartorial impediment to physical activity, proved so durable within and without the sporting community and why few people of either sex had the boldness or perceptivity to predict its demise. In addition it is clear why advertisements for sports costumes went to great lengths to emphasise the sportswoman's need to remain feminine in appearance, why they stressed the elegance and beauty of garments more than their utility, and why during the Edwardian period they often depicted sportswomen with most unnatural and unathletic-looking pigeon chests and pinched waists.[72]

Deciding what to wear must have created considerable tension in early games players between their desire to be fashionable and feminine and their desire to be free, for utility and safety were in apparent conflict with morality and womanliness. When stylishness and propriety clashed with comfort and safety the former usually triumphed. Like campaigners for the vote, sportswomen realised their appearance had a powerful effect on the responses of observers, and that the more attention they paid to the requisites of ideal womanliness the more acceptance they and their activities would gain.[73] Participants who 'looked well' and inconspicuous were a positive advertisement for sporting ladyhood, while those who did not inflicted serious damage to the fragile reputation of the whole sporting sorority. Most therefore regarded it as a point of honour to dress like ladies. To win approbation and to reconcile the contradictions between sport and the feminine ideal, they were prepared to make compromises by adopting sports costumes that allowed more movement but were still constraining and cumbersome. Was it not preferable, they asked, to play in attractive though restricting costumes to applause than in rational but unbecoming ones to jeers and condemnation?[74]

At the same time, however, although sportswomen continued to be limited considerably by fashion's tyrannical hold over the appearance of ladylike behaviour, the influence of sport on women's dress and on women's self-perception was of critical importance. More than anything else sport encouraged a utilitarian attitude towards female dress and the actual development of more functional costumes. Under sport's influence women began to shed restrictive clothing and to adopt styles permitting freer movement; and in the course of doing so some experienced for the first time a liberating sense of their own bodies. The loosening of corsets, the enlarging of armholes, the simplification or abandonment of hats and the moderate elevation of hemlines signified an important challenge to the physical and symbolic encumbrances of the past. Even limited changes in dress reflected the changing attitudes of society and of women themselves towards women's abilities and place in society, which accompanied women's movement into worlds such as sport that had previously been dominated by men. By threatening the Victorian era's standards of decorum and the immutability of its sexual world view, they made a contribution to the process of female emancipation as important, it can be argued, for its impact on women's daily lives as the acquisition of the vote.

Notes

1. Advertisement for J & B Athletic Girl Corset, *Ladies' Golf*, vol. 1 (June 1912), p. 52.

2. John W.G. Lowe and Elizabeth D. Lowe, 'Cultural Pattern and Process: A Study of Stylistic Change in Women's Dress', *American Anthropologist*, vol. 84, no. 3 (1982), pp. 521–41; Roberts, 'Exquisite Slave', pp. 544, 551.

3. Roberts, 'Exquisite Slave', p. 557. See also C.W. Cunnington, *English Women's Clothing in the Nineteenth Century* (London, 1937), p. 131.

4. Kunzle, *Fashion and Fetishism*, pp. xvii–xviiii, 18–30. See also Mel Davies, 'Corsets and Conception: Fashion and Demographic Trends in the Nineteenth Century', *Comparative Studies in Society and History*, vol. 24, no. 3 (1982), pp. 619–24; David Kunzle, 'Dress Reform as Antifeminism: A Response to Helene E. Roberts's "The Exquisite Slave: The Role of Clothes in the Making of the Victorian Woman"', *Signs*, vol. 2, no. 3 (1977), p. 574; Helene E. Roberts, 'Reply to David Kunzle's "Dress Reform as Antifeminism: A Response to Helene E. Robert's 'The Exquisite Slave'"', *Signs*, vol. 3, no. 2 (1977), p. 518–19; Helene E. Roberts, 'Submission, Masochism and Narcissism' in Virginia L. Lussier and Joyce J. Walstedt (eds), *Women's Lives* (Newark, Del., 1977), pp. 39–40.

5. *Lancet* (10 January 1880), p. 75. See also *British Medical Journal* (8 April 1882), p. 526; *Lancet* (2 February 1878), p. 179, (8 December 1883), p. 1004, (25 June 1887), pp. 1296–7, (15 June 1889), p. 1179, (14 June 1890), p. 1316.

6. F.A. Schmidt and Eustace H. Miles, *The Training of the Body for Games, Athletics, Gymnastics, and other forms of Exercise* (London, 1901), pp. 114–19; Davies, 'Corsets and Conception', p. 619; Kunzle, *Fashion and Fetishism*, pp. xvii–xviii, 18–30; Roberts, 'Submission . . . and Narcissim', p. 49; Veblen, *'Theory of the Leisure Class'* in Abbott (ed.), *Masterworks of Economics*, pp. 130–46.

7. Phillis Cunnington and Alan Mansfield, *English Costume for Sports and Outdoor Recreation* (London, 1969), p. 339.

8. Thomas K. Chambers, *A Manual of Diet in Health and Disease* (London, 1876), pp. 177–8.

9. *Rational Dress Society's Gazette* (April 1889), p. 6. See also Stella M. Newton, *Health, Art and Reason* (London, 1974), p. 116.

10. *Rational Dress Society's Gazette* (July 1889), p. 3.

11. Ada S. Ballin, *The Science of Dress in Theory and Practice* (London, 1885), p. 181; Gertrude M. Douglas, *The Gentlewoman's Book of Dress* (London, c. 1890), pp. 116–27; *Lancet* (26 May 1883), p. 921, (30 June 1883), pp. 1134–5; *Pall Mall Gazette* (14 October 1884), p. 6; *Rational Dress Society's Gazette* (April 1888), pp. 1–7, (October 1888), p. 2.

12. Ada Ballin, quoted in Cunnington and Mansfield, *English Costume*, p. 333.

13. Ballin, *Science of Dress*, p. 212. See also Ada Ballin, 'Introduction' in Sir Howard Spicer (ed.), *Sports for Girls* (London, 1900), pp. 8–10.

14. Douglas, *Gentlewoman's Book of Dress*, pp. 120–2.

15. *Rational Dress Society's Gazette* (October 1888), p. 1. See also *Sanitary*

Record (15 October 1888), pp. 149–50.

16. *Sanitary Record* (15 December 1888), pp. 163–5. See also *Rational Dress Society's Gazette* (January 1889), pp. 1–4.

17. Ann Pagan, *St George's Chronicle* (May 1894), quoted in May, *Madame Bergman-Osterberg*, p. 45.

Bergman-Osterberg insisted that for the good of their health players must change into dry clothing after matches. Dartford was one of the few institutions that provided changing rooms and showers for home and visiting players.

18. Hargreaves, 'Playing Like Gentlemen', p. 98; Okely, 'Privileged . . . and Finished', pp. 125, 130; Pointon, 'Growth of Women's Sport', p. 159.

19. *Chelsea College . . . 1898–1958*, pp. 10–11.

20. *Anstey Physical Training College Magazine* (Christmas 1907), p. 22, (Christmas 1909), pp. 28–30.

21. North London Collegiate School, Headmistresses' Reports, vol. 1 (7 June 1880), pp. 149–50, vol. 3 (5 December 1898), pp. 121–2, (6 February 1899), p. 130; North London Collegiate School, Staff Meeting Minutes (5 October 1896), p. 135, (29 May 1899), pp. 243, 286, (4 March 1901), p. 275, (10 February 1902), p. 197; *Our Magazine*, vol. 6 (July 1877), pp. 136–7, vol. 10 (March 1885), p. 27, vol. 17 (November 1892), p. 112, vol. 22 (April 1897), p. 32; Sara Burstall, *Frances Mary Buss* (London, 1938), pp. 54–5; Elizabeth Ewing, *Women in Uniform through the Centuries* (London, 1975), pp. 68–70.

22. *Our Magazine*, vol. 15 (March 1890), pp. 10–13; Ellis, *Man and Woman*, p. 211.

23. *Ladies' Field* (9 September 1911), p. 57; Lumsden, *Yellow Leaves*, p. 29; White interview; Grant, McCutcheon and Sanders (eds), *St Leonards School*, pp. 91, 99–102.

24. Ewing, *Women in Uniform*, p. 70.

25. Raverat, *Period Piece*, p. 71.

26. Evelyn M. Perry, 'School Games', *Teachers' Guild Quarterly* (March 1910), pp. 17–19.

27. Peck, *A Little Learning*, pp. 121–2.

28. Atkinson, 'Fitness . . . and Schooling', p. 120.

29. Smith and Robson (eds), *Hockey*, p. 324.

30. Ibid., p. 316.

31. AEWHA, Minutes (23 November 1895), (29 April 1898); *Hockey Field* (11 January 1906), p. 177.

32. AEWHA, Minutes (28 April 1899); *Hockey Field* (31 October 1901), p. 42, (11 January 1906), p. 177, (14 October 1909), p. 7.

33. *Hockey Field* (27 January 1910), p. 254. After the First World War the gymnastic tunic for women's hockey emerged triumphant. It was worn by all the first teams in England until it was ousted by short skirts and shorts in the 1960s and 1970s.

34. Smith and Robson (eds), *Hockey*, pp. 316–17.

35. Thompson, *Hockey*, pp. 12–13.

36. Pollard, *Story of the AEWHA*, p. 10. See also Smith and Robson (eds), *Hockey*, pp. 314–15; Pointon, 'Growth of Women's Sport', pp. 133, 157–8.

37. LLA, Minutes (16 July 1913); *Hockey Field* (24 November 1910), p. 93, (12 December 1912), p. 113.

38. Roger Longrigg, *The English Squire and his Sport* (London, 1977), p. 284.

39. Lady Milner, 'Cricket' in Beatrice Violet Greville (ed.), *The Gentlewoman's Book of Sports* (London, c. 1892), p. 655; Rheinberg, 'Women's Cricket — The Fashion', pp. 1–5.

Trousers still are not worn by many women cricketers, the policy remaining that women playing what is by tradition a man's game should look as feminine as possible.

40. *Illustrated London News* (24 May 1890), p. 655; Permanent Exhibition, Cricket Museum, Lord's Cricket Ground, London.

41. Ted Tinling, *The Story of Women's Tennis Fashion* (London, 1977), p. 1.

42. F.G. Aflalo (ed.), *The Sports of the World* (2 vols , London, 1903), vol. 1, p. 618. See also Cunnington, *English Women's Clothing*, p. 293.

43. James Laver, *Taste and Fashion*, rev. edn (London, 1945), p. 71.

44. Longrigg, *English Squire*, p. 287.

45. Tinling, *The Story of . . . Tennis Fashion*, pp. 1–6.

46. *Pastime* (19 May 1886), p. 329.

47. Ibid. (17 August 1883), p. 185, (19 May 1886), p. 333, (26 May 1886), p. 351.

48. *Young Woman* (1893–4), p. 371.

49. Dod, 'Ladies' Lawn Tennis' in Heathcote *et al.*, *Tennis, Lawn Tennis*, p. 312.

50. Chambers, *Lawn Tennis*, pp. 64–8.

51. Ross [Hezlet], 'Ladies' Point of View' in Hutchinson (ed.), *New Book of Golf*, p. 346.

52. Douglas, *Gentlewoman's Book of Dress*, pp. 61–2.

53. Stringer, *Golfing Reminiscences*, p. 27.

54. Hezlet, *Ladies' Golf*, p. 236.

55. *Ladies' Golf* (7 September 1907).

56. Ibid. (June 1912), p. 52, (26 February 1914), cover, (30 April 1914), p. 18, (6 August 1914), cover.

57. Ross [Hezlet], 'Ladies' Point of View' in Hutchinson (ed.), *New Book of Golf*, p. 352.

58. Cunnington and Mansfield, *English Costume*, pp. 71–9.

59. Davidson, *Handbook*, p. 114.

60. F.J. Erskine, *Tricycling for Ladies* (London, 1885), p. 12.

61. Lightwood, *Cyclists' Touring Club*, p. 199; Marie Pointon, 'Factors Influencing the Participation of Women and Girls in Physical Education, Physical Recreation and Sport in Great Britain During the Period 1850–1920', *History of Education Society Bulletin*, no. 24 (Autumn 1979), p. 50.

62. *Review of Reviews*, vol. 10 (July–December 1894), p. 222. See also Rubinstein, *Before the Suffragettes*, pp. 217–19.

63. *Badminton Magazine of Sports and Pastimes* (August–December 1895), p. 411; Erskine, *Bicycling for Ladies*, pp. 27–33; *Ladies' Gazette* (18 April 1896), p. 56; Malmesbury, 'Bicycling For Women' in Graves, Lacy and Malmesbury, *Cycling*, p. 93; Pemberton *et al.*, *Complete Cyclist*, p. 54; *Punch*

(18 May 1895), p. 239, (3 August 1895), p. 59, (11 September 1897), p. 110, (6 September 1899), p. 114.

64. *Cycle Magazine*, vol. 1 (November 1896), pp. 22–5; Pemberton *et al., Complete Cyclist*, pp. 51–4; *Review of Reviews*, vol. 12 (July–December 1895), pp. 149–50; *Wheelwoman* (9 January 1897), p. 3, (14 January 1899), p. 10.

65. Erskine, *Lady Cycling*, p. 22.

66. Ibid., pp. 19–22.

67. G. Patience Thomas, 'Clothing and Sports: A Psychological Analysis', *Quest*, vol. 19 (January 1973), pp. 101–2.

68. Doreen Yarwood, *English Costume From the Second Century B.C. to 1960* (London, 1961), p. 241.

69. Corset manufacturing was big business. The production of rust-proof stays for swimmers was only an extreme example of a commercial response to changing realities that saw the corset trade produce for women devoted to open-air pursuits such products as Dr Jaeger's knitted and woven woollen corsets, the J & B Athletic Girl Corset, the Royal Worcester Boneless Sports Corset, the Khiva Corselet and Sandow's Corset. These garments were advertised as ideal in that they provided support and preserved beauty by moulding the form to the lines of grace and elegance without undue pressure. Douglas, *Gentlewoman's Book of Dress*, p. 19; *Hockey Field* (19 January 1911), p. 220; *Journal of Scientific Physical Training*, vol. 3 (Autumn 1910), pp. 8–16, vol. 5 (Spring 1913), p. 20; *Lady Cyclist*, vol. 1, no. 1 (1895), p. 25; *Ladies' Golf* (June 1912), pp. 25, 52, (26 February 1914), cover.

70. Cunnington and Mansfield, *English Costume*, p. 359.

71. J.C. Flugel, *The Psychology of Clothes*, 2nd edn (London, 1950), pp. 147–53.

72. *Badminton Magazine of Sports and Pastimes*, vol. 38 (January–April 1914), pp. 149–59.

73. June Kennard, 'Sport Costume for Englishwomen in the Nineteenth Century', *Abstract: Proceedings and Newsletter, North American Society for Sport History, Seventh Annual Meeting* (Austin, Tx., 1979), p. 18.

74. Hezlet, *Ladies' Golf*, pp. 234–5.

9

The Literature of Women's Sport

When a man wants looking after he doesn't want to find his wife playing a round of golf.[1]

Accompanying the nineteenth-century revolution in sport was the development of an abundant sporting literature. For the obvious reasons that sport and men were almost synonymous and that for three-quarters of the century there was very little involving women on which to report, its primary focus was male. When women did begin to 'play the game', however, the manner in which their activities were treated provided striking testimony to the extent of sportswomen's progress and impediments.

The fight for women's sporting rights was more actional than verbal, with the result that there is no great corpus of literature defending women's athletic rights such as exists in the educational, legal and political spheres. There was still a women's sporting literature, however, for, as we have seen, during the late-nineteenth century a considerable amount of written advice was offered to women about the physiological and social benefits and detriments of sport by doctors, clerics, educators, popular writers and feminists. In addition, various literary media — some directed at an exclusively female audience, some at a mixed audience and some at a primarily male one — accepted sport of certain types as compatible with socialisation for femininity, and so began to feature female sporting subjects.

In a history of women's magazines, Cynthia White reports a remarkable expansion in the field of publishing during the Victorian era, especially in its later stages, as a result of complex social, economic and technological changes. She notes particularly the increase in the number and circulation of journals directed towards women of various social classes, which apparently acted as a forum for the discussion of subjects of interest — or perceived by editors who were mostly male to be of interest — to women, and provided women with opportunities for exchanging ideas and seeking assistance and advice. They thus became a medium of mass communication with the potential for considerable social and economic influence.[2]

In the early-Victorian period few editors or readers of respectable journals were much concerned about the emancipation or intellectual improvement of the female sex. Contents included articles on fashion, etiquette, handicrafts, personal beauty and the domestic arts, which reinforced the *status quo* by emphasising the innocent, amusing and genteel. Occasional articles featured female archers and riders of horses or advised women to take more exercise, albeit of an unstrenuous type. But on the whole, their ideal woman was a weak, helpless creature whose physical activity was properly confined to a leisurely walk.

Women's magazines usually followed rather than initiated changes, with the result that it was some time after females began to participate in sport and to obtain more practical physical education that they took to featuring sporting ladies. And even when the realities of women's widening sphere provided magazines with the confidence to report on such subjects as sport, and to portray women in more active and public capacities, they continued to present traditional views about women's rights and roles being based most naturally on the home. As a result, while sport was depicted as a legitimate female interest, they continued to impose conservative values on their readers by projecting the view that women's sports were acceptable only if feminine standards of dress and behaviour were observed.[3]

The contents of several magazines are representative of the tension between the forces of change and tradition that frustrated and typified emancipators of women; and they offer insights into how publishers viewed women and the varying ways in which women viewed themselves, and into women's changing priorities.

The *Queen* was the foremost late-Victorian periodical for ladies of rank and breeding. Begun in 1861 by Samuel Beeton, the husband of the legendary Mrs Isabella Beeton of household management fame, it rejected revolutionary ideas about women's sphere and rights and was dedicated to promoting traditional virtues among upper- and upper-middle-class women who remained at home, through articles on the court, society, travel, the arts, fashion, design, social problems, domestic management and interior decoration.

Towards the end of the century the *Queen* could offer the elderly Mrs Lynn Linton an opportunity to rail against the New Woman, her untidy dress, hockey sticks and bicycles, and her liking for 'the more violent bodily exercise of boys'.[4] Yet at the same time the journal had a progressive streak that manifested itself, albeit for health reasons, in support of women's sport and in criticism of tight lacing and 'the languid dawdling which often passes by the name of exercise'.[5] As early as the 1870s, in a regular feature on 'Pastimes', it included articles on croquet, lawn tennis, swimming and ice- and roller-skating, and the proper garb for participants. By the 1890s it had added hunting, angling, riding, sailing, curling, golf, hockey, cricket, rowing, gymnastics and cycling to the roster; and by 1905 it had moved with the times sufficiently to introduce a separate feature on 'Sports and Games'.

A number of other magazines for genteel ladies also chronicled society at play at home and abroad, and provided commentaries on sport. Among the leaders were the *Gentlewoman* (1890) and the *Ladies' Field* (1896).

The *Gentlewoman*, launched as a 'quality' weekly, quickly became a society favourite. Along with commentaries on the theatre, the arts and fashion, it offered its leisured and affluent readers a steady diet of sport that ran the gamut from croquet, archery and tennis, to riding, hunting, driving, boating, yachting, cycling, walking, fishing, fencing, skating, swimming, hockey and cricket.

The first issue included a column on 'Sports and Sportswomen' by 'Diana', who assisted women to improve and develop their bodies and thus create new life and happiness, but who also had regressive attitudes. Diana argued that women's physical weakness was due to a lack of physical education and exercise rather than natural incapacity. She connected the development of physical fitness through sport to the survival of the race and the development of character. She approved of rational dress for sport, anticipated the popularity of the safety bicycle and identified the cultivation of strong, healthy bodies as a female birthright. Simultaneously, however, she opposed women 'becoming like men', was sceptical about the efficacy of women striving to break records in athletic competitions, and constantly stressed that dignity, grace, moderation and the avoidance of exhibitionism were essential in the true sportswoman.[6]

After ten years Diana's column was replaced by regular articles on a variety of sports that continued the progressive-conservative orientation of their predecessor. They customarily praised sport for teaching self-dependence, a quality that 'a few years ago . . . would have been condemned as masculine and unbecoming'.[7] But in the same revealing breath, they condemned women riding astride and sitting in parliament and the association between their enthusiasm for sport and their becoming 'modern'.[8] The *Gentlewoman*'s gentlewoman might have been independent and athletic, but she knew that her true interests lay in the home.

The leading late-Victorian magazine for sportswomen, and the one that best demonstrated the degree to which fashionable ladies of the affluent classes considered it necessary to claim sporting accomplishments, was the *Ladies' Field*, the sports editor of which from 1907 was the famous male sporting journalist, Eustace White. In addition to the court, society, fashion, gardening, pets and the arts, it featured 'illustrated notes on hunting, tennis, golf, croquet, hockey, archery, and all the sports in which Ladies are interested'.[9] The latter took the form of weekly articles on 'Sports and Pastimes' that ran to several pages and went into great detail on the lawn tennis and golf championships and 'important contests' in other sports. Field sports, particularly hunting and riding, were treated separately and in similar detail. On occasion special features, usually focusing on a single activity, were published in special supplements. In addition, the magazine issued handbooks on hockey and croquet, and sponsored contests in hockey, croquet, tennis and archery. The *Ladies' Field* approved of almost any sport that ladies took up. From a wealth of photographs and articles on 'Society Sportswomen', 'Distinguished Sportswomen' and 'Leading Sportswomen of the Day' readers learned about ladies of position who were masters of hunts, good shots, anglers, equestriennes, yachters and golfers. They learned as well that the *Ladies' Field* approved of women playing polo, albeit with slightly modified rules, of ladies throwing the discus, after the fashion of some in France, of mixed yachting races, of mixed cricket and golf as 'excellent means of combining fresh air, exercise, and society', of ladies golfing on full-length courses, of ladies participating in motor launch races at Cowes, and even of ladies ballooning.[10]

None the less, despite its advanced views, the *Ladies' Field* was far from oblivious to the rules of propriety, and often reflected the conservative attitudes of the classes to which it catered. It certainly considered football and competitive rowing off-limits; and although it encouraged competition and winning, it described 'the spirit of excessive competition' as 'one of the greatest dangers' pervading women's games.[11] It defended women's sports on the grounds that they would give women greater energy for the performance of domestic duties; and it argued that ideally women's games should be pursued moderately and retain some of the characteristics of pastimes entered into for sheer pleasure, since 'a woman gives up her invaluable prerogatives if she takes up athleticism uncompromisingly'.[12]

From time to time articles of a distinctly cautionary nature were offered, such as that in which Lady Jeune, the cyclist, expressed the view that, while athletics had produced a race of strong, vigorous, healthy women, violent exercise and the abnormal development of muscle that accompanied them were incompatible with beauty and grace; and worse still, because women's strength and powers of endurance were limited, they damaged their constitutions and threatened the health of future generations. It gave a male contributor the opportunity to rue women's 'mad rush to sports without consideration of whether they mar the figure or jeopardise grace', or whether they required a number of purely masculine qualities of which the fair sex was devoid and which would be unbecoming. When an anonymous 'Diana' issued a rebuttal, she was careful to oppose the type of excesses epitomised by compulsory games in schools, and to advocate that, in athletics as in book learning, women acquire a sense of proportion.[13]

A number of magazines also catered to women lower down the middle-class ladder. Their forerunner was the *Englishwoman's Domestic Magazine*, the first cheap magazine for women of the lower-middle class, 50,000 to 60,000 copies of which were issued monthly from 1852 to 1879, under the editorship originally of Samuel Beeton. While it promoted quiet domestic virtues and the cultivation of morals, the *Englishwoman's Domestic Magazine* was committed to a cautious degree of female emancipation; and its advocacy of the improvement of women's minds and bodies through intellectual and physical education challenged traditional cultural constructs.

Later in the century the *Young Woman* (1892) and the *Woman at Home* (1894) carried on the *Englishwoman's Domestic Magazine*'s mission. The *Young Woman* attempted to cut across the limits imposed by social stratification and to appeal to serious-minded women who shared similar attitudes. Although sport was not one of its major preoccupations, it frequently offered readers articles on boating, cycling, ice-skating, fencing, swimming, golfing and lawn tennis, on sports costumes, and on the general benefits to women of regular physical exercise; but it reminded them simultaneously that women should not overdo an interest in sport. Rather, they should follow the example of:

> Clarisse, a rosy-cheeked, high spirited girl of eighteen, who, in defiance of the restrictions of femininity, indulged her passion for cycling, climbing, rowing, and golfing, but, who, upon becoming engaged to be married, immediately lost her taste for 'horsey and mannish things'.[14]

The *Woman at Home* too was interested in sport, because of a conviction that sports participation did much to improve women's physiques and general health provided that overstrain was avoided. It regularly gave its readers the opportunity to enjoy vicariously such upper-crust sports as hunting and riding, archery and fishing, and motoring, yachting and mountaineering. Once in a long while it even featured authors with insight and feminist inclinations. Witness the views of a Miss M.E. Hughes, who, when asked 'Should Women Climb Snow Mountains?', responded in the affirmative on the grounds that the psychological and physical benefits more than compensated for the risk of accidents and over-fatigue.

> I used to think that men only could succeed in mathematics, Latin, and snow-climbing [she said]. I have been forced by experience to grasp the refreshing idea that all three are possible to women; . . . there remains to men still the privilege of fighting, which they may keep, and the privilege of parliamentary representation, which some day we mean to share with them.[15]

Commercial possibilities prompted publishers to turn their attention to young readers as well. The *Girls' Own Paper* and the *Girl's Realm* were magazines directed towards the type of juveniles who as ladies would be apt to read the *Queen*. Launched following the success of the Religious Tract Society's *Boys' Own Paper* (1879), the *Girls' Own Paper* (1880) eschewed the heroic sagas and epic adventures that were the *Boys' Own Paper*'s staples, believing in separate spheres for males and females, and attempting to condition its readers to motherhood and home-making. Like its adult counterparts, it offered fiction, the latest royal and aristocratic intelligence and extensive domestic guidance. When editors grudgingly recognised that girls could cope with mental stimulation, pieces on education at public schools and women's colleges were also included. But they too supported girls' participation in a variety of sports because of the health- and character-building properties of physical exercise; and while they condemned false notions of gentility, they portrayed the excessively athletic girl as a creature deficient in womanliness, mental power and domestic skills and likely to become an old maid.[16] Until it acquired a more liberally-minded editor in 1908, the *Girls' Own Paper* generally supported the view that, 'To keep girls' complections and spirits good, to preserve grace, strength, and agility of motion, there is no gymnasium so valuable, no exercise more beneficial in result than sweeping, dusting, making beds, washing dishes, and polishing brass and silver.'[17]

The *Girl's Realm* (1898) was aimed at a younger age-group than the *Girls' Own Paper* and initially was more progressive. Although it repeatedly emphasised that the duties of home life and motherhood were woman's natural destiny, it encouraged girls to obtain good educations, consider new roles and train for careers. Convinced of the beneficial effects of sport on girls' health and character, it published forward-looking articles on gymnastics, physical culture and various sports and exercises, along with regular interviews with 'Girls Who Excel at Sports' and features on famous schools where sport was important. By 1906, apart from football, there was scarcely a sport it considered inappropriate, and it presented respectable girls doing everything from playing hockey and taking long cycling tours to ballooning, canoeing, climbing cliffs and shooting big game.

Inspired exclusively by the revolution in women's sports were the journals that catered to specific female sporting sub-groups, for example, the *Lady Cyclist* (1895) and its successor, the *Wheelwoman* (1897), the *Hockey Field* (1901), *Ladies' Golf* (1912) and the *Golfing Gentlewoman* (1914). Their readership was inevitably narrower than that of general magazines, but their very existence was a revealing sign of changing times.

Part of a vast cycling literature including novels, poems, journals, newspapers, manuals, guidebooks and magazine articles, the *Lady Cyclist* and the *Wheelwoman* were intended 'to instruct the women of England in the art and pastime of cycling . . . and to be a medium of intercommunication between women who cycle'.[18] Although edited by men, most of their contributors were women who, to an extent that now seems absurd, provided information on how to ride, choose, care for and maintain a bicycle; how to mount, dismount, sit, steer and pedal; how to dress in a functional yet stylish manner; how to care for the skin; how to ride safely in towns; how to climb hills; how to ride long distances; and how to 'ankle' gracefully. They also included correspondence, cartoons, gossip, fiction, society news, interviews with notable wheelwomen, articles on royal and aristocratic cyclists, medical advice, and information on weddings on wheels, cycling clubs, cycling abroad, cycling tours, cycling picnics, cycling schools, Sunday cycling, cycling shows and gymkhanas, accidents and their causes, the rules of the road, and elaborate lists of do's and don'ts.

As indicated in Chapter 5, the *Hockey Field*, the premier women's sports journal, was established to promote the game and to bring players into contact with each other through the provision of information on players, the AEWHA, match schedules and results and so on. Ambitious to consolidate its reputation, it soon expanded to include cricket, lacrosse, netball, golf, tennis, archery, sculling and swimming. Between April 1908 and April 1909 it acted as the official organ of the Ladies' Golf Union under the title, the *Hockey Field and Golf Green*, since the LGU felt the need for a means by which lady golfers could communicate with each other and gain a knowledge of each other's play, and by which the union could publicise 'its notes, its notices and its chastening nostrums'.[19] The experiment was unsuccessful because of jealousy between the AEWHA and LGU, but with its ambitions intact the *Hockey Field* added Lacrosse and Net-ball to a subtitle in October 1909, and after the formation of the Ladies' Lacrosse Association published an official page for its news.

From 1902 the LGU issued a year book containing rules, course maps, tournament results and players' names and addresses; and from 1912, in response to numerous golf journals' relegation of ladies' sections to the back pages, the union published its own journal under the editorship of Mable Stringer, the only successful female sports journalist in England. *Ladies' Golf*, included everything from golf gossip, handicaps and reports on competitions and clubs to information on union meetings, rules, how to dress, where to shop and the history of the game.

Both general and specialised women's magazines contained considerable advertising, since the growth of the women's periodical press in the late-Victorian period was underwritten by advertisers whose activities testified to a large expansion in mass-produced consumer goods, to rising incomes, and to the potential of the women's press as a selling medium and of the sporting lady as a lucrative source of revenue.[20] By the early-twentieth century, magazines carried extensive advertisements — often sponsored by new sportswomen's departments of such great stores as Gamages, Burberry's and Lilley and Skinner — for yachting gowns, riding habits, shooting and angling suits, walking skirts, tennis dresses, cycling garb, motoring dresses, golfing attire, swimming costumes and gymnastics tunics, and the appropriate corsets, under-garments, hats, gloves and footwear to accompany them. They also featured advertisements for sports equipment, ladies' sports clubs and women's physical training colleges, for fencing and seeds for tennis lawns, for Beecham's pills and potions and embrocations designed to keep the skin becomingly soft and relieve muscular pain, and for Bovril, a 'recuperative beverage' useful for sportswomen because it 'refreshes, strengthens, stimulates and invigorates without deranging the most delicate constitution'.[21] In almost all instances models embodied the essence of femininity rather than athleticism.

Stress on femininity also characterised the monographs and anthologies on women's sport and exercise — in general and particular — that issued from the pens of women from the 1880s, partly as a result of frustration with the omission or cursory treatment of women's activities in books of instruction for men. Notable were Lady Greville's *The Gentlewoman's Book of Sports* (1892) and *Ladies in the Field* (1894), and Frances Slaughter's two-volume *The Sportswoman's Library* (1898).[22]

Greville's anthologies were prepared by and for ladies who were well-off. The first included a dozen chapters by female authorities on such sports as trout fishing, sailing, ice-skating, archery and cricket, while the latter concentrated on more elite activities — riding, hunting and shooting everything from deer to kangaroo and tigers. Both offered the reminiscences of contributors and encouraging instructions to women who were beginning to interest themselves in sport; and both insisted that sport improved women's character and health, taught valuable lessons and skills, and was no threat to feminine thought and behaviour.

They also made it clear that certain activities were unacceptable, and that in her role as a sportswoman it was incumbent on the lady to behave in an exemplary fashion and to display womanly traits at all times. Finally, they paid deference to the tradition of female subservience and domesticity by providing, as among the most important justifications for women's sports participation, that it would add to their menfolk's enjoyment by making women bright and cheerful companions and would improve women in a manner that would benefit their families and nation. In other words, sportswomen were to perform only 'certified' activities, and in a feminine manner, for the good, primarily, of others.

Frances Slaughter's *Sportswoman's Library* — a compendium of articles by female experts on fox, hare and deer hunting, shooting, fishing, archery, ice-skating, golf, croquet, punt racing, cruising, small yacht racing, driving, cycling, tennis, and riding — was a more ambitious project. Dedicated to the Marchioness of Worcester, a keen sportswoman and wife of one of the foremost sportsmen of the age, it aimed to provide women with information on the history and practice of outdoor recreations unlikely to be found in material written from a male perspective. In the preface to volume one, anticipating a negative response, Slaughter specifically requested a hearing from 'the great body of sportsmen, who so far held almost undisputed sway in the realm of sporting literature'.[23] She also did her sex considerable service by urging it to play a larger role in the life of the nation, and by relating the extent of women's participation in outdoor exercise to the amount of freedom and independence allowed it by the unwritten laws of the age, and to the stimulus provided by the contemporary women's movement.[24]

Another literary medium that revealed the growth of female sport was girls' school fiction. During the early-nineteenth century, novels for girls usually centred on home and family, and were characterised by condescending simplicity and sticky sentimentality. Later, however, accompanying the proliferation of good girls' schools, tales of school life began to replace domestic ones. They inevitably left the impression that school days were exciting and liberating, and lent glamour to such aspects as the hockey field. The 'hockey girl' became an identifiable type, for their heroine was likely to be a healthy, outdoor girl who kept her 'jolly hockey stick' beside her bed.[25]

Pre-eminent among writers of girls' school fiction were L.T. (Elizabeth Lillie Thomasina) Meade and Angela Brazil. The remarkably prolific Meade wrote over 300 books between 1886 and 1914, many sentimentalising school days during which young ladies played games in a decorous manner and had any tomboyish edges removed, for most 'sweet girl graduates' were destined for the home.[26]

Angela Brazil's novels were much the same. Brazil had attended a school in Manchester that made no provision for games or exercise other than weekly classes in drill and callisthenics, and as a result she developed a profound feeling of having missed something important. Her book covers frequently featured girls in tunics holding hockey sticks; and her characters were often games-playing, boarding school types, who used their own sporting lingo and were — like the ideal public school boy — honest, loyal, unintellectual and all-round 'good chums'. Brazil particularly championed hockey because of its controlled release of adolescent energy and the bridge it provided between staff and students. Her games mistresses were portrayed as a type of adult games captain, adored by pupils and useful as a role model for quality, discipline and orderliness.[27]

Although Brazil's early books reflected new attitudes to girls' education, on the whole they were unprogressive. Her characters played all the new games and sports, but underneath they were still ladies concerned about social niceties, and they constantly sought the approval of males in anticipation of matrimony rather than independent careers. In Brazil's first book, for example, the heroine was sent to a school where championship hockey players were developed and cricket, swimming and gymnastics were compulsory. But when her father returned home after an extended stay in the colonies, her highest ambition upon graduating was to become his own 'little housekeeper'.[28] Patty Hirst, the heroine of Brazil's most popular novel, went to a school where two hours of outdoor exercise were compulsory daily. She excelled in all games and sports, and ended up being the 'best bat in the school', a tennis champion, a prefect and head girl.[29] The conditioning she received, however, destined her, not for feminist activism, but for marriage to a 'decent chap' or in a pinch for training as a games mistress.

Perhaps even more important to an understanding of society's reactions to women's sport was the treatment accorded it in a variety of forms of literature addressed primarily to a male audience — literary and sporting periodicals, books on sport, encyclopaedias of sport and newspapers — for they showed conclusively what form male reactions to the new breed of sporting women took.

Some of the most distinguished literary journals of the late-Victorian period considered the sportswoman a subject worthy of serious discussion, if only occasionally. Their range of opinions ran the gamut from total support to total disapproval, with the majority falling somewhere in between, that is, supporting women's sport as long as excesses were avoided and moderation and femininity were observed, for reasons that had more to do with the good of others than of women themselves.

The first discussions usually were related to the debate on the higher education of women, and involved the inextricable connection between healthy minds and bodies. Later, after women had taken up sport in considerable numbers, writers mostly male but occasionally female put a cautious seal of approval on certain types of activities as beneficial to future mothers and their children if violence were avoided and womanliness cultivated. Women owed it to society, they implied, not to do anything that might pollute 'feminine influences' or distract them from their duty to produce worthy sons and daughters for England and the Empire. Women's sport was thus justified, not for its own sake or that of individuals, but because it was perceived as having a higher purpose. Participation was turned into another female duty.

The articles on sportswomen and women as athletes in the *Fortnightly Review* and the *Nineteenth Century* around the turn of the century are fascinating examples of the debate on women's sport that occurred at the highest literary level.

Unenlightened and enlightened views on the sportswoman were expressed in the *Fortnightly* by Pleasaunce Unite and F.G. Aflalo in 1900 and 1905. The former described athletics, even in moderation, as unhealthy for girls and unwholesome and unbecoming for women in middle life. A sound mind and a sound body were much more likely, Unite said, if the brain were rested not by violent exercise but by such manual labour as needlework.[30] On the other hand, Aflalo, a well-known sports journalist, after dissociating the emergence of sportswomen from the 'independent products' of the movement for female emancipation, commented positively on the 'emancipated position in the world of sport' that women had recently achieved, and chastised 'the majority of men' for their inability

258

. . . to discuss a subject of such importance in its bearing on our social evolution in any spirit other than one of either patronage or derision, for their unnecessary inhospitality has inspired in women themselves a corresponding attitude of sarcastic apology that is no apology at all.[31]

Aflalo then criticised his sex further for 'our unchivalrous gibing at the modern woman', and concluded by arguing that 'women can play the game as honourably and as sportingly as men', and that there were few sports, apart from violent ones like shooting, boxing and football, from which they should be excluded.[32]

The debate on 'Woman as an Athlete' conducted in the *Nineteenth Century* in 1899 by two very different women, Arabella Kenealy the anti-feminist eugenist and physician and Laura Ormiston Chant a writer and feminist, was even more fascinating.

As indicated in Chapter 7, Kenealy believed that while exercise was essential to the building of healthy bodies, minds and emotions, it destroyed the qualities of true womanhood and inclined women to forsake their natural roles when overdone. Athletic women sometimes were good-looking and exuded poise and strength, she conceded, but their voices were usually loud and assertive and their body movements unwomanly. They also often suffered from damaged health as a result of a depletion of their limited store of energy, which jeopardised their ability to achieve woman's noblest goal — to be the mother of men — and threatened to neuter the race.[33]

In a coldly logical fashion, Laura Ormiston Chant demolished Kenealy's arguments, and presented female athleticism as increasing rather than squandering sportswomen's femaleness and the potential of the race. She dismissed the 'subtle elusiveness' that Kenealy identified as tragically threatened by female athleticism and the likelihood that female athletes would neglect their familial duties, on the grounds that no woman played games or cycled all the time or took her duties so casually that she could be easily distracted. She observed that muscular vigour and the moral qualities which usually accompanied it were more valuable commodities in times of crisis than 'elusiveness', and that sportswomen anticipated the creation of a nobler and happier home life and the production of healthier, happier children. She urged modern women to ignore the denunciations hurled their way and to continue to cycle, row, climb mountains and play hockey, full of confidence that in strengthening their bodies they were becoming more useful and no less womanly human beings. Finally, Chant asked, who had the right to decide that it was not woman's province to be muscular?[34]

The debate concluded with Kenealy dismissing Chant as a 'clamouring reformer' who exemplified the 'disorderly muscularity' against which her original article was directed, and dismissing her arguments as worthless because they were not supported by medical training. Still not content, she presented a complicated explanation of how over-indulgence in sport gave the male qualities in women an artificial stimulus that could make them dominant, and she warned that repose was the most valuable factor in physical development, that defective children were likely the result of their mother's excessive athleticism, that cancer was frequent in women with robust physiques and that athletic women lacked the magnetic charm that epitomised health and physical perfection. Contrary to Chant's claim that woman's highest goal should be to do things that men did, Kenealy argued that her true value lay in her capacity for doing things men could not and in cherishing her womanliness. If woman ignored this, Kenealy concluded, she would become superfluous and subject to regressive deterioration. She should remember at all times that such rights as her sex possessed had been given to her through the chivalry and generosity of men.[35]

A journal of a different sort from the *Fortnightly* and *Nineteenth Century* was *Punch*, whose pages illuminate the debate on women's rights and women's sport in an inimitable way. Although prepared to give credit to women where credit was due, on the whole Mr Punch shared the conventional view of the female role in society and usually portrayed women's rightists as aggressive and unattractive. For years many aspects of the campaign for the emancipation of women provided him with an abundant source of mirth, none more so than women's sport.

An astute observer of the contradictions in Victorian society between established norms and the transition that was occurring to new ones, Mr Punch was quick to perceive women's sport as part of a larger process of emancipation and social change that threatened the sexual *status quo*. From his early days he supported women taking healthy, outdoor exercise, and he never objected to sporting women in the way he did to learned ones. When intrepid horsewomen were presented side by side with ladies who were tightly laced and took no exercise, the latter were lampooned more vigorously. Nevertheless, during the 1850s and 1860s he revelled in impugning the motives and competence of lady riders, archers and croquet players and laughing at their ridiculous fashions and hair-styles in poems and cartoons that depicted them as incompetent and ignorant. In the 1870s he directed his athletic wisdom at lady bathers and ice- and roller-skaters; but it was the advent of lawn tennis that opened up to him a whole new world.

Punch's first cartoon featuring a female tennis player, in September 1874, compared the scoring system, in which love meant 'nothing', with women's main interest in life. For years thereafter he poked fun at inappropriately clad, tennis-playing ladies who were much more interested in flirting with the opposite sex than in improving their game, and who used their womanly wiles to try to persuade male umpires to make calls favourable to their side.[36]

Scarcely a sport to which women turned their hands escaped Mr Punch's eagle eyes. He laughed at the ignorance of lady spectators at cricket matches. He qualified his support for girls' gymnastics by presenting it as a forerunner to their taking boxing and fencing lessons in order to threaten husbands who ill-used them. He satirised lady golfers, lady cricketers, lady hockey players, lady mountaineers, ladies on horse-back and of course lady cyclists. The latter in particular offered him an inexhaustible supply of opportunities to laugh at 'sighcling creatures' and to ridicule the New Woman and her fastness, fads, fashions and fickleness.[37]

Punch eventually presented women playing croquet, tennis, golf, hockey, cricket, rowing, punting, canoeing, ice- and roller-skating, hunting, shooting, angling, riding, cycling, fencing, hiking, mountain climbing and swimming. He thus testified to the evolution of women's sport to a place of apparent importance in the female social world, at the same time as he made clear his suspicions of sportswomen, and their potential for subverting the female role, by depicting those who excelled and those who wore rational dress as assertive, unattractive, mannish and single. By implying that women were too emotional, illogical and incompetent to master complicated rules and develop genuine skills, by indicating that when their paths crossed with men's they spoiled the latter's sporting fun and by repeatedly portraying sportswomen as masculine and their motives as frivolous, *Punch* perpetuated the contradictory views that women's sport was not really serious, and yet that it masculinised women and so threatened the dominance of men, and hence the social order.

The world of male sporting journalism also bears exploring, for late in the century it too began to pay some attention to women. One of its roots was the *Sporting Magazine* (1794), a journal devoted largely to field sports for gentlemen. From the outset it occasionally included articles on women, but to amuse not inform. It tended to feature subjects like 'female pugilism' and 'amazonian cricket matches', and so confirmed the view that women in sports were aberrations of the masculine norm. It also began a trend of long standing — reporting women's activities anecdotally and as oddities in a spirit of disapproval or amused tolerance.

Notable among later sporting periodicals were *Baily's Monthly Magazine of Sports and Pastimes* (1860), the *Badminton Magazine of Sports and Pastimes* (1895) and *C.B. Fry's Magazine of Sports and Outdoor Life* (1904), which demonstrate clearly the reaction of sportsmen to the new breed of sporting women.

Baily's viewed sport as the ideal diversion for men from the workaday world. On the whole it virtually ignored women until the 1890s, apart from the occasional broadside against the unsuitability of sportswomen's costumes and against the 'amazons' who took up sport other than quietly and unostentatiously.[38] Between 1893 and 1914, its attention diverted slightly, *Baily's* published 25 articles on women's sport, on rare occasions by female authors such as Frances Slaughter. Although little more than a drop in the bucket, in comparison with the hundreds of features on and by men, their tone is important.

Male contributors by the 1890s generally accepted that ladies on horse-back and in the hunting field were there to stay, some even advocating cross-saddle riding. They welcomed lady cyclists and anglers; and a few hailed 'the adoption of sport in almost every phase' as one of the 'great features' of the movement for the emancipation of women.[39] But most believed that men and women had separate sporting spheres; and in a condescending tone they implied that it was men's right to determine the physical capabilities of women, and that in 'allowing' women to disport themselves men were the very souls of generosity. Besides, as some asserted, women's sport was a welcome diversion from the feminist movement, that had 'done more for the gentler sex than . . . all the women reformers put together'.[40]

Baily's last word on women's sport before the outbreak of war was issued by Dr T. Claye Shaw, a lecturer in psychological medicine at St Bartholomew's Hospital, who commented that it was perfectly natural for women of the leisured classes to devote considerable time to sports and games, and that their admission to the world of sport had improved their health and promoted companionship and a better understanding between the sexes. He called the myth of female physical incapacity a bluff by the male sex to keep sport exclusively to itself; he identified men and women as much more similar than previously thought; and he insisted that women were not unsexed by joining men in some of their pursuits. But his use of the phrase 'some of their pursuits' was the real give-away, implying a male possessiveness that allowed women only limited participation.

Whatever women's courage, Shaw said, they lacked the strength and endurance to participate in sport really effectively. If they insisted on 'having-a-go' at such 'dangerous' activities as cricket and rowing, they would have to be satisfied with half-hearted competitions among members of their own sex that would never be taken seriously; and like many men who feared a successful challenge to their sporting monopoly, Shaw couched his qualifications in such a way as to make them appear to be for women's own good, warning them not to exchange the peace of home life for the rebellious spirit of competition. Finally, in a swipe at the militant suffragettes who attacked the male sporting establishment, he reminded women that they were 'much indebted to sport for the opportunities it has afforded of exercising what they are capable of', and that out of gratitude they ought to quietly 'play the game' instead of wreaking vengeance on golf-greens and grandstands.[41]

The reactions to women's sport of the *Badminton Magazine* and *C.B. Fry's Magazine* were similar if somewhat more liberal. The *Badminton Magazine* included articles on women's sport from its foundation, some by female writers, and by 1914 it had a special ladies' section. It asserted that 'the athletic woman . . . may be occasionally marred by one or two minor peculiarities, but even so, she is an infinitely more beautiful spectacle than the lackadaisical hypochondriacal woman of the last generation'.[42] It declared that women did not always go to pieces in crises, and that most sportswomen were feminine to their fingertips. Finally, it praised women for having accomplished so much in only a single sporting generation rather than being humbled by their inability to equal the standards of men in sports that demanded strength.

On the other hand, underlying the *Badminton Magazine*'s support of women's participation in sport was a bedrock of conventionality. In 1900, for example, a writer asserted that:

For women . . . beauty of face and form is one of the chief essentials . . . unlimited indulgence in violent outdoor sports, cricket, bicycling, beagling, otter-hunting, paper-chasing, and — most odious of all games for a woman — hockey, cannot but have an unwomanly effect on a young girl's mind, no less than her appearance . . . Let young girls ride, skate, dance and play lawn tennis and other games in moderation, but let them leave field sports and rough out-door pastimes to those for whom they are naturally intended — men.[43]

C.B. Fry's Magazine was the enterprise of England's most famous male athlete, a man who at one time or another captained the England Cricket XI, boxed, was a football international and world record holder in the long jump. Its aim was to see that every man, woman and child got the opportunity to participate in sport. Although men received the lion's share of *Fry's* attention, like the *Badminton Magazine*, in articles mainly by women writers, it also featured women playing tennis, badminton, golf, cricket, croquet, squash rackets, hockey, bicycle polo, swimming, rowing, ice-skating, cycling, skiing, motoring and even flying. Also like the *Badminton*, however, *Fry's* had a limited perspective. It therefore advised women that smart attire signified good taste and was essential to the reputation of a game; that the best sports required grace and non-violence and did not overtax their strength; and that sports like croquet and lawn tennis, in which they could hold their own against men, were not really manly or prestigious.

In a classic example of male sporting chauvinism, an 'Oxford Blue' observed that the women's sporting craze was but one feature of the life of the New Woman whose advances in sport paralleled advances in other areas, 'particularly in the matter of the assertion of women's rights and a certain kind of independence'.[44] The athletic girl was straying too far from the traditional female role and seeking too much public attention, he argued. Normal women's physical and temperamental deficiencies prevented them from playing any sport as well as men, no matter how much expertise improved, and the gap was widest in activities requiring the most skill.

Man has been, is, and will be easily first in athletic sports and games because in the first place he has a natural instinct for them, which is the primitive combative instinct of the warrior and the hunter watered down to suit modern

civilization; in the second place, he has the physical formation which is in every respect perfectly adapted for such
pursuits, and was meant by nature to be so; and in the third
place, he has the right temperamental qualities. He is
naturally a sportsman, has the right even balance of nerves
and moods, and the capability to put the severest strain upon
himself. He knows how to try. Women fail in all three
particulars. They may get over their deficiencies in the first
respect, and again, in exceptional cases and in the process
of time, in the third; but how about the second?[45]

The late-nineteenth century also saw the publication of
monographs, anthologies and multi-volume encyclopaedias on
sport, which were directed primarily towards men but included
chapters on women's activities by male and female writers.[46] The
three most prominent encyclopaedias were the *Isthmian Library of
Sports and Pastimes*, the *Encyclopaedia of Sport* and the *Badminton
Library of Sports and Pastimes*.[47]

The *Isthmian Library*, edited by B. Fletcher Robinson and Max
Pemberton, appeared between 1896 and 1902 in twelve volumes
covering all the major sports. The second volume, on cycling, was
co-edited by a woman, Mrs Harcourt Williamson, and included
a chapter by her on society ladies' cycling, dress, clubs and touring. The third volume, on golf, contained a chapter on ladies' golf
by Amy Pascoe dealing with the LGU, notable players and the
past and future of the lady's game. The sixth volume, on ice
sports, contained two chapters by a Mrs Alec Tweedie on cross-
country skiing and ice-boat sailing, while the ninth gave considerable attention to women's hockey, and the tenth, on croquet,
featured numerous women in photographs. These concessions to
the distaff side were a small part of the total contents, accurately
reflecting the minor place of women's sport in society, but the fact
they existed at all was significant.

The proportion of male to female subjects in the *Encyclopaedia
of Sport* was similar to that in the *Isthmian Library*. The first two-
volume edition was published in 1896 under the primary editorship of the Earl of Suffolk and Berkshire. It covered sport all over
the world,[48] and contained articles on, for example, women's
cycling by the Countess of Malmesbury, women's golf by Louis
Mackern and women's lawn tennis by Lottie Dod.[49]

When the *Encyclopaedia* was expanded to four volumes in 1911,
its coverage of women included curling, cycling, croquet, hockey,

tennis, climbing mountains, riding, rowing, skating and swimming. Adverse comment was reserved only for astride riding and inappropriate dress, but the new edition reflected no significant extension of the coverage of women's activities and included articles by male authors only and mainly male illustrations.

The most influential and extensive sporting encyclopaedia was the unique *Badminton Library of Sports and Pastimes*, edited by Alfred E.T. Watson and the Duke of Beaufort, one of the most distinguished sportsmen in the land, and exquisitely published by Longmans in 29 volumes between 1885 and 1902. The *Badminton* series was intended to supply the want of a succession of volumes which treated virtually all the sports and pastimes indulged in by English men and women. It covered everything from fishing and motor driving to dancing and the poetry of sport. Almost the only sports excluded were lacrosse, hockey and other ball games because they were not thought to appeal to a sufficiently large class. Each volume was edited or authored by an authority on the subject, the only female being a Mrs Lilly Grove who was responsible for Volume 21 on *Dancing*. Women did, however, write a few individual chapters.

Since the volumes were aimed primarily at inexperienced men seeking guidance in the practice of various activities, their male orientation was overwhelming. The legitimacy of women's participation in some sports, however, was acknowledged in articles on fishing, hunting, riding, cycling, lawn tennis, golf, mountain climbing, ice-skating, swimming, archery, yachting, billiards, motoring and dancing.

In the first edition of the volume on golf there was no separate chapter on women's golf, an omission the editor later conceded was an oversight;[50] but this was little wonder considering Lord Wellwood's expression of distinct reservations about the suitability of golf for women and women for golf, as a result of his perception of the women's game solely in relation to that of men and to the pleasure or pain it gave the 'superior' sex.[51] When the efficacy of ladies' lawn tennis was discussed by several authors, the tone was at best condescending.[52] They conceded, however, that

> . . . those ladies who are not prevented from playing in tournaments by the publicity and excitement, do give an immense amount of pleasure to the spectators, and the largest crowd is nearly always to be found round the court where ladies are engaged.[53]

In a chapter devoted exclusively to 'Ladies Lawn Tennis' the ubiquitous Lottie Dod observed enthusiastically that no championship meeting was complete without ladies' events and that these attracted almost as much interest as men's. She urged women to adopt practical clothing and to play the volleying game as hard as they possibly could; and so as not to spoil mixed doubles for men, to concentrate on improving their play.[54]

Consideration of the effects of women's participation on men was also evident in the volume on fishing, in which ladies were encouraged to take up the sport, not because of its benefits to women, but because the 'graceful companionship' of lady fishers by lake or stream would double their husbands' pleasure of success.[55] And in other volumes women riders were described as vain, and women archers as slow learners, even though the sport was 'a gentle and elegant amusement . . . lacking in hurried movements, violent exertion, and ungraceful attitudes', which provided 'a good opportunity to show off their dress'.[56]

The general impression left by the *Badminton Library* and the other encyclopaedias was that sport was innately masculine, and that women's participation was acceptable only as long as charm, grace, decorum, moderation and attractive dress prevailed, and as long as it did not interfere with the 'gentlemen's province'.

Finally, the significance of sport in general and women's sport in particular was shown by the increasing frequency with which it was covered by the daily press. In *The Times* between 1862 and 1892 women's sports were mentioned perhaps once or twice a year, and then only when some exceptional event occurred, such as a rowing or walking race involving women of the lower ranks, the Empress of Austria hunting in England or a lady cricketers' match. From the early 1890s, however, while it would be an exaggeration to claim that women's sport became 'big news' in *The Times*, reports on women's tennis, golf, cycling, hockey, fencing, hunting, fishing and motoring multiplied by such an extent that it is difficult to keep track of them.

The growing interest of *The Times* in sportswomen characterised other major dailies. The *Daily Telegraph*, for example, gave extensive and fascinating coverage to 'The Athletic Girl' through a series of letters to the editor that appeared daily between 29 July and 23 August 1913, from medical doctors, military officers, clergymen, hard-up bachelors, public school boys, school examiners, lovers of effeminate women, school-mistresses, schoolgirls, athletic girls, women workers, girls' club leaders, open-air enthusiasts, athletic and unathletic mothers, gymnasts and games mistresses. They expressed every possible shade of opinion, and focused particularly on the athletic girl's attractiveness to men and usefulness to society; and they epitomised the debate on women's rights in general.

The controversy was sparked by a prize day address at Princess Helena College by a Colonel Sir Thomas Holdich in which he described the athletic girl as untidy, crude and bad-mannered, and by a letter to the *Daily Telegraph*'s editor from 'A Woman' who agreed that athletic girls represented excess and exaggeration, were the antithesis of grace and elegance, were unqualified to preside over a household and as a result had dim marital prospects.

Correspondents who took the negative side, like people opposed to other women's causes, believed that the world was created for men, and women for reproduction and men's enjoyment. Women had neither the time nor strength nor qualifications for sport. Furthermore, they argued, vigorous exercise and competitive sport strained the female constitution by sapping vital energy needed elsewhere. It produced invalidism, appendicitis, the inability to breast feed and the deterioration of the race; and it jeopardised feminine grace, refinement and delicate complexions and turned women into mannish, over-muscled, slovenly and rude hoydens.

Correspondents on the affirmative side, on the other hand, claimed that sport contributed to the healthy development of mind and body, prevented or cured neuroses by relieving boredom, and made women strong, supple, graceful and agile. Rather than detracting from femininity and domestic duties, it produced fitter wives and mothers by strengthening their characters, heightening their self-confidence and teaching them self-respect, self-control, unselfishness and endurance. In no way, they argued, was a desire to develop and control one's body an exclusively masculine trait.

People in similar professions revealed strikingly dissimilar opinions. One medical doctor might argue that the slightest over-exertion could produce a host of ailments in growing girls and that the fairer sex was fitted for domestic tasks rather than hard physical exercise, while another doctor might insist that the modern games-loving girl was a far finer specimen than her mother or grandmother and much more likely to produce fit children. Most clergy and military men preferred old-fashioned, domestically-oriented ladies who knew their place, to the 'half male' sportswomen who masqueraded as females; others considered fresh air and exercise as good for women as for men. Schoolmistresses disputed whether athletic girls exuded 'graceless muscularity' and endangered their reproductive capacity and academic performance, or whether they were the nicest, brightest and best-rounded of students. Mothers disagreed on whether sport and the independence it might engender were good or bad for their daughters. Even athletic and formerly-athletic girls were at odds, most defending sports for improving health and character and as entirely compatible with femininity, but some attributing chronic semi-invalidism to an over-emphasis on games at school.

The majority of correspondents of both sexes preached moderation. As was traditional, they perceived women not as individuals, but in relation to men, and their ideal was the sporting girl with domestic skills who avoided extremes. Since she would be able to share some of her husband's sporting interests, she was much more likely to be a better companion than the sedentary and boring 'fashionable butterfly' type. The majority of English women, they noted, did not pursue sport fanatically, nor did the majority of sportswomen present a masculine, aggressive appearance or carry their interest in sport to extremes, so it was grossly unfair to condemn all athletic girls. Exercise of some sort was as essential for women as men, and there was nothing innately incompatible between womanliness and athleticism. Rather, games' good or harm depended on how they were performed.

Most interesting of all were the opinions of feminists who perceptively identified the chief motives of the male opponents of the athletic girl as selfishness and the fear of threats to their masculinity. Men, they argued, wanted to control women, when it was actually none of their business whether women chose to devote their free time to sport. Why, they asked, was there a double standard in sport? Why was physical development considered the exclusive prerogative of the male sex? Why, when men went to extremes with sports, were complaints muted? Why did no one think that athletics made men awkward and ungainly? Why were men allowed to set standards for women? Why was what was considered legitimate for women evaluated according to how it pleased men rather than women themselves?[57] 'What right', one woman asked,

> . . . has any man to say 'You shall progress no further; you
> must mould yourself to our ideals, for we know what is best
> for you?' Why should men consider that certain games are

graceful and others not, and that only the ones they consider suitable for women should be played?[58]

Feminists went on to damn as an abomination the tendency to treat women like 'glass dolls' with no brains or strength. They insisted that sports, by producing the health and characteristics essential for success in life, helped females to come into their own and to realise that they had no obligation to bow to men. If a few sportswomen went to extremes, they concluded, it was only because they 'were very natural products of the violent reaction in favour of a healthy and athletic life for women which is one of the sides of the great woman movement of this and the preceding centuries'.[59]

There is scarcely a more eloquent statement in the entire corpus of feminist literature than the letter of one K.S. Birnstingl, who passionately damned the 'incurable obtuseness' of some supposedly enlightened men who were incapable of grasping the fact that women were equally entitled to independence and freedom to choose for themselves how to spend their time. Such men, Birnstingl asserted, seemed to think that every woman should be forced into motherhood and a lifetime spent winning male approbation, when in fact they

> . . . should realize that it is possible for women to have an equal distaste for being limited to wife and motherhood as it would be to men to be allowed only the attributes best suited to fatherhood . . . It is none of men's business if women choose to use their free time in athletics. To the liberty-loving, athletic girl I say, 'Go on and prosper, and prove to the world that woman free is the exact equal if not counterpart of man, neither superior nor inferior, but precisely alike in intellect and wishes and ambition.'[60]

The factors determining content and the messages communicated to readers are of prime significance in all the literary cases cited. The reason women's sport became newsworthy was that the numbers of participants increased in a seemingly geometric progression in the late-nineteenth century. There was therefore a ready-made and largely untapped audience for material on women's sport that accorded with tastes already in place. As for the messages communicated, some people, including some women, believed that women were 'inherently incapable of being athletes',[61] and considered the sports phenomenon an aberration that threatened men's and women's proper spheres and thus the social order. Some believed, with feminists, that sport was another of the areas, hitherto monopolised almost exclusively by men, in which women had a legitimate role to play. Literature which damned sportswomen with faint praise, or disparaged them as oddities and objects of humour, confirmed the comfortable prejudices of men about male superiority and female inferiority, and the less comfortable ones of some women about the same thing. Writers who congratulated sportswomen, on the other hand, identified sport as a legitimate feminine interest; but even they usually agreed that this was so only if certain rules were observed.

Female readers, who were mainly leisured members of the upper and middle classes and the products of public schools and colleges, learned from sporting literature what they learned in life: that it was socially acceptable for women to participate in a wide variety of sports and that, because of sport's health-giving properties, women serious about their higher destiny — maternity — had a duty to take exercise. Simultaneously, however, they were reminded that they could play only certain games, and then only in restrictive dress and in a feminine fashion. The use of terms like 'athletic amusements', 'pretty players', 'weaker sex' and 'fair sex', conjured up stereotypical images of femininity and lack of ability and seriousness of purpose that dogged women's sport into the second half of the twentieth century. It also reflected a basic concern for the unthinkable — that women might some day actually equal and even surpass men and so make them appear ridiculous.

Most writers — of both sexes — who defended the right of women to participate in sport rarely considered the broader question of women's emancipation and the place of sport within it. In defending women's 'playing the game' and in pleading for understanding, they cautiously acknowledged a necessity for women to cultivate moderate and aesthetically pleasing images, and to consider the pleasure of men and their duty to men and the race rather than their own 'selfish' interests; and they denied the connection between an enthusiasm for sport and the production of 'modern women'. A minority, however, appreciated that there was an important link between women's taking up 'athletic amusements' and their efforts to emulate and compete with men in the wider world. They spoke of the evolution of the

271

sportswoman as one of the most notable and radical changes of the late-nineteenth century; and they described the age as one of 'athletic emancipation' for women, when active and responsible women, not content to sit at home, sought freedom and disputed man's authority in spheres he deemed peculiarly his own — law, medicine, art, university education and sport.[62]

By 1914 the numbers of different sports pursued by both men and women that were reported in the daily and periodical press and other literary media were legion. Relatively speaking, the coverage given to women's activities as opposed to men's was still extremely limited. But that there was such a thing as a literature of women's sport at all was a sign of at least a degree of acceptance and of the progress that women had made along the road to physical liberation during the previous half-century. Its limitations, of course, revealed the distance yet to go.

Notes

1. *Daily Telegraph* , 11 August 1913.

2. Cynthia L. White, *Women's Magazines 1693–1968* (London, 1970), pp. 17–78.

3. Ibid., pp. 88–90.

4. *Queen* (18 June 1896), p. 1039.

5. Ibid. (3 January 1880), p. 22.

6. *Gentlewoman* (12 July 1890), p. 5, (22 November 1890), p. 714, (6 August 1892), p. 170, (24 September 1892), p. 394, (20 October 1894), p. 504.

Diana supported the *Gentlewoman's* sponsoring an inter-club golf tournament in 1894 and had no qualms about ladies' boating races in public, but she felt ladies' swimming championships should be held in private, on the grounds of taste, and she justified archery as a pastime for gentlewomen because they could achieve excellence without a loss of dignity.

In July 1914, the *Gentlewoman* began publishing a weekly supplement, the *Golfing Gentlewoman*, which featured golf gossip and news about resorts, championships, match results, coming events and the Ladies' Golf Union.

7. *Gentlewoman* (18 July 1914), p. 78.

8. Ibid. (3 September 1910), p. 305.

9. *Ladies' Field* Handbooks, *Croquet Annual* (1901–2), p. 143.

10. *Ladies' Field* (25 February 1899), p. 493, (1 July 1899), p. 127, (9 September 1899), p. 630, (28 March 1903), pp. 93–4, (22 August 1903), p. 446, (9 March 1907), p. 22.

11. Ibid. (20 August 1902), p. 477.

12. *Ladies' Field Supplement* (28 October 1899), p. 14.

13. *Ladies' Field* (12 October 1901), p. 183, (12 July 1902), p. 192, (26 July 1902), p. 269.

14. *Young Woman*, vol. 5 (October 1896–September 1897), pp. 332–4.

15. *Woman at Home*, vol. 7 (October 1897–September 1898), pp. 930–3.

16. *Girls' Own Paper*, vol. 20 (20 May 1899), pp. 534–5. See also vol. 24 (25 October 1902), pp. 61–2; Mary Cadogan and Patricia Craig, *You're a Brick, Angela!* (London, 1976), pp. 73–5.

17. *Girls' Own Paper*, vol. 23 (9 November 1901), pp. 84–5.

18. *Lady Cyclist*, vol. 1, no. 1 (1895), pp. 3–4.

19. *Hockey Field* (8 April 1908), p. 445.

20. White, *Women's Magazines*, pp. 63–7.

21. *Lady's Realm* (December 1896), p. 17. See also review of Beatrice Violet Greville (ed.), *The Gentlewoman's Book of Sports*, in *Saturday Review*, vol. 73 (1892), p. 369–70.

22. See also Theodora Johnson, *The Swedish System of Physical Education* (1897); Theresa D. Stempel, *Physical Exercise for Girls* (1904); F.J. Erskine, *Tricycling for Ladies* (1885), *Bicycling for Ladies* (1896) and *Lady Cycling* (1897); Lillias Campbell Davidson, *Handbook for Lady Cyclists* (1896); Susan, Countess of Malmesbury, *Cycling for Women* (1898); May Hezlet, *Ladies' Golf* (1903); Cecil Leitch, *Golf for Girls* (1911); Dorothea Lambert Chambers, *Lawn Tennis for Ladies* (1910); Mrs Aubrey Le Blond, *The High Alps in Winter* (1883), *True Tales of Mountain Adventure for Non-Climbers Young and Old* (1903), *Adventure on the Roof of the World* (1904) and *Mountaineering in the Land of the Midnight Sun* (1908); Mrs Power O'Donaghue, *Ladies on Horseback* (1881); Alice M. Hayes, *The Horsewoman* (1893); Gertrude M. Douglas, *Rifle Shooting for Ladies* (1910); Mrs Stuart Menzies, *Women in the Hunting Field* (1913); Edith Thompson, *Hockey as a Game for Women* (1904). Women also authored and edited works on women's sport and exercise with men, for example, Alexander Alexander and Mrs Alexander, *British Physical Education for Girls* (1909); H. Graves, G.L. Hillier, and Susan, Countess of Malmesbury, *Cycling* (1898); Louis Mackern and Margaret Boys, (eds), *Our Lady of the Green* (1899).

23. Slaughter, *Sportswoman's Library*, vol. 1, p. xiv.

24. Ibid., pp. 8–9.

25. Cadogan and Craig, *You're a Brick*, pp. 44–5, 57, 76–7.

26. See, for example, L.T. Meade, *A World of Girls: The Story of a School* (London, 1886), *A Sweet Girl Graduate* (London, 1891) and *The Girls of Merton College* (London, 1911).

27. Angela Brazil, *My Own Schooldays* (London, 1925), p. 149; Fletcher, *Women First*, p. 78; Gillian Freeman, *The Schoolgirl Ethic* (London, 1976), p. 17.

28. Angela Brazil, *The Fortunes of Philippa* (London, 1907), p. 206.

29. Angela Brazil, *The Nicest Girl in the School* (London, 1909), pp. 44–6, 186–7.

30. Unite, 'Disillusioned Daughters', *Fortnightly Review*, vol. 77 (1 November 1900), p. 854.

31. F.G. Aflalo, 'The Sportswoman', *Fortnightly Review*, vol. 77 (May 1905), p. 891.

32. Ibid., p. 903.

33. Kenealy, 'Woman as an Athlete', pp. 636–45.

34. L. Ormiston Chant, 'Woman as an Athlete: A Reply to Dr Arabella Kenealy', *Nineteenth Century*, vol. 45 (May 1899), pp. 745–54.

35. Kenealy, 'Woman as an Athlete: a rejoinder', pp. 915–19.

36. *Punch* (12 September 1874), p. 104. See also (7 July 1877), p. 302, (17 August 1878), p. 66, (18 October 1879), p. 124.

37. Ibid. (17 June 1876), p. 241, (16 July 1881), p. 15, (22 September 1883), p. 138, (10 June 1882), p. 270, (8 March 1884), p. 177, (6 March 1886), p. 114, (6 April 1895), p. 49; (18 May 1895), p. 239, (15 June 1895), p. 279, (3 August 1895), p. 59, (7 September 1895), p. 120, (30 May 1896), p. 255. See also Adburgham, *Punch History*, p. 39; Constance Rover, *The Punch Book of Women's Rights* (New York, 1970), pp. 13–15, 67.

38. *Baily's Monthly Magazine of Sports and Pastimes*, vol. 4 (March 1862), pp. 163, 167, vol. 32 (July 1878), pp. 200, 202, vol. 43 (March 1885), pp. 397–8.

39. Ibid., vol. 63 (May 1895), pp. 373–4, vol. 64 (July 1894), pp. 26–9, vol. 75 (March 1901), pp. 179–81.

40. Ibid., vol. 71 (February 1899), pp. 103–4. See also (March 1901), pp. 179–81, vol. 83 (January 1905), p. 27, vol. 85 (March 1906), p. 237, vol. 86 (July 1906), p. 66.

41. Ibid. (June 1913), pp. 409–10. See also pp. 403–10.

42. *Badminton Magazine of Sports and Pastimes*, vol. 14 (January–June 1902), pp. 496–7.

43. Ibid. (1900), quoted in Brian Dobbs, *Edwardians at Play* (London, 1973), p. 177.

44. *C.B. Fry's Magazine*, vol. 16 (November 1911), pp. 209–15.

45. Ibid., pp. 214–15.

46. For example, Amy Bennet Pascoe, 'Lady's Golf' in Garden Smith *et al.*, *The World of Golf* (1898); Amy Bennet Pascoe, 'Ladies' in Horace G. Hutchinson, *The Book of Golf and Golfers* (1899); Mary E.L. Hezlet, 'The Expenses of Golf' in Henry Seton-Karr *et al.*, *Golf* (1907); Mrs Ross [May Hezlet], 'From the Ladies' Points of View' in H.G. Hutchinson (ed.), *The New Book of Golf* (1912); Miss Toupie Lowther, 'Ladies' Play' in R.F. and H.L. Docherty, *Lawn Tennis* (1903); Ethel M. Robson, 'Women's Hockey' in J. Nicholson Smith and Philip A. Robson (eds), *Hockey, Historical and Practical* (1899). Similarly, in F.G. Aflalo's *The Sports of the World* (2 vols , 1902–3) women were included in chapters on fencing, archery, tennis, croquet, riding and roller- and ice-skating, while Muriel Lucas wrote the chapter on 'Badminton', Mrs Aubrey Le Blond, on 'Mountaineering from a Woman's Point of View', Lottie Dod, on 'Ladies' Lawn Tennis' and Ethel Robson co-authored 'Hockey for Men and Women'. See also H.E. Vandervell and T.M. Maxwell, *A System of Figure Skating* (1869); Alexander Alexander, *Healthful Exercises for Ladies* (1885); Oscar Jennings, *Cycling and Health* (1890); Howard H. Spicer (ed.), *Sports for Girls (1900); S.M. Massey, Badminton* (1911); Claude Benson, *British Mountaineering* (1914).

47. The encyclopaedia of sport has only recently been recognised as a literary landmark of considerable academic significance. Gerald Redmond, 'Sport History in Academe: Reflections on a Half-Century of

Peculiar Progress', *British Journal of Sports History*, vol. 1, no. 1 (1984), p. 25.

48. The alphabetical listing in Volume 1 went from aardvark to leopards and panthers.

49. Countess of Malmesbury, 'Bicycling for Women' in the Earl of Suffolk and Berkshire, Hedley Peek and F.G. Aflalo (eds), *Encyclopaedia of Sport* (2 vols , London, 1897–8), vol. 1, p. 292; Louis Mackern, 'Ladies Golf', vol. 1, pp. 470–1; Lottie Dod, 'Lawn Tennis for Ladies', vol. 1, p. 619.

50. Pointon, 'Growth of Women's Sport', p. 82.

51. Beaufort and Watson (eds), *Badminton Library*, vol. 11: *Golf*, by Hutchinson, pp. 51–2.

52. Ibid., vol. 12: *Tennis; Lawn Tennis; Rackets; Fives* (1890), by J.M. Heathcote, C.G. Heathcote, E.O.P. Bouverie and A.C. Ainger, p. 81.

53. Ibid., p. 292.

54. Ibid., pp. 343–4.

55. Ibid., vol. 1a: *Fishing* (1885), by H. Cholmondeley-Pennell, p. 112.

56. Ibid., vol. 20: *Archery* (1894), by C.J. Longman and H. Walrond, pp. 423–8.

57. *Daily Telegraph*, 18 and 25 August 1913.

58. Ibid., 6 August 1913.

59. Ibid., 9 August 1913.

60. Ibid., 11 August 1913.

61. *Physical Culture*, vol. 2, no. 2 (1899), p. 102.

62. *Baily's Monthly Magazine of Sports and Pastimes*, vol. 71 (February 1899), p. 100, vol. 75 (March 1901), pp. 178–82, vol. 99 (June 1913), p. 405; *Daily Telegraph*, 6, 9, 11, 16, 18 August 1913; *C.B. Fry's Magazine*, vol. 16 (March 1912), pp. 670–2; *Gentlewoman* (28 March 1891), p. 427, (10 December 1892), p. 786, (3 September 1910), p. 305; *Golfing Annual*, vol. 7 (1893–4), pp. 37–8; *Ladies' Field* (27 April 1907), p. 328, (9 October 1909), pp. 188–9.

10

Conclusion

The interaction between feminism and the growth of women's sport is important to the conclusion of this study, for sport was an important site of feminist intervention, albeit indirectly.

The leaders of the Victorian women's movement were an ambitious and intellectually thwarted minority of middle-class women, tormented by enforced idleness and dissatisfied with the sentimentality that was supposed to give meaning to their lives. Concern about the fate of thousands of 'redundant' women and anger over women's general lack of rights and the degrading assumptions about the biological and divine origins of their intellectual and physical inferiority led them to challenge a social system in which the important rules were made by men, and to envisage a future in which women would be respected as persons in their own right. They were not radicals, for they sought to reform and integrate rather than overthrow the established order. But freedom was their cry, and to achieve it they questioned traditional concepts concerning women's nature and proper sphere.

By attacking the sacred ideal of femininity and women's lack of opportunities for self-development outside the home, the women's movement fostered changes in gender divisions and sexual hierarchies in the direction of greater equality, and it awakened in women a consciousness of their rights as human beings. This in turn produced modifications in the conception of women's position in society and a dynamic of changing options that allowed them more active roles in a variety of areas. While feminists did not organise to fight directly for women's sporting rights, the acquisition of such rights was an important consequence of their activities in other areas. In turn, sporting activities made a substantial contribution to emancipating females from physical and psychological bondage and to altering the image of ideal womanhood.

Although the circumstances of the period between 1870 and 1914, and the nature, aims and achievements of its women's movement, differed markedly from those of the modern era, the changing patterns of Victorian women's participation in sport can be more clearly understood if they are placed against the backdrop of current feminism, which has also seen women making progress away from the narrow bonds of domestic life in sport and other spheres. Then as now the separation of the sexes in sport was based on the premise of women's physical and emotional inferiority. Then as now, although leading feminists did not initially focus attention on sport, feminism acted as a catalyst that stirred interest in physical liberation and stimulated sporting changes. Then as now sport was a logical arena to demonstrate the falseness of assumptions about women, and women's participation was a response to oppression and expanded opportunities for activity. Then as now, in counteracting the stereotype of female frailty and expanding the meaning of being female to include qualities and skills previously thought to be exclusively male, sportswomen reflected feminist hopes of diminishing the significance of gender-based definitions of appropriate behaviour, providing women with new opportunities to develop all their powers and enabling them to gain control of their own lives and bodies. Then as now, too, the growth of feminism, and the accompanying changes in perceptions of women and their roles, led to the realisation that women's exclusion from sport was culturally determined. Victorian sportswomen, like those at present, were therefore important contributors to and products of a larger movement to achieve female autonomy and self-respect.

It is interesting and perversely logical that the most militant early twentieth-century feminists focused on sport in a negative context.

Because sport was such a pronounced symbol of masculine exclusivity, suffragettes turned some of their frustration and violence against the male sporting establishment. Throughout 1913 they damaged turf and burned buildings at race courses, bowling greens, tennis, croquet and golf clubs and cricket and football grounds, thereby infuriating sportsmen and prompting equations of suffragette activity with the 'explosive fury of epileptics'.[1] Shortly before midnight on 26 February 1913, for example, the groundsman at Wimbledon apprehended on the centre court a woman carrying incendiary materials and a piece of paper containing the words, 'No peace till women have the vote'. In the aftermath of her 'outrage', she was convicted of intending to commit a felony and sentenced to two months imprisonment; and the council of the AELTC decided to enclose as much of the ground as practical with barbed wire, to hire extra night-watchmen and to search the bags and parcels of spectators at the annual championships.[2] Later the same year the suffrage movement obtained a much more spectacular martyr, when on 4 June Emily Wilding Davison threw herself under the hooves of the king's horse during the Derby and was killed.

As for the interest in the general issue of women's rights on the part of women involved in sport, while some sporting pioneers certainly had a feminist sense and an awareness that their activities were influenced and promoted by a rebellion against traditional stereotypes and restrictions, only a small minority were active supporters of the women's movement. Physical educators were much keener than 'mere' games-players, probably because they were career women and had a more pronounced sense of women's rights and wrongs than did sportswomen whose activities were largely recreational. The heads of the physical training colleges certainly did not completely reject traditional assumptions about gender-roles, but they strongly supported the extension of women's educational, employment and political rights; and the Gymnastic Teachers' Suffrage Society, which sought the franchise for women on the same terms as men and sent contingents to march in suffrage processions in London, was the only organisation of physical educators and sportswomen to participate directly in 'the cause'. Other prominent women's sports organisations, such as the AEWHA and the LGU, stayed carefully out of the 'votes for women' controversy; and, while 'many a woman [rode] to suffrage on a bicycle',[3] few sportswomen were moved by their athletic success to conclude that women were fit for the privilege of parliamentary representation. Most appear to have evinced little interest in the franchise issue and to have been indifferent to whether they could vote or not.

Modern research has shown, contrary to expectations, that female athletes often hold more conventional views on women's roles than non-athletes, which suggests that the non-traditional role of women in sport does not necessarily carry over into other gender issues. Since participation in sport has been seriously inconsistent with society's view of femininity, and since sportswomen have been judged more on aesthetic and social considerations than performance, some apparently reconcile conflicting desires to be both feminine and active in sport by espousing orthodox attitudes to women's place in society at large.[4] The parallels with the late-Victorian period are striking. Even at the Oxbridge women's colleges, where support for the vote was strong, and sport in the form of occasional mixed doubles tennis tournaments was used to raise money for 'the cause', there was no evident correlation between sports participation and pro-suffrage sympathies. The majority of women who took up sport did so because sport was enjoyable, fashionable or companionable, not because they rejected patriarchal notions of female frailty and inferiority or because they viewed sports participation as a means of emancipating themselves and their sex from restricting social norms.

'What made the whole issue notable was the attention given to sportswomen by anti-feminists, who contrived to see a sharp contradiction between femininity and sports participation.'[5] Some were female themselves, like Mrs Lynn Linton to whom the New Woman in all her manifestations was anathema, Dr Arabella Kenealy who equated excessive female athleticism with race suicide, and ordinary women who disapproved of 'ladies' spending their Saturdays at hockey matches instead of looking after their homes.[6] More were men.

'It is difficult to understand the ordeal which each advancement and expansion into the sporting world cost and meant to the women who dared to venture.'[7] In nearly every sport, men were 'apt to resent the encroachments of the opposite sex',[8] for they saw women's sport as a disruptive force and one which, by apparently challenging men physically, trespassed on an even more intrinsically masculine field than when they challenged them academically; and they worried that an extension to women of 'men's' sporting rights would lead to fundamental changes in the definitions of masculine and feminine and in the whole social order which men had controlled hitherto. Women in sport represented females in highly non-traditional roles, and they inspired warnings that if allowed to proceed unhindered they might apply elsewhere the toughness, self-reliance and competitiveness acquired on the playing field. Just as it was predicted that if women received the right to vote they would soon want to be judges and members of parliament, it was predicted that if women were allowed to play cricket and hockey they would take up boxing and football. These considerations explain why a good many men believed that the outcome of golf and tennis matches between men and women had a direct bearing on the suffrage question and the superiority of the male sex, and why, in anticipation 'before many years pass . . . [of] daring ladies knocking at the gate of our amateur championship', they sympathised with the Asquith government over its suffragette difficulties.[9]

'Myths reflect and sacralise the dominant tendencies of a culture, thereby sustaining social institutions and life-styles;'[10] and this was demonstrated by the fact that, to preserve the male monopoly on sporting power and privilege, to maintain sport as a socialising agency that prepared men for leadership in the public domain and to safeguard the hierarchical ranking of gender roles,[11] conservative Victorians developed a series of myths centred on two main themes: women were physically and emotionally unfit for sport and sport was unsexing. Moral judgements supporting traditional ideas about propriety and innate female weakness were presented as medical, historical and aesthetic evidence. Women were deemed to be physically inferior and were defined by their sexual function in a way that men never were; and because factors which affected 'the purpose of womanhood' were perceived as positive and negative, conservatives argued at one and the same time that it was women's duty to their future children to take regular exercise in order to make themselves healthier, and that it was their duty, for similar reasons, to restrict their participation in vigorous and competitive outdoor sports that required physical strength and endurance beyond women's normal capacities.

Victorian sportswomen were warned, therefore, that an overly zealous pursuit of sport would endanger their reproductive capacity, that it would jeopardise their 'mystical feminine essence', that it would masculinise them and hence could prejudice their chances of attracting a mate. They were reminded that their irrationality, immaturity and inability to concentrate on or commit themselves to serious things were psychological deficiencies which militated against success in sport and against their ability to join, run and enjoy sports clubs or understand complicated rules. In addition, although patience was considered a peculiarly womanly quality, they were advised that they were too impatient to persevere and learn to play a sport well. Limitations on women's role in sport were thus rationalised by perceptions of their responsibilities to others and of femininity defined both physically and psychologically; and the evaluation of every sport and physical activity women participated in according to how it was perceived to impair or enhance sanctioned feminine norms effectively affirmed the worth of traditional gender-role values. Sport was definitely not to be allowed to become a major contributor to female independence and self-development.

Other devices were used by men to relieve the stress and uncertainty engendered by threats from female sport and to keep sport to themselves. One was humour, which camouflaged fears that skilled sportswomen might actually put men to shame and so threaten male dominance of sport and guardianship of its basic integrity. The female enterprise was frequently damned with faint praise or trivialised and disparaged as a mere caricature of the real masculine version, and its practitioners were treated as objects of fun or denigrated as masculine-looking oddities who were unattractive to men — as if this were the ultimate stigma.[12] All this had the desired effect of glorifying men's sport and sportsmen, and acting as a powerful disincentive to women's participation.

Another tactic was to encourage women to experience the pleasures of competition vicariously in their traditional role as spectators who would applaud male competitors, award prizes and elevate the tone of events. Since spectating offered women welcome new social outlets and identification with a large group, they responded positively and became an obvious if always minority presence at race meetings and tennis, golf and cricket matches. Spectating in fact proved an important step for women in the transition from physical recreation to real sports participation, for by providing opportunities to be present during competition it legitimised their connection to sport, and by familiarising them with sport it perhaps eased their discomfort when the chance came to take an active part. On the other hand, the idea that spectating was women's proper role re-emphasised their 'natural passivity' and justified the separation of the sexes in sport that was manifested elsewhere by restrictions on what they were permitted to wear, to watch and to play, and on their membership in sports clubs that either excluded them completely or relegated them to an auxiliary role whose first duty was to cater to men.[13]

It was also to women's disadvantage that their sporting achievements were inevitably compared to men's.

From 1870 to 1914 — and long after — the sporting standards of men provided the absolute criteria against which women's performances were judged, with the result that women's activities were rarely evaluated as an autonomous and significant type of experience through which women could explore their physical potential without threat to their female identity or exposure to irrelevant comparisons with male performances. The ultimate irony was, of course, that while women were not expected to compete against men, their efforts were considered inferior for the very reason that they did not, or because on the rare occasions when women did compete with men they almost always lost. As long as male performances were taken as absolute measures, the tendency among many of the most skilful women was to try to narrow the gap, which admitted the stigma of femininity and the legitimacy of male norms; and the continued existence of any gap at all seemed to prove the inferiority of female activities.[14]

These remained marginalised and separated from the sporting mainstream. They continued to be perceived by the public at large as more like play than serious athletic activity — which it must be acknowledged some of them certainly were — and their low status retarded women's sports' development. While through sport men achieved identity, esteem and position, the opposite held true of women. The view endured that masculine and feminine were opposites, and that the latter was not conducive to power or status, which meant that despite advances in many areas the main avenues of authority and prestige remained closed to women, and that in turn women's achievements — sporting and otherwise — continued to be undervalued. The philosophy that real sport was essentially masculine endured.[15]

Still another problem was that the sports encouraged for females in the educational realm were not readily pursued into adult life. The acceptance of physical activity for school and college students was a major factor in the development of team games such as hockey and lacrosse; but young women often found that their educations had trained them in games they could neither continue nor identify with when grown. The acceptance of team games-playing by adult women outside educational settings was achieved only with difficulty, for it represented an unladylike accomplishment that was supposed to be abandoned after school and a potential strain on delicate organs on the eve of their going into action. It also presented a threat to male dominance of the important world of team sports. The birth of the AEWHA, of course, indicated that strictures were often ignored by women who were determined to continue to 'play the game'; but most, even of these women, conformed to convention when they got married.

With only the rarest of exceptions, married women — and those engaged to be so — gave up hockey as incompatible with domestic responsibilities and a mature, womanly image.[16]

In this connection in the modern anthropological context, Edwin Ardener and Judith Okely employ the useful concept of muted female groups being allowed to express themselves only in ways permitted by the dominant male culture,[17] which in sport meant limiting women's participation to activities that were not considered overtly male and defeminising, and so could be encouraged without signifying dangerous social change.

The case of individual sports such as tennis and golf was somewhat different. Because they were less identifiably masculine than team games, because the female way of playing posed little threat to men or to 'delicate' female physiques, and because they had an attractive social component involving class segregation and periodic gender integration, they seemed at least partially fitted to the cultural and aesthetic image of womanhood; and thus the participation of women — both single and married — was generally condoned.

The women who participated in sport were mainly from middle- and upper-middle-class families. Many had been sent to schools and colleges where games were emphasised and afterwards enjoyed the leisure time and financial means that continued play demanded. But they had been raised according to social rules and gender definitions that largely originated with men, and to believe that they must please men and consider the effect of just about everything they did on men and their marital chances. So even those with 'advanced' educations rarely thought they had any choice but to adapt to prevailing norms and try to reconcile them with their own needs and purposes, in other words, to reinterpret and redefine rather than reject Victorian myths about womanhood; or, as Jane Frances Dove and Jennifer Hargreaves so succinctly put it, 'to play like gentlemen while behaving like ladies',[18] always with one eye on males of their own social group 'to see how far they could go without being ostracised'.[19]

The result was that at the same time as women determined to take advantage of the expanding opportunities to participate in sport, they knew that the ultimate test they had to pass was womanliness, and that if they failed their whole future could be affected. They appreciated that they would be judged more on appearance than sporting performance, and thus that the greater the attention they paid to the requisites of femininity — although these were the antithesis of the behavioural and physical demands of competitive sport — the more acceptance they were likely to find. Not surprisingly, their responses were usually pragmatic and discreet — to accept moderation as their watchword; to accommodate and adjust to rather than revolutionise the arenas they entered, in a spirit of conciliation that aimed to temper the tacit admission of male dominance but to show that no offence was intended to the superior sex and that femininity and more active involvement in physical exercise were compatible.[20]

To assure that they projected an image of respectable femininity, the majority of sportswomen accepted the idea of limited sport, with special rules and techniques and cumbersome costumes that may have hindered skilful play, but safeguarded modesty and avoided 'unhealthy' strain and so won approval. They espoused different ends and aims involving a much stronger health-producing and 'play' element than was the case with men, as well as at least partially subscribing to the prevailing ideology that attributed women's athletic shortcomings to their basic nature. They also denounced as hoydens the few sports-crazy females who eschewed conformity and went to extremes by exhibiting the roughness and off-handed manners of young men, striding about in heavy boots and short skirts and talking loudly of nothing but hockey or cricket. For — like that of the bra-burning feminists of more recent times — the minority image stuck in the public mind and did the cause of women's sport serious harm.[21]

Whereas in the academic realm female variants were rejected by many pioneers on the grounds that they would perpetuate the belief in women's inferiority, in sport it was accepted that women should stop at a certain point in order to preserve their feminine image and conform to women's assumed or desired physical limitations. Sportswomen themselves thus reinforced and re-emphasised the separate and different — and thus inferior — character of the female sex and its sporting abilities and activities.

In the perceptive words of Jennifer Hargreaves:

The story of women's sport and physical recreation during the later part of the nineteenth century comprises themes of continuity as well as change; contradictions and ambivalences, advances and compromises characterised the complicated processes of its history. The biologically determined stereotype co-existed along with the more vigorous model of the sporting woman. There continued to be common opposition to sport for women because of its believed negative effects on sexuality and childbirth, at the same time as it became an increasingly popular and acceptable pursuit. By their actions in sport women were effecting a change in public opinion about their physical image at the same time as they were having to accommodate to social pressures.[22]

This accommodation clearly reflected the tension between the images of sport and ideal womanhood and between a woman's responsibilities to others and to herself and her own ambitions. It worked in the short run in that it gained for women's sport a degree of approval, and it was probably the only viable alternative at the time. However, it created problems over the long term. The acceptance of the basic masculinity of sport meant that for generations its female devotees adopted an apologetic tone when they justified even a modest invasion of 'man's domain', 'man's pastimes', 'man's games', as if men owned the whole sporting world. Whatever their age females came to understand that they could play games but only if they took great care to demonstrate their basic femininity; and they learned that there would be no automatic assessment of their real sporting worth as long as the standards of men were the universal criteria of excellence. Women in sport thus remained the 'other', the 'second sex', well into the twentieth century.

Because English sportswomen represented only a small, privileged sector of the female population, because their scope in sport remained limited, because the majority of middle-class women remained physically underdeveloped as a result of an inability or unwillingness to take proper exercise or engage in sport, and because sport continued to be a potent sign of male sexuality and power and thus of the inequality of the sexes, the material gain for women overall can be considered rather limited.[23] For years — some would argue to the present — the philosophy behind women's sport participation continued to imply restriction and control. The images and activities of women's sport remained circumscribed by outworn social values and sanctions that reinforced a negative attitude to women and reproduced traditional gender divisions by perpetuating myths about male superiority and female weakness and inferiority.

While sport could act as the ultimate idiom of conformity,

however, it could also be a deviant activity, a channel for challenging and expressing hostility to existing social arrangements. Women's sport grew steadily between 1870 and 1914; and the relationship of women to sport changed substantially, as the idea that sport was a form of human behaviour that should be accessible to both sexes was increasingly accepted, and sport was recognised as beneficial and worth encouraging in women as well as men. Despite the restrictions which social convention continued to place on women's sport, despite its confinement to a minority, despite its separation and difference from the male enterprise, and despite its confirmation of gender inequalities and prevailing ideologies, women's participation in sport was much more than a reflection of the preservation of traditional values. It was a critical manifestation of liberation and an extremely important part of the larger movement for female autonomy.

Victorian sportswomen had the capacity to stand at least partly aside from the behavioural norms they had been conditioned into accepting. They may not have been feminists, and they may not have appreciated the implications of their activities, but they were innovators or at the very least acceptors of innovation. Their determination, in increasing numbers, to participate in physical activities, with far greater physical freedom and competence than ever before, was in direct opposition to those of both sexes who clung for security to the sanctity of supposedly immutable biological and social norms. Whatever their motivations, sportswomen were far from passive observers of a larger social drama. They actively effected change by creating new roles for women, albeit within socially acceptable limits. Simply by 'playing the game' they transformed and redefined expectations of women; their trespassing on activities identified culturally as male provided an important element of social discontinuity that successfully challenged the stereotypes and system which restricted the potential of their sex.

Although the evidence is only circumstantial, sport probably brought to Victorian participants what it has brought to modern ones — real mental and physical gains in the form among other things of greater self-confidence and improved health. And this probably explains why, despite prejudice, discrimination and restrictions, despite considerations of costume, propriety and physical risk, the lure of sport was irresistible to a number of women, who apparently found the rewards of participation sufficient to counteract whatever social costs were involved, and sufficient to offset the stress and role conflict they must have experienced as a result of the clash between their own desire to play and social norms to the contrary. But the benefits were not confined to participants alone, for, by symbolising the larger game women were playing in the arena of social change, sport held considerable emancipatory potential for the female sex in general.

While sport involved an integration of the physical, social and mental, the physical aspect best explains the relationship between sport and women's oppression and emancipation. As late-nineteenth-century advocates of contraception appreciated, control over the body's use was central both to women's subordination and liberation, since women were defined by biology and the subjection of their bodies was a powerful symptom of their subjection in society at large. Because body control meant social control, the struggle for the legitimate use of the female body through sport and exercise was crucial to women's struggle to control their own destiny.

Notwithstanding continuing limitations on their scope in sport, women's progress from archery and croquet to tennis and golf to cycling and hockey saw their alienation from their own physicality diminish as a result of the increasing strength and bodily freedom they experienced. Every sporting breakthrough stimulated others and helped to erode long-held prejudices. Victorian sportswomen were potent role models who showed that, whatever the physiological differences between the sexes, women were not innately frail and did not have a physical structure inherently unsuitable to strenuous exercise. They demonstrated that sport did not masculinise their appearance or damage their hearts or reproductive organs or shorten their lives, thereby revealing that women's exclusion from sport had been more culturally than physiologically determined and so could be safely revoked. By extending the call for greater equality into the fundamental area of the physical, by challenging gender inequality, outworn stereotypes and patriarchal privilege, women's participation in sport was a major attack on the physical barriers to their sex's liberation, and was bound to have a broad transforming effect.[24]

Victorian sportswomen demonstrated that females had abilities of which they and others rarely dreamed. They ventured beyond normative boundaries and violated the traditional gender-role expectations of the dependent female in an effort to free themselves from the strict control of social convention. Even when they performed with moderation and in activities denied the status of men's, participation required them to behave in a competitive and aggressive manner considered inappropriate in everyday reality. This suspension of normal role-playing raised the possibility of suspensions in other areas and redefined and broadened the range of behaviour that was available and acceptable to members of their sex. Women's sporting activities between 1870 and 1914 defied a system that restricted opportunities for development to males. They gave evidence that women were finally taking initiative in defining themselves and their own proper sphere, and in insisting that they be treated less as 'women' and more as individual human beings with a right to freely express and develop all their talents.

In conclusion, then, even if for years women's sport was confined to a small, elite group and largely to educational and club settings which insulated it from public view, and even though it had to compromise with the traditional concept of femininity in order to gain acceptance, its evolution was most important to the emancipation of women, for it contributed to a revised definition of woman's nature, rights and abilities. The battle may have been far from won by 1914, but by then delicacy was no longer considered an essential sign of high breeding. 'Ladies' were no longer thought of exclusively in still-life attitudes; and it was no longer necessary to speak apologetically of the girl who was fond of outdoor games. Society had become prepared to accept less rigid stereotypes of womanly behaviour than the artificial mid-Victorian ideal had imposed, with the result that female sport had effectively come out of the closet, and its validity, propriety and moral and physical safety had been at least partly vindicated. By presenting women in nontraditional roles and by replacing an image of lassitude and frailty with a splendid new one of energy and activity, sport contributed significant modifications to the image of feminine perfection and laid the foundations for further changes. A New Woman, whose strength and vitality would allow her to act independently and decisively and take advantage of new opportunities for personal and professional advancement seemed at last to be within reach.[25]

It can thus be argued with some justice that 'few changes in Queen Victoria's reign are more complete than the position of the fair sex in modern sport'.[26] The range of women's sporting activities and the attitudes towards them were in marked contrast to the severe constraints of the past, and symbolised the great changes that were affecting women in society as a whole. Whereas the physical amusements considered sufficient exercise for the young lady of the 1860s — a little walking, croquet and gentle callisthenics — were but a pale reflection of those of young men, her grand-daughter if she chose could escape from the confining reality of the drawing room. She could run, bicycle, climb mountains, play tennis at Wimbledon, golf at St Andrews, hockey for England and any number of team and individual games at school and college, and then she could read about doing so in features on 'The Sportswoman' or 'The Outdoor Girl' in respectable periodicals and newspapers. She could even pursue a relatively well-paying career as a games and physical training instructor.

Sports participation, hedged in as it was by compromises with the social system, was certainly important as a constraining experience and as a powerful symbol of the female sex's continuing repression; but in the last analysis, during the late-nineteenth century the positive effects of even limited activity were ultimately more significant. Sport mirrored the degree of middle-class women's acceptance outside the home and their release from the restraints of Victorian prudery, for there was a direct relationship between women's acceptance in sport and in other social situations. Sport gave women the opportunity to be physically active, to be mobile, to be vigorous and hardy, to compete, to strive for excellence, to be congratulated for success, to accept honourable defeat, to extend comradeship to other women, to aspire to increased independence and self-fulfilment, to make important choices freely, and to experience and get to know themselves — in other words to try almost anything with a reasonable hope of succeeding. It provided a unique taste of freedom, and likely whetted appetites for more and increased confidence that it could be achieved. Sport also heightened women's consciousness of and control over their own bodies, through dress reform and greater physical activity, and in turn by doing so likely produced feelings of greater self-assurance, self-identity and self-esteem.

As English women became more active in the public sphere and as the women's movement gained credibility and recruits, women's sport became increasingly widespread, strenuous and competitive, and also more plausible. The emergence of the Victorian sportswoman was part of the same broad movement for social transformation that saw middle-class women contradict received definitions of their sex's true nature and challenge a system that restricted opportunities for development to males by becoming university students, medical doctors and municipal voters. In its own way sport was just as significant to the ultimate goals of feminism.

Notes

1. *Baily's Monthly Magazine of Sports and Pastimes* (June 1913), p. 410. See also *Golf Monthly*, vol. 3, No. 1 (1913), pp. 46–7; *Ladies' Golf*, vol.1 (October 1912), p. 12 and vol. 2 (February 1913), p. 16; *The Times*, 1 February 1913; Adburgham, *Punch History*, p. 252; Dobbs, *Edwardians at Play*, p. 178; Caroline Ramsden, *Ladies in Racing* (London, 1973), p. 55; Wray Vamplew, 'Sports Crowd Disorder in Britain 1870–1914: Causes and Controls', *Journal of Sport History*, vol. 7, no. 1 (Spring 1980), p. 10.

2. AELTC, Minutes (5 March and 14 April 1913); *Lawn Tennis* (3 July 1913), p. 503; *The Times*, 27 February 1912, 5 March 1913.

3. Elizabeth Cady Stanton, quoted in Janice Kaplan, *Women and Sports* (New York, 1979), p. 76.

4. Patricia Del Ray, 'In Support of Apologetics for Women in Sport', *Psychology of Motor Behaviour and Sport* (1977), pp. 56–60; E.E. Snyder and J.E. Kivlin, 'Perceptions of the Sex Role among Female Athletes and Non-Athletes', *Adolescence*, vol. 12, no. 45 (1977), p. 27; E.E. Snyder and E. Spreitzer, *Social Aspects of Sport* (Englewood Cliffs, NJ., 1978), p. 117.

5. Pointon, 'Feminine Image', p. 21.

6. *Hockey Field* (18 February 1909), p. 323.

7. Darwin *et al.*, *History of Golf*, p. 229.

8. *Hockey Field* (10 September 1908), p. 360.

9. *Golf Year Book* (1912), p. xxix. See also Stringer, *Golfing Reminiscences*, pp. 30-1, 199-200.

10. Michael R. Real, 'Super Bowl: Mythic Spectacle' in Andrew Yiannakis, Thomas D. McIntyre, Merrill J. Melnick, Dale P. Hart (eds), *Sport Sociology: Contemporary Themes*, 2nd edn (Dubuque, Ia., 1979), p. 24.

11. Mary A. Boutilier and Lucinda SanGiovanni, *The Sporting Woman* (Champaign, Ill., 1983), pp. 100-1; Theberge, 'Toward a Feminist Alternative', p. 195.

12. For example, Barrie, *Greenwood Hat*, pp. 100-4; cartoons and poems in *Punch* (1870-1914). See also Munrow, *Physical Education*, pp. 155-6.

13. Gerber *et al*, *American Woman in Sport*, pp. 14-7; Helen King, 'The Sexual Politics of Sport: An Australian Perspective' in R. Cashman and M. McKernan (eds), *Sport in History* (St Lucia, Queensland, 1979), p. 79.

14. Boutilier and SanGiovanni, *Sporting Woman*, p. 21; M. Ann Hall, 'Sport and Feminism: Imperative or Irrelevant?' in John J. Jackson, *Theory and Practice* (Victoria, BC., 1979), p. 55; Dorothy V. Harris, 'Female Sport Today: Psychological Considerations', *International Journal of Sport Psychology*, vol. 10, no. 3 (1979), p. 170-1; Marie Hart, 'Sport: Women Sit in the Back of the Bus', *Psychology Today*, vol. 5, no. 5 (1971), p. 66; Gladys I. Stone, 'On Women and Sport' in March L. Krotee (ed.), *The Dimension of Sport Sociology* (West Point, NY., 1979), p. 43; Paul E. Willis, 'Women in Sport in Ideology' in Jennifer Hargreaves (ed.), *Sport, Culture and Ideology* (London, 1982), pp. 122, 132.

15. Harry Edwards, *Sociology of Sport* (Homewood, Ill., 1973), p. 227; Felshin, 'Triple Option' in Hart (ed.), *Sport*, p. 433; King, 'Sexual Politics' in Cashman and McKernan, *Sport in History*, p. 78.

16. 'Are Athletics Over-Done?', pp. 251–2; Brown, *Silver Cord*, p. 45; Munrow, *Physical Education*, p. 159; Pointon, 'Feminine Image', pp. 22–3.

17. Shirley Ardener (ed.), *Perceiving Women* (London, 1975), pp. xii–xvii.

18. Dove, 'Cultivation of the Body', p. 407; Hargreaves, 'Playing Like Gentlemen', p. 138.

19. Eleanor Metheny, *Connotations of Movement in Sport and Dance* (Dubuque, Ia., 1965), p. 168.

20. Hargreaves, '"Playing . . . While Behaving"' pp. 43–4.

21. Burstall, *English High Schools*, p. 101; Perry, 'School Games', *Teachers' Guild Quarterly* (March 1910), pp. 16–17; Thomas (ed.), *Athletic Training*, pp. 109–17; Felshin, 'Triple Option' in Hart (ed.) *Sport*, pp. 432–3.

22. Hargreaves, 'Playing Like Gentlemen', p. 87.

23. Ibid., p. 85.

24. See Theberge, 'Toward a Feminist Alternative', pp. 201–2.

25. See Metheny, *Connotations*, p. 150; Patricia Vertinsky, 'God, Science and the Market Place: The Bases for Exercise Prescriptions for Females in Nineteenth Century North America', *Canadian Journal of History of Sport*, vol. 17, no. 1 (1986), p. 38.

26. *Harmsworth Magazine*, vol. 3 (August 1899–January 1900), p. 173. See also *Woman's World* (1889), p. 233.

Select Bibliography

The sources listed below represent only about a quarter of those consulted. The notes which appear at the end of each chapter contain a more extensive list.

I. Primary Sources: Archival Material, Unpublished and Published

All England Women's Hockey Association, London. *Hockey Field*, 1901–15; minute books

All England Women's Lacrosse Association, London. General and council meeting minutes; newspaper cutting record book

Anstey Physical Training College, City of Birmingham Polytechnic, Birmingham. *Anstey Physical Training College Magazine*, 1904–14

Association of Head Mistresses of Endowed and Proprietary Schools, London. Minutes

Bedford Physical Training College, Bedford College of Higher Education, Bedford. Students' Association Minutes and reports; taped and written reminiscences of Old Students

Chelsea College of Physical Training, Brighton Polytechnic, Eastbourne. College histories; miscellaneous addresses and articles; photographs

Cheltenham Ladies' College, Cheltenham. *Cheltenham Ladies' College Magazine*, 1880–1914; principals' reports and prospectuses.

Dartford College of Physical Training, Thames Polytechnic, Dartford. Kingsfield Book of Remembrance; miscellaneous articles and addresses; prospectuses and reports; scrapbook of college history

Girls' Public Day School Trust, London. Miscellaneous addresses, letters pamphlets, reports and school histories

Girton College, Cambridge. Brown, Violet E.L. *The Silver Chord (c. 1954)*; college songs; *Girton College Clubs, etc.* (1898); *Girton Review*, 1882–1914; *Register, 1869–1946*, photograph album; reports; tennis club minutes

Kenneth Ritchie Wimbledon Library, Wimbledon Lawn Tennis Museum, London. Minutes of committee, All-England Lawn Tennis Club; *Pastime* and *Lawn Tennis and Croquet* and *Lawn Tennis and Badminton*, 1883–1914

Lady Margaret Hall, Oxford: Annual reports; boat club minutes; *Brown Book*, 1891–1914; council minute books; *Daisy*, 1890–1; *Fritillary*, 1894–1914; log book; Miller, Leonard (ed.) 'Unpublished Diary of Irene M. Martin, c. 1894–1970'; principals' reports; sports and students' committee minute book; photographs; *Register, 1879–1966*

Newnham College, Cambridge. Letters; Newnham College Club, Cambridge Letter and Newnham College Letter; Newnham Roll; North Hall Diary; photographs; *Register, 1871–1971*; *Thersites,*

1901–14; unpublished reminiscences

North London Collegiate School, London. Governors' minutes; gymnasium medical notes; head mistresses' reports; hockey, netball, swimming and tennis clubs' minutes; letters; *Our Magazine*, 1875–1914; photographs; prize day reports; staff meeting minutes

Roedean School, Brighton. Photographs; *Wimbledon House* and *Roedean School News*, 1889–1914

St Anne's College, Oxford. Association for Promoting the Education of Women in Oxford, reports; principals' reports; Oxford Home Students Committee, annual reports and minute books; photographs; *Ship*, 1911–14

St Hilda's College, Oxford. Burrows, Christine M.E. 'History of St Hilda's College' (c. 1952); Chronicle of Old Students' Association; house rules; photographs

St Leonards School, St Andrews. Photographs; *Register, 1877–1895*; rules and record of challenge shield competitions; *St Leonards School Gazette*, 1887–1914; school songs

Somerville College, Oxford. Annual reports; letters; log book; *Register, 1879–1971*; Students' Association reports

II. Primary Sources: Books, Articles, Pamphlets and Addresses

Aflalo, F.G. (ed.) (1903) *The Sports of the World*, 2 vols, Cassell & Co., London

—— (1905) 'The Sportswoman' *Fortnightly Review*, vol. 77 (May), pp. 891–903

Alexander, Alexander (1896) *Healthful Exercise for Girls*, 5th edn, G. Philip & Son, London

Anderson, Elizabeth Garrett (1874) 'Sex in Mind and Education: A Reply', *Fortnightly Review*, vol. 15 (January–June), pp. 582–94

'Are Athletics Over-Done in Girls' Colleges and Schools? — A Symposium' (1912) *Woman at Home*, vol. 6 (April), pp. 247–52

Armstrong, Annie (1898) *Physical Exercises for Girls*, Iliffe & Son, London

Ballin, Ada S. (1885) *The Science of Dress in Theory and Practice*, Sampson Low, London

Beaufort, Duke of and Watson, Alfred E.T. (eds) (1885–1902) *The Badminton Library of Sports and Pastimes*, 19 vols, Longmans, Green & Co., London

Bernard, Franz (1860) *The Physical Education of Young Ladies*, Simpkin, Marshall & Co., London

Blackwell, Elizabeth (1859) *The Laws of Life: With Special Reference to the Physical Education of Girls*, Sampson Low, London

Brenner, Lucie (1870) *Gymnastics for Ladies*, London

Burstall, Sara (1907) *English High Schools for Girls: Their Aims, Organisation, and Management*, Longmans & Co, London

Butler, Ruth F. and Prichard, M.H. (eds) (c. 1930) *The Society of Oxford Home Students: Retrospects and Recollections 1879–1921*, Oxford

Chambers, Dorothea Katherine Lambert (1910) *Lawn Tennis for Ladies*, Methuen & Co., London

Chant, Laura Ormiston (1899) 'Woman as an Athlete: a Reply to Dr Arabella Kenealy', *Nineteenth Century*, vol. 45 (May), pp. 745–54

Clarke, Edward H. (1873) *Sex in Education*, James R. Osgood, Boston, Mass.

Cobbe, Frances Power (1870) 'Ladies Amusements', *Every Saturday* (12 February), pp. 101–2

Davidson, Lillias Campbell (1896) *Handbook for Lady Cyclists*, Hay Nisbet Co., London

Douglas, Gertrude M. (c. 1890) *The Gentlewoman's Book of Dress*, Henry & Co., London

Dove, Jane Frances (1901) 'Cultivation of the Body' in Beale, Dorothea, Soulsby, Lucy H.M. and Dove, Jane Frances (eds) *Work and Play in Girls' Schools*, Longmans, Green & Co., London, pp. 396–423

Ellis, Henry Havelock (1894) *Man and Woman: A Study of Human Secondary Sexual Characters*, Walter Scott, London

Erskine, F.J. (1885) *Tricycling for Ladies* Illiffe & Son, London

—— (1896) *Bicycling for Ladies*, Iliffe & Son, London

Faithfull, Lilian M. (1924) *In the House of My Pilgrimage*, Chatto & Windus, London

Fenton, W.H. (1896) 'A Medical View of Cycling for Ladies', *Nineteenth Century*, vol. 39 (May), pp. 796-801

Fletcher, J. Hamilton (1879) 'Feminine Athletics', *Good Words*, vol. 20, pp. 533–6

Graves, H., Hillier, George Lacy and Malmesbury, Susan, Countess of (1898) *Cycling*, Lawrence & Bullen, London

Greville, Beatrice Violet (ed.) (c. 1892) *The Gentlewoman's Book of Sports*, Henry & Co., London

—— (ed.) (1894) *Ladies in the Field: Sketches of Sport*, Ward & Downey, London

Hezlet, May (1907) *Ladies' Golf*, 2nd edn, Hutchinson & Co., London

Hutchinson, Horace G. (1899) *The Book of Golf and Golfers*, Longmans, Green & Co., London

—— (ed.) (1912) *The New Book of Golf*, Longmans, Green & Co., London

Kenealy, Arabella (1899) 'Woman as Athlete', *Nineteenth Century*, vol. 45 (April), pp. 636–45

—— (1899) 'Woman as an Athlete: a rejoinder', *Nineteenth Century*, vol. 45 (June), pp. 915–29

—— (1904) 'The Curse of Corsets', *Nineteenth Century*, vol. 55 (January), pp. 130–7

—— (1920) *Feminism and Sex-Extinction*, T. Fisher Unwin, London

Leitch, Cecil (1911) *Golf for Girls*, George Newnes, London

Linton, Lynn (1891) 'The Wild Women: As Social Insurgents', *Nineteenth Century*, vol. 30 (October), pp. 596–605

Lumsden, Louisa (1933) *Yellow Leaves: Memories of a Long Life*, William Blackwood & Sons, London

Mackern, Louis and Boys, Margaret (eds) (1899) *Our Lady of the Green: A Book of Ladies' Golf*, Lawrence & Bullen, London

Malim, Mary Charlotte and Escreet, Henrietta Caroline (eds) (1927) *The*

Book of the Blackheath High School, Blackheath Press, London

Malmesbury, Susan, Countess of (1898) *Cycling for Women*, Lawrence & Bullen, London

Maudsley, Henry (1874) 'Sex in Mind and in Education', *Fortnightly Review*, vol. 15 (January–June), pp. 466–83

Mullins, Mrs Roscoe (1893) 'The North London College School for Girls', *Sylvia's Journal* (September), pp. 498–505

Pearson, Norman (1885) 'Athletics for Ladies', *London Society*, vol. 48 (July), pp. 64-71

Peck, Winifred Knox (1952) *A Little Learning: or A Victorian Childhood*, Faber & Faber, London

Romanes, George J. (1879) 'Recreation', *Nineteenth Century*, vol. 6 (September), pp. 401–24

Saleeby, Caleb W. (1912) *Woman and Womanhood: A Search for Principles* William Heinemann, London

Scharlieb, Mary (1909–10) 'Adolescent Girlhood under Modern Conditions, with Special Reference to Motherhood', *Eugenics Review*, vol. 1 (April–January), pp. 174–83

―――― (1911) 'Recreational Activities of Girls During Adolescence', *Child*, vol. 1 (April), pp. 571–86

Schofield, Alfred (1889) *The Physical Education of Girls*, London

Slaughter, Frances E. (1898) *The Sportswoman's Library*, 2 vols, Archibald Constable & Co., Westminster

Smith, J. Nicholson and Robson, Philip A. (eds) (1899) *Hockey, Historical and Practical*, A.D. Innes & Co., London

Spencer, Herbert (1861) *Essays on Education and Kindred Subjects*, Dent & Sons, London, 1910

―――― (1864) *The Principles of Biology*, 2 vols, Williams & Norgate, Oxford 1898

Spicer, Howard H. (ed.) (1900) *Sports for Girls*, Andrew Melrose, London

Stringer, Mabel E. (1924) *Golfing Reminiscences*, Mills & Boon, London

Suffolk and Berkshire, Earl of, Peek, Hedley, and Aflalo, F.G. (eds) (1897–8) *The Encyclopaedia of Sport*, 2 vols, Lawrence & Bullen, London

Suffolk and Berkshire, Earl of (ed.) (1911) *The Encyclopaedia of Sport and Games*, 4 vols, William Heinemann, London

Thomas, C.E. (ed.) (1912) *Athletic Training for Girls*, Pitman & Sons, London

Thompson, Edith (1904) *Hockey as a Game for Women*, Edward Arnold, London

Waldron, Kathleen (1901–2) 'Won on the Playing Fields: the Story of Some School and College Challenge Trophies', *Girl's Realm*, vol. 4 (November–October), pp. 678–81

Walker, Donald (1837) *Exercise for Ladies: Calculated to Preserve and Improve Beauty and to Prevent and Correct Personal Defects, Inseparable from Constrained or Careless Habits: Founded on Physiological Principles*, 2nd edn, T. Hurst, London

III. Primary Sources: Periodicals and Newspapers

Dates cited indicate years studied for compiling this list and not dates of publication of journals, magazines etc., most of which are now defunct.

Badminton Magazine of Sports and Pastimes (1895–1914)
Baily's Monthly Magazine of Sports and Pastimes (1860–88), also known as *Baily's Magazine of Sports and Pastimes* (1889–1914)
British Medical Journal (1858–1914)
C.B. Fry's Magazine (1904–12)
Child (1910–14)
Cycle Magazine (1895–7)
Cyclists' Touring Club Gazette (1884–99)
Daily Telegraph (1913)
Educational Review (1890–8)
English Woman's Journal (1858–63)
Englishwoman's Review (1866–1902)
Eugenics Review (1909–11)
Fortnightly Review (1874–1914)
Gentlewoman (1890–1913)
Girls' Own Paper (1880–1914)
Girl's Realm (1898–1914)
Girls' School Year Book (1906–14)
Golf Monthly (1911–14)
Golf Year Book (1904–14)
Golfing Annual (1887–1909)
Hockey Field (1901–15)
Journal of Education (1869–1914)
Journal of Scientific Physical Training (1908–22), also known as: *Journal of School Hygiene and Physical Education* (1923–32); *Journal of Physical Education and School Hygiene* (1933–44); *Journal of Physical Education* (1944–54); *Physical Education* (1955–69)
Ladies' Field (1896–1914)
Ladies' Field Handbooks (1900–2)
Ladies' Golf (1912–14)
Ladies' Golf Union Year Book (1902–14)
Lady Cyclist (1895–7)
Lady's Pictorial (1891–2, 1919–20)
Lady's Realm (1896–1909)
Lancet (1860–1914)
Nineteenth Century (1879–1904)
Pastime (1883–95), also known as: *Lawn Tennis and Croquet* (1895–1905); *Lawn Tennis and Badminton* (1905–19)
Physical Culture (1898–1901)
Punch (1870–1914)
Queen (1861–1914)
Rational Dress Society's Gazette (1888–9)
Review of Reviews (1890–1914)
Sporting Magazine (1794–1870)

Strand Magazine (1894–1911)
Transactions, National Association for the Promotion of Social Science (1858–84)
The Times (1870–1914)
Wheelwoman (1897–9)
Woman at Home (1894–1914)
Woman's Beauty and Health (1902–14)
Woman's World (1888–90)
Wycombe Abbey School Gazette (1897-1914)
Young Woman (1892–1903)

IV. Secondary Sources: Books, Booklets, Articles, Papers, Theses and Dissertations

All England Women's Hockey Association (1954) *Women's Hockey from Village Green to Wembley Stadium*, Macdonald & Evans, London
Atkinson, Paul (1978) 'Fitness, Feminism and Schooling' in Sara Delamont and Lorna Duffin, *The Nineteenth-Century Woman: Her Social and Physical World*, Croom Helm, London, pp. 92–133
——— (1985) 'Strong Minds and Weak Bodies: Sports, Gymnastics and the Medicalization of Women's Education', *British Journal of Sports History*, vol. 2, no. 1, pp. 62–71
Bailey, Gemma (ed.) (1923) *Lady Margaret Hall: A Short History*, Oxford University Press, Oxford
Bailey, Peter (1978) *Leisure and Class in Victorian England: Rational Recreation and the Contest for Control, 1830–1885*, Routledge & Kegan Paul, London
Baker, William J. (1979) 'The Leisure Revolution in Victorian England: A Review of Recent Literature', *Journal of Sport History*, vol. 6, no. 3, pp. 76–87
——— (1983) 'The State of British Sport History', *Journal of Sport History*, vol. 10, no. 1 pp. 53–66
Battiscombe, Georgina (1978) *Reluctant Pioneer: A Life of Elizabeth Wordsworth*, Constable & Co., London
Bedford Physical Training College (1953) *Margaret Stansfeld*, Bedford
Bell, Pauline C. (1978) 'A History of Physical Education in Girls' Public Schools, 1870–1920, with particular reference to the influence of Christianity', unpublished MEd thesis, University of Manchester
Boutilier, Mary A. and SanGiovanni, Lucinda (1983) *The Sporting Woman*, Human Kinetics Pubs., Champaign, Ill.
Burstyn, Joan (1980) *Victorian Education and the Ideal of Womanhood*, Croom Helm, London
Cadogan, Mary and Craig, Patricia (1976) *You're a Brick, Angela!: A New Look at Girls' Fiction from 1839–1975*, Victor Gollancz, London
Claydon, Jane (1980) 'Lacrosse at St Leonards School', *Lacrosse*, vol. 34, no. 1, pp. 9–10
Crunden, Colin (1974) *A History of Anstey College of Physical Education 1897–*

1972, Anstey College, Birmingham
—— (1975) 'The Care of the Body in the Late Nineteenth and Early Twentieth Centuries in England', *Bulletin of Physical Education*, vol. 11, no. 1, pp. 17–21
Cunningham, Hugh (1980) *Leisure in the Industrial Revolution c. 1780 — c. 1880*, Croom Helm, London
Cunnington, Phillis and Mansfield, Alan (1969) *English Costume for Sports and Outdoor Recreation*, A. & C. Black, London
Davies, Mel. (1982) 'Corsets and Conception: Fashion and Demographic Trends in the Nineteenth Century', *Comparative Studies in Society and History*, vol. 24, no. 4, pp. 611–41
Delamont, Sara and Duffin, Lorna (eds) (1978) *The Nineteenth-Century Woman: Her Cultural and Physical World*, Croom Helm, London
de Zouche, Dorothy E. (1955) *Roedean School, 1885–1955*, Dolphin Press, Brighton
Dixon, J.G., McIntosh, P.C., Munrow, A.D. and Willetts, F.F. (1957) *Landmarks in the History of Physical Education*, Routledge & Kegan Paul, London
Dyhouse, Carol (1976) 'Social Darwinistic Ideas and the Development of Women's Education in England, 1880–1920', *History of Education*, vol. 5, no. 1, pp. 41–58
—— (1978) 'Towards a "Feminine" Curriculum for English Schoolgirls: the Demands of Ideology, 1870–1963', *Women's Studies International Quarterly*, vol. 1, no. 4, pp. 291–311
—— (1981) *Girls Growing Up in Late Victorian and Edwardian England*, Routledge & Kegan Paul, London
Elsworth, Margaret (1981) 'Women's Participation in Physical Recreation in the Nineteenth Century with Particular Reference to North-West England' in David McNair and Nicholas A. Parry (eds) *Readings in the History of Physical Education*, Czwalina, Hamburg, pp. 85–94
Ewing, Elizabeth (1975) *Women in Uniform through the Centuries*, B.T. Batsford, London
Felshin, Jan (1973) 'The Social Anomaly of Women in Sports', *Physical Educator*, vol. 30, no. 3, pp. 122–4
Fletcher, Sheila (1984) *Women First: The Female Tradition in English Physical Education 1880–1980*, Athlone, London
—— (1985) 'The Making and Breaking of a Female Tradition: Women's Physical Education in England 1880–1980', *British Journal of Sports History*, vol. 2, no. 1, pp. 29–39
Flint, Rachael Heyhoe and Rheinberg, Netta (1976) *Fair Play: the Story of Women's Cricket*, Angus & Robertson, London
Freeman, Gillian (1976) *The Schoolgirl Ethic: The Life and Work of Angela Brazil*, Allen Lane, London
Gathorne-Hardy, Jonathan (1977) *The Public School Phenomenon, 597–1977*, Hodder & Stoughton, London
Gerber, Ellen W., Felshin, Jan, Berlin, Pearl and Wyrick, Waneen (1974) *The American Woman in Sport*, Addison-Wesley, Reading, Mass.
Gorham, Deborah (1982) *The Victorian Girl and the Feminine Ideal*, Indiana University Press, Bloomington, Ind.
Grant, Julia M., McCutcheon, Katherine H. and Sanders, Ethel F. (eds)

(1927) *St Leonards School, 1877–1927*, Oxford University Press, Oxford

Haddon, Celia (1977) *Great Days and Jolly Days: The Story of Girls' Schools Songs*, Hodder & Stoughton, London

Haley, Bruce (1968) 'Sports in the Victorian World', *Western Humanities Review*, vol. 22, no. 2, pp. 115–25

Hall, M. Ann (1971) 'The Role of the Safety Bicycle in the Emancipation of Women', *Proceedings of the Second World Symposium on the History of Sport and Physical Education, Banff, Alberta*, pp. 245–9

—— (1978) *Sport and Gender: A Feminist Perspective on the Sociology of Sport*, Canadian Association for Health, Physical Education and Recreation, Ottawa

—— (1981) 'Sport, Sex Roles and Sex Identity', *Canadian Research Institute for the Advancement of Women Papers*, Ottawa

Hargreaves, Jennifer A. (1978) 'Playing Like Gentlemen While Behaving Like Ladies: The Social Significance of Physical Activity for Females in Late Nineteenth and Early Twentieth Century Britain', unpublished MA thesis, University of London Institute of Education

—— (1982) (ed.) *Sport, Culture and Ideology*, Routledge & Kegan Paul, London

—— (1985) ' "Playing Like Gentlemen While Behaving Like Ladies": Contradictory Features of the Formative Years of Women's Sport', *British Journal of Sports History*, vol. 2, no. 1, pp. 40–52

Harris, Dorothy V. (1975) 'Towards a Better Understanding of the Female in Sport', *New Zealand Journal of the History of Physical Education and Recreation*, vol. 8, no. 3, pp. 91–6

Harrison, Brian (1981) 'Women's Health and the Women's Movement in Britain, 1840–1940' in Charles Webster (ed.) *Biology, Medicine, and Society*, Cambridge University Press, Cambridge, pp. 15–71

Hart, M. Marie (ed.) (1976) *Sport in the Socio-Cultural Process*, 2nd edn, Wm. C. Brown, Dubuque, Ia.

Hendry, A.E. (1968–9) 'Social Influences Upon the Early Development of Physical Education in England', *Journal of Physical Education*, vol. 60, no. 182, pp. 78–82 and vol. 61, no. 182, pp. 17–20

Hunt, Felicity (1984) 'Secondary Education for the Middle Class Girl: A Study of Ideology and Educational Practice 1870 to 1940 with special reference to the Harpur Trust Girls' Schools, Bedford', unpublished PhD thesis, University of Cambridge

—— (1985) ' "Divided they Fall": The Educational Implications of Opposing Ideologies in Victorian Girls' Schooling, 1850–1914'. Paper presented at the meeting of the History of Education Society, Atlanta, Ga. (9 November)

Jones, Greta (1980) *Social Darwinism and English Thought: The Interaction between Biological and Social Theory*, Harvester Press, Brighton

Joy, Nancy (1950) *Maiden Over: A Short History of Women's Cricket and A Diary of the 1948–49 Test Tour of Australia*, Sporting Handbooks, London

Kennard, June A. (1974) 'Women, Sport and Society in Victorian England', unpublished PhD dissertation, University of North Carolina, Greensboro, NC.

—— (1979) 'The History of Physical Education', *Signs*, vol. 2, no. 4, pp. 835–42

Kunzle, David (1982) *Fashion and Fetishism: A Social History of the Corset, Tight-Lacing and Other Forms of Body-Sculpture in the West*, Rowman & Littlefield, Totowa, NJ.

Lowe, John W.G. and Lowe, Elizabeth D. (1982) 'Cultural Pattern and Process: A Study of Stylistic Change in Women's Dress', *American Anthropologist*, vol. 84, no. 3, pp. 521–44

McCrone, Kathleen E. (1984) 'Play Up! Play Up! and Play the Game! Sport at the Late Victorian Girls' Public School', *Journal of British Studies*, vol. 23, no. 2, pp. 106–34

────── (1986) 'The "Lady Blue": Sport at the Oxbridge Women's Colleges from their Foundation to 1914', *British Journal of Sports History*, vol. 3, no. 2, pp. 191–215

McIntosh, Peter C. (1952) *Physical Education in England Since 1800*, G. Bell & Sons, London

────── (1963) *Sport in Society*, C.A. Watts & Co., London

Macaulay, Julia S.A. (ed.) (1979) *St. Leonards School 1877–1977*, Blackie & Son, Glasgow

Mangan, J.A. (1973) 'Physical Education as a Ritual Process' in J.A. Mangan (ed.) *Physical Education and Sport: Sociological and Cultural Perspectives*, Basil Blackwell, Oxford, pp. 87–102

────── (1981) *Athleticism in the Victorian and Edwardian Public School*, Cambridge University Press, Cambridge

────── (1981) 'Social Darwinism, Sport and English Upper Class Education', *Stadion*, vol. 7, no. 1, pp. 93–116

────── (1984) '"Oars and the Man": Pleasure and Purpose in Victorian and Edwardian Cambridge', *British Journal of Sports History*, vol. 1, no. 3, pp. 245–71

────── (1987) and Park, Roberta J. (eds) *From 'Fair Sex' to Feminism: Sport and the Socialization of Women in the Industrial and Post-Industrial Eras*, Frank Cass & Co., London

May, Jonathan (1969) *Madame Bergman-Osterberg*, George G. Harrap, London

Meller, Helen E. (1976) *Leisure and the Changing City, 1870–1914*, Routledge & Kegan Paul, London

Mitchell, Juliet and Oakley, Ann (eds) (1976) *The Rights and Wrongs of Women*, Penguin, Harmondsworth

Molyneux, D.D. (1959) 'Early Excursions by Birmingham Women into Games and Sports', *Journal of Physical Education*, vol. 51, no. 153 pp. 46–54

Mosedale, Susan Sleeth (1978) 'Science Corrupted: Victorian Biologists Consider "The Woman Question"', *Journal of the History of Biology*, vol. 11, no. 1 pp. 1–55

Munrow, Albert D. (1972) *Physical Education*, George Bell, London

Newton, Stella M. (1974) *Health, Art and Reason: Dress Reformers of the Nineteenth Century*, John Murray, London

Okely, Judith (1978) 'Privileged, Schooled and Finished: Boarding Education for Girls' in Shirley Ardener (ed.) *Defining Females: The Nature of Women in Society*, Croom Helm, London, pp. 109–39

Park, Roberta J. (1983) 'Research and Scholarship in the History of Physical Education and Sport: The Current State of Affairs', *Research*

Quarterly, vol. 54, no. 2, pp. 93–103

Pederson, Joyce Senders (1975) 'Schoolmistress and Headmistress: Elites and Education in Nineteenth Century England', *Journal of British Studies*, vol. 15, no. 1, pp. 135–62

—— (1979) 'The Reform of Women's Secondary and Higher Education: Institutional Change and Social Values in Mid- and Late-Victorian England', *History of Education Quarterly*, vol. 19, no. 1, pp. 61–91

—— (1981) 'Some Victorian Headmistresses: A Conservative Tradition of Social Reform', *Victorian Studies*, vol. 24, no. 3, pp. 463–88

Phillips, Ann (ed.) (1979) *A Newnham Anthology*, Cambridge University Press, Cambridge

Physical Education Association (1964) *Nine Pioneers in Physical Education*, Physical Education Association, London

Pointon, Marie (1978) 'The Growth of Women's Sport in Late Victorian Society as Reflected in Contemporary Literature', unpublished MEd thesis, University of Manchester

—— (1979) 'Factors Influencing the Participation of Women and Girls in Physical Education, Physical Recreation and Sport in Great Britain During the Period 1850–1920', *History of Education Society Bulletin*, no. 24 (Autumn), pp. 46–56

—— (1981) 'The Feminine Image' in David McNair and Nicholas A. Parry (eds) *Readings in the History of Physical Education*, Czwalina, Hamburg, pp. 20-5

Pollard, Marjorie (1965) *The Story of the AEWHA 1895–1965*, AEWHA, London

Rader, B.G. (1979) 'Modern Sports: In Search of Interpretation', *Journal of Social History*, vol. 13, no. 2, pp. 307–21

Reekie, Shirley H.S. (1982) 'The History of Sport and Recreation for Women in Britain, 1700–1850', unpublished PhD dissertation, Ohio State University

Roberts, Helene (1977) 'The Exquisite Slave: The Role of Clothes in the Making of the Victorian Woman', *Signs*, vol. 2, no. 3, pp. 554–69

—— (1977) 'Submission, Masochism and Narcissism', in Virginia L. Lussier and Joyce J. Walstedt (eds) *Women's Lives: Perspective on Progress and Change* (University of Delaware, Newark, Del., pp. 27–66

Rosaldo, Michelle Zimbalist and Lamphere, Louise (eds) (1974) *Women, Culture and Society*, Stanford University Press, Stanford, Cal.

Rubinstein, David (1977) 'Cycling in the 1890s', *Victorian Studies*, vol. 21, no. 1, pp. 47–71

—— (1978) 'Cycling 80 Years Ago', *History Today*, vol. 28, no. 8 pp. 544–47

—— (1986) *Before the Suffragettes: Women's Emancipation in the 1890s*, Harvester Press, Brighton

Sandiford, Keith (1981) 'The Victorians at Play: Problems in Historical Methodology', *Journal of Social History*, vol. 15, no. 2, pp. 271–88

—— (1983) 'Sport and Victorian England: Review Article', *Canadian Journal of History*, vol. 18, no. 1, pp. 111–17

Sayers, Janet (1982) *Biological Politics: Feminist and Anti-Feminist Perspectives*, Tavistock Publications, London

Simon, Brian and Bradley, Ian (eds) (1975) *The Victorian Public School*, Gill & Macmillan, Dublin

Smith, W. David (1974) *Stretching Their Bodies: The History of Physical Education*, David & Charles, Newton Abbot

Smith-Rosenberg, Carroll and Rosenberg, Charles (1973) 'The Female Animal: Medical and Biological Views of Women and her Role in Nineteenth Century America', *Journal of American History*, vol. 60, no. 2, pp. 332–56

Snyder, E. and Spreitzer, E. (1978) *Social Aspects of Sport*, Prentice-Hall, Englewood Cliffs, NJ.

Stephen, Barbara (1933) *Girton College 1869–1932*, Cambridge University Press, Cambridge

Sutherland, Gillian (1980) 'The Social Location of the Movement for Women's Higher Education in England, 1840–1880'. Unpublished paper

Theberge, Nancy (1985) 'Toward a Feminist Alternative to Sport as a Male Preserve', *Quest*, vol. 37, no. 2, pp. 193–202

Tinling, Ted (1977) *The Story of Women's Tennis Fashion*, Wimbledon Lawn Tennis Museum, London

Vertinsky, Patricia (1986) 'God, Science and the Marketplace: The Bases for Exercise Prescriptions for Females in Nineteenth Century North America', *Canadian Journal of History of Sport*, vol. 17, no. 1, pp. 38–45

Vicinus, Martha (1982) '"One Life to Stand Beside Me": Emotional Conflicts in First Generation College Women in England', *Feminist Studies*, vol. 8, no. 3, pp. 603–28

—— (1985) *Independent Women: Work and Community for Single Women, 1850–1920*, Virago, London

Walvin, James (1984) 'Sport, Social History and the Historian', *British Journal of Sports History*, vol. 1, no. 1, pp. 5-13

Watson, Roderick and Grey, Martin (1978) *The Penguin Book of the Bicycle*, Penguin, Harmondsworth

Watts, K.M. (1980) *A History of the Blackheath High School*, Blackheath High School, London

Webb, Ida M. (1967) 'Women's Physical Education in Great Britain, 1800–1966, with reference to teacher training', unpublished MEd thesis, University of Leicester

—— (1976) 'Women's Hockey in England' in Roland Renson, Pierre Paul de Nayer and Michel Ostyn (eds) (1976) *The History, the Evolution and the Diffusion of Sports and Games in Different Cultures*, Brussels, pp. 490–6

—— (1977) 'The History of Chelsea College of Physical Education', unpublished PhD thesis, University of Leicester

White, Cynthia L. (1970) *Women's Magazines 1693–1968*, Michael Joseph, London

Index

advertisements 235–6, 241, 246n69, 255
All-England Lawn Tennis and Croquet Club 158–63, 278
  lady champions 158–62, 165–6, 233–4
  ladies' championships 158–61, 186n12
  ladies' and mixed doubles 162–3
All England Women's Hockey Association 30, 36, 66, 77, 84, 128–35, 137, 150n5, 150n14, 150n18, 229–30, 278, 282
  and women's emancipation 137
  dress 229–30
  formation, structure and rules 128–31
  publicity 132–3
  sexually and socially mixed play 133–4
Anderson, Elizabeth Garrett 23, 195
Anne, Queen 4
Anstey, Rhoda 113–15, 118, 214n41, 224
  aims and personality 113, 115
  feminism 115
Anstey College of Physical Training 100, 110, 113–15, 124n15, 124n31, 224
  aims and curriculum 113
  dress 224
  regime 114–15
  sports 114
archery 7, 154–5
Association of Head Mistresses 62
athleticism 12, 59–60, 63, 87–8, 100
Atkinson, Paul 227

Austen, Jane 5
Ayrton, Hertha 31

Badminton Library of Sports and Pastimes 169, 265–7
Badminton Magazine of Sports and Pastimes 262–4
Baily's Monthly Magazine of Sports and Pastimes 262–3
Ballin, Ada 221–2
Beale, Dorothea 46, 81–4, 87, 226
Bedford Physical Training College 110, 116–18
  aims and curriculum 116–18
  dress 117
  regime 117
  sports 116–17
Bell, Gertrude 48
Bergman-Osterberg, Martina 73, 104–10, 113, 116, 118, 121, 123n20, 223, 244n17
  achievements 109
  aims and personality 104–6, 108
  feminism 109–10, 123n20
Bergman-Osterberg Physical Training College *see* Dartford Physical Training College
Berners, Dame Juliana 3
Blackheath High School 69
Blackwell, Elizabeth 194–5
Bloomer, Amelia 219–20
blues 24, 44, 48, 52–3
bluestockings 5
Bodichon, Barbara Leigh Smith 31
Brazil, Angela 256–7
British Medical Journal 196–8, 206
Brown, V.E.L. *see* Violet Cooper
Bryant, Sophie 66–7, 95n19, 225
Burstall, Sara 87, 184, 205